Culture and the Judiciary

How can jurists resolve multicultural conflicts? Which kind of questions should judges ask when culture enters the horizon of the law? Are they then called to become anthropologists? Through the analysis of hundreds of cases produced through decades of multicultural jurisprudence, this book reconstructs the constitutional and anthropological narratives and the legal techniques used by Western judges to face the challenges posed by multiculturalism: from Japanese parent–child suicide to the *burqa*, from Jewish circumcision to Roma begging, from kissing a son on his genitals to the claim of indigenous people to fish salmon in natural parks, the book brings the reader into a fascinating journey at the crux of the encounter between the relativism of anthropology and the endeavor toward a democratic coexistence pursued by the law. After identifying the recurrent themes or *topoi* used by judges and lawyers, this book critically analyzes them, evaluates their persuasive power and suggests a "cultural test" that gathers together the crucial questions to be answered when resolving a multicultural dispute. The "cultural test" is a matrix that guides the judge, lawyers and legislatures across the intricate paths of multiculturalism, to assure a relational dialogue between the law and anthropology.

Ilenia Ruggiu is Professor of Constitutional Law at the University of Cagliari. She holds a PhD in European and Public Law from the University of Palermo. She is the author of *Interpreting Culture in Italian Courts: A Proposal of a Cultural Test* (LEHR 2016).

> "This book is a must-read for judges and lawyers who want to deepen their anthropological knowledge and ready themselves to face the challenges posed by the multicultural transformation of their societies."
>
> *Giacinto Bisogni, Judge, Italian Court of Cassation*

Cultural Diversity and Law

Around the world, most states are faced with difficult issues arising out of cultural diversity in their territories. Within the legal field, such issues span across matters of private law through to public and constitutional law. At international level too there is now considerable jurisprudence regarding ethnic, religious and cultural diversity. In addition, there are several layers of legal control – from communal and religious regulation to state and international regulation. This multiplicity of norm setting has been variously termed legal pluralism, inter-legality or internormativity and provides a fascinating lens for academic analysis that links up to cultural diversity in new and interesting ways. The umbrella of cultural diversity encompasses various population groups throughout the world ranging from national, ethnic, religious or indigenous groupings. This series particularly welcomes work that is of comparative interest, concerning various state jurisdictions as well as different population groups.

Series Editor:
Prakash Shah, School of Law, Queen Mary University of London, UK

Also in the series

The Challenge of Legal Pluralism
Local Dispute Settlement and the Indian State Relationship in Ecuador
Marc Simon Thomas

Access to Justice and Human Security
Cultural Contradictions in Rural South Africa
Sindiso Mnisi Weeks

The State and the Paradox of Customary Law in Africa
Edited by Olaf Zenker and Markus Virgil Hoehne

Law, Cultural Diversity, and Criminal Defense
Craig L. Carr and Lisa Johnson

Culture and the Judiciary
The Anthropologist Judge
Ilenia Ruggiu

For more information about this series, please visit:
www.routledge.com/Cultural-Diversity-and-Law/book-series/CULTDIV

Culture and the Judiciary

The Anthropologist Judge

Ilenia Ruggiu

Routledge
Taylor & Francis Group
LONDON AND NEW YORK

First published in English 2019 by Routledge

2 Park Square, Milton Park, Abingdon, Oxfordshire OX14 4RN
52 Vanderbilt Avenue, New York, NY 10017

Routledge is an imprint of the Taylor & Francis Group, an informa business

First issued in paperback 2020

Translated by Jeremy Daw

Published in Italian by FrancoAngeli 2012

British Library Cataloguing-in-Publication Data
A catalogue record for this book is available from the British Library

Library of Congress Cataloging-in-Publication Data
Names: Ruggiu, Ilenia, author. | Daw, Jeremy, translator.
Title: Culture and the judiciary : the anthropologist judge / Ilenia Ruggiu ; translated by Jeremy Daw. Other titles: Giudice antropologo. English
Description: Abingdon, Oxon ; New York, NY : Routledge, 2019. | Series: Cultural diversity and law | Includes bibliographical references and index.
Identifiers: LCCN 2018034592 | ISBN 9781138359833 (hardback)
Subjects: LCSH: Multiculturalism—Law and legislation—Cases. | Law and anthropology. | Minorities—Legal status, laws, etc.
Classification: LCC K487.C8 R8413 2019 | DDC 340/.115—dc23
LC record available at https://lccn.loc.gov/2018034592

ISBN: 978-1-138-35983-3 (hbk)
ISBN: 978-0-367-53409-7 (pbk)

Typeset in Galliard
by Swales & Willis Ltd, Exeter, Devon, UK

Disclaimer

This publication has received funding from the European Union's Horizon2020 research and innovation programme H2020-DRS-2015, under grant agreement No. 700385 Project CLISEL, Climate Security with Local Authorities, and by the Swiss State Secretariat for Education, Research and Innovation (SERI) under contract number 16.0038. This book reflects only the author's view and the Agency is not responsible for any use that may be made of the information it contains. The opinions expressed and arguments employed herein do not necessarily reflect the official views of the Swiss Government.

This book has received funding from the Sardinian Region under law 7/2007, and from the *Fondazione di Sardegna* under the project "Multiculturalismo e conflitti. Le risposte del diritto".

In loving memory of my uncle Gianni Mele
(1944–2018)

Contents

Acknowledgments

Many people and institutions have supported this work with invaluable intellectual and material help. I would like to thank all my colleagues of the Department of Law at the University of Cagliari and particularly Pietro Ciarlo, Gianmario Demuro, Silvia Niccolai and Giuseppe Lorini for their constant support. I thank the University of Glasgow, in particular Noreen Burrows, Maria Fletcher, John Finlay and Tom Mull for the hospitality in the years 2004 and 2006 when my research on cultural identity began; the University of Victoria-British Columbia, and in particular Avigail Eisenberg, for many generous exchanges during the two periods of research on Canadian multiculturalism in 2008 and 2011, and for her helpful suggestions on the manuscript, as well as Taiaiake Alfred, Paul Bramadat and James Tully; the University of Edinburgh, particularly Eve Hepburn, Michael Rosie and David McCrone, for supporting research on theories of identity in 2009; Georgetown University in Washington DC where I researched the US cultural defense in 2010; the University of Southern California, and in particular Alison Dundes Renteln, who sponsored a visiting scholarship in 2012, essential to completing the work, as well as Nomi Stolzenberg and anthropologists Nancy Lutkehaus, Erin Moore, Jean Cooper and Thomas Ward; the University of California, Berkeley and in particular Sarah Song, who sponsored a visiting scholarship at Berkeley in 2015 on the intersections between patriarchy and culture, as well as Laura Nader and Kathryn Abrams.

I wish to thank Justice Giacinto Bisogni and lawyer Paola Lovati for promoting the creation of the Observatory on Justice, Transcultural Dialogues and International Protection by Italian judges and lawyers and for inviting me to co-coordinate it in order to test the possible application of the cultural test proposed in this book in Italian courts.

I wish to thank Jeremy Daw, for engaging the challenging task of translation with his competence with the American system.

Last, but not least, my thanks go to the many librarians for their assistance and to the funding sponsors of the research: the University of Cagliari, the Sardinia Foundation, the Sardinia Region, the European Union, the Embassy of Canada in Italy and the Royal Society of Scotland.

Translator notes

It has been a true pleasure to work with Professor Ruggiu to bring her urgent work to the English-speaking world; both her insightful analysis and strong command of English aided me to render the most faithful translation of *Il Giudice Antropologo* that I could.

Given the comparative nature of this work I inevitably had to make some tough translation choices, and in particular with regard to the different judicial structure of common law and civil law systems between the Italian- and English-speaking worlds.

Unlike common law court systems, such as those of the US or UK, which combine conflict resolution with rule-making under the unifying doctrine of *stare decisis*, the Italian court system has two high courts: the Constitutional Court which rules on the validity of laws, and the Supreme Court of Cassation, also called the Supreme Court, which is the final arbiter of disputes. Similar divisions are present in Germany and in other civil law systems. The reader will therefore find a double use of both "Constitutional Court" and "Supreme Court" when applied to civil law systems; this is intended to refer to two distinct courts. In Italy, the terms "Court of Cassation" and "Supreme Court" refer to the same high Court.

The Italian court system also differs from the one in the US in that Italy is a regional state (not federal) and therefore unifies the judicial power at the national level. There are three levels of ordinary jurisdiction:

1. Trial courts in civil, criminal or minors matters called *Tribunali* (*civili, penali, minorili*).
2. Courts of appeal: the *Corti d'appello* which have the power to analyze facts *de novo*.
3. Supreme Court of Cassation: the *Corte di Cassazione* or *Corte Suprema*, divided into criminal or civil sections, acts as the final arbiter of legitimacy. It cannot re-analyze the facts, but it can overrule the appellate opinion if it finds that the Court of Appeal badly reasoned or misapplied the law.

Separate from these ordinary jurisdictions are special jurisdictions such as the administrative one. It is articulated in two levels:

1 Administrative Trial Courts: *Tribunali amministrativi regionali* (TAR), comprising a total of 20 Trial Courts, one per region.
2 Council of the State: *Consiglio di Stato*, based in Rome which has the power to re-analyze the facts and is the final arbiter of disputes.

I translated to English all the names of the courts in the body of the book, accompanied by the Italian name in parentheses. I chose to leave their original names in the table of judgments for the benefit of those who want to find the original opinions in Italian databases.

In Italy, civil law judgments are referred to with a number or, for lower courts, only by the date of the judgment, and often the names of the parties are, by their request, anonymized. But since this is an international, comparative study, I chose to indicate the case also in the common law style with the names of parties when possible, or with the name of the subject treated when the protagonist of the case was anonymized, so as not to jar the reader with constantly shifting naming conventions.

Finally, although I am aware that the word "multiculturalism" is charged with criticism and conflicting meanings in the American debate, I chose to leave it as is in the text, because of the word's still mostly valued European currency.

Jeremy Daw
Juris Doctor, Harvard Law School

Preface

I decided to update and translate *Il Giudice Antropologo*[1] after the so-called "migration crisis" in Europe started in 2015. I live in Sardinia, an island in the middle of the Mediterranean Sea that is right along the route that thousands of migrants take from Africa and Asia. I saw, in 2017, the Italian courts transformed with the creation of 26 migration sections, one for each Court of Appeal, to try to accelerate and specialize the analysis of asylum applications, many of which are culturally based. The number of migrants fleeing wars, climate change or poverty (200,000 per year in Italy alone since 2015) added to those already living in Italy (6 million out of a total 60 million) compelled me to act.

I was also inspired by the Italian judges who were very active in finding solutions to the "migration crisis." In 2015, the Italian Supreme Court of Cassation organized an international conference on *Il multiculturalismo e le corti* (Multiculturalism and the Courts) and the judges showed interest in the cultural test I presented in the Italian version of this book. Following this conference the Observatory on Justice, Transcultural Dialogues and International Protection was founded as part of a broader system of Observatories formed by Italian judges and lawyers.

I wrote this book with a practical aim in mind: to provide judges with a handy tool that could guide them when resolving a multicultural case. I chose judges because I think they are on the front line of multiculturalism and the ones most in need of such a tool. While legislatures can decide to leave the questions of multiculturalism unregulated, a member of the judiciary cannot say "*non liquet*": she must give an answer, one that satisfies justice.

In order to accomplish this practical aim, I may have trampled on some pristine academic theory. I am aware of the complexity of the concept of culture, of its intersections with other behavior- and identity-markers such us class, race, gender, poverty, psychology, colonialism etc. I am aware of the turning away from culture, even within anthropology. I beg the pardon of the readers who might find parts of the book far from such important deconstructions and in-depth analysis. I recognize the validity of their criticisms, but I chose to address the present work to judges, who face isolated behaviors that belong to the "complex whole" that

1 *Il Giudice Antropologo. Costituzione e tecniche di composizione dei conflitti multiculturali*, Milano: FrancoAngeli (2012).

is a culture. No bench affords an omniscient view, and judges may find helpful recourse in a synthesis of the main questions to ask when facing a new problem of social coexistence. As a jurist, I was compelled by the need to stop the current random approach to culture in the judiciary and to find some predictability in the law. The cultural test I propose is conceived as a synthesis of the most persuasive theories on culture and judicial *topoi* which have emerged so far in the debate. I hope that also the academic reader might appreciate this effort of bringing into the law, although in an apparently simplified manner, the critical debate around culture current in anthropology, feminism and other social sciences.

Today, I feel again the lesson of Antonio Gramsci on subalternity and hegemony, and the role of intellectuals in denouncing it. I see cultural recognition as important, both to preserve the Western constitutional values of pluralism and the centrality of the person, and as a mitigation action toward the effects of neocolonialism: after obliging people to migrate, destroying their food sovereignty, grabbing their land and water and generally polluting the Earth, to impose on migrants the extra burden of renouncing their culture is indeed morally unacceptable. I believe that the debt of the global North toward the global South should be paid, at least, through guaranteeing cultural rights – and the most fundamental of these is the right to present a cultural defense.

Introduction

How can jurists resolve multicultural conflicts? In a time of unprecedented cross-cultural migration, predicted to increase even more with climate change,[1] finding a workable answer could hardly be more urgent.

"If for centuries constitutionalism had to elaborate a theory of equality, today this is accompanied by the need for an efficient constitutional theory of difference" (Palermo, Woelk 2011: 1). But the constitutional uncertainty in framing multiculturalism under the theory of fundamental rights (Sigler 1983; Barry 2001; Margalit, Halbertal 2004; Kurt Barth 2008) and the absence of shared patterns for cultural recognition (Taylor 1992; Habermas 1992; Tully 1995; Benhabib 2002; Shweder, Minow, Markus 2002; Foblets, Dundes Renteln 2009) would seem to prove that an effective "constitutional theory of difference" is still stuck at an *impasse*. The concept of culture in an anthropological sense entered a judicial document for the first time in 1966, with art. 27[2] of the International Covenant on Civil and Political Rights. The category of cultural rights has been debated ever since (Dundes Renteln 1988). While civil, political and social rights are settled in the constitutional tradition of Western democracies, cultural rights still have an uncertain status: Are they group rights or individual rights? Are they universal or special rights? All these questions generate an uncertain theoretical framework that does not favor normative recognition. The result is that only fifty constitutions (out of one hundred and ninety-four existing in the world) recognize cultural rights, and only thirty have a multicultural clause (Appendix: the status of culture in constitutions). Few of these constitutions belong to Western democracies – the

1 Future forecasts vary from twenty-five million to one billion of environmental displaced people, by 2050, in the world, escaping drought, floods, changes in the agricultural rhythms or wars and conflicts related to environmental changes. IOM, International Organization for Migration www.iom.int/complex-nexus#nearfar

2 International Covenant on Civil and Political Rights, G.A. 2200A (XXI), art. 27, 21 UN GAOR, Supp. No. 16, at 52, U.N. Doc. A/6316 (Dec. 16, 1966): "In those States in which ethnic, religious or linguistic minorities exist, persons belonging to such minorities shall not be denied the right, in community with the other members of their group, to enjoy their own culture, to profess and practise their own religion, or to use their own language."

majority of them are from South America and Africa – with few exceptions, such as Canada (art. 27 Charter of rights and freedom). The majority of the European Constitutions recognize only linguistic rights for internal minorities, and freedom of religion as an individual right, completely ignoring any right to culture.

In the absence of a precise theoretical and regulatory framework, courts have tackled the question, mainly, on a case by case basis. Judges have had to look for solutions from time to time, conflict to conflict.[3] However, the virtuality potentially and abstractly implied in this approach – eg. flexibility in the search for an individual judgment – has clashed, and often, with complicated reality, creating judges who decline cultural arguments as unconvincing; who "culturalize" common crimes simply because they are committed by foreigners; who issue irreconcilably different rulings from case to case; or who write judgments that exacerbate rather than mitigate multicultural coexistence, through rulings based on stereotypes or essentializing attitudes. In some cases, the potential of a careful and aware judicial approach yields inexorably to the unresolved issues of a constitutional theory of difference.

This work shows one of the possible ways out of this double impasse. Lack of a clear theory of difference combined with the disparate outcomes are the hallmarks of the predominant case by case approach; the consistent application of a "cultural test" designed to resolve multicultural conflicts can eliminate them. The test consists of a set of questions, the answers to which judges, lawyers[4] and, with perspective, legislatures, could employ for a more conscious approach to the concept of culture. This technical legal instrument, which has its origins in the North American constitutional courts, is obtained through a survey of the most pervasive doctrines and recurring arguments found in comparative judicial analysis engaging with the concept of culture.

I aim, therefore, to retrace how Western judges are made into anthropologists. With this expression I mean any judge who may find herself facing different cultural practices and who decides (on her own initiative) or is induced (by the lawyer) to confront the concept of culture, in civil, criminal or administrative jurisdictions and in trial, appeal or supreme courts. I analyze the figure of the "anthropologist judge" on three levels: the descriptive, deconstructive and prescriptive. These three elements define the pedagogical structure of this book.

3 The protagonism of judges within the ambit of multiculturalism can be explained by the fact that "liberalism has eliminated from the political agenda of the state parliament . . . the identitarian elements of religion, ethnicity, language and culture." In this context: "just as the parliamentary debate for the 'culturally homogenous' citizens, judicial litigation is, for the minority citizen, the place in which the bonds of the State are consolidated . . . through the reasoning contained in the judicial opinion" (Guazzarotti 2001: 85–88).

4 As lawyers play a crucial role in helping the judge in his *iuris dicere* (to declare the law) task, the cultural test proposed in this book is conceived for them as well. The fact that an "anthropologist lawyer" so often stands behind an "anthropologist judge," stimulating and instructing the judge of the controversy's cultural aspects, should not be overlooked.

The first level of analysis is descriptive and is intended to reconstruct the use of culture by judges, i.e. the solutions of each case, paying particular attention to the recurring elements, the fixed points, the *topoi* (Aristotle's word[5]) that these solutions present (Chaps. 1 and 2). The work explores the figure of the anthropologist judge by describing, from the earliest decisions, the different arguments produced when confronted with different cultures. In particular, I analyze the analytical tools of the test – in the double variant of cultural and religious tests – such as standardized procedures which predetermine the conditions under which courts may grant cultural recognition (Chap. 2).

The second level of analysis is the critical, deconstructive type (Chap. 3). Looking at the law as a historically located phenomenon, the survey asks what kind of narratives, contexts of meaning and power relations underlie the different uses of the concept of "culture" within legal argument. The spread of the anthropologist judge figure throughout several jurisdictions is presented in this section, itself theorized as a cultural and historical fact: "culture" is one of the current ways of perceiving the other, but it can be a double-edged sword: a way to either recognize or fail to realize him. This concept is constructed sometimes in an intersectional way and sometimes in competition with other lenses – gender, race, social or economic class – in categorizing difference.

I deconstruct the uses of cultural argument mainly by examining how different cultural concepts, developed in anthropological thought, "return" to the law. Research shows that the broad varied landscape of comparative jurisprudence contains not a single concept of culture, but many. All correspond to certain ideas of culture, more or less current, circulating in society and theorized by anthropology since the discipline's onset in the nineteenth century. For these reasons, this work does not aim to provide an ultimate definition of culture, but rather intervenes in the debate on multiculturalism by analyzing multiple concepts of "culture," which osmotically filter from society and from anthropology into the law.

The third level of the analysis is prescriptive and aims to answer the question: How should a judge who wants to be a competent anthropologist avoid *ad hoc* improvisation, but instead address the issue of diversity from a consistent jurisprudential foundation?

To answer this question, I elaborate an operative instrument for jurists consisting of an apposite "cultural test" (Chap. 4). I think it is a task of the law, as a practical social science, to approach multiculturalism precisely and with a practical attitude, offering solutions and tools. The problem is particularly urgent for judges and lawyers. While legislatures may decide to leave multiculturalism unregulated simply by not intervening, a judge cannot say "*non liquet* – I do not know how to resolve this case." The judge must decide. Similarly, the lawyer cannot frustrate her client's right to a defence. The cultural test can be a useful instrument to guide them in balancing and solving the case.

5 Aristotle (384–322 B.C.E.) defines *topos* (in Greek: place) or *topoi* (in plural) as the shared points reached in a discourse on which there is a stable consensus (Viehweg 1962; Aristotle 2012: book 5).

The legitimacy of this legal tool comes from the fact that it embodies the most recurring and persuasive questions that judges have been asking – although in an erratic way – in many Western democracies when resolving multicultural conflicts. Thus it is like a fresh photograph of an emerging – although still blurry – common judicial/legal tradition which forms through a stratified complex of choices, rethinkings and corrections. Thus this test imbues the law with anthropological knowledge.

There are clear possible objections to an instrument of this kind, including neo-positivist critiques, the bureacratization of conflicts and warnings of the subordination of judicial prudence to predetermined evaluations. My analysis will address possible remedies to prevent the proposed cultural test's transformation into a formalist instrument which drains all life from concrete cases. The test will, rather, be a guide for judges, lawyers and other operators which does not trammel the reasoning of ***modus iuridicus*** or the search for just solutions but rather proceeds by providing standards of orientation among the intricate paths of multiculturalism.

The elaboration of the test benefits from the use of two methodologies crucial to multicultural studies: the comparative and the interdisciplinary.

An issue like multiculturalism demonstrates how effectively comparative approaches must now be integrated into constitutional inquiry: judicial experience of multiculturalism has found full understanding only through a vigorous comparison of various regulations and decisions. If I had limited this investigation to the Italian courts or American courts, this research would not have succeeded. Not only would it have provided an incomplete perspective, but it would have been impossible to find any guiding principle on how to resolve conflicts, to deconstruct concepts of culture which penetrate legal reasoning, or to develop new tools such as the cultural test. The fact that "the judges of the world face similar problems, especially in the field of fundamental rights" is urging jurisdictions to look at case law "drawn from foreign experience" (Cartabia 2009: 547; Markesinis, Fedtke 2006).

The comparative perspective, traversing disparate conflict resolution techniques, indicates the basic elements of what could be a unifying method in the present historical moment, to resolve conflicts. Analyzed comparatively, in fact, Western jurisprudence permits a far-flung introduction of available legal topics and techniques as well as a reflection of an interpretative horizon amplified and legitimized by the experiences of others. Comparison also permits a reflection on which elements to expunge from legal argument because they may be historically trapped in particular socio-political contexts, because they are not persuasive or because they are not sufficiently relational. In this sense, comparative descriptive tools can become prescriptive instruments. Comparison acquires the role prophesied by Peter Häberle (1999) of a fifth interpretive method.[6] Furthermore, it

6 After the four already identified by Friedrich Carl von Savigny (1779–1861): the historical, the literal, the systematic and the teleological.

becomes a source of law.[7] In fact, the comparative method supports the proposal of a new cultural test elaborated by merging different comparative judicial experiences (Chap. 4).

Another method crucial to this work is interdisciplinarity which, while well settled in the English language academy[8] within fields like "law and society," "law and literature," "law and emotion" and "critical legal studies," still strives for full recognition in European schools of law; continental schools still favor Hans Kelsen's pure theory of law, which views the law as norm produced according to certain procedures and ignores all the social, cultural, political, economic aspects brought to the formation of the norm and to its interpretation.

In this book, the interdisciplinary approach is used, in particular, to cross-pollinate the cultural ideas that circulate between anthropology and judicial reasoning (Chap. 3). The interdisciplinary investigation started, perhaps, from a banal consideration. At a moment when "culture" has become one new lens through which to read social interactions, it has become unavoidable to look at the social science discipline that invented the concept and make it the object of study *par excellence*: anthropology (Ferlito 2005). To address the themes of culture without the contribution of anthropology is a scientific suicide, as it is necessary for the jurist to leverage maximum knowledge of the key concepts of multicultural issues.

But the expression "anthropologist judge" does not propose a position of the law subordinate to anthropology, as if the judge faced with other cultures should uncritically adopt the tools of anthropology and apply them passively; rather it aims to indicate a new possibility of interaction between the two disciplines. At a time when "cultural discourse," developed in society and conceptualized by anthropology, penetrates the law, it is important that this discourse have the participation of active protagonists, better informed, less casual and more predictable. Also because, as the artful composition of social conflicts (Azzariti 2012), as a discipline that longs for justice, and as a science that helps build a society with the kinds of choices which make life worth living, the law has, undoubtedly, very much to say. A renewed interaction between the two disciplines, respecting both the peculiarities of legal reasoning and the scientific validity of anthropology, can answer the question – how to resolve multicultural conflicts? – that has agitated legal systems for decades.

While tracing the methodology of this book, I quickly encountered the thorny questions of the style with which to present the collected data and the choice of expositive plan.

7 Against Bognetti (2009: 10), according to which "the comparatist – for the nature of his work . . . is not . . . a 'practical' jurist . . . he is simply a describer of normatively accepted facts . . . a historian." For a function of the comparative law as a source of a cosmopolitan constitutional law see Camerlengo (2007: 239–274 and *passim* for the problem of "democraticity of the source" implied by these new methods of formulating the law).

8 On the need to arrive at a post-disciplinary approach see Goldberg, Musheno, Bower (2001: xi).

On the matter of style, I tried to take account of new parlances lately widespread in the social sciences: specifically, of narrative. Thus I resort, at times, to storytelling which aims to describe the law in a narrative way in order both to present the case and to suggest how the law is itself one of the many discourses around a fact. Some cases are therefore presented as if they were tragedies performed in the theatre of life.

Pedagogically, I adopted an inverted technique. I opted to begin with a case by case, rather than theoretical, analysis to introduce the reader to the topic area, showing all its heterogeneity and complexity. The first chapter may have a certain de-centering effect which is nonetheless useful to show the many ways in which judges have handled the concept of culture and also the empirical, almost "experimental" modes with which jurists have undertaken these questions at their caution. The second chapter completes the descriptive part in a more analytical way by proceeding to describe multicultural jurisprudence in individual states. The third chapter deconstructs the use of "culture" as employed by judges. At the conclusion of this part of the research the reader has before her an overview of the most significant arguments that judges have elaborated over the last six decades to resolve multicultural conflicts. The book ends, therefore, with a working proposal of the test's application.

In an age of mass migrations, the future will be multicultural, whether welcomed or not. Instead of indulging security anxieties or building walls as Fortress Europe, the US and the majority of states are doing worldwide, the task of the law should be to find peaceful coexistence through pragmatic solutions.

Part I

Descriptive analysis

The use of culture by judges

1 *In medias res*

The cases

1 Parents who kill their children

1.1 The Kimura *case:* Oyaku Shinju *– Japanese infanticide between culture and madness*

On a morning in January 1985 a woman walked along the beach in Santa Monica, California, holding her newborn daughter in her arms and her four year-old son by the hand. Then turning decisively toward the sea, she plunged into the cold surf. She came to drown. She brought her children.

A group of students from the shore saw the three submerged under the water and came to the rescue. They saved the life of the mother – but arrived too late for the two young children.

Before the Superior Court of California, Fumiko Kimura – the name of the woman the students pulled from the ocean – was charged with second-degree murder, the most serious charge available under the facts, for which state law permitted a sentence of death.

What drove this woman into the waves?

One Chorus – the prosecution – blames a spirit of vendetta against a cheating husband. When Kimura learned of her husband's infidelity, she became filled with anger. As Medea faced with Jason's betrayal, she tried to avenge her dishonor by killing both herself and their children: an extreme act of revenge towards her husband, to wipe every trace of his generation. Fumiko Kimura wanted to reaffirm, with this gesture, her most primal conjugal rights (Bryant 1990).

The government's briefings filed with the court urged the application of the severest penalty available: the woman, they argued, let her passion drive her to destroy two innocent lives.

Not so, objects a second Chorus. The woman loved her children too much to entangle them in such a vendetta. So then insanity was her motive – they suppose. Perhaps Fumiko Kimura is crazy. As the sixth child of a troubled home, driven by a failed musical dream in Japan to seek her fortune in California, weighed by another marriage of eight years which also failed, isolated in her house in a country in which she never learned the language, with neither a job nor any life outside of family, the news that Itsuroku Kimura, her second husband with whom she was married for six years and with whom she believed she had rebuilt her damaged domestic life, had thrice cheated on her may have triggered a latent psychic weakness which had smoldered for some time. Fumiko Kimura, they speculated, became incapable of sound mind while she dove, with their children, into the ocean waves.

Perhaps, the lawyers speculated, Kimura suffered from a temporary insanity.

Not so, whispers a third Chorus. Perhaps it was neither madness nor vendetta which motivated Kimura. Do not limit your point of view to what you can see. Kimura came from Japan, not Greece, not from America. She is no contemporary Medea; she is not insane. The woman produced in this gesture the only reasonable solution to her domestic doom – an act under a cultural impulse. She was practicing, consciously, the *Oyaku Shinju*, an ancient practice that is still echoed in contemporary Japan. In the presence of a betrayal, Japanese women have traditionally suffered a strong social humiliation to make the gesture of suicide an inevitable outcome. Perhaps it is culture, then, that pushed Kimura and her children into the sea.

Such became the argument of the Japanese community in California, submitted in a petition of twenty-five thousand signatures, asking the judge to take cultural factors into account and explaining that Kimura deeply loved her children (McCaslin 1985a).

"But why the children?" asked the broader public (Woo 1989). What terrible culture is this, which hounds mothers to kill innocent children? Even in Japan the practice is now illegal, although punished leniently by the criminal justice system (typically through reduced charges such as manslaughter which implies a maximum of five years in prison) and the act receives full sympathy at all Japanese social strata. Yet, Fumiko Kimura had lived in the US for fourteen years when she committed the act. For these reasons, thought many Californians, the culpability of Kimura's actions was clear. She should have been able to "see" other ways to solve her drama.

Not quite, a fourth Chorus interjects. To concentrate too myopically on this ancient ritual, the *Oyaku Shinju*, can risk missing elements of the broader Japanese cultural system which still persist. What drove the woman is not so much ancestral custom, but non-Western ideas of maternity, child care, ideas about the value of life, and about the way to suicide that shaped her way of seeing the world. Cultures are not mere sums of single practices, but rather "whole systems" (Tylor 1871). To understand the individual cultural behavior, we must go to the wider cultural system. The decision to kill herself was Fumiko Kimura's, perhaps spurred by her failed life or by the news of her husband's betrayal; but once she made it, her culture would not permit her to leave her children in this world. They are not perceived as separate subjects: "Japanese mothers kill their children when committing suicide because they do not consider it murder. They would be surprised to be accused of murder and would respond to the accusation: 'how can killing myself and a part of myself be murder?'" (Kawanishi 1990: 32[1]). For these reasons, "Japanese society in general very rarely accuses a mother of infanticide" (Yoshitomo Takahashi, Douglas Berger 1996: 248). As in the West a pregnant mother who attempts suicide and survives is not accused of attempted murder of her fetus, an equivalent logic should apply to Kimura.

While there is, therefore, a symbiotic relational concept in Japanese parenting, it would be unthinkable for Kimura to entrust her living children to the care of others (perhaps even her husband's new lover) because children without their mothers are destined for misery. To bring her children with her, pleads this Chorus, is an act of love.

The judge calls a cultural expert to explore the socio-cultural background of Fumiko Kimura. He explained how in Japan orphanages are very rare and that no mother would entrust their children to a substitute. Such a gesture would be seen as irresponsible. Paradoxically, explains the cultural expert, the *Oyaku Shinju* is still common in Japan not as a ritual response to social humiliation (betrayal), but as a result of the strong bond between mother and child, a visceral bond that does not end with the fetus stage of development because the woman perceives the offspring as one with herself for a prolonged period of childhood. In this perspective, according to Japanese logic, a loving mother would not be able to even think about leaving a child in the world to survive alone.

The expert adds that suicide, in the Japanese cultural system, is not seen as a traumatic choice, as in the West where it is almost pathologized; a resort to suicide is not only an extreme solution to an unsolvable problem, but also a path to rescue honor, to express repentance or express love for another.[2] Suicide, in essence, requires a lower motivational impulse because it is one of many ways to solve a crisis and is considered an honorable way to die. It is no coincidence, then, that at the news of the death of his children, Kimura's husband Itsuroku threatened suicide; nor that Kazue Tanahashi, the rival lover whose relationship prompted Fumiko's decision, sent a letter offering to kill herself as well if it would ease the pain of the family.

1 Kawanishi (1990: 34–35) proceeds to observe: "Most mothers in all cultures feel to some extent that their children are a part of themselves. The degree of maternal identification with children depends upon the culture. However, this extremely intense identification as manifested in mother-child joint suicide may be a phenomenon found in a uniquely Japanese context . . . Japanese mothers often have an extreme form of ego extension with respect to their children. They often lack the sense of boundaries between themselves and their children as separate individuals. Not only do they feel 'personally affected by what happens to their children', but they also sometimes require that their children follow the same path they take. In short, Japanese mothers feel 'oneness' with their children. To a Japanese mother, a child is not a separate individual, but an important component of the mother's self." See also McCaslin (1985b).

2 These divergent types of suicide exist in Japan because, in that country, suicide is not considered a consequence of depression and "there seem to be greater 'vocabularies of motives' for suicide. One can commit suicide not only for self-destruction or self-hatred, but also from such motivations as punishing others, saving face, expressing apology, or loving another with such strong attachment that taking that person's life with one's own is necessary" (Kawanishi 1990: 43).

From concepts of motherhood to those on suicide, wide high-level differences between individualism and interdependence emerge between the two divergent cultures. This explains why the Japanese society conveys a lenient understanding toward those who choose *Oyaku Shinju* and how even the transformation of the practice into a crime in Japan (evidence indeed of profound internal cultural change) still harbors its practitioners with the reduced charge of involuntary manslaughter. It is this complexity of factors in which was forged Kimura's identity, in which her gesture becomes understandable, reasonable and even compassionate, according to the Japanese mentality.

Whatever her reasons, Kimura sought death. She reported after being discharged from the hospital: "I wanted to be with my children" (Dolan 1985).[3]

This tragedy's Choruses dissonantly diverge. No clear values guide the judge. The horizon of law is torn by new voices, appealing to new anthropological knowledge: that all do not become human beings in the same way, but are all "situated" individuals, actors driven by cultural inputs, with even the human unconscious differing greatly depending on the culture in which it is socialized. Would we, too, have acted as Kimura did if we had been raised in Japan? In addition, the cultural expert's "translation" of the woman's gesture further disrupts the Western sense of justice by presenting it as an act of care.

Thus does doubt insinuate.

To condemn Kimura would significantly obscure what has already been stated: the woman could not have acted otherwise, seeing no other viable solution but a gesture which is not only reasonable in her culture, but which even signifies an act of love. And the Japanese community concurred in her judgment.

Yet to absolve the woman would be to ignore the fact that two lives have been snuffed out. Would this not disrupt the values of coexistence, by refusing to protect one of the most important of all legal interests – that of life itself?

Where is the just solution? How is the court supposed to find it?

There is no *deus ex machina* to unravel the knot. The judge, in this story, is compelled by the petition from Japanese public opinion to don the role of an anthropologist, so much so that he decides to hear from a cultural expert on Japan. Kimura's attorney, however, abandons the path of the cultural defense,[4] because admitting that she wanted to kill her children for love would be equivalent to a full assumption of responsibility, a premeditated murder that exposes his client to the death penalty. The insanity defense appeared to be a preferable trial strategy.

3 The case profoundly shocked the United States and was widely covered in the media (Dillow 1985a, 1985b; Reese 1985a, 1985b).

4 The "cultural defense" is a kind of defense used in criminal proceedings, although not officially recognized in the US. From the side of the defendant the "cultural defense" is the invocation to the court to consider the cultural background underlying a behavior; from the side of the court the "cultural defense" is a requirement for judge to consider the cultural background of litigants in the disposition of cases before them, for instance to ascertain the *mens rea* or elements of provocation. The applying of a cultural defense could lead the judge to acquit the defendant or to mitigate the punishment. This concept is diffusively theorized by Dundes Renteln (2004).

The case is resolved according to the theses of the defense. Fumiko Kimura was found incapable of sound mind at the time of the act: madness, agreed the parties, not culture, pushed her with her children into the ocean waves. After her attorney reaches an agreement with the prosecution, she pleads no contest to two counts of voluntary manslaughter and is sentenced to time served and five years of probation, with mandatory psychological support.[5]

1.2 The **Saleem** *case: "honor killings" between culture, individual responsibility and patriarchy*

In the summer of 2006, in Sarezzo, a village near Brescia, Italy, Mohammed Saleem called his twenty-year old daughter, Hina, home and, with the help of a cousin, killed her with a knife. A few days later he claimed: "It was me, alone. I did it in a moment of anger. I did not want her to become like the girls here. I asked her to change her life, but she would not." A chorus of critical voices immediately rose within the Italian press and public opinion, accusing Saleem of acting under a cultural impulse. Since he is from Pakistan, these voices claimed, Hina's death must be an honor killing, premeditated within the family clan in order to restore its offended dignity. She had gone to live with an Italian man and refused to marry her cousin, to whom she was betrothed in Pakistan. The meeting of the men of the family to decide her death, mere days before the crime and the declaration of Hina's mother who told the press: "My daughter was not a good Muslim: Mohammed has rendered justice."[6] all seemed to confirm this logic.

The first Chorus of this tragedy maintained it was his culture that moved Saleem's hands, a culture that must be forcefully rejected to affirm the fundamental rights, of which life is the first. While the Pakistani community living in Italy declared that the conduct of Mohammed Saleem was disproportionate and that an average Pakistani father would not have killed his daughter for this kind of conduct, the lawyers who defended the man, using data of honor killings in Pakistan and

5 *People v. Fumiko Kimura*, no. A-091133, California Superior Court 1985 (unpublished decision). The judge condemned Kimura to one year in prison but observed that she had already been held for 297 days and waived the remaining time for "good conduct." Even from a distance of 40 years, the *Kimura* case, despite being unpublished, continues to be cited as one of the most complex multicultural cases. Critics of cultural argument use it to highlight the risk that the acceptance of culture could become a cause of justification of otherwise criminal behavior. The supporters of the cultural argument, conversely, accuse the attorney and judge of pathologizing what elsewhere would be normal. As observed: "if Kimura's actions constituted temporary insanity, despite their being in keeping with Japanese culture, wouldn't that make Japanese culture similarly insane?" (Goel 2004: 443–444). In this sense, Reddy (2002), analyzes, in critical points, the tendency of multiple jurisdictions, and in particular the United States, to pathologize cultural diversity. Ten years later another woman, Helen Wu, would revive the *Kimura* story: on this occasion the appellate judge would "officially" use the cultural argument and would condemn the woman to a lesser form of homicide and five years of detention (*People v. Wu*, 235 Cal. App. 3d 614, October 24 1991).

6 "É tornata la madre di Hina, 'Mohammed ha fatto giustizia'" ("Hina's mother is back: 'Mohammed brought justice'") in *La Repubblica*, August 21st, 2006, www.repubblica.it.

explaining the importance of honor in that culture, decided to present the case as one of "culturally motived crime" and therefore requested the application of mitigating circumstances, which would reduce the applicable sentence to eighteen years. They claim that, according to Mohammed Saleem's culture, the rescue of honor could be considered a "motive of particular high moral or social value" recognized as extenuating circumstance by the Italian criminal code (Art. 62 no. 1). Saleem's lawyers invited the judge to adopt this cultural logic.

But a second Chorus also raises its voice. Feminist critiques vigorously dispute the defense's characterization of the Hina case, observing how violence against women, which manifests itself as femicide (Caputi, Russell 1992)[7] and pervades in both domestic and public spaces, is not just a matter of individual responsibility nor a fact limited to traditional cultures but rather a universally widespread practice, better read under the category of patriarchy or gender oppression (Phillips 2005; Reddy 2008).

The judge heeds this Chorus. Urged to assume the role of the anthropologist by defense briefs asking him to take into account the cultural context in which Saleem's decision matured, he disposes of such arguments immediately by countering that in this case culture is not involved. Mohammed Saleem acted, according to the trial court, driven by his personal conception of the role of father.

As stated by the trial court:[8]

> [W]eighing also the crime's motive . . . in the cultural connotations of the subject and the social context in which the event occurred, the motive appears futile: to the Pakistani community these facts appear completely out of proportion, and the reprehensible motives are absolutely insufficient to justify forcing his beliefs into reality.

The appellate court[9] reiterates that the cultural argument is

> misleading . . . because a crime like the one committed is not justified in Pakistan, because he [Mr. Saleem] has been a resident of Italy since 1989 and has had ample time and opportunity to learn and live the national customs and our rules, and finally because attempts to rely on the cultural motivation in this case is rather an attempt to conceal what is only the attitude of the father-master [*padre-padrone*] who takes revenge of a serious insult suffered by his daughter, as it might be for any subject with the same character and the same nature, whatever their ethnic or cultural affiliation.

7 The term indicates a form of patriarchal control, not due to the pathology of perpetrators but rather to the projection of male supremacy. According to the authors "femicide includes mutilation, murder, rape-murder, battery that escalates into murder, the immolation of witches in Western Europe and of brides and widows in India, and 'crimes of honor' in some Latin and Middle East countries, where women believed to have lost their virginity are killed by their male relatives" (Caputi, Russell 1992: 15).

8 Trial Court of Brescia (Tribunale di Brescia) January 19th, 2008, which condemned the man to thirty years in prison, with the aggravating factor of abject and futile motives.

9 Court of Appeal of Brescia (Corte d'appello di Brescia) December 5th, 2008, which confirmed the thirty-year sentence.

This is confirmed by the Supreme Court: "the absorbing motivation of the accused's action has come from a pathological and distorted attitude of possessive parental entitlement."[10] Although not explicitly mentioned, the shadow of patriarchy appears to underlie the opinion. The sentence of thirty years imprisonment is confirmed in all three instances.

Why and how the judiciary and public opinion have read similar facts in such different ways merits further discussion. Perhaps the judge has a piece of Italian history in mind. "Murder for cause of honor" as a separate criminal category was repealed in Italy only in 1981. Before that date any man in Italy who killed his wife, daughter, sister for reasons of "honor" received a maximum of five years of imprisonment. Even in 1982 the Supreme Court of Cassation reduced the sentence of a young Italian man who beat his sister to death because she went out at night. The sentence for this "honor killing" was mitigated by an inner-cultural argument: the younger brother had intended to take upon himself the paternal role. Perhaps changes in public attitudes toward women's rights which had occurred since then pressured the judges to consciously decide the Hina case the opposite way. Even judges, after all, are culturally situated. They must have recognized that mitigation based on cultural factors would mean legitimizing a number of past Italian behaviors as well, but such a move was still too close to the 1982 case to be bearable for the public. Perhaps the trial court's reference to the fact that Mohammed Saleem "is resident in Italy since 1989 and has had ample time and opportunity to learn and live the national customs and our rules" is intended as a way to stress that these rules are irreversibly changed since that "distant" period of Italian history. The intuition of the judge in declining the role of anthropologist in this case, despite the pressure of the defense and the public, is certainly commendable and perhaps even follows from an anti-discriminatory purpose, in the sense that the decision avoids stereotyping the entire Pakistani community.

The *Kimura* and *Saleem* cases of the United States and Italy, respectively, represent two difficult exemplary cases. They serve to introduce fundamental theoretical problems in dealing with multicultural conflicts, which will be taken up in detail later in the work.

Each case presents a high water mark in reference to the concept of culture then reformulated and ultimately rejected by the judges, showing that there is a "competition" between different classifications of human behavior, including anthropology, psychology and gender (Chap. 4 sec. 5.1). When, therefore, should the category of culture be used? When should individual responsibility? When patriarchy?

How much, for example, should the peculiar and distinct nature of a behavior count toward its classification *sub specie* of culture? Should the fact that in Italy as well as in other European countries a woman is killed by her lover almost every two days – a statistic not far from the rate of honor killings in Pakistan – be an argument to deculturalize the behavior? But would then the fact that infanticide can also be found around the world influence the outcome of the *Kimura* case (Marinopoulos 2008)?

10 Supreme Court of Cassation (Corte di Cassazione) sec. I penal, February 18th, 2010, no. 6587.

Each case grappled with the fundamental right to life, yet their solutions were opposite: Kimura has not served a day in prison, and Saleem was sentenced to thirty years. One might ask, how important is the legal right affected by the alleged cultural practice? But since in both cases the right in question is the right to life, is there, therefore, some other consideration that moves the judge?

Since 1980, with certain anticipations in place since 1950 in Western legal systems, there have accumulated hundreds of judgments in which the court was forced to wear the clothes of the anthropologist, in order to handle the complex category that is culture.

In this chapter, the reader is invited to take a first journey through these texts and the facts from which they originated – a journey yet unguided, not yet systematized (that must wait for Chapter 2), but one which offers a kaleidoscopic overview of the ways in which the judge has become an anthropologist. This chapter does not give answers yet, but it does show some of the most significant cultural arguments used in different legal traditions. The selection of cases among the hundreds analyzed, while never insouciant,[11] must still inevitably be partial. The omission in this chapter of such usually crucial conflicts for multiculturalism as genital mutilation/circumcision, polygamous marriage, prescriptions of the *burqa* or veil, *purdah* and so on is not due to any supposed minor importance, but due to a mere necessity to distribute the discourse; these subjects, in fact, will be treated in detail later in the course of the work.

2 Men who abuse women

2.1 The Kassam *case: the idea of family in Morocco*

What prompted Mohammed Kassam, who immigrated to Italy with his family, to beat and rape his wife? Moroccan culture, said his lawyer.

Kassam was sentenced to two years, six months and twenty days imprisonment for abuse, kidnapping, sexual assault and breach of the obligations of family assistance both to this spouse and his young son. The lawyer who defended him appealed to the Italian Supreme Court,[12] contesting that the judge erred in applying the subjective motive elements of the alleged offenses: not only does Kassam not confer any negative value to his conduct, but rather sees it almost necessitated

11 I have, for example, deliberately opened with a case which involves a woman not in the typical role of the victim covered, usually, in multicultural conflicts, and more generally with cases that conclude with judicial refusal to use culture (in the *Kimura* case, perhaps, strategically) to demonstrate the ambiguity underlying the concept of culture. Among the substantially similar hard cases (which deal with homicides) I have juxtaposed cases in which the reasoning of the parties are, sometimes, alien to our horizon of values (family honor) and at other times are instead respected (the feeling that children are part of us), to see the type of pre-comprehension of the case which determines the outcome. Totally irrelevant is, instead, the territorial provenance of the cases. In this sense, the globalism of multicultural conflicts (Kymlicka, Baogang 2005) does not frame the *Kimura* case as less "European" than others. Actually, all conflicts here described in the work could have happened anywhere.

12 Supreme Court of Cassation (Corte di Cassazione), sec. VI penal, op. 1520/2008.

in the face of his wife's rejection of the "conjugal debt." The lawyer argued that the appellate judge should not, in fact,

> in point of familial and socioeconomic relationships between spouses and parents/children . . . apply Western valuation schemas, without respect for the necessity of racial integration and without weighing, concerning the conduct of the offender, a Moroccan citizen, how cultural and religious diversity have shaped and informed his actions considered illegal here.

According to the lawyer, the judges "had concluded the prosecution on the basis of value assessments based on an ethnocentric prejudice, unable to ascertain the *mens rea*." Mohammed Kassam, any more than Kimura, according to this argument, could not have acted otherwise.

The judges of the Italian Supreme Court, in considering this argument, agreed to immerse themselves in the role of the anthropologist. The court analyzes, then, what it calls "the suggestive profile" raised by the applicant:

> the situation evokes the well-known phenomenon of "cultural crimes" that scholars have defined as the fruit of a normative conflict, suggestively using the expression "inter-legal" to indicate the condition of those who, having to make a choice, are forced to refer to a complex framework of norms, simultaneously existing and interacting between different legal systems.

The Supreme Court therefore focuses diffusively on the influences of multiculturalism on legal categories. They consider two models – the assimilationist, and the multiculturalist.[13] After this theoretical excursion the Supreme Court provides, finally, this response:

> it is quite clear that both prospects [the assimilationist and multiculturalist models] can be implemented in our criminal justice system if and to the extent they are not in conflict with the basic principles of it or the constitution, in themes of family, personal relationships and sexual coercion that in our system was rigidly and innovatively regulated by law no. 66/1996.[14]

13 In the words of the Court: "such reality has determined in various states, interested in massive fluxes of migrants, two different perspectives on multiculturalism. The first, 'assimilationist' type, pursues the inclusion of the foreigner into the national fabric and demands of the counterpart a substantial renunciation of his ethnic-cultural roots; the second, instead, its protocols oriented toward 'integration-inclusion' (symbolic and practical), is generally willing to accept the identitarian request and is sensitive to the cultural specificity of the 'other.' In this last model, founded in multi-relational logic and forms of 'evolutive co-learning,' the result is to propose as realizable a political society (deprived of a dominant or majoritarian cultural identity) constituted of multiple cultural identities, with equal right to recognition."

14 Entitled "Norms against sexual violence" this law transformed rape from being a crime against "public morals and good habits" (*pubblica morale e buon costume*) to a crime against "the person," thus increasing the penalties

The Court recalls art. 2 (protection of human rights) and 3 (equality principle) of the Italian Constitution and observes that they

> constitute an insurmountable barrier against the introduction, in law and in fact, into our civil society, of any practices or customs which present themselves as "anti-historical" in the face of the results obtained over the centuries, to assert the rights of the person, whether citizen or foreigner.

The Supreme Court seems not to close the door against open perspectives of legal pluralism and admits that, in the abstract, there may be circumstances in which it applies. But not this case. Hypotheses such as those of domestic violence collide with cardinal principles of the Italian legal order, and therefore the Moroccan "culture" cannot find recognition.

2.2 The **Pusceddu** *case: maltreatment as a Sardinian cultural attitude*

In the same period, Maurizio Pusceddu, a twenty-nine year old man from Cagliari, the provincial capital of Sardinia, who had emigrated to Stadthagen, Germany to work as a waiter, became convinced that his Lithuanian girlfriend had betrayed him. He kept her prisoner for three weeks, repeatedly subjected her to sexual violence, injected heroin against her will, extinguished cigarettes on her body and urinated on her. The German court[15] donned the role of the anthropologist without receiving any input from the defense, and reduced the penalty taking into account "the particular cultural and ethnic prints;" Mr. Pusceddu, in fact, "is a Sardinian. The picture of the role of man and woman which exists in his own country can hardly count as an excuse, but it must be taken into account as a mitigating factor."[16]

This decision immediately aroused disapproval in Italy, almost to the point of creating a diplomatic incident. The lawyer of the accused, instead of celebrating the lenience, commented: "this is a racist judgment." The political and intellectual Sardinian world mobilized, insisting on the incongruence of the reading given by the judge and accusing him of being an improvised anthropologist, one who ignored one of the pillars of the Sardinian culture: matriarchy.[17]

The disparate responses of the two judges, the Italian for the *Kassam* case and the German for the *Pusceddu* case, are opposite in their conclusions, but are identically legible, in my view, through the premises which motivated them. As Kassam and Moroccan culture are to Italy, Pusceddu and Sardinian culture are to Germany. But

15 Trial court of Bückeburg, January 25th, 2006.

16 They condemned him to six years in prison, instead than eight, thanks to the "ethno-cultural" mitigating circumstances. The decision was overturned on appeal after Italian protests.

17 The characteristic of a pastoral society which saw the man far from home for many months out of the year – explained Sardinian politicians and intellectuals – meant that the women assumed a central role in Sardinian society. In my view, this cultural counter-argument contributes more to tie the knot than to unravel it. The appeal to matriarchy, in fact, may be disputable on the merits, because it is present only in certain zones of the island and because it coexists with indubitable forms of patriarchy. What should have been contested is the "cultural" reading of the case itself.

neither of these two judges ask: was culture really evocable in these two cases? What happens, in both legal systems, when a Herr Schmidt or Signore Rossi, members of their respective majority cultures, happen to commit the same crimes? The cultural argument disappears immediately from the core of interpretations surrounding the judge, to give way to individual responsibility. In essence, what is left "unsaid" by any of the choruses intervening in the *Kassam* and *Pusceddu* cases is that domestic violence is not an exclusively Moroccan or Sardinian peculiarity, but rather one affecting almost all legal systems. Again, as seen in the drama of Hina Saleem (*supra* sec. 1.2), the gender issue is more suitable to frame the two cases under consideration and to defuse the potential toward stereotyping and possibly even racism.

Another question which arises is, in fact, how would the Bückeburg court have decided the case if the woman who had been the victim of violence had been German instead of Lithuanian? Could the attitude of the judge unconsciously conceal a form of racism not only to Pusceddu and the Sardinian culture that eventually favors the reduction in his sentence, but even (or especially) to the victim of this story: his partner? Are the two cultures, the Sardinian and Lithuanian, perhaps perceived as distant and incommensurable with the German one, abandoned in the name of giving a value to "culture," when in fact the use of the term subtly proscribes a lower value to the people who are part of it?

These cases thus intersect a further issue that surrounds multiculturalism: the culturalization of any conduct by the mere fact that its perpetrator is a foreigner (Volpp 2000).

3 Concepts of child care

3.1 The begging case: the Roma child who went to manghel *with his mother*

In 2008 the Italian Supreme Court pronounced a judgment[18] that inflamed public opinion, provoking a subsequent intervention in the legislature.

A Roma woman was denounced because she was found twice by police "begging on a street . . . sitting on the sidewalk with a child in her lap, while the other four-year-old son . . . begged nearby and then handed the money to his mother." The Court of Appeal in Santa Maria Capua Vetere (Naples) condemned the woman to the penalty of five years imprisonment pursuant to art. 600 of the Italian criminal code, which, amended by art. 1 of law no. 228/2003, introduces the new offense of "reduction to servitude," with the aim to combat racketeering by begging.

The decision was appealed to the Supreme Court by the defendant, with two arguments.

First, the appeal denied the existence of the offense, lacking coercion, the purpose of economic exploitation and the requirement for full and total subjection of the child's life. According to the defense, therefore, the facts, at most, support

18 Supreme Court of Cassation (Corte di Cassazione), sec. V, penal, September 17th, 2008, no. 44516.

a breach of art. 671 of the criminal code, which provided the offense of begging with a child with lesser penalties (from three months to a maximum of one year of prison), not a crime but a misdemeanor.

Second, the defense offered the cultural argument which claimed that: "the impugned decision would criminalize the *manghel* usually practiced by the Gypsies."

The Supreme Court partially upheld the claim of the defense, holding that the crime of reduction to servitude fit imperfectly, but recognizing, in its place, the crime of maltreatment. Let us follow the Supreme Court in its line of argument.

First, courts must identify whether or not there is an "abuse of authority," as a necessary element to reduction to servitude. It is not easy in general – notes the Supreme Court – but

> this is particularly true of some ethnic communities where, for example, the alms is part of a traditional lifestyle deeply rooted in the culture and mentality of this population . . . It is necessary to pay attention to the actual situation in order not to criminalize conduct that falls within the cultural tradition of a people.

After affirming that wherever there is a cultural element, the law cannot criminalize, the Supreme Court, however, states:

> it is understood, however, that if certain practices, perhaps even customary and traditional, jeopardize other individual's fundamental rights guaranteed by our Constitution or conflict with criminal laws that seek to protect such rights, criminal repression is inevitable. It is all too evident, in fact, that customs which are against criminal law cannot be allowed.

The reference to the Roma culture, along with the peculiarities of the case, move the Supreme Court to say that in this case the Court of Appeal erred in recognizing the crime of reduction to servitude in art. 600 criminal code. This rule has the purpose to prevent the exploitation of children:

> the situation is quite different, however, in the case of the woman, the mother of the children who are carried with her, who practices begging for a few hours per day – or who practices this as part of a cultural tradition of the ethnic group to which she belongs or because she is found in conditions of severe economic hardship (or for both reasons, often overlapping) – and who asks help from her son. In this context, it is difficult to set up the offense under art. 600 criminal code because it is quite possible that, after conducting the begging in the morning hours, in the remaining part of the day the woman takes care of the children properly trying to meet their needs and allowing them to play and associate with other children; it means, that there was not the radical negation of human freedom and dignity of the child necessary to prove a state of complete servitude, thus legitimately providing for the serious sanctions foreseen by art. 600 of the criminal code.

At this point, the court could frame the case as part of the misdemeanor of art. 671, but prescribed, however, just the opposite; observing that the woman

> used a four year old child to beg to passersby on a continuous basis, i.e. each day . . . thus forcing him to stand for more than four consecutive hours in winter, without being, however, properly dressed . . . There is no doubt that such conduct is detrimental to the physical and moral integrity of the child and causes a severe distress situation.

The court, therefore, sustains the offense of maltreatment (art. 572 of the Italian criminal code), based on their own doctrine that no cultural practice can violate fundamental rights.[19]

Despite the conviction, the opinion has been perceived by the Italian public opinion as favorable toward the *manghel*. Presented as a decision authorizing "part-time baby begging" or "begging as a cultural practice,"[20] it has aroused adverse reactions from all the major political figures, in defense of children's rights. So much so that a few months later the legislature passed the law no. 94/2009. This has introduced art. 600 *octies* which repealed the previous art. 671 of the criminal code, increasing the sanction against child begging: from a misdemeanor "against public order," begging with a child becomes a "crime against the person;" from the previous "three months to a year" of prison now child-begging is punished to "up to three years" of prison with the automatic penalty of loss of parental authority.

Yet among all the Choruses to have spoken, one still has not been heard: the Roma community. They have almost unanimously denied that the *manghel* was a custom for them. The *manghel* is part of their history but not of the Roma culture. They did not always beg: first they pastured horses, worked copper, dealt with circus activities, recycled old iron scrap. Engaging in begging they said, was on the contrary a product of the collapse of their culture; they started to beg in Italy after 1960 when the industrialization of the country brought about the demise of their nomadic lifestyle and their traditional jobs. But though this Chorus whispered, the courts remained deaf to it.[21]

At the end of the book we will see how the judge could have stated the reasons by taking into account the truly cultural practices underlying this case (Chap. 4 sec. 5.2). What we can say for now is that, even in this case, as in the above

19 This decision is in line with the Italian "living law" (i.e. the prevailing judicial interpretations of the written law), which has over time seen a substantial disapplication of the misdemeanor of art. 671 of the criminal code, as a constant subsumption of the begging of minors within the crime of maltreatment of art. 572.

20 See, for example, the comments in "Mendicante a quattro anni. I giudici: non é schiavitú. 'É la tradizione dei Rom'. Insorge il centrodestra," ("Begging at four years old. Judges: it is not slavery. 'It is Roma tradition.' Center-Right parties protest,") and in "Se era italiano la donna sarebbe in cella," ("If she were Italian the woman would be in jail,") both in *Il Corriere della Sera*, November 29th, 2008.

21 See the declaration of the *Federazione Rom e Sinti Insieme* ("Roma and Sinti Together Federation") at http://sucardrom.blogspot.com/search?q=manghel+sentenza. The Court of Cassation (Corte di Cassazione) sec. V penal returned to the subject of *manghel* with the judgment September 28th, 2012 no. 37638 in which it subsumed the fact that the parents who obliged a ten-year old child to beg the whole day under the crime of *riduzione in schiavitú* ("reduction to slavery"). Also in this case the defense maintained that "the culture of the Roma people accords the practice of begging the value of a true and proper system of life, based on a thousand-years history." And the Supreme Court replied that culture should yield to human rights, perpetuating a disputable cultural reading of *manghel*.

mentioned *Kassam* and *Pusceddu* cases, the anthropologist judge has constructed the story as a multicultural conflict, although on the cultural nature of *manghel* there is disagreement, a disagreement that comes, in the first place, from the same group to which the practice is attributed. But how could the Supreme Court notice this? After all, it was the mother's defense attorney who spoke of *manghel* as part of Roma culture. Two other cases involving the care of children reveal how judges have proceeded in other jurisdictions to investigate the nature and characteristics of a practice.

3.2 In re Peter L., Jr.: *the Greek grandmother denied custody for mourning too ardently*

A trial court in the State of New York, United States, found itself confronted with the following case of contentious foster care: a Greek child had been orphaned after his father died during a shootout in the neighborhood where the family lived; his mother, shortly after this event, gave up parental authority over the child, thus opening the procedure for foster care.[22] The child's paternal grandmother, who at the time of his abandonment assumed his care, proposed to become his permanent guardian but social services rejected her request with these arguments: the woman did not seem appropriate because she had an over-protective attitude toward her grandson, did not let him come out to play, told him that it was his duty to avenge his father, and generally seemed incapable to overcome a tragic loss as shown by, among other things, the fact that she left many photos of her dead son (the Greek boy's father) in the house, adorned with small lamps and black ribbons. Social services believed since this over-protective woman was not the biological mother, they should look for more acceptable pairings.

According to the court of first instance, which validated the decision of social services: "the isolated existence of a lonely and embittered grandmother (whose first son was also killed in a street violence episode) could not be an appropriate home for the child."

The woman appealed; the trial court largely observed that her custodial behavior "stood by cultural practices that are quite pronounced, part of the personality of the grandmother, and certainly part of the cultural heritage of the child." The anthropologist judge arrives at this decision after consulting with a Greek psychologist who explains how in Greece mourning "is very ceremonial and lasts a long time." Black is worn by adults for three to five years, there is "a lot of discussion about death, about where the person goes after death," a "picture of the deceased on the grave and in the home with black crepe around them" may be displayed forever, and people wear or keep in their pocket a picture of the deceased. At the judge's question "Has the keeping

22 *In the matter of Peter L. Jr., Christina L., v. James Krauskopf, as Commissioner of Social Services*, 460 N.Y.S.2d 578, 1983.

of a picture of the deceased parent been found to be detrimental to a child's development?" the psychologist responds:

> I have to answer this generally. Given that these are the Greek cultures, with a ceremonial way of dealing with death, and given that we all go through the experience if somebody in the family dies, as people we don't have higher incidents of mental disturbances than any other nation. As a matter of fact we have less, but in general this is the custom of the country, and as far as I know there is no study that would suggest that this is "detrimental" as you put it.

The judge concluded by accepting the cultural reading and allowing the child to be entrusted to his grandmother.

This solution is "understandable" in all Southern Europe where there are similar forms of mourning and where there is a concept of extended family in which the child's relatives are basically seen as subjects preferred over anyone else for the purpose of care and dependence. But in the Northern American context where, by contrast, the mononuclear family model is more pronounced and there are different forms of mourning, the task of translation to decode the grandmother's behavior, otherwise perceived on the brink of pathology, must be accomplished. The resolution of the conflict occurred through the figure of a cultural mediator, in this case a Greek psychologist, who also acted as an expert on the meanings of a cultural system to which he himself belonged. The success of the solution relies on the fact that the judge asked for a full and informed description of the cultural practice (objective cultural analysis) and its impact on the litigants (subjective cultural analysis).

3.3 The Kargar *case: the Afghan father who kissed his son on the genitals*

In 1993 Mohammad Kargar, a refugee from Afghanistan to the United States, was seen by a neighbor's daughter putting his mouth on the penis of his son, an eighteen-month-old baby. The daughter tells her mother, who recalled that in Kargar's house she had already observed, in an album that he had shown her, a photo in which he and his wife kissed the genitals of their infant child. Convinced that she had found a pedophile, she filed a complaint with the police. When the man and his wife departed from the house, police searched it and recovered the photos. Kargar was accused of the charge of "sexual abuse."

The Superior Court of Maine[23] applied an article of the Criminal Code of Maine, which identifies in detail what is meant by sexual act and punishes "direct physical contact between the genitals [. . .] and the mouth" between an adult and any person under the age of fourteen years. Kargar's defense, however, called

23 *State of Maine v. Mohammad Kargar*, 679 A.2d 81, 1996.

for the application of the *de minimis* (*non curat lex*) standard (Pomorski 1997), trying to prove that his conduct does not in fact encompass sexual abuse. Inviting the court to become an anthropologist, the defense explains that Afghan

> culture views the penis of a child as not the holiest or cleanest part of the body because it is from where the child urinates. Kargar testified that kissing his son there shows how much he loves his child precisely because it is not the holiest or cleanest part of the body.

Other members of that culture confirm this reconstruction:

> Kargar's witnesses, all relatively recent emigrants from Afghanistan, testified that kissing a son's penis is common in Afghanistan, that it is done to show love for the child, and that it is the same whether the penis is kissed or entirely put into the mouth because there are no sexual feelings involved. The witnesses also testified that pursuant to Islamic law any sexual activity between an adult and a child results in the death penalty for the adult.

A professor of Islamic religion, called as well by the defense as an independent expert, reiterates the actual existence of such a custom in Afghanistan.

Nevertheless, the judge rejected the request to apply the *de minimis* standard and condemned Kargar, who lost custody of his baby.

The opinion of the judge is based on the originalist-textualist interpretation of the article of the criminal code which incriminates as sexual abuse the behavior of "anyone who handles the genitals of a child under 14 years with the mouth." Before 1985 this provision contained an additional requirement: the action must be carried out "in order to obtain sexual gratification;" but this last phrase had been repealed by the legislature in 1985. The fact that the latter had left the requirement for other cases (for example, the case of "touching the genitals" of a child still requires "sexual gratification," so as to permit medical treatment) and had explicitly repealed it in this case, according to the court, made it clear that the legislature had intended to punish any kind of contact between the genitals and mouth, without exception. The textualist argument, according to the judge, did not allow any other interpretations in this case.

The decision is appealed

> in point of law because the court fails to consider culture, the absence of damage (the child was an infant, therefore, unable to perceive or suffer any adverse consequences from the gesture) and the absence of willful misconduct as relevant for the application of the *de minimis* standard

in the Supreme Court of Maine – which grants the appeal, sets aside the lower court decision and orders a reevaluation of the case in light of the *de minimis* standard.

The holding of the Supreme Court of Maine reads: "Although it may be difficult for us as a society to separate Kargar's conduct from our notions of sexual abuse, that difficulty should not result in a felony conviction in this case." The appellate court thus replies to the textualist argument raised by the state lawyer and accepted by the court of first instance:

> The State is concerned, however, with the potential harm caused by courts using the factors of this case to allow for even more exceptions to the criminal statutes. It argues that exceptions should be made by the Legislature, which can gather data, debate social costs and benefits, and clearly define what conduct constitutes criminal activity. The flaw in the State's position is that the Legislature has already clearly defined what conduct constitutes gross sexual assault.

The court states the conditions under which the cultural argument can be used to justify the *de minimis non curat lex* standard:

> Application of the *de minimis* statute does not nullify the gross sexual assault statute nor does it reflect approval of Kargar's conduct. The conduct remains criminal. Kargar does not argue that he should now be permitted to practice that which is accepted in his culture. The issue is whether his past conduct under all of the circumstances justifies criminal convictions.

Among the reasons stated: "culture, lack of harm, and [Kargar's] innocent state of mind."

Thus only after a long legal battle the cultural argument was evaluated; but in the meantime the child had been definitively assigned to another family.

In this case cultural "translation" was necessary as the majority American culture stands for a strong puritanism and has cancelled forms of bodily affective relations involving the genitalia, which persist, however, in other groups, including Western societies such as the Albanian where kisses and caresses on the genitals of infants are not unusual.[24]

24 In Italy the Trial Court of Reggio Emilia (Tribunale dei minori di Reggio Emilia) November 21st, 2012 acquitted an Albanian father who kissed, touched and suckled his five year old son's penis and was accused of sexual abuse. The court stated the reasons saying that, although the gesture was clearly sexual according the Italian criminal code, the father lacked sexual intention with the behavior being a culturally motivated crime based on a tradition of rural Albania (as it was a cuddle and a form of homage to the penis). The Court of Appeal of Bologna (Corte d'appello di Bologna) April 19th, 2017 upheld the decision, adding that the behavior could not even be considered a crime because "it was a gesture of love and paternal pride toward the male offspring, completely lacking any sexual connotation and conforming to cultural tradition of rural Albania." The Italian Supreme Court of Cassation (Corte di Cassazione) sec. III penal, 29 January 2018, no. 29613 reversed and ordered a new trial in which the man would be condemned, as the sucking and kissing of the penis, concerning an erogenous zone, is inherently sexual and the cultural defense cannot be used when it affects crucial rights of the child.

What is striking in the dramatic outcome of this case, which was not isolated,[25] are the diverse bonds between parents and children, subordinated to compliance with standardized ways of expressing affection. Also in Western cultures there are debates on how to show affection, but they are almost never solved by the loss of parental rights of Western parents. Consider, for example, the nudist philosophy that aims to free children from any taboos by the open display of the parents' bodies, or to those positions that criticize the de-sexualization of the mother–child relationship, stressing its fundamentally erotic nature (Rodrigañez 1995).

The cases analyzed so far show that it is sometimes easy for anthropologist judges to fall into a culturalist fallacy (in the *Kassam*, *Pusceddu* and begging cases), while sometimes it is only the appreciation of cultural variations that can avoid committing an injustice (the *In re Peter* and *Kargar* cases).

4 Culture and indigenous peoples

An important chapter in the reconstruction of the role of the anthropologist judge and argumentative techniques drawn from her analyses concerns the case law on indigenous peoples. Although seemingly far from the migrants' reality (Kymlicka 1995; Grandi 2009: 183), this case law which has developed primarily in the first contemporary Western multicultural nations – Australia, Canada and the United States – is important because it has seen the development of further requirements and conditions for the acceptance of culture. Actually, the very first cultural test, in fact, was elaborated (in Canada in 1996) to resolve cases regarding indigenous peoples.

25 In 1983 in the US (in the case *In Re Jertrude O. 466 A.2d 885 (Md App 1983))*, a family of the Republic of Central Africa lost, temporarily, their three children, on the grounds of leaving them alone and because one of them, Jertrude, was found with oval bruises on various parts of her body. The cultural expert demonstrated that it was a cultural fact that older children deal with those who are younger and that the bruises were not the consequence of maltreatment, but rather of a traditional medical practice consistent with pressing various parts of the body with an oval mug. The appeal judge affirmed that these practices "did not provide ordinary and proper care and attention by our standards," but decided that instead of taking them from their parents as the trial judge had decided, the children would be better served through social services. In 1989 in Texas, Sadri and Sabahete Krasniqi, two Albanian parents, lost their parental rights to their two children because the father was accused of molesting his daughter, as he caressed her pubis more than once during a school sporting event. Despite the testimony of the cultural expert that, in Albania, it is an accepted way of showing affection, the children were adopted by custodial parents and converted from Islam to Christianity. The judge expressly said that the children would be better raised in a Christian family [*Krasniqi v. Dallas Cty. CPS Unit TX*, 809 S.W.2d 927 (Tex. App. 1991)]. In the same period in which the *Krasniqi* case was discussed, the daily papers had publicized the case of a Danish mother accused of abandoning a minor for the fact of leaving her baby carriage outside the entrance of a restaurant in America. The woman quickly recovered her child after demonstrating that in Denmark this practice is usual. A few days later the papers spoke of "cultural diversity" and showed a photo in Copenhagen with baby carriages left outside of stores while the parents made purchases. The two examples reveal a double standard (Sultana Brelvi 1996–97; Volpp 1994, 1996).

In some of the cases that follow, I present a new configuration of multicultural conflicts argued over culture as a constitutionally recognized right and not a mere tradition or custom or factor to be taken into account in the interpretation of an applicable standard.

4.1 The Muddarubba, Rankin *and* Noboi-Borsi *cases: reasonable killing, reasonable cannibalism*

We are in Australia; it is 1956; the Northern Territory Supreme Court is faced with the case of an aboriginal member of the tribe of Pitjintjara who killed a woman belonging to his own tribe, reacting to an insult with this retaliation.[26] The court would apply all of a series of common law precedents, under which the mere words are not suitable to integrate a "provocation," and thus inapplicable as a mitigating factor. However, the judge refuses recourse to them, wearing instead the clothes of the anthropologist. He explains that in each finding of provocation, the general principle of law is to create a standard that is observed by the average person in the community in which the accused person lives. Finding a cultural equivalent (Chap. 4 sec. 5.9) the judge observes that what in the white community a hundred years ago was considered as a sufficient provocation could not be considered sufficient today, suggesting that the standard is unfixed and changing. This leaves open the ability to see the tribe of Pitjintjara as a separate community with regard to the consideration of the average person's reaction. Based on this premise, the judge instructs the jury that if they think that the average person of Pitjintjara tribe would react to the woman's offensive words by flinging a javelin against her, then the act is not first-degree murder (murder, worst case), but second-degree murder (manslaughter, a lesser charge).

In a similar case,[27] another Australian judge instructed the jury as follows:

> The accused was born in the settlement of Aboriginal Woorabinda in central Queensland, where he lived most of his life and where the murder was committed. I propose to direct the jury in the sense that the question to be considered is whether the sudden provocation was sufficient to deprive an average Aboriginal man who lives in an Aboriginal settlement of his power of self-control. [A group of Aborigines appeared and gave testimony to that effect before the jury.]

In a case which occurred in Papua New Guinea,[28] faced with two indigenous accused of having eaten parts of a corpse, the judge again recourses to the standard of the "reasonable person" according the criterion of that specific culture. He believes, in fact, that the conduct of cannibalism of the dead should be measured not by Western standards, but with those of an average Gabusi

26 *R. v. Muddarubba* [1956] NTJ 317, 322, quoted by Morris, Howard (1964: 96).
27 *R. v. Rankin,* [1966] QWN 16.
28 *R. v. Noboi-Bosai* [1971–1972], P. and N.G.L. R. 271.

man of primitive tribes, as he would have acted in a village of Daldabili and Yulabi in 1971. Applying this criterion, the judge notes that the decision to "eat the dead body of the village inhabitants was not an improper or indecent behavior, being rather a normal and reasonable behavior." He chooses not to condemn the accused.

In the cases cited the diversity of aboriginal peoples is recognized through the "reasonable cultural person" instrument, which declines to take the behavior of the majority as its parameter but rather uses the agent model, the average reasonable person who is culturally located. There is thus a strong anthropological matrix undergirding the judge's reasoning.[29]

4.2 The Thomas *case: initiation by force into the spirits' dance*

In 1992, in British Columbia, David Thomas, a member of the Coast Salish First Nation, was taken by some people of his community to an indigenous ceremonial hall (Long House), where he was held for three days, beaten, forced to fast and subjected to several ablutions, while his companions sang and exhaled over his body. Once freed, Mr. Thomas sued Daniel Louie Norris and the other companions for assault, battery and false imprisonment (Eisenberg 1994).

What motivated these people to take away their companion against his will? What happened inside the Long House?

The British Columbia Supreme Court[30] observes that the case must be examined "through the eyes of indigenous people" by adopting the cultural group's point of view: one needs to understand that we are faced neither with an act of bullying, nor a possible revenge. What David Thomas faced is a behavior which has a certain meaning in Western culture – an assault with injuries – and a totally separate meaning for the indigenous communities – an initiation, performed to fulfill a ritual. The companions of David Thomas are, in fact, three of the dancers of the dance of the spirits, who were performing a ritual that would serve to make Thomas a dancer too. An ancient initiation. To help dancers find their own voice, their own "song," their hidden inner self, they must endure an ordeal. The tradition requires that, once identified by those who already know the dance, the person involved in transmitting the secret of the steps can initiate the rite even against the will of the chosen.

Through various appeals, the case arrives to the British Columbia Supreme Court. The court observes, in the abstract, that the civil rights of the applicant

29 Forms of "reasonable killings" were discussed in the following cases; *Gadam v. R.*, 14 W.A.C.A. 442 (1954) Nigeria (murder of witches); *Philip Muswe s/o Musele v. R.* 23 E.A.C.A. 622 (1956) Kenya (murder of witches); *R. v. Mbombela*, 1993 South Africa (murder of a person mistaken for an evil creature).

30 *Thomas v. Norris*, [1992] 2 C.N.R. 139 B.C.S.C. (Canadian Native Law Reporter-British Columbia Supreme Court), 139–163.

against the assault, beatings and imprisonment are subordinated and have to leave room for the collective rights of the Aboriginal nation to which he belongs and which are protected by sec. 35 of the Canadian Constitution. As long as certain conditions are met.

The British Columbia Supreme Court ascertains the origins of the practice and find that they are very ancient: the dance of the spirits was practiced long before the contact between the indigenous and the Europeans who colonized Canada. But this is not enough. The subjects were motivated by a cultural imperative to perpetuate a long-lasting tradition; however, the dance of the spirits is not something that can be said to be "essential and integral" to the survival of the Coast Salish as a distinct group. The dancers of the Coast Salish Tribe are, therefore, condemned.

But what would happen if, instead, the dance of the spirits had been an essential and integral practice for the Coast Salish? Can a cultural practice, if essential and binding, be enforceable against the will of someone who does not recognize it as such? The reasoning in the British Columbia Supreme Court would seem to support such a reading.

Such cases are part of the dozens of judgments that were handed down in Canada to resolve conflicts with Aboriginal people. There are as many in the United States and even some in Europe with reference to the only existing Indigenous people who remain: the Samis. One can already appreciate the vastly different approaches of the Australian judge in 1950–1960 who accepts, anthropologically, to read the facts through the eyes of the reasonable indigenous person standard, and the Canadian who demands a broader series of requisites through the 1996 cultural test (Chap. 2 sec. 5.1): the practice must have been established pre-contact, it must be distinctive, essential and often supported by evidence from archaeologists or anthropologists. This is a very rigid proceduralization of the conditions for the recognition of Aboriginal rights enshrined in sec. 35 of the Constitution. A similarly standardized approach to the questions a Canadian judge should ask is used with respect to religious claims. Since 2004, in fact, the Canadian Supreme Court has adopted a "religious test" (Chap. 2 sec. 5.2), deeply different from the "cultural test." This clear distinction of remedies, depending on whether the claim is cultural or religious, is a feature of many other legal systems as well.

After this presentation, deliberately kaleidoscopic, of the heterogeneous ways in which the courts may decline the cultural argument, it appears indispensable to enter within individual legal traditions to systematically verify which techniques worked and which models of the resolution of multicultural conflict models are deducible.

The survey will continue to be performed in comparative manner, with a focus on North American, English, Italian and German jurisprudence. The US and Canada were some of the first to confront the challenges of multiculturalism and, not surprisingly, have made numerous attempts to systematize the legal reasoning in the face of a conflict.

Thus the aim of the following analysis will be to extrapolate some common trends within the multiplicity of multicultural jurisprudence (Foblets, Renteln 2009), to check if it is possible to foresee the emergence of a common legal tradition in solving multicultural conflicts. I will explore recurring elements (or *topoi* according to Aristotelian dialectic) in Western judicial reasoning, such as the importance accorded to the residence time in the host culture (UK), the element of physical damage (Italy and Germany) as well as the historicity of the cultural practice and its essential and integral nature for the survival of the group (Canada).

2 The resolution of multicultural conflicts in Western comparative jurisprudence

In search of a common tradition and reliable legal techniques

1 *Topica*: finding recurring themes (*topoi*) in Western judicial reasoning

The cases discussed in the previous chapter reveal a phenomenon diffused, with various levels of intensity, in all Western societies which are, in fact or under law, multicultural: the consideration, by the courts, of the culture of the protagonists of a case as an element which calls into question the application of a general and abstract rule which would normally apply to a national member of the majority culture.

The scope of this chapter is to analytically complete the cursory descriptions of the previous one, and to verify the divergences and the analogies within the prevalent judicial doctrines using the concept of culture. To understand whether a common legal tradition is emerging from the various case by case approaches, and to compare the several arguments developed by judges in different Western jurisdictions appears, in fact, to be an operation essential to the elaboration of a tool to resolve multicultural conflicts.

The *topoi* (singular *topos*) signify, in dialectic and rethoric tradition, "the points of view which constantly return, the fixed themes" (Viehweg 1962; Cavalla 1992), that is, the shared points reached in a discourse on which there is a stable consensus (Mootz, Cerrone, Niccolai, Repetto, Bascherini 2013). The term was used by Aristotle and reprised by Cicero (44 B.C.E.), who called them *loci*. The *stagirite* considered *Topica* (title also of one of his works gathered in the *Organon*) as a branch of the *Dialectica*, that is the art of discussion (Aristotle 2012). Translated as the "theory of common points," and in certain cases directly as "rhetoric," *topica* expresses the fact that judicial reasoning has a non-deductive-systematic structure, but practices oriented toward concrete cases.[1] Opposite

1 Theodor Viehweg (1962) reaffirms the distinction between systematic thinking, typical of hard sciences and problematic thinking, typical of the law. *Topica* or topical approach is defined as "the technique of thinking problematically" and as "those techniques of thought that are addressed toward the problem" (31). Overall, this adherence and strict liaison with the concrete case, or the problem, does not signify total absence of systems. Defining the problem as "whatever question that apparently consents more of a response" (32), Viehweg observes, in fact, that the task of *Topica* is to furnish the *topoi*, the tools to resolve the problem (33). Applying Viehweg's *Topica* to our times, an emblematic example of thinking on problems is the affair of the Sikh dagger: faced with a normative system that prohibits the carrying of arms, the Canadian judges have said that the knife could be worn by adult persons, except within airports, and also by children at school if sealed, showing attention to the practical aspect of accommodation (Chap. 3, sec. 7). An example, *vice versa*, of thinking on systems is the French prohibition of the veil in schools (Chap. 2, sec. 10) in the name of the abstract principle of laity (*laicitè*) and neutrality (Laffaille 2010).

to a view of the law as a formulaic science, which pervaded European civil law from the Pandettian movement up to the *Begriff Jurisprudenze* (Jurisprudence of concepts), the approach suggested by *Topica* was resurrected, after centuries of oblivion, by the work of Theodor Viehweg *Topik und Jurisprudenz* (1953) and by the new rhetoric movement launched by Chaim Perelman and Lucie Olbrechts-Tyteca with the *Traitè de l'Argumentation: La Nouvelle Rhètorique* published in 1962 (Perelman, Olbrechts-Tyteca 1969).[2]

According to Theodor Viehweg, legal reasoning is not formulaic, but instead consists in:

> the activity of a speaker, which cannot proceed deductively from an axiom held true by the whole audience, and therefore seeks to identify the points (or *loci*, *topoi*) with which to begin, through their examination, a discursive procedure to make them appear convincing.
>
> (Viehweg 1962: 38)

Against this background, my goal is to investigate whether Western judges' reasoning around culture produce some *topoi* that can be considered stable references to resolve conflicts. Once collected, the main *topoi* will be assessed to see which of them are more recurring and persuasive toward the view of building a new multicultural coexistence and to see which of them can be stably incorporated into judicial reasoning (through the "cultural test" proposed in Chap. 4).

This journey through the "recurring themes" produced when culture appears in court will take us to comparatively analyze several legal systems. The use of the cultural argument appeared first around 1950 in American, Australian and British jurisprudence. Until 1980 it remained, however, confined to a few cases, and did not raise particular theoretical attention. Its record thereafter gradually increased. It is, therefore, a recent phenomenon, whose symbolic birth dates vary from system to system. In the United States it took the *Kimura* case (1985) to initiate an intense season of recourse to the use of the cultural argument in courts and an ongoing debate on the formalization of the cultural defense. Canada, which had constitutionalized multiculturalism and indigenous cultural rights since 1982, began to actually use it in 1996. Other realities, such as the Italian, faced significant transformations in the multicultural sense of their social fabric later, so the question has arisen especially strongly since 2000.

2 Perhaps the most important work on the structuration of non-scientific discourse, the *Traitè de l'Argumentation* gave legitimacy to the anti-positivistic movement within the law sustaining that, as social science the law, more than authoritatively reaching a truth, wants to persuade. Perelman revitalized the tradition of law as dialectic and rhetoric, that is the art of persuasion, which had suffered a decline, at least in the civil law tradition, in favor of a mathematical vision of judicial reasoning.

Each of these jurisdictions has struggled to resolve their individual cases in a structural vacuum,[3] a situation that can be contemplated at a glance today to comprehend what Theodor Vieweg (1962) considered the aim of *topica*: connecting "thinking problematically" to "thinking systematically," that is, finding a bridge between the peculiarity of each case and a systematic matrix for solving multicultural conflicts.

2 The distinction between culture and religion in constitutional law: the *topos* of God

In all the countries covered by this analysis there is a difference hinging on whether the principal issue of the case is "culture" or "religion." Both are non-juridical concepts which have been conventionally defined by the law as follows: "Culture should be regarded as the set of distinctive spiritual, material, intellectual and emotional features of society or a social group . . . it encompasses, in addition to art and literature, lifestyles, ways of living together, value systems, traditions and beliefs."[4]

Definitions of religion vary from those that include all the beliefs and practices expressing a connection with a transcendent or immanent divinity, to broader definitions including any sincere and meaningful belief that occupies in the life of its possessor a place which is equally important to that held by God in the lives of other persons.[5]

Religious conflicts are generally resolved with argumentative techniques partially different from cultural conflicts in the strict sense.

The reason for this distinction is primarily historical. At the dawn of the constitutionalism era, in fact, "religion" was considered the main factor of "alterity."[6] For Catholics the other, the different *par excellence* was the Protestant. Religion

3 Conversely, an example of legal recognition of the cultural defense is the Criminal Code of Peru, which was amended in 1991 (legislative decree 3 April 1991 no. 635): art. 15 introduces the concept of "cultural error" as a circumstance exempting from liability in sentencing or mitigating the criminal penalties. Art. 15: "Culturally motivated miscomprehension (*Error de comprensión culturalmente condicionado*). He, who commits a punishable act without being able, because of his culture or customs, to understand the criminal relevance of his act or to behave according to that understanding, will be exempted from liability. When, for the same reason, said possibility (to understand the criminal relevance of his act) is diminished, the penalty will be mitigated."

4 Preamble of the UNESCO Universal Declaration on Cultural Diversity, 2 November 2001. This is one of the few legal definitions of culture. For other anthropological definitions see Chap. 3 sec. 1 of this book.

5 *United States v. Ballard*, 322 U.S. 78, 64 S. Ct. 882, 88 L. Ed. 1148 (1944).

6 Scholars stress the "religious roots of democratic constitutionalism" (Spadaro 2008: 93–150), and observe: "just as the modern state, as it emerged from the compromise of Westphalia, was initially a tool to resolve religious conflicts, in the same way the concept of minority was intimately born from and bound to religious factors. The first minorities in the juridical sense, thus, were religious ones" (Palermo, Woelk 2011: 82).

was one of the first freedoms recognized in constitutions because across Christian Europe so many had killed over it. Religion receives separate treatment for another historical reason: the legitimacy it received in Europe depended in part on the existence of highly structured historical nexus between ecclesiastical and political power and on the idea of the religious roots of human rights (Prisco 2011).

For these reasons, therefore, religion has long been recognized as a constitutional right to be protected. It is no coincidence that there are currently around fifty constitutions to have codified cultural rights (Appendix: the status of culture in constitutions), and one hundred and ninety-four to mention religious rights.[7] For this, when faced with religious diversity, the judge is facilitated by a number of normative parameters and a rich tradition of constitutional interpretation. We can say that an indisputable *topos*, recurrent theme, which emerges in Western courts is that of God:[8] the transcendent divine elicits more recognition from the legal systems than the more immanent "human cultures."

This distinction between culture and religion, which can be justified historically and which may be found in the greater part of judicial opinions, is yet revealed today as more and more questionable – for three principal reasons.

Philosophically, both culture and religion are constituent elements of identity (Taylor 1989). Indeed, following the era of secularization, religion is losing its role as a key source of identity in the process of construction of the self (Taylor 2007).[9]

Anthropologically, the concepts encounter very similar dynamics and have no ontological autonomy. Both concepts pose similar problems with regard to, for example, the relationship between culture/religion in the abstract and their concrete incarnations within individuals (each one of which embodies both a lived culture and a lived religion), as well the transformations that over time a culture and a religion can face. Further, the distinction now appears to anthropologists a result of a Western mindset as similar categorizations do not exist in many other semiotic systems. The result is that within anthropology religion, as well as language, is a *species* of the wider *genus* of culture.

Legally the different treatment of culture and religion is problematic as well, because of the many aspects they share. Both represent areas of discrimination to

7 Constitutions differ between those which recognize religion in its individual dimension as freedom of religion, and those which recognize the collective dimension, giving recognition to "religious groups," their representatives and institutions.

8 I am conscious that I am referring to the divine with a culturally conditioned word – God – which belongs only to monotheistic religions. The choice is stylistically motivated by the need to find a concise word that can be understood by the audience of this book, which is mainly Western. Moreover I could not find a more appropriate culturally inclusive word: "the *topos* of the divine," for instance, does not include Indigenous religions, which do not separate nature from the divine.

9 Historically, religion, race or social class have filled the role of main identity-markers. They are still categories utilized in the social sciences and are relevant to the law, but in secular and post-industrial society they have lost their dominant role. Alternatively, the emergence of culture as an identity-marker is an historical fact often contested, in respect to which there are still uncertainties, and perhaps in the future it will surrender its place to other classifications although, in my opinion, the cultural element will remain for at least another century a strong identity-marker relevant for all policy makers and judges.

be removed. Both appear to have a value inherent to the democratic principles of pluralism and diversity that every open society promotes. Conversely, the issue of the claims of so-called "illiberal minorities" (Stolzenberg 2002) touches across both cultural and religious minorities (Stolzenberg, Myers 1992; Stolzenberg 2010; Shah 2015a).

With these observations I do not intend to contest the validity of a stipulative distinction between culture and religion; I can, in fact, concur that the concept of religion indicates all aspects of a culture that are relevant to the spiritual sphere. What seems questionable is the different legal treatment of "culturally motivated crimes" (Van Broeck 2001) on the one hand, and "religiously motivated crimes" on the other hand.[10]

The bias in favor of religion that exists in all the examined laws is likely to create situations of inequality, primarily in borderline cases. If the judicial techniques or the regulatory structure present in a legal system to resolve a religious or cultural conflict do not coincide, one risks different solutions according to the judge, faced with practices that are both religious and cultural (eg. male circumcision, the *burqa*), who chooses to catalog the behavior in one rather than the other category.

Indeed, it is argued that the problem would be more apparent than real in the sense that many cultural practices coincide with religious practices; therefore one would find the maximum legal protection, under the theory of fundamental rights, in each case. However, this approach is belied by the fact that there are several areas of behavior that would remain uncovered. Consider all the eating and dressing habits that have no connection with religion, the concept of honor, or the practices of child care or intergenerational relationships, or the myriad secular rites of passage or the role of the family.

Even in cases where the classification of the practice as religious would not involve any preferential treatment – think of female genital mutilation,[11] which

10 For a contrary view, see Bramadat (2005a), who favors a juridical treatment separated for religion. At the same time, the author recounts other situations in which it is difficult to trace a neat boundary between the two concepts. Sometimes we cannot precisely determine which part of identity of a person or a group or which motivations derive from religious sources and which from ethnic sources. For example, many studies of Sikhism would sustain that the turban is not explicitly required as one of the traditional five pillars (see note 102) of Sikhism (as is the requirement to cut one's hair): the turban is a cultural addition, an element of the culture or ethnicity of the Punjabi that has been absorbed into Sikhism as a religion (18). The author reveals, furthermore, that religions are internally diversified and subject to change over time, for which reason we cannot affirm a paradigm of more stability of religion than culture (13).

11 On the configuration of female genital mutilation (FGM) as a cultural instead than religious practice see Fornasari (2008: 179), with these arguments: "The origin of FGM cannot be traced back to Islam, because there is, according to the references of anthropologists, a multi-millennial history rooted in East Africa, in which it was practiced, over all these territories, also by Christians and Jews (the Coptics and the Ethiopian *falasha* are classic examples)." To this the author adds that FGM is not "a religious precept unanimously recognized, being absent in different areas of Islamic prevalence, such as the Maghreb, Libya and Iran." In sum, "the Koran does not provide any imposition in this regard." The fact that FGM is not founded in religious principles is used, in the public debate, as an argument to differentiate it from male genital mutilation (circumcision). In my opinion, the parallel between the two practices reveals that, to maintain a double standard toward their legal statuses, we should not rely on their classification within the category of culture or religion, but should use other types of evaluations.

could not find coverage in most jurisdictions even under religious freedom – the distinction seems inappropriate. Indeed such practices precisely reveal how religion and culture pose substantially similar problems, and thus should be addressed using similar argumentative criteria.

All this tends to make more apparent how tangled the constitutional difference in treatment between these two concepts has become. The close proximity of the issues that arise in the face of these two concepts suggests the opportunity of taking the best legal techniques used to solve cultural conflicts, on the one hand, and religious conflicts, on the other hand, and reflecting in a unified way on the two issues toward homogeneous treatment of the two types of conflict. On the other hand, analogies between the problems imply a jurisprudential convergence already underway. Some questions that judges raise are, in fact, identical: When is the practice (cultural and religious) obligatory? When does it cause damage? Is it shared by the whole religious or cultural group? What is reasonable in a democratic society? And so on. The resolution techniques for religious and cultural disputes are, therefore, subject to mutual comparison in the following section, in order to reconstruct the main argumentative approach to multicultural conflicts nowadays.

With these preliminary warnings, we can now move on to the analysis of the ways in which different legal traditions resolve cultural and religious conflicts, starting with one of the most interesting legal techniques elaborated in the context of judicial reasoning: the cultural and religious tests.

3 The emergence of cultural and religious tests

What is a cultural test? It is a matrix of pre-determined questions a judge may ask in order to decide whether and at what level to give recognition to cultural frames to resolve a case. It is a way to proceduralize the argumentative *iter* of the judge into a standard set of inquiries. The same definition can be applied when religion is at stake, when religion is used in the law as a concept distinct from that of culture.

The cultural test has its roots in North American jurisprudence.

The first tests in constitutional law were balancing tests born around 1910, at a precise moment in the history of American legal thought (Vespaziani 2001, 2002).[12]

12 "Starting from 1910, the 'rule of reason' within antitrust law . . . the reasonable standard to evaluate how diligent is a person in accomplish his contractual duties . . . and the 'clear and present danger' test under constitutional scrutiny over the limits of free speech are all manifestations of balancing logic practiced by US courts. In 1921 Roscoe Pound wrote that a new legal doctrine should encourage the 'balancing of social interests' although it was only after 1930 that balancing tests explicitly appeared as a method of constitutional interpretation. The solicitation to center the judicial decisions on the considerations of social interests reflected the general aspiration of the realist movement to liberate judicial reasoning from the *jus naturalis* paradigm of common law, in which the traditional logic of property law became mechanically applied to the institutions of public law, thus keeping the law isolated from the reality of social transformations of a society which is undergoing a rapid industrialization process" (Vespaziani 2002: 6).

This period assisted the passage from a formal syllogistic logic to a controversial and practical one, under the influence of American legal realism. The origin of the balancing tests reflects a powerful process of distancing from textual formalism that requires strict adherence by the judge to constitutional texts. Textualism became openly contested by the "realist school and the apologists of sociological jurisprudence" (Scaccia 2000: 321). In this context, the test is a passing solution that:

> represented the tool adopted to overcome the formalistic method without risking to be blocked in the shallows of legal nihilism and the ultra-realist positions that denied any logic to constitutional decisions, reduced to manifestations of an arbitrary personal power on the part of the judge.
>
> (Scaccia 2000: 321)[13]

The tendency to develop recurrent standards to measure interests at stake is also present in the European dimension. One prong of the test on the margin of appreciation elaborated by the European Court of Human Rights (ECHR)[14] uses the consensus standard; that is, the ECHR must ascertain to what extent a given solution to a multicultural conflict is shared among the forty-seven state members. Other prongs of the test ask if the restrictions are necessary and proportionate in a democratic society.

Cultural and religious tests were developed comparatively, starting in 1963, by constitutional courts and international parajurisprudential bodies and are quite heterogeneous. Some apply only to specific minorities, constitutionally recognized (eg. indigenous peoples), while others are more generalized, covering also acts performed by immigrants, and all persons who belong to diverse cultures (eg. European minorities as Roma people, national minorities, tourists and temporary residents). Significant differences also may be found in subjects called to give an answer to the various test steps. The presence of some of the test requirements (eg. descriptions of the cultural or religious practice, its relevance for the group) is, in fact, sometimes ascertained directly by the judge and other times with the support of another figure to speak for the minority. This figure may be the cultural expert, usually an anthropologist or a qualified

13 Regarding the capacity of the balancing test to remove arbitrariness from decisions, the author observes: "a touch of ambiguity remains immanent in the balancing test, as it . . . can bend toward different utilizations and to constitutional politics very distant, not to say opposite" (Scaccia 2000: 323). An analogous passage from formalism to a fully balancing logic happened also in the history of the Italian Constitutional Court (Bin 1992: 56).

14 The "margin of appreciation" test of the ECHR aims at establishing when the sovereign states can make their own informed decisions on how to respect human rights protected by the Convention. As an example, France may ban *burqas* insofar as the French state is best informed as to whether they may or may not pose risks to social coexistence, *S.A.S. v. France*, ECHR 695, July 1st, 2014.

member of the culture in question (such as a religious leader or activist), or an official organ of the cultural group (eg. a consulate or embassy) or sometimes a *quisque de populo* who belongs to that culture and who is called as a witness, to confirm the veracity of the practice. Another fundamental difference, as mentioned above (*supra* sec. 2), appears, depending on whether the test is forged around the concept of culture or religion.

The tests are therefore heterogeneous and influenced by the historical and social peculiarities of each jurisdiction in which they were produced. At the same time, though, they also reveal the presence of some *topoi*, which – when combined with other doctrinal exercises performed by the judges in the legal systems examined – will form the starting point to find a "common legal tradition" to resolve conflicts in multicultural Western law (*infra* sec. 12).

On the one hand, the presence of a cultural test leads to greater consistency and certainty in judges' decision-making. The fact of being subject to rigorous steps avoids a wavering jurisprudence. It also helps avoiding a stereotypical concept of culture in which any behavior, by the mere fact that it is performed by a foreigner, is necessary due to culture. The tests, in fact, must be addressed in all of their questions before they can allow the application of cultural exception.

On the other hand, the test could hinder a proper account of the peculiarities of cases which may sometimes prevent a fair resolution of the dispute. It may become a mere formulaic tool.

Each of the tests we examine appears as a historical product, also reflecting the legal tradition and historical-political conditions in which it is produced. Considered of themselves, the existing cultural tests appear to us incomplete and only able to intercept part of the problems that other people's cultures present, but read in a comparative perspective, several suggestions appear.

4 The cultural test of the United Nations Human Rights Committee: the *topos* of graduation

The Human Rights Committee of the United Nations has, since the 1980s, progressively elaborated a systematic cultural test, although not explicitly defined as such (Eisenberg 2009: 127–131).

Despite being basically denied a judicial nature, this organ, composed of eighteen independent experts, can receive individual communications with respect to those states that have given consent and express themselves with advisory opinions on whether rules violate articles of the International Covenant of Civil and Political Rights (ICCPR) of 1966 or other instruments. Formally not binding, decisions of the Committee have a strong political influence. Several advisory opinions were produced in relation to the right to culture.

The fact that it was an international body that first paid attention to the cultural factor in a standardized way is not coincidental. Unlike state legal systems, which still falter in the face of recognition of cultural rights, international law has recognized them since 1966 (Appendix: the status of culture internationally). The test here proposed, in fact, finds its basis in art. 27 of the Covenant (ICCPR).[15]

The Human Rights Committee went on to define a precise set of steps to verify compliance with art. 27, ensuring the presence, in order, of the following requirements:

1) *Identification of the cultural practice.* First, the Committee should identify the cultural practice under which the individual alleges infringement under art. 27. The practice must be identified with the "perspective" of the cultural minority; it does not have to be traditional or historically rooted, being able to consist of "contemporary" activities of that community. Also included are "economic" practices.
2) *Essentiality.* The cultural practice for which protection is sought must be "essential and integral" to the identity of the group; it should be a practice that is not incidental or secondary, but defining of the group, without which their cultural survival would be placed at risk.

15 The first case to apply art. 27 was *Lovelace v. Canada*, Communication No. R.6/24, U.N. Doc. Supp. No. 40 (A/36/40) at 166 (1981). In this phase, the Human Rights Committee had not forged a standardized test. The case regarded Sandra Lovelace, native of a tribe of Maliseet, in Canada, who had lost the status of "Indian" in 1970, following her marriage to a non-native spouse. Art. 12, Chapter 1 of the Indian Act of 1867 forbade, in fact, that an Indian woman who married a non-Indian could continue to be Indian, in order to preserve the identity of the tribe. In 1977 the marriage of Sandra Lovelace came to an end and she returned to the Tobique reservation where her parents lived. The woman intended to permanently relocate and acquire a home, but the Band Council opposed this, claiming she had lost all her Indian rights, including the right to reside on a reservation. Because there did not exist in the Indian Act of 1867 an analogous provision for an Indian man who married a non-indigenous person, Lovelace sued the law for gender discrimination. The Committee did not frame the case that way but held, instead, that Canada had violated art. 27 ICCPR: "in the opinion of the Committee, the right of Sandra Lovelace to access to her native culture and language 'in community with the other members' of her group, has in fact been, and continues to be interfered with, because there is no place outside the Tobique Reserve where such a community exists (sec. 15)." There is also, however, the concrete dimension of the controversy over how the judge oriented the decision: "The case of Sandra Lovelace should be considered in the light of the fact that her marriage to a non-Indian has broken up. It is natural that in such a situation she wishes to return to the environment in which she was born, particularly as after the dissolution of her marriage her main cultural attachment again was to the Maliseet band. Whatever may be the merits of the Indian Act in other respects, it does not seem to the Committee that to deny Sandra Lovelace the right to reside on the reservation is reasonable, or necessary to preserve the identity of the tribe (sec. 17)." The Committee concluded by affirming that Canada should change its legislation (as indeed, Canada did after 1985, when it abrogated the disposition of the Indian Act).

3) *Reasonableness of limits.* The obstacle that the state poses to the enjoyment of the right to culture, limiting or preventing altogether the cultural practice, must have a "reasonable and objective justification."[16]
4) *Consultation.* When the rights of minorities are in play, the state should proceed to consult them. If the state shows that it met the "criteria of consultation and effective participation" of the group whose practice is impaired, its actions are more likely to be upheld.
5) *Graduation.* It is possible to distinguish between mere "alteration" and the more radical "destruction" of a cultural practice. By using this test item, the Human Rights Committee has considered harmless to the right to culture those state actions affecting a practice by reducing it without letting it totally disappear. For example, while acknowledging that native peoples have a special relationship with the land and that this relationship is essential for the cultural survival of the group, the UN Committee considered that a partial compression of land may be legitimate.[17] Decisions of this kind have also been pronounced in respect of Sami, Europe's only indigenous people, who several times opposed the Finnish government's plans for the construction of dams or cutting of trees in Lapland.

The first of the test's peculiarities under examination is that its basis lies in an express "right to culture" under art. 27 of the Covenant. In other jurisdictions such as the Italian, British or German, conversely, the production of cultural arguments takes place outside of an explicit constitutional recognition of culture.

The second feature of the test under examination is the rather broad notion that the concept of culture has adopted, which comes to encompass even economic practices. It is a significant definition, given that other tests (Canada, *infra* sec. 5.1), *vice versa*, exclude the possibility of counting economic practices within the scope of the test's protection as failing to pertain to culture. Another broad

16 On this requirement, see how the Committee affirmed in *Ivan Kitok v. Sweden*, Communication No. 197/1985, UN Doc CCPR/C/33/D/197/1985, IHRL 2484 (UNHRC 1988), 27th July 1988, UN Human Rights Committee, resolving the case of a Sami who contested a Swedish law which permanently stripped Sami rights from those who did not pasture reindeer for three consecutive years. The Committee affirmed that pasturing reindeer is an essential element of the Sami community, but "to restrict the number of reindeer breeders for economic and ecological reasons" serves "to secure the preservation and well-being of the Sami minority" and is therefore "reasonable and consistent with art. 27 of the Covenant." The Committee also stressed the importance of reading the case in context: as the Sami community permitted Mr. Kitok to pasture his reindeer and to be part of the community anyway, his right to enjoyment of community with the rest of the group of his own culture is not compromised.

17 The criterion was fixed in the case of *Lubicon Lake Band v. Canada*, Communication No. 167/1984, (26 March 1990), U.N. Doc. Supp. No. 40 (A/45/40) at 1 (1990), UN Human rights Committee, in which Chief Ominayak, leader and representative of the Lubicon Lake Band, a tribe of Cree Indians in the modern province of Alberta, contested a series of state actions of industrial exploitation of the land. Applying the test, the Committee held that the state's "formal offer would, if accepted, enable the Band to maintain its culture, control its way of life and achieve economic self-sufficiency and, thus, constitute an effective remedy" that the Committee deemed appropriate, holding the exploitation actions therefore admissible because they were partial and did not entirely destroy the zone.

dimension of the concept is to be found when the Committee appears disposed to recognize newly arisen practices or those carried out with modern methods, without providing for an investigation on their historicity or permanence over time (contrary to the Canadian cultural test *infra* sec. 5.1).

Another test element worthy of note concerns the requirement of "consultation." To entirely omit consultation with the minority whose practice is impaired stigmatizes the state behavior. Had the state, on the contrary, proceeded to consult, as well as having good reasons to compress a cultural practice, this could be a weighty reason in favor of the state. On the one hand, this element of the test may appear highly relational: the practice is read in its interactions with the majority culture on which it imposes the burden of considering the reasons of the minority, but, on the other hand, it also extends a possible waiver in the presence of a wider collective interest such as, for example, that of enjoying the mineral or oil resources present in an ancestral territory. However, one should not overlook the downside of this requirement with which the Committee seems to outline a process that, if followed by the government, would distance it from the controversy and the responsibility of violating the 1966 Covenant. Participation in such proceedings ensures that the minority is also distanced from the process, because in the administrative procedure there is already a public good to be pursued which was identified as such by the public authorities. The minority shall be consulted, but not on the public good.

Of note, finally, in respect to other tests (*infra* sec. 5.2 Canadian religious test and 6.1 US religious test), is the fact that the UN Committee test is marked by an investigation of a purely objective nature, meaning they do not involve any kind of assessment on the way the collective cultural identity is concretely embodied in individuals. Once established that a subject is part of the minority, this test does not seek to ascertain how his personal identity is forged as part of that culture and how the subject is sincere and consistent in his life, compared to the culture to which he professes to belong. The "essentiality" requirement is measured in relation to culture, perceived almost as an ontological entity in its own right, and to the group, perceived as giving its own life to its individual components.

5 Canadian jurisprudence

The Canadian legal system has developed three different tools to resolve cultural conflicts (Tierney 2007; Eisenberg 2009).

The first is a cultural test forged by the Supreme Court in 1996 for a well-defined cultural group: aboriginal peoples, also referred to in the legislation as First Nations or Indigenous peoples. Aboriginal peoples are constitutionally recognized by Section 35 of the Constitution (the Constitution Act of 1982), which divided them, in turn, into three sub-groups: the Inuit, also known as Eskimos, inhabitants in the sub-Arctic region; the Indians, divided into over six hundred First Nations scattered in all of Canada (some of whom reside on reservations); and the Métis, a group that is the fruit of unions between settlers and indigenous people, mainly located on the prairies (eg. Red River, Manitoba).

The cultural test has been developed to realize Section 35 of the Constitution, which provides:

> 1. The existing aboriginal and treaty rights of the aboriginal peoples of Canada are hereby recognized and affirmed. 2. In this Act, "aboriginal peoples of Canada" includes the Indian, Inuit and Métis peoples of Canada. 3. For greater certainty, in subsection 1 "treaty rights" includes rights that now exist by way of land claims agreements or may be so acquired. 4. Notwithstanding any other provision of this Act, the aboriginal and treaty rights referred to in subsection 1 are guaranteed equally to male and female persons.

Section 35 distinguishes between two categories of rights: first the "rights arising from the Treaties," which were signed during the colonization between the First Nations and the Crown, and, second, "aboriginal rights." The latter category – unlike the first that refers to the content of existing or future treaties – is an open clause, its content is unwritten and unspecified, including indigenous prerogatives, prevalently cultural, which, while not having been the subject of any treaty are, nevertheless, abstractly recognized by the Constitution. The content of the "aboriginal rights" has been specified through court rulings.

A second legal instrument on the Canadian model concerns religious conflicts, to resolve which the Supreme Court has applied, since 2004, a religious test that has very different characteristics compared to the cultural test for aboriginal peoples – focused, as we shall see, on subjective rather than objective elements, and having a more general application, toward anyone (including immigrants) claiming a religious practice. Religious freedom, as opposed to aboriginal rights, is not a right of the group, but of the individual (Eisenberg 1994).

A third legal instrument is the "reasonable accommodation" which applies to all minorities that make up the Canadian mosaic and is also characterized by standardized assessments in a kind of test, albeit not explicitly named as such.

Canada expressly rejected in 1994, during a debate on the reform of the criminal code, the possibility to formalize the "cultural defense," for any person belonging to any minority. This, however, does not mean that cultural conflicts are ignored, as they are addressed on a case by case basis (Wong 1999) that produce *topoi*: recurrent themes and persuasive arguments.

The Canadian model, as indeed those of other jurisdictions, is characterized, therefore, by the diversification of the methods of resolving conflicts depending on which groups (immigrants or national minorities) and which kind of diversity – culture or religion – is at play (Eisenberg 2006).

5.1 The cultural test for indigenous peoples: the topos *of authenticity*

In 1996, the Canadian Supreme Court forged a "distinctive culture test," also referred to as the "integral to a distinctive culture test," to resolve disputes regarding cultural practices of aboriginal peoples. It was the first time that, in Western law, the specific *nomen iuris* "cultural test" was used. The test and its formulation were foreseen by some cases from 1990[18] and reflected a turning point for the Supreme Court, which had hitherto ruled out the possibility of recognizing a differential treatment for indigenous peoples; despite sec. 35 of the 1982 Constitution anticipating "aboriginal rights," these remained essentially devoid of meaning until 1996.

The case giving rise to the test is the story of Dorothy Marie Van Der Peet, a member of the *Sto:lo* nation, who sued after she was caught selling ten salmons without a license, at a price of $50 – salmon which she had caught in a protected area (Barsh, Henderson 1997; Asch 2000; Luther 2010). Dorothy Van Der Peet defended herself by advancing the special relationship with the salmon that her community had, from time immemorial, within the ancestral lands in which she lived, to justify a derogation from federal fisheries legislation. The *Sto:lo*, in fact, consider salmon a part of their community and revere it as a sacred animal, an expression of the life cycle. According to their chthonic spirituality, the animals are not created to serve man, but rather all living beings are children of Mother Earth, in fully equal position: salmon fishing is not for the *Sto:lo* an economic issue, but rather an integral part of their identity as a group. Dorothy Van Der Peet claimed to exercise her aboriginal right under sec. 35 of the Constitution.

The Supreme Court,[19] to resolve the case, forges the "integral to a distinctive culture" test, articulated according to the following steps:

1) *Identification of the cultural practice*. The first part of the test is to identify a concrete cultural practice. A generic appeal to culture is not sufficient; the party must circumscribe a particular expression of a well-defined custom, describable in detail: "Courts considering a claim to the existence of an aboriginal right must focus specifically on the practices, customs and traditions of the particular aboriginal group claiming the right. Claims to aboriginal rights are not to be determined on a general basis."[20] In addition, only behaviors which are cultural in the strict sense can find protection and if the practice has an economic dimension, the test cannot be applied. The choice of what constitutes a cultural practice and what does not should be made taking

18 The first was *R. v. Sparrow*, [1990] 1 S.C.R. 1075 which considered the case of a native of the Musqueam Indian Band who was found fishing, in 1984, with a net longer than what was regularly accorded to his community's fishing licenses. Mr. Sparrow defended by sustaining that the limits imposed by the licenses were unconstitutional insofar as he "was fishing in ancient tribal territory where his ancestors had fished 'from time immemorial'." The Court of Appeals called an anthropologist, Dr. Suttles, an expert in the Musqueam culture, who explained the importance of the salmon for the life of that community. The judge, however, held that the "aboriginal right is not to take fish by any particular method or by a net of any particular length." The Supreme Court reversed and remanded, finding that the limitation on the net could effectively compromise the right of the fisher to attain the ceremonial scope of procuring food that was, therefore, recognized in the abstract. As already seen, even the case of *Thomas v. Norris* (1992) contains these embryonic requirements that will become the future test (Chap. 1 sec. 4.2).

19 *R. v. Van Der Peet* [1996], 2 S.C.R. 507.

20 A principle reaffirmed also in *R. v. Pamajewon* [1996], 2 S.C.R. 821 sec. 25, in which the Court affirmed that the judge "must first identify the exact nature of the activity claimed."

into account the "perspective" of the indigenous people. The Court uses the expression "through the eyes," to express how the judge must read the behavior of the *Sto:lo* by wearing their cultural lenses, to finally stabilize the meaning that the practice plays. In this case, for example, it would be incorrect to say that salmon fishing is an economic and not a cultural practice, because that would apply Western standards of interpretation, not those of the *Sto:lo* for which the relationship with the salmon is ritualized and it is connected to a wider cosmic vision.

2) *Essentiality*. The second element that the Canadian Supreme Court requires to establish the existence of an aboriginal right is a demonstration that cultural practice be identified as both "integral and essential," that is, central, crucial for the self-identity and self-preservation of the group. The practice must be a salient feature and defining of the culture that "makes the culture what it is." Non-essential behaviors, mere accessories, do not count: "those aspects of the aboriginal society that are only incidental or occasional" cannot receive protection.
3) *Distinctive nature*. Once these elements are established, the third requirement is the "distinctive" character of the practice. Distinctive does not mean to be "distinct, meaning 'unique' to the aboriginal culture in question. The aboriginal claimants must simply demonstrate that the custom or tradition is a defining characteristic of their culture." The Supreme Court specifies, again in the 1996 *Van der Peet* decision, that "a court cannot look at those aspects of the aboriginal society that are true of every human society (eg. eating to survive) . . . the court must look instead to the defining and central attributes of the aboriginal society in question."
4) *Pre-contact origin*. The fourth of the test elements is the fact that the practice has its roots in the period "prior to contact between aboriginal and European societies." On this point the Supreme Court specifies that it is sufficient that the customs rose prior to contact, even if the practice did not endure contiguously across the centuries: "the concept of continuity does not require aboriginal groups to provide evidence of an unbroken chain of continuity between their current practices, customs and traditions, and those which existed prior to contact. It may be that for a period of time an aboriginal group, for some reason, ceased to engage in a practice, custom or tradition which existed prior to contact, but then resumed the practice, custom or tradition at a later date. Such an interruption will not preclude the establishment of an aboriginal right." This criterion takes into account the fact that many of the aboriginal practices were aborted because they were prohibited by the Canadian government (eg. the sun dance, the potlatch) yet came to flourish again. Nor is it necessary that the cultural practices remain in archaic stasis: it can be repeated in modern forms subsequent to contact. In this sense, the canoe may be replaced by a motor boat for fishing or the traditional nets of rattan can be replaced by modern, nylon fishing nets. However, it is essential that the practice existed before the moment of contact, so that the community can claim fishing was ever an essential element of its identity. The moment of contact, as the Court states, varies

from group to group depending on the historical movements of the border line indicating the advance of European settlers. Canada was colonized over the course of over two centuries. So, for instance, for the Indigenous People Ts-meeun-is (Chemainus) who first met Europeans in 1859, only practices existing before this time are eligible for the test.

Applying the "integral to a distinctive culture" test, the Supreme Court rejected Dorothy Van Der Peet's request. All test requirements are met – believes the Court – except the last.

It is true that the salmon fishing is a "cultural" (and not merely economic) practice of the *Sto:lo*.

It is also true that the practice in question is "essential and integral" to the cultural survival of the group, in the sense that the *Sto:lo* would not be *Sto:lo* without salmon fishing.

It is likewise true that it has a "distinctive nature" compared to other communities for the special relationship that the tribe established with the salmon. Though other Canadians also fish for salmon, they do not do it with the same cosmic vision and web of significance that supports this activity with the *Sto:lo*.

However, before contact with Europeans, while the *Sto:lo* fished, they did not sell fish. Had the case concerned only the fishing of salmon in a protected area, such activity – or so it appears according to the reasoning of the Supreme Court – would have received the protection of the test: but the fact that Mrs. Van Der Peet had been caught in the act of selling ten salmon prohibits her actions to be considered an aboriginal right, because the sale of salmon by the *Sto:lo* is a practice that they undertook only after the arrival of the first Europeans, and as a direct result of such contact. It was the cultural change implied by the arrival of settlers that introduced this practice in tribes, which therefore does not fulfill the essential "pre-contact" requirement of the cultural test. As we will better see when analyzing the primitivist attitudes into which judges who become anthropologists might fall (Chap. 3 sec. 3), the Canadian court-created test was accused of freezing rights in the past (Borrows 1997–98), taking no account of how aboriginal cultures have evolved as a result of contact with colonists. Denying these changes means, according to some scholars (Chienhan Cheng 1997; Vallace 2011), perpetuating a colonial attitude that does not consider that the indigenous peoples have had to adjust to unrequested colonization.

Returning to the descriptive analysis, it should be noted that in 2004,[21] a fifth element was added to the test in question:

21 In the case of *Haida Nation v. British Columbia (Minister of Forests)* [2004] S.C.R. 511, sec. 20. The case regarded a decision of the provincial government in favor of cutting woods to expand agricultural land. This part of the test was crucial to solve the following cases: *Tsilhqot'in Nation v. British Columbia*, 2014 SCC 44, [2014] 2 S.C.R. 256; *Beckman v. Little Salmon/Carmacks First Nation*, 2010 SCC 53, [2010] 3 S.C.R. 103; *Mikisew Cree First Nation v. Canada* (Minister of Canadian Heritage), 2005 SCC 69, [2005] 3 S.C.R. 388; *Taku River Tlingit First Nation v. British Columbia* (Project Assessment Director), [2004] 3 S.C.R. 550, 2004 SCC 74.

5) *Consultation*. There is an obligation on the Canadian government to consult aboriginal peoples before making any decision that could undermine their cultural practices. Consultation is an element that, as one may recall, also appears in the cultural test used by the UN Human Rights Committee (*supra* sec. 4) and that is well articulated by the Canadian Supreme Court in the *Haida Nation v. British Columbia* case of 2004: "Canada's Aboriginal peoples were here when Europeans came, and were never conquered. Many bands reconciled their claims with the sovereignty of the Crown through negotiated treaties. Others, notably in British Columbia, have yet to do so. The potential rights embedded in these claims are protected by s. 35 of the Constitution Act, 1982. The honour of the Crown requires that these rights be determined, recognized and respected. This, in turn, requires the Crown, acting honourably, to participate in processes of negotiation. While this process continues, the honour of the Crown may require it to consult and, where indicated, accommodate Aboriginal interests."

The Canadian test's principal characteristic is its objective nature. The focus of the findings of the Supreme Court revolves entirely around the characteristics of a cultural practice, whose boundaries are well defined across specific choices made in advance: the practice must be accurately described, essential to the survival of the group, distinctive, non-economic and pre-contact. The presence of these rigorous standards ensures that the cultural argument is not expendable in general terms. Conversely, in other jurisdictions (eg. Italy), often the argument "my culture made me do that" triggers formulaic respect from the judge, without any kind of verification of the practice or its nature or the conditions under which it can be recognized: the magic words "my culture made me do that" may activate the anthropological sensitivity of the judge, but in the absence of a serious study on the practice in question, and of certain standards, it is likely to lead only to improper cultural reasoning.

Returning to the test in question, it does not provide, unlike almost all the others that we will examine, a balancing analysis. The only time when the reasons of the indigenous peoples are compared with those of the other inhabitants of Canada is at the stage of consultation, the fifth element added to the test in 2004. For the rest, if the indigenous peoples show willingness to support activity equipped with all the features required by the test, it seems that this is in itself sufficient to grant protection. Missing, in essence, is a relational dimension. This often produces rather formalistic arguments, centered on objective categorizations of "culture" instead of on the real reasons underlying the decision. This closes the resolution of the case to novel possibilities of coexistence between aboriginal peoples and European descendants who colonized Canada. Thus, in the arguments of the Supreme Court, the Indian dancer cannot be forcibly initiated into the dance of the spirits (Chap. 1 sec. 4.2) not because his freedom of choice must be respected, but rather because the practice is not essential for the survival of the Coast Salish; so too the Mohawk who wants to traverse the Canada–US border without paying duties cannot do it, not because there may be other current interests with which his conduct is to be measured, but rather because the court does not consider sufficient the archaeological evidence presented on the routes followed by his ancestors[22] (MacIntosh 2009); so too the Shawanaga and Eagle Lake tribes cannot open casinos not because gambling can cause serious social harm, but rather because in the past these tribes played cards and dice only occasionally and thus the practice cannot be said to form an "essential and integral" part of their culture.[23]

Alternatively, the test as it is structured presents a real obstacle to recognition, so the Supreme Court has had an easy time excluding several claims, alleging that they did not meet the difficult conditions imposed by the test when in fact perhaps the real reason was not made explicit: that the Supreme Court, bereft of any explicit balancing requirement of the test, found hidden ways to compare aboriginal rights against other rights or interests that came into play in the dispute. To avoid this ambiguity and to make manifest all the arguments which lead to the decision, a relational and dialectical comparison of the rights of the minority and the majority should be explicitly present in every cultural test (Chap. 4 sec. 5.10–13).

Another feature that confirms the exclusively objective nature of the test is that it does not query any type of connection between cultural practices and the identity of the individual who brings them into being. The scenario, however, changes completely for the Supreme Court's religious test (*infra* sec. 5.2).

To fully understand the examined test, we cannot analyze it in the abstract, without accounting for historical reality and Canadian politics. As with any doctrinal exercise conducted by judges, in fact, also in this case it is essential to understand the context in which it takes place.

Against the background of such a rigid test is the fact that, in Canada, struggles for cultural recognition conceal the question of political power lost by the indigenous peoples (Macklem 2001). It is not culture which is the real issue behind this attitude in Canadian jurisprudence, but sovereignty.

In this context, it is argued that cultural rights are a Western tool to quell what are the real struggles of indigenous peoples: to recover lost territories, to create enclaves inside the sovereign state. According to these positions, culture is only a veil dropped over the "real" problem which is that of power, so that a part of indigenous scholars and activists remain stalwart against framing the rights of aboriginal peoples within cultural discourses, preferring instead the

22 The case was decided first as *Grand Chief Michael Mitchell, also known as Kanantakeron (Plaintiff) v. Canada* (Minister of National Revenue – M.N.R). [1997], Federal Court of Canada-Trial Division Ottawa Ontario, in favor of the indigenous, then the Supreme Court, in *Minister of National Revenue v. Grand Chief Michael Mitchell* [2001], 1 S.C.R. 911, reversed.

23 *R. v. Pamajewon* [1996] 2 S.C.R. 821.

discourse of renewed sovereignty over the historically lost territory (Alfred 2005).[24] All this brings one to see in cultural rights the same problems present in anti-discrimination protections or affirmative actions. They guarantee access to power to persons who were previously excluded: indigenous people, women, people with disabilities or LGBT orientation. If this is doubtlessly a positive aspect, it also suggests us to take a look at the conditions imposed by those who allow such access. They often require that the hierarchical relationships, hierarchies of values, do not change and continue to be managed by those who were already (and remain) the holders of the symbolic and material power. More than "guaranteeing," recognition "domesticates." Just like women's claims are "sedated" by affording women a "protected" status at work or in politics, but in forms which are the expression of the same competitive hierarchical patriarchal order that they intended to remove, so the recognition of an indigenous culture takes place under conditions decided by the Canadian government that has no intention, for example, to review its policy of exploitation of natural resources to adapt to the idea of the indigenous mother land as a living being.

In this sense, the test examined is accused, by some, of being a neo-colonial legal product (Borrows 1997–98; Alfred 2005). For example, in choosing to exclude economic practices from the test, a choice that differs with respect to the test of the Human Rights Committee of the United Nations, is expressed a clear political goal: to prevent indigenous peoples full control of the resources present in the ancestral territories and close the door to a debate over the Canadian-Western model of development.

Another track that reveals the neo-colonial matrix of the test is found when one requires the hyper-restrictive element of the essentiality of the practice for

24 However, in respect to this dichotomy, Canadian philosopher James Tully presented another point of view to me in an interview I conducted in April 2008 at the University of Victoria. To my question "do you think indigenous claims fit better in the cultural discourse or in the sovereignty discourse?" the Canadian thinker observed: "it is possible to answer in two ways: the first is that there are 'culture-related claims' from one side and 'sovereignty related claims' from the other. Nevertheless this is our Western way to frame the issue. I think an indigenous person does not see the issue so separated because sovereignty and identity, they fit together through the land. Aboriginal people do not separate, but say: we don't own the land, the land owns us. Their identity would not exist without the land as they are intimately connected. Moreover: they could not be defined as what they are without the land. There is no identity without territory, there are no Aboriginal people without the Great Mother Earth. Therefore the issue of the ancestral territories which we read as a sovereignty issue is for them a question of identity." To my other question: "Does this special relation with the land still exist or is it operate at a mere level of historical memory and is used mainly as a tool for a political fighting?" Tully responded: "It does exist. Maybe somebody can say that Aboriginal people make a strategic use of it. I cannot exclude that some of them do not believe anymore in it and use it in a utilitarian way. But if you go, for instance, to Queen's Charlotte Island, and speak with the Haida, they would tell you that the Haida would not exist without Haida Gwaii, their island. And this is the same with all the First Nations of Canada, especially those which live rurally. Now we could say 'this is a primitive vision, a people can exist without a territory,' but this is not the indigenous way of understanding peoplehood, and this ecosocial view is not 'primitive'" (amended version of the 2008 Interview, publication authorized by Prof. Tully).

the survival of the group. With this test Canada says to the aboriginal people: "we will spare you, will not exterminate you more, your identity as a group is preserved," placating the sense of post-colonial guilt. It would, however, make much more sense to look at the issue in a relational way, recognizing also an "accessory" indigenous practice (eg. sweat lodges) if it enriches society or, reversing the requirement by asking what is essential for the rest of Canadians, through a new dialectic of mutual accommodation.

But also wanting to read the cultural test *in bonam partem*, as a Canadian attempt to establish criteria (which in 1996 could appear sensible to erect safeguards to any aboriginal claim) it is impossible not to note that the nature of this test's questions in some ways cheapens the function of the litigation and its ability to be a place of knowledge and a virtuous transformation of conflict.

The result is such a restrictive test that several lawyers suggest that aboriginal peoples advance their claims on the basis of religious freedom instead. In this field, as we will soon see, courts apply a less rigid test which likely conveys a better chance of success.[25]

5.2 *The religious test: the* topos *of individual sincerity*

If 1996 saw the birth in Canada of the "integral to a distinctive culture" test for the three categories of aboriginal peoples (Inuit, Indians, Métis) recognized by sec. 35 of the Canadian Constitution, 2004 saw the structuring of a second test, forged to resolve religious conflicts that concern any minority.[26] The opinion of the Supreme Court in *Syndicat Northcrest v. Amselem*[27] encodes it, in part through a process of importing into Canadian law the existing religious test (the *Sherbert* test) of the United States[28] (*infra* sec. 6.1).

The Canadian religious test consists of the following steps:[29]

1) *Identification of the religious practice.* First, the party must prove that the practice or belief has a nexus with religion in the sense that the subject adheres to "the practices of which allow individuals to foster a connection with the divine or with the subject or object of that spiritual faith." The

25 Scholars skeptically observed that none of the tools currently available in Canada (the cultural test based on sec. 35 of the Constitution of 1982 and the religious test based on sec. 2 of Part I of the Charter of Freedom) would guarantee natives adequate protection. This prediction is confirmed in one of the first aboriginal claims under freedom of religion: *Ktunaxa Nation v. British Columbia* (Forests, Lands and Natural Resource Operations), 2017 SCC 54, [2017] 2 S.C.R. 386.

26 Religious liberty is codified in art. 2 of the Charter of Rights, that states: "2. Everyone has the following fundamental freedoms: (a) freedom of conscience and religion."

27 *Syndicat Northcrest v. Amselem* (2004) 2 S.C.R. 551.

28 The religious test was first affirmed in Canada in 1985, but at that time reference to the element of sincerity imported from the US was not constant; it was after 2004, with the *Amselem* case, that the test solidified (Beaman 2008).

29 All of the quotations in the following text come from *Syndicat Northcrest v. Amselem* (2004) 2 S.C.R. 551.

behavior need not be mandatory according to religious authorities, but may be so subjectively. As the Supreme Court states: "This understanding is consistent with a personal or subjective understanding of freedom of religion. As such, a claimant need not show some sort of objective religious obligation, requirement or precept to invoke freedom of religion. It is the religious or spiritual essence of an action, not any mandatory or perceived-as-mandatory nature of its observance, that attracts protection. The State is in no position to be, nor should it become, the arbiter of religious dogma."

2) *Non-trivial limitation and possible alternatives.* Second, the party must prove that the obstacle or limit to the practice is a non-trivial burden.[30] In general, the test can be used against all restrictions provided they are not clearly negligible. Where there are other interests to balance, if the limitation imposed by the legislature leaves room for an alternative meaningful choice, making it possible to remain faithful to their own religion, restrictions can be justified even if they are particularly intrusive.
3) *Sincerity of the subject.* Third, courts must ensure the honesty of the claimant, who has to prove that s/he has a sincerely held belief. [31] As seen in part 1 of the test, no demonstration of any sort of objective religious obligation or precept is necessary to invoke protection, but it must be ensured that the practice is claimed "in good faith, neither fictitious nor capricious, and that it is not an artifice." In assessing sincerity, the judge must, among other things, consider the credibility of the testimony and the consistency of the creed with the overall life of the subject.
4) *Criterion of damage.* This element of the test will emerge, as we shall see in subsequent cases, and is still being developed: it implies that a religious practice cannot find protection if it causes physical or mental harm to others. This policy has been the key argument of British Columbia's Supreme Court's opinion in 2011 against polygamy (*infra* par. 11).
5) *Balance.* Fifth, there should be no competing rights or democratic principles that conflict, otherwise judges must proceed to find balance and not automatically allow religious freedom to prevail. As the Canadian Supreme Court observes: "respect for and tolerance of the rights and practices of religious minorities is one of the hallmarks of an enlightened democracy" – yet in practice this can create such a multitudinous democracy that the religious rights of minorities "must also coexist alongside societal values that are central to the make-up and functioning of a free and democratic society."[32]

30 This requirement is established since *R. v. Jones* (1986), 2 S.C.R. 284.

31 In *Syndicat Northcrest v. Amselem* (2004) one reads that "a claimant need not show some sort of objective religious obligation, requirement or precept to invoke freedom of religion" (sec. 48) but that instead it is fundamental to "demonstrate that he or she sincerely believes in a practice or belief that has a nexus with religion" (sec. 65).

32 With this argument the Supreme Court rejected the the request for an exemption from the obligation of a driver's license photo by the Hutterian religious community of Alberta, *Alberta v. Hutterian Brethren of Wilson Colony*, [2009] 2 S.C.R. 567.

6) *Reasonableness and proportionality of limits.* Finally, again in connection with democratic principles, jurists must ensure that the limitation imposed on religious practice is proportionate and "reasonable in a free and democratic society."

Through the application of this test, the Supreme Court ended the long case of Mr. Moïse Amselem, an Orthodox Jew, a fervent practitioner, who in September 1996 had constructed on the balcony of his apartment a *succah*.

We are in Quebec, in Montreal, in the Outremont district, a residential area inhabited by an upper-medium bourgeoisie that, compared to a homogeneous socio-economic class, mixes significant religious differences that have made it the hub of several clashes. The neighborhood is, in fact, partly "sophisticated, secular and francophone" and in part "traditional, religious and Yiddish-speaking" (Van Praagh 2008).

Amselem lives in the luxury condominium Le Sanctuaire, and it is here, on his terrace, that he builds a *succah*, a traditional Jewish hut open on one side, to pray, eat and perform other daily activities in order to celebrate the religious festival of Succot. As stated in the judgment, "[t]his nine-day festival, which begins in late September or early to mid-October, commemorates the 40-year period during which, according to Jewish tradition, the Children of Israel wandered in the desert, living in temporary shelters."

Except that the structure seemed to violate the condominium rules that Mr. Amselem had signed at the time of buying the flat. The condominium rules, in addition to general prohibitions against decoration and alterations of the facade, explicitly states that "[n]o owner may enclose or block off any balcony, porch or patio in any manner whatsoever or erect thereon constructions of any kind whatsoever." In September 1997, following protests from the condo association from years before, Amselem along with other condominium owners submitted a formal request to the condominium association.

The *succah*, although removable, was considered not comparable to a tent, a trellis with a climbing plant or a parasol that perhaps other condo owners built on their terraces. The condo association rejected the request, proposing instead to concede to the erection in the garden of a common *succah* to which all the Jewish inhabitants of the building could go. Dissatisfied with this accommodation, Amselem built his hut and was denounced by the condo association.[33]

The court of first instance decided to consult a rabbi to understand the degree of importance that the practice assumes in Judaism. The rabbi explained that there are no specific religious obligations to perform the prayers and live during Succot within a personal enclosure; the communal *succah* proposed by the association would do. In light of this expert testimony – that the practice exists, but it is not required to be achieved in this specific form – the trial court refuses to accept Amselem's request.

Through various levels of courts, who had all sided with the condo association, the case finally arrives at the Supreme Court of Canada.

33 Professor Avigail Eisenberg, in an interview I conducted in May 2011 at the University of Victoria, observes that Mr. Amselem claimed not only his religious identity but also his identity as a member of the Jewish high bourgeois and class enclave which could not mix within a common *succah*.

The compulsory nature of a practice is often a key element of the solution, one of the *topoi*, one of those recurring persuasive fixed points in the comparative case law that resolve multicultural conflicts. It is so even in the cultural test developed by the Canadian Supreme Court itself for aboriginal peoples (*supra* sec. 5.1). However, this time the Canadian Supreme Court forged another policy, in which the subjective assessment prevails over the objective. Applying the new religious test, the Supreme Court recognizes for Mr. Amselem the right to preserve his personal *succah* as an expression of religious freedom protected by sec. 2 of the Canadian Charter of Rights. Although, in fact, a personal building is not compulsory according to the Jewish religion, the sincerity, the fervor, the special relationship that Amselem has with his God justify the constitutional protection:

> freedom of religion consists of the freedom to undertake practices and harbour beliefs, having a nexus with religion, in which an individual demonstrates he or she sincerely believes or is sincerely undertaking in order to connect with the divine or as a function of his or her spiritual faith, irrespective of whether a particular practice or belief is required by official religious dogma or is in conformity with the position of religious officials.

Similar to what we will see in the United States (*infra* 6.1), the test for the recognition of a religious practice is independent of the "essential and integral to the culture" test (*supra* 5.1) and is based on a powerful subjective factor, focused on the evaluation of how intimately the subject adheres to and believes in the practice.

The religious test exalts, therefore, the personal requirement of sincerity; although, in hindsight, it cannot wholly dismiss objective components, otherwise the law would be inundated with "do-it-yourself religions."[34]

This choice of the subjective sincerity of religious test becomes fully understandable when seen within the historical context of Canada: it is a legal precipitate of Protestantism and battles fought in its name to determine a direct relationship between the faithful and God, without the mediation of clerical authorities. An

34 An amusing model hinting at what courts might face under more permissive subjective rules comes from the movement of "Jediism" which began to attain some renown, especially in Great Britain, after the advent of the internet. Inspired by the fictional Jedi religion of the *Star Wars* films, novels and other media which recognize "the Force" as an immanent spirit, a number of British citizens felt moved to write in "Jedi" as their creed on the British census, beginning in 2001. Other than two minor disputes between Jedi adherents asserting their religious right to appear in public while hooded and stores citing security concerns, Jediism has had no real impact on British religious law. The manager of one of the stores in the mentioned disputes, incidentally, publicly defended his ejection of the hooded Jedi by questioning the hood's supposed mandatory nature, pointing out that Luke Skywalker, Obi-wan Kenobi and even Yoda are all depicted hoodless in the films, while the only character never shown removing his hood is the evil Emperor (Carter 2009; Levy 2010). The broad and ardent popularity of *Star Wars* lends a patina of plausibility to such subjective claims, but even on the objective axis a double standard may be somewhat unfair. If a judge recognizes creeds based, for instance, on the Book of Mormon circa 1830 A.D. which is based at least in part on visions witnessed inside a hat, perhaps she should also recognize a creed which matured after the release of *Star Wars* in 1977 and based on visions seen inside a cineplex.

evident effect of the test at issue is the weakening of the leading role of religious institutions to the benefit of the individual faithful as well as the reaffirmation of the idea that faith is a personal experience.

As also seen in the case of the "integral to a distinctive culture" test, many cultural arguments are historical/political products incorporating the peculiarities of legal systems. In the search for a common legal tradition and a shared way of resolving cultural conflicts, it is important to discern these historical peculiarities that may seem in contrast to the consolidation of a common criterion – like the mandatory nature of a practice – or which may be too connected to the history of one place to be "exported" or "persuasive" in another (eg. the pre-contact requirement discussed in the previous sec. 5.1).

Alternatively, although historically located, some of the requirements found in a concrete judicial setting can have their autonomous uses. Like any text, judicial opinions are also "open works" – *opere aperte* (Eco 1962), which can have their life outside of the semiotic context in which they operate. For example, the attention to the subjective element in the Canadian test can be exportable to the extent that it is considered that the anthropologist judge's attitude should also enhance the relationship between collective and personal identity, including objective evidence of a culture and its individual incarnations (Cohen 1996). The concepts of lived religion and embodied culture are echoed in the most modern conceptions of human nature, very different from those in which religion or culture appeared as something with their own ontology (Chap. 3 sec. 2). The fact that Mr. Amselem wants to adhere to a more stringent level of one's faith corresponds to his level of spirituality in the abstract Jewish religion, beyond what any religious authority can say. The concept of lived religion seems implicitly evoked in the Canadian Supreme Court's reasoning.

An explanation as to why there may be such a clear difference between the cultural test and the religious test when both were forged from the same organ resides in the different historical backgrounds of the two instruments: the indigenous question that has been domesticated with a guarded cultural recognition on the one hand; and Protestantism and the need to free the faithful from religious elites on the other.

Another reason for the distinction between the two tests can also be found in the fact that the cultural test is based on sec. 35 of the Canadian Constitution, which encodes aboriginal rights as group rights, while the religious test is based on sec. 2 of the Charter of Rights, which codifies religious freedom as an individual right. After building culture as a group right, the importance of concrete incarnations it has in the individual identity diminishes. What matters is whether that culture exists and if that group needs to perpetuate those concrete activities to culturally survive. Conversely, when constructing religious recognition on a model of individual rights, the embodiment in individual identities becomes relevant.

It is a thesis of this book that there are not persuasive reasons to maintain such a level of difference between the resolution of religious and cultural conflicts, and that one of the tasks of a multicultural jurisprudence should be to homogenize them.[35] The Canadian system brings out the incongruences of treating the type of conflicts differently.

Returning to the *Amselem* case, in the opinion balance plays a fundamental role to measure the interests of others by passing through the fourth part of the test: the criterion of damage. Once satisfied that the construction of the *succah* did not create any safety issues for the condo as it did not hinder any escape route, the Supreme Court assessed the interest of the owners not to see the aesthetics of the facade affected, or any subsequent decrease in the value of the property. We follow the Supreme Court in its reasoning. They ask:

> In practice, to what degree would the respondent be harmed were the appellants allowed to set up a *succah* for a period of 9 out of 365 days a year? . . . Even if I were to consider the possibility that the economic value of the property might decrease if a substantial number of co-owners were allowed to set up *succahs* on their balconies for a lengthy time period throughout the year, any drop in value caused by the presence of a small number of *succahs* for a period of nine days each year would undoubtedly be minimal. Consequently, in this case, the exercise of the appellants' freedom of religion, which I have concluded would be significantly impaired, would clearly outweigh the unsubstantiated concerns of the co-owners about the decrease in property value . . . Although residing in a building with a year-long uniform and harmonious external appearance might be the co-owners' preference, the potential annoyance caused by a few *succahs* being set up for a period of nine days each year would undoubtedly be quite trivial.
>
> (par. 85–86)

Unlike the cultural tests previously examined, the religious test, in its relational structure, allows a broad measurement of interests disputed before the court: there is a practice of a non-compulsory nature, but in which an individual believes firmly and sincerely, and that, after all, being temporary, does not affect significantly the rights and interests of others. Thus the court finds balance.

Weighing the interests at stake, the Court, however, calls for a settlement effort also from the minority who receives recognition in this case: "the appellants should set up their *succahs* in a manner that conforms, as much as possible, with the general aesthetics of the property in order to respect the co-owners' property interests." It is a practical, rational settlement of law.

There is also another aspect to take into account to fully appreciate the present dispute, which brings us to the socio-political context in which it is issued. A reading, not emerging from the holding, but that might be considered the

35 Against those who sustain that religion, in general, faces slower changes than culture and that for this reason merits a greater judicial protection not accordable to an entity destined in itself to change, Beaman (2008) rebuts that within religions occur many schisms, transformations, a constant competition between leaders who seek to define the significance of their practices. In sum, religions have transformative processes analogous to cultural dynamics.

"true" reason of the judgment is that the Supreme Court wanted to "counteract" the existing racist attitudes in the area (Robinson 2013). Given traces of anti-Semitism present in the Outremont neighborhood of Montreal where Mr. Amselem resided, the protective judgment of such an intense yet not mandatory practice could have had the intention to send a political message of Jewish minority protection. Even behind this case, as well as among the roots of the cultural test forged for aboriginal peoples, there would, therefore, be an injustice to be removed (Markell 2003; Murphy 2005), a discriminatory situation that the judge knows well and wants to remedy. The theme of historical injustice and discrimination (Lear 2006) is one of the factors that drive the experience of the judge and that often intersects with the new anthropological knowledge that beings become human beings in different ways.

The fact that a judge takes into account whether behind the multicultural conflict there are situations of discrimination is a relevant *topos*, which will be included in the test suggested in this book (Chap. 4 sec. 5.6).

A problematic example of the application of the religious test regards the case of Ktunaxa First Nation, which opposed the construction of a year-round ski resort claiming that the resort would drive Grizzly Bear Spirit from a mountain (Qat'muk in British Columbia) of spiritual significance. The Canadian Supreme Court rejected the claim based on two arguments. The Court said that, while the "sincerity" part of the test was met, the Ktunaxa Nation was not able to prove "that the impugned state conduct interferes, in a manner that is non-trivial or not insubstantial, with his or her ability to act in accordance with that practice or belief." In fact, according to the Court:

> The Ktunaxa must show that the Minister's decision to approve the development interferes either with their freedom to believe in Grizzly Bear Spirit or their freedom to manifest that belief. Yet the Ktunaxa are not seeking protection for the freedom to believe in Grizzly Bear Spirit or to pursue practices related to it. Rather, they seek to protect the presence of Grizzly Bear Spirit itself . . . The state's duty under s.2(a) (freedom of religion) is not to protect the object of beliefs or the spiritual focal point of worship, such as Grizzly Bear Spirit.

I think this reasoning is formalistic since, by driving away Grizzly Bear Spirit from the mountain, the construction of the resort would actually impair the ability to perform any ritual or cult connected to it.

Another argument used by the Canadian Supreme Court is that:

> The Minister's decision is reasonable . . . because it reflects a proportionate balancing between the Ktunaxa's s.2(a) Charter right and the Minister's statutory objectives: to administer Crown land and dispose of it in the public interest . . . the Minister had two options before him: approve the development or permit the Ktunaxa to veto the development on the basis of their freedom of religion. Granting the Ktunaxa a power to veto development

> over the land would effectively give them a significant property interest in Qat'muk—namely, a power to exclude others from constructing permanent structures on public land. This right of exclusion would not be a minimal or negligible restraint on public ownership.

This argument too seems disproportionate; the decision fully demolishes the aboriginal interests in favor of the majority.

Beyond this controversial application, what is worthy to note is that, in general, the religious test is better than the cultural test in exalting the qualities of common law: isonomy, balancing and the dialectical use of reason, whereas in the cultural test for aboriginal people, the judge is compelled into a straitjacket through which she is called upon to be an archaeologist of ancient indigenous customs, insulated by the present living relations between aboriginal peoples and other Canadians.

It seems opportune that the comparison between the interests at stake be better explained in the test, with findings relative to the proportionality of a measure, the possibility of alternatives, the intensity level of truncation, the impact on the community, and the possibility of the adaptation of the minority to new rules of coexistence (Chap. 4 sec. 5.10–12).

5.3 The reasonable accommodation: the topos *of undue hardship*

Canada has prepared a cultural test reserved to the aboriginal peoples and a religious test for all minorities who apply the protection of a belief. But Canada also protects cultural and religious diversity via a third instrument: the reasonable accommodation.

The principle of reasonable accommodation was born in the context of labor law jurisprudence and the term was used for the first time by the Canadian Supreme Court in 1985.[36] Subsequently, the mechanism was extended to resolve conflicts both religious and cultural, and applies not only to employers and businesses, but all stakeholders, including institutional, which interact in the public sphere (Eisenberg, Kymlicka 2011). The principle of reasonable accommodation is aimed to force the state, the institutions and businesses to change policies or practices in order to accommodate reasonable needs and to avoid indirect discrimination (Milot 2009). In 2007 a Consultation Commission on Accommodation Practices Related to Cultural Differences (also known as the Bouchard-Taylor Commission) was instituted to release a report in which reasonable accommodation is so defined:

> a legal notion which stems from jurisprudence in the realm of labour and indicates a form of relaxation aimed at combating discrimination caused by the strict application of a norm, which, in certain of its effects, infringes on a citizen's right to equality.
>
> (Bouchard, Taylor 2008)

36 The case was *O'Malley and Ontario Human Rights Commission v. Simpsons-Sears* (1985) 2 S.C.R. 536 in which the judge recognized the obligation of an employer to change some general rules for certain employees unless they caused an undue hardship on the company.

The courts are free to impose or promote reasonable accommodation in each of the areas where there are prohibited forms of discrimination in accordance with sec. 15 of the Canadian Charter of Rights.

The criteria that guide the judicial application of reasonable accommodation include:

1) *The case by case approach*. Requests for reasonable accommodation must be examined on a case by case basis. This is necessary in order to understand the specific circumstances in which the exercise of religious and cultural practice takes place and how it can possibly collide with other interests.
2) *Double reasonableness*. The courts and institutions must ensure that the restriction of a practice is reasonable on the part of any public or private authority, but the minority at issue must also present her own reasons to show that she wants to engage in a behavior that is "reasonable in a democratic society." There is, therefore, a double reasonableness detection on both sides, to determine whether the legal rule or the custom of the minority will prevail.
3) *The efforts made by the institution* or by the employer to reach an accommodation with the applicant must be taken into account.
4) *The undue hardship* that the arrangement would impose on the establishment or the employer must also be weighed.
5) A *balancing* evaluation of the level of restriction of the rights of others is the final judicial exercise.

This tool allows for very flexible conflict resolution. The nature of the case by case approach, for example, allows jurists to distinguish within the same cultural practice, rather than being bound by overly abstract assessments. For example, in Canada the rite of wearing the *kirpan* has been recognized in schools, but not in airports where security needs are considered prevalent. Despite the same religious freedom being at play, the case by case approach may lead to an opposite arrangement depending on the context. Also significant is the factor relating to the reasonableness of a custom that avoids reifying and fixing cultures in time and place, recognizing that the other can give up his practice.

The principle of reasonable accommodation has been used in an opinion enacted in 2001 by the Quebec Superior Court[37] regarding the Hebrew *eruv*. The *eruv* is the placement of a series of overhead wires (eg. fishing lines, plastic cables), typically linked to existing light poles or poles placed *ad hoc* in order to circumscribe a group of houses and streets; in this way Orthodox Jews extend, through a fiction, the domestic space to be able to move and exercise some transport activities from space to space, activities that would otherwise be precluded by the strict observance of the Sabbath. The municipality of Outremont, a neighborhood of Montreal, wanted to dismantle the *eruv* built by a group of Hasidic Jews, claiming that Quebec law requires a city to remain strictly secular. According to the judge, to dismantle the *eruv* manifests a lack of reasonable accommodation of the practice.

37 *Rosenberg v City of Outremont* [2001] Q.J. No. 2858; [2001] R.J.Q. 1556 (Quebec Sup. Ct).

The arguments raised by neighbors were that the *eruv* signified the entire area as a religious zone and it would put undue hardship on the secular neighbours such as the prevention of their children to play with kites. The judge's first objection replied that:

> the City of Outremont is not being asked to expend public funds, to advance the precepts of Orthodox Judaism, or to associate itself or its citizens in any way with the erection of *eruvim*. It is being asked to tolerate the barely visible wires or lines traversing city streets and not to take them down when they are erected. In doing so, it is not being asked to associate itself with the Orthodox Jewish faith any more or less than it associates itself with Christianity when it allows Christmas decorations to be displayed on city property, including city hall, or when it tolerates the ringing of church bells on Sunday morning to summon Christians to worship. . . The accommodation the Petitioners seek does not purport to require the City of Outremont to endorse or in any way to be associated with Orthodox Judaism, but only to tolerate a religious practice that has not been shown to cause any inconvenience or undue hardship to Outremont residents. To the extent that some residents in the affected area contend that the granting of the Petitioners' claim will involuntarily place them in some kind of religious zone from which they cannot escape as long as they live there, counsel for the Petitioners is right to point out that the area within an *eruv* is only a religious zone for those who believe it to be one. That belief is limited to the practitioners of Orthodox Judaism, and not to residents who do not belong to that faith.

The second objection raised by the neighbours (the "kite argument") is rejected by the judge observing that the area is already full of trees which would prevent the game of flying kites in any case: therefore the demonstration that the *eruv* would cause an "undue hardship" has not been reached.

This reasoning provides an anti-discrimination touch that could have also had a hand in moving the court's decision,[38] but the centerpiece of the decision is the weight of reciprocity: the Jews would be "imprisoned in the house" without the *eruv*, while its presence does not affect the interests of the majority in any major way. Finding the cultural equivalent of the Christmas decorations and revealing the instrumentality of the obstacles put forward by the majority, the court considers the request of the Jews to be accommodatable.

Another case that has been resolved by resorting to the instrument of reasonable accommodation concerned a taxi firm in which a Muslim taxi driver refused to pick up people with dogs for religious reasons. A blind citizen accompanied by a guide dog, who was refused the opportunity to get on board and became aware of himself as a victim of discrimination, sued the company and won the following arrangement: while the Muslim taxi driver can refuse to pick up people with dogs even if they are

38 Julius Grey, the lawyer representing five Hasidic Jews in the case, told Justice Allan Hilton: "There is no evidence of harm. What you've got here is evidence that some people don't like it" (Hamilton 2001).

blind, he still must stop, call another taxi and wait along with the blind person until his needs may be served.[39]

The concept of "accommodation" has only lately germinated and, although it can apparently be similar to that of balancing, presents different peculiarities (Bouchard, Taylor 2008). If, in fact, most balancing is a technical instrument that judges usually apply to resolve conflicts between rights, this arrangement is a more purely practical tool, closely connected to the case, which can have different outcomes from the balancing test in the sense that can provide more articulated and diverse answers depending on the circumstances.

Summing up, the Canadian model of multicultural conflict resolution employs a distinction between cultural and religious tests, wherein the cultural test is reserved to a specific minority – the aboriginal peoples – and imposes quite stringent requirements in order to obtain recognition, whereas the religious test is much more open to individual peculiarities. The fact of granting a special test to aboriginal peoples can appear as a symbolic "support" to their culture, but in fact, as has been observed, the cultural test represents a limit, since religious tests often ensure greater protection. Alongside these two tests, the mechanism of reasonable accommodation is used in Canada, which is in turn assisted by a sort of test, while a commission's proposal for criminal code reform in 1994, which would have introduced official recognition of a cultural defense, was never enacted.

The Canadian experience consents already to draw initial conclusions on legal techniques to resolve multicultural conflicts. If these techniques are limited to only seize the anthropological dimension of the dispute (focusing objectively to define what is culture, the type of practice, who is part of the group and who is not) or limited only in respect of the individual dimension (asking whether a subject is sincere) it would provide an incomplete picture. In fact, the crux of a decision is the moment of encounter between opposing interests to resolve controversy, and to provide reasons in support of that interest. The objective and subjective elements of a test can illuminate this dialectic phase, but they cannot be left alone to provide all the answers and, above all the relationship between the two cultures must be given a central role to seek a solution that opens up new possibilities of coexistence. The Canadian cultural test fails in this endeavor, while its religious tests and the reasonable accommodation doctrine succeed. The point, therefore, is to maintain in the test a method, a controversial and dialectic use of judicial reason, and not resort to mere administrativistic or *ex post facto* rationales.

The Canadian experience also provokes thought about whether it is preferable to use homogeneous argumentative technique which applies equally to all groups, including eventually the majority, in order to reassure the majority of its own "at risk" cultural practice in the face of multicultural contact, instead of developing myriad techniques for minorities and for classificatory categories of culture and religion.

39 Analogous cases include those of taxi drivers who refuse to drive passengers with bottles of alcohol or to pick up clients from clubs or places where liquor is consumed.

6 US jurisprudence

In the United States of America there is not, at least not formally, a so-called cultural test. Indeed, there are a number of instruments that consent to give relevance to culture in courts by combining objective, subjective and relational assessments.

First, the US model is characterized by the presence of a religious test that has also been transformed into a *de facto* cultural test, ever since the US Supreme Court referred to such a wide concept of religion that it allows for the inclusion of many practices which in other jurisdictions would be defined as purely cultural. For example, the test served to vindicate the use of ancestral lands by natives, the ability to keep a certain look (hair, clothes) and the ingestion of peyote.

Second, US courts were pioneers in experimenting with forms of cultural defense in criminal cases and in civil cases have assisted in increasing compensation of damages on the grounds that the conduct had a certain significance for the member of that culture. The cultural defense is not official and has not yet stabilized as a real test presenting various steps for judges who use the cultural argument to follow. This aspect creates a rather fragmented system with uncertain precedent, but at the same time allows progressive adjustments of the conditions for granting legal protection to culture. A comparison between all those different uses can reconstruct some key elements or *topoi* that for US judges are of crucial relevance.

The US model, too, preserves the distinction between religion and culture, but is sensitive to their interactions within personal identity and not merely, therefore, to their purely objective definition.

Unlike Canada, the United States has not seen the emergence of test applications specific to certain groups: even indigenous peoples see their cultural rights recognized through the same religious tests or cultural defenses available to any minority.[40]

6.1 The religious test: the topos *of a compelling state interest*

The religious test of US law is rooted in the decision of *Sherbert v. Verner* of 1963[41] in which the Supreme Court framed one of its central elements: the so-called

40 However, the native populations enjoy a kind of special recognition across some laws or on the basis of rights present in stipulated treaties from the times of colonization. The *Indian Child Welfare Act* of 1978, for example, provides preferential assignation of Indian children to Indian couples and values the different concept of first care to revoke the parental power; a rich legislation of natural parks and sites of historical interest provides that protection is no obstacle to native practices, and makes it mandatory to consult the indigenous population.

41 *Sherbert v. Verner* (1963), 374 U.S. 398, for which the test is also known as the *Sherbert* test. The case was that of a woman, belonging to the Seventh-Day Adventist church, who had been firstly laid off because she refused to work on Saturday, a holiday in her religion, and then had refused different jobs, each because they required work on Saturdays. A law of South Carolina prevented her from accessing unemployment benefits because she had refused to work. The Supreme Court declared relevant parts of the South Carolina Unemployment Compensation Act unconstitutional.

compelling interest test, ruling that even laws which are facially neutral but which had an effect, albeit indirect, of limiting religious freedom were unconstitutional, unless the state could demonstrate a compelling interest in their adoption.

Through a complex history that has seen one of the most bitter institutional clashes between the Supreme Court and Congress, the test was deleted by judicial decision in 1990, then re-introduced by legislation in 1993 and again partially suppressed by the Supreme Court in 1997 (*infra*). It currently applies to federal legislation and in thirteen states and consists of the following steps:

1) *Identification of the practice.* The first element is to ascertain the identification of a belief or practice that has a religious origin. The assessment of "religiosity" attaches with very broad criteria. The concept of belief can also embrace practices alien to traditional religions and it is not necessary that the activity be practiced by all the members of that religion; internal variances are also acceptable. These assumptions mean that a large number of practices can find protection under this test. Also in this case, as in the UN Human Rights Committee' test and in that of the Canadian Supreme Court, identification must be performed from within the "perspective" of the other.
2) *Sincerity of the subject.* The second element is that the court should assess the sincerity of the individual claiming the creed or practice. It is not enough to present an objective element given by the discovery of a religious behavior; the claimant must also promote the subjective element of her intimate adherence to that creed, to be ascertained by assessments of the consistency in the overall behavior of the subject with other spheres of her life. If there are current or past assessments (for example, the fact that the subject years ago refused a job in order to remain faithful to his religion) these are examined, but in the latter case, the assessment is not rigid: the fact that a claimant had changed religion later in life, for example, has never been an obstacle to recognition.
3) *Substantial burden and mandatory practice.* The third element of the test is to see whether the state regulation imposes a significant restriction – or, in the words of the Supreme Court, a "substantial burden" – on that religious belief. Such evaluation shall include an assessment of how mandatory the practice may be; the most obvious case of substantial burden is that in which the state requires conduct prohibited by religion or, conversely, prohibits conduct that is religiously required. The more a practice is mandatory and essential within the religion, the greater the burden imposed and thus the higher the proof that the state must provide to satisfy this element.
4) *Compelling state interest and minimal restrictions.* The fourth element is to ensure that there is a cogent, compelling state interest to pursue,[42] for which

42 The religious test initially consisted exclusively of the compelling interest test, which was cited in the decision of *Sherbert v. Verner* in 1963.

no less restrictive solution is available. If this interest exists, even religious practices can be restricted.[43] Introduced in 1963 (*Sherbert* test), the requirement dictates that a religious practice can be affected only if the state advances a compelling interest, which is a high hurdle to surmount. In any case, the state must demonstrate that the least restrictive measures have been used to achieve that interest, thus burdening the religion with the lightest possible weight.

The described religious test, as mentioned, has been the subject of a complex institutional exchange. After decades of refinement, in 1990, following the judgment of *Oregon v. Smith*[44] – handed down by Justice Scalia – the test was suppressed. The case had settled the dispute between Mr. Smith, a Native American member of the Native American Church, and his employer. The employer, after having dismissed Smith for ingesting peyote, refused to contribute to his unemployment benefits. The employer, in fact, claimed to have applied the law that denies this right to anyone who consumes illegal drugs. In concrete terms, the Native American Church to which Smith belonged perpetuated the practice of using peyote for their prayers and rituals, which for them had ancient roots. According to the native, the law indirectly violated, therefore, his religious freedom as it did not consider that some religions may involve the use of drugs for ritual purposes. Although the *Sherbert* test should apply, the Supreme Court radically changed its orientation, abandoned the test, and noted that if a law had a neutral content and it was generally applicable to all citizens without having an explicitly discriminatory or harmful intent against a religion, its indirect effects, collateral restriction of a religion could not be taken into account. The Supreme Court described the religious test as "the most demanding test known to constitutional law" for the legislature, and then overturned *Sherbert*. It is left to the legislature and not to the judiciary – so says the Supreme Court – to identify any exceptions to the application of a law to ensure the protection of particular religious practices. In a ruling in which the court is more conservative than Congress and waived part of its prerogatives, Justice Scalia reaffirmed his loyalty to the textualist interpretation: a general and abstract legislation must be applied as such, and there is not space for any recognized or indirect discrimination or violations of constitutional rights.

In the absence of the *Sherbert* test, in the following years the court created a situation in which, in more than sixty cases, judges had to deny protection to religious claims as the laws used neutral wording. In particular, the following cases aroused the public attention: the case of Orthodox Jews who could now be subjected to autopsy, despite the opposition of the families for religious reasons; the

43 The requirement of a clear and compelling state interest is developed on a case by case basis. For example, in *Cheema v. Thompson*, 61 F.3d 734, 9th Cir. (1995), the state, faced with a case of the use of a *kirpan*, a ritual knife, brought by a Sikh child as part of his school uniform, had sought to demonstrate that there was a clear and compelling state interest of security, but the judge imposed the view that, up until that moment, the *kirpan* had never been used, in any circumstance, as a weapon as proof that the state's fears were unfounded.

44 *Employment Division, Human Resources of Oregon v. Smith* (1990) 494 U.S. 872.

case of Catholic hospitals that had lost their accreditation because they refused to practice abortion; and the case of different lands of the Natives who could be expropriated by laws which had a general and abstract content.

Following this situation, the test was reinstated by Congress with the Religious Freedom Restoration Act of 1993 (known as RFRA):[45] it is therefore one of the few existing tests that has been supported with a legislative foundation.

Perceiving the reintroduction by legislation of the test as a forceful act of the Federal Congress, the RFRA was declared partly unconstitutional by the Supreme Court with the decision *City of Boerne v. Flores* in 1997, on the grounds that the law violated the prerogatives and responsibilities of the individual states.[46] The actual test, therefore, is applied only to federal legislation.[47] It should, however, be reported that thirteen states have enacted similar laws (known as mini-RFRAs) that enable the completion of the test also at the state level.

Moving to a deeper analysis of the contents of the test, it should be noted that it has as an essential component ascertaining a subjective element: the sincerity of the claimant. To find religious practice in the abstract says nothing to the US judge of whether there is an intimate adherence by the claiming party. In this sense, the test creates an encounter between the concept of religion/culture and that of personal identity. Because religions and cultures do not live as an entity ontologically distinguishable from the individuals who practice them, but in fact are part of the individual's personal identity, the incarnations of religion and culture in the individuals are to be evaluated by the judge.

As in Canada, this test reflects the historical context in which it was forged. Also in the United States, the Protestant matrix plays a key role. In addition, many

45 Congress instated RFRA with the explicit intent to contest the erosive effect that the *Oregon v. Smith* decision of 1990 had on the protection of religious liberty. According to RFRA's text, in fact the judgment "virtually eliminated the requirement that the government justify burdens on religious exercise imposed by laws neutral toward religion" (42 USC 2000bb(a)).

46 The decision in *City of Boerne, Texas v. P.F. Flores Archbishop of San Antonio, and United States*, 521 U.S. 507 (1997) was pronounced by the majority of the court (six to three). In the opinion they write that, as a consequence of RFRA, "Any law is subject to challenge at any time by any individual who claims a substantial burden on his or her free exercise of religion . . . Requiring a State to demonstrate a compelling interest and show that it has adopted the least restrictive means of achieving that interest is the most demanding test known to constitutional law. 494 U.S. at 888. Furthermore, the least restrictive means requirement was not used in the pre-*Smith* jurisprudence RFRA purported to codify. All told, RFRA is a considerable congressional intrusion into the States' traditional prerogatives and general authority to regulate for the health and welfare of their citizens." The case regarded a request by a Catholic archdiocese to enlarge a church which fell under the laws for the protection of the cultural heritage that prohibited the enlargement of historical monuments.

47 The religious test was used, for instance, in *Gonzalez v. O Centro Espirita Benecifiente União do Vegetal*, 546 U.S. 418 (2006), a decision in which the Supreme Court reaffirmed the right of a religious sect originating from the Amazon forest that, in a syncretism with Catholicism, assumed a communion ritual by drinking a sacramental tea, made with a plant unique to the region and which contained a hallucinogen, the *ayahuasca*, listed in Schedule I of the Controlled Substances Act. The Supreme Court held that the reasons which determined in favor of the native peoples' use of peyote in 1993, thanks to RFRA, could be applied also for this religious group, composed of about one hundred and fifty people, who could seek the protection of the free exercise of religion clause.

religions practiced in North America are characterized by frequent schisms, and by the phenomenon of sects which have no comparable institutionalization level to that of Catholicism, for example. In the latter religions the tenets are more certainly settled regarding which practices are essential and which are not, and its doctrines define the boundaries of the believer's prohibitions and obligations in greater detail.

Nevertheless, recognizing such a weighty element as sincerity does not mean that the way in which the individual lives his religious experience prevails over everything. Even in the case of the US religious test, in fact, an objective connection with a group and with an external religious rule is required.

There is an interesting case that shows how the anthropologist judge can disentangle subjective and objective elements. The case of Mr. Burks Bey – a member of the Moorish Science Temple of America,[48] a religious sect – who sued the prison in which he was detained because it kept him from practicing his religion whose rites, *prima facie*, appear characterized by significant syncretism between the major monotheistic religions.

The first recurring violation contested by the applicant to the prison authority was the cancellation of some rites and study programs. On this point, the court observed that Mr. Burks-Bey, in fact, did not constantly attend all the rites. To justify, for example, his absence from the ceremony on Good Friday, he replied that since he was not a Christian he did not have to attend mass. The court found this inconsistent with his statement that his religion consisted in honoring "all true prophets of God (Buddha, Confucius, Mohammed and Jesus)" and in participating in all the religious programs of "all these faiths."

A second violation contested by Mr. Burks-Bey to the administration of the prison was that they denied him "the right to worship his God on February 14, 2003" due to the absence of a chaplain, who was ill. The court observes, of its own initiative, that his sect "does not require the intercession of a priest and his adherents pray directly to Allah. See the Holy Quran of the Moorish Science Temple of America, divinely prepared by the Prophet Noble Drew Ali, Chapter 10."

The need for an objective foundation for Mr. Burks-Bey's claims is also apparent in another part of the opinion which responds to the appeal in which Burks-Bey complained that he had been denied the acquisition of sacred oils. Having established that the Holy Quran of the Moorish Science Temple of America does not speak of such oils, the judge observed:

> Though Mr. Burks-Bey might enjoy using prayer oils, because their use is not a fundamental belief of Moorish Science Temple of America (MSTA), the prison has no obligation to accommodate this demand. Even if prayer oils are fundamental to Islam, even if *kippot* are fundamental to Judaism, even if holy water is fundamental to Catholicism, none of these items are fundamental to MSTA. Mr. Burks-Bey complains that Sunni Muslims are permitted

48 *David M. Burks-Bey v. Sally Stevenson, et al.*, 328 F. Supp. 2d 928 (2004).

> to purchase "Muslim Prayer Oils" . . . but in yet another inconsistency, this argument does not seem to recognize that he is not a Sunni Muslim . . . the question is not whether Mr. Burks-Bey sincerely believes and practices his belief in the religion of MSTA (though such questions might reasonably be raised); here the issue is what are the beliefs of MSTA and what does it require of its adherents. As a member of MSTA, prayer oil is at best an optional item which is not essential to the practice of the MSTA religion. Mr. Burks-Bey, like all other MSTA members, was no less able or effective in the worshiping of his god without prayer oil than he would have been had he had it.

In this reasoning the recurring theme of mandatory practice returns. This *topos* is offered by the judge, although, as we have seen, it is not officially incorporated in the American test. This provides evidence that the mandatory nature of a practice, from a comparative point of view, is an element that is often established, and that has an important weight to move the decision in one direction or another.

In this case, indeed, the court is faced with practices that seem to be used instrumentally, and, in fact, concludes by noting that the guarantee offered to any religious group, even newly established, encounters an objective limit. Mr. Burks-Bey thought he could get by "individually inventing religious practices and holidays and then ascribing them to MSTA without any regard for the historical, theological, or logical consistency of the traditions of that religion."

The balance between the objective and the subjective parts of the test and the attention to the relational dimension of the interests of the majority as well (measured with the compelling interest standard) make this test a good tool to balance different reasons at play in a religious conflict.

6.2 The cultural defense in criminal trials: the topos *of enculturation*

In the United States the religious and cultural practices which may fall in the wide concept of religion are governed by a religious test. But what happens to other practices that have no religious trait? They are not backed by a certain test, but the courts have often considered the cultural elements of a dispute through the instrument that takes the name of the cultural defense.

This concept is defined in the seminal work of Alison Dundes Renteln both as "a defense strategy in criminal cases", according to its classical meaning,[49] but also as a "pervasive phenomenon" which may arise in civil cases as well and which "affects many more stages of legal process than just the guilt phase of the trial", according to a "broader interpretation" supported by the scholar (Dundes Renteln 2004: 6). The cultural defense is, according to Dundes Renteln, an argument raised in any

49 In its traditional meaning "[a] cultural defence is a rule of state law which constitutes a complete or partial defence to a crime or mitigation which reduces the punishment, and which takes effect where the defendant would not have committed the criminal act had they not belonged to a particular culture" (Woodman 2009: 14).

trial or pre-trial phase, the premise of which is "enculturation – the notion that culture shapes cognition and conduct" (Dundes Renteln 2004: 7). Moving from this definition we can distinguish, first, a more restricted technical meaning of the term which is translatable as a cause of justification, mitigating or extenuating cultural circumstances that have an influence in determining both the objective and the subjective element of the criminal offense. In these more technical, criminal, meanings

> in US law the exemption (or quasi-exemption) never operates independently, but always within other defenses recognized by law (for example, self defense, the insanity defense, a mistake of fact, the provocation defense, etc.), since, at the present time, US law does not expressly recognize the cultural defense.
>
> (Sorio 2008)[50]

At present, therefore, although the lawyers often label their appeals as a cultural defense, there is no obligation on the part of judges to implement it. We are thus speaking of a phenomenon that takes place outside a normative framework. Whereas the religious test is formalized in its steps and is regularly applied by judges within the argumentative logic detailed above, there is no actual cultural test used as an officially recognized defense. What I seek shortly to explain, therefore, is a complete inductive reconstruction of the most common factors (*topoi*) in the US case law though they are not established by reformist Supreme Court action. So if the test exists at all, it is neither well established nor binding. This analysis, however, allows us to bring to light the most relevant elements which attempt to address culture and add an important piece to the puzzle of our comparative approach, to see whether a shared approach may be under way and whether any doctrine can be taken as a starting point for the resolution of disputes (*infra* sec. 12).

The presence of investigations and more accurate analysis by the court around the concept of culture was not, even in the United States, an immediate phenomenon. A first season of cases saw judges approaching culture in a very formulaic fashion: the presence of a cultural element has influenced judges, indirectly in *Kimura*, and more explicitly in some extremely controversial cases: the *Chen* case,[51] involving a Chinese man who had killed his wife with a hammer upon finding out that she had betrayed him, and the *Moua* case,[52] of a Hmong man who had raped his girlfriend, convinced that the resistance that she opposed to sexual intercourse was part of a ritual that involves fake reluctance on the part of the woman (*zij poj niam*, marriage by capture). In both cases the judges acquitted the defendants, taking into account their cultural background. Although not explicitly formulated as such, what the judges took into account

50 Those that are currently recognized in the American legal system are the "cultural offense" and the "cultural evidence," namely the possibility to present before the judge the cultural context of the defendant (De Maglie 2010: 71–79).

51 *People v. Dong Lu Chen*, No. 87-7774, N.Y. Sup. Ct., Dec. 2, 1988.

52 *People v. Moua*, No. 315972–0, Cal. Sup. Ct., 1985.

was the idea of "enculturation:" the impossibility for Mr. Chen and Mr. Moua to see other paths of action given the powerful shaping that culture had exerted on their minds (Beger, Hein 2001). Following critical reactions to these decisions, the consideration of culture in the courts has been the subject of more careful evaluations which lead to some fixed standards. The reasoning of US courts can be rebuilt inductively and show the emergence of those *topoi*:

1) *Identification of the cultural practice.* The judge is not limited to simply naming a practice, as was the case until the early 1990s, but proceeds to its accurate description. Some judgments incorporate real anthropological reports. This description is partly taken from the same evidence collected in the process, but more often is the result of consultations with anthropologists (Rosen 1977); rarely, it is presented as the result of an intuition or pre-knowledge of the judge or his passive acceptance of whatever the defense suggests.
2) *The reasonable (cultural) person standard.* In several decisions the court has established the reasonableness of the conduct by measuring the behavior that the average person belonging to that group would evince. This element is the adaptation of the already existing "reasonable man" (Lee 2003) test to a culturally characterized person and leads the judge to ask: how would the "reasonable Mexican man," the "reasonable Japanese woman" or the "reasonable Danish mother"[53] behave in that circumstance?[54]
3) *Residence time in the host culture.* A third issue that has a certain recurrence is the assessment by the judge of how long the immigrant has lived in the United States, what level of integration and contact with majority culture he has reached, his knowledge of the rules in force in the United States and his intention of continuing or abandoning the cultural practice in the future. A wide diffusion of the time factor is revealed, as is seen also in the resolution of multicultural conflicts in the English case law (*infra* sec. 7) and is not even alien to Italian law (*Saleem* case, Chap. 1 sec. 1.2).

Regarding the first element, an accurate description of the practice allows the court to dismiss the cultural argument when used purely and simply, without determining the content. On this point, a significant appellate decision decided the case of a married couple, Aurora and José Luis Gonzalez, convicted in the first degree and sentenced respectively to two years and twenty-five years in prison for abuse and murder of a nineteen-month-old baby who had been entrusted to their

53 The case of a Danish mother accused of abandoning a minor for the fact of leaving her baby carriage outside the entrance of a restaurant in America was resolved by considering that in all of Denmark, even in big cities such as Copenhagen, this is a perfectly accepted and reasonable behavior (Sultana Brelvi 1996–97).

54 This aspect is defined by the Italian criminal law doctrine as "coincidence of reaction" of the plaintiff/defendant and her cultural group: "it will be necessary to demonstrate that the cultural motivation of the individual has an 'objective dimension' that, in other words, the cultural motive is not the only part of the individual ethic of the agents, but is also an expression of a cultural baggage well consolidated within the group to which they appertain" (De Maglie 2010: 31).

care by neighbors.[55] The child, who had received a beating, had been brought late to the hospital and the lawyer for Aurora Gonzalez had set the defense arguing that "to evaluate the appellant's judgment based on a reasonable person standard in the defendant's position, one must also take into consideration the traditional role of women in Mexican households." As one may guess, the lawyer evoked the role of subordination of women and the Mexican *machismo*: after her husband beat the child, Aurora Gonzalez, who first asked to take the child to the hospital, was so intimidated by his authority that she refrained from insisting. But the judge observes that the cultural argument is "undeveloped" as

> Aurora doesn't bother to explain what that traditional role is or how it affected this case, what evidence was presented at trial to make out a cultural defense, or what legal authority supports a cultural defense. The failure to properly develop an argument is fatal on appeal.[56]

Incidentally, it is useful to note how these grounds are fully in line with a controversial/dialectic approach, which requires rigor in identifying the connection between the theory of cultural defense and the concrete controversy.

Unlike what happens in Italy (*infra* sec. 8), therefore, the US judge refuses to consider the cultural factor for the mere fact that a party requests it. The lack of a clear identification of the practice and resorting to the "it's my culture" argument is no longer enough. A party must demonstrate, with an accurate description, the content of his behavior, just as in Canada (*supra* sec. 5.1). The consolidation of this *topos* in comparative jurisprudence is, in my opinion, very important both for the benefit of the minority to avoid misattribution of false cultural practices (as wife-beating to Sardinians or the begging to Roma, seen in Chap. 1 sec. 2.2. and 3.1 respectively) and for the benefit of the majority which can better understand the reasons underlying the behavior thanks to a more accurate description.

With regard to the second standard recurring in the American case law – the reasonable "cultural" (i.e. Mexican, Japanese, Danish) person test – on the one side it reveals an anthropological sensitivity on the part of the American judge, capable of measuring the reasonableness of a behavior through other "cultural lenses"; and, on the other side, it prevents the "blaming culture for bad behavior" (Volpp 2000) risk, especially when that behavior is condemned by the same minority group or is quite unusual.

A famous case in which this standard was applied, was decided by a California Court of Appeal in 1994[57] against a Mexican citizen accused of shooting an

55 *The People v. José Luis Gonzalez et al.*, Court of Appeal of California, 2nd Appellate District, Division 3, January 23, 2009.

56 A series of other considerations urge the judge to hold that the behavior of Aurora was not culturally motivated. As, according to the judge, proves the testimony of a doctor who affirmed how "even non medically trained persons, if they saw how ill David [the child] was, would recognize that the patient was in a grave situation and bring the patient in."

57 *Trujillo Garcia v. Rowland*, U.S. 6199 (Dist. Ct., 1992); U.S. 30441 (App. Ct., 1993), 114 S. Ct. 2145; U.S. 4219 (Dist. Ct. 1994).

acquaintance. Convicted of murder, the defendant appealed, claiming the cultural argument: Trujillo Garcia would, in fact, have responded in an altered mental state, as the "*chinga tu madre*" expression that had been uttered by the victim represented a very strong challenge in the Mexican culture, which had not been properly appreciated by resorting to the American agent model parameter. The appeal court changed the standard, from asking how a reasonable US person would have acted in that circumstance, to asking how a reasonable Mexican man would behave if faced with an insult of that kind in Mexico. Using this criterion, the judge came to the conclusion that no average Mexican man would react to that provocation by killing and, therefore, upheld the conviction. If the premise of the judge proves founded,[58] reasoning of this kind is appropriate. They also freed the Mexican group from a stereotypical vision which attributes a readiness toward crime to their culture, rather than to individuals' tempers.

The cultural reasonable person *topos* deserves contextualizing attention. The requirement in question, in fact, is forged from a more general standard: that of the reasonable man under all circumstances. This very general standard has, in recent decades, received several clarifications by American judges. The most significant four are: the reasonable "cultural" person standard just analyzed; the reasonable woman standard; the reasonable battered woman standard; and the reasonable black person standard.[59] These clarifications were developed at a time when some judges found that the apparent neutrality of the overall standard of the reasonable man was always assessed on the basis of an average white, Anglo-Saxon, Protestant male (the so-called WASP) and not necessarily from the point of view of the main parties of the event, the victim or the accused.

The reasonable woman standard has been developed in order to determine whether a woman is subjected to sexual harassment in the workplace. The presence of office calendars with naked women, gazing insistently to bosoms or undeterred love letters from the employer were measured on the basis of an assessment made by the reasonable average woman, and as such, sanctioned (Mootz 2010a).

The standard of the reasonable battered woman derives from the acceptance in the legal sphere of what has been recently recognized by psychiatry as a disease, identified as the battered woman syndrome (Walker 1979). Thus the battered woman defense was created, also founded on the assumption that legal rules – supposedly interpreted only along the lines of a neutral individual, the reasonable person – in fact coincided with the male. In this sense, the rules of self-defense have been applied by the courts even in cases of women who had killed their husband in his sleep after having been beaten, if they were aware

58 The decision was, indeed, criticized for the fact that the judge did not care to hear from any anthropologist of Mexican culture, nor undertake any particular investigation (Dundes Renteln 2004: 34–35).

59 We may debate whether those standards should be considered as autonomous standards, in which case they would require some recognition at the legislative level or on the part of the Supreme Court or, *vice versa*, whether they are nothing other than specifications and articulations of the more traditional "reasonable man under all circumstances" standard, in which case they would not represent a significant innovation.

of the likelihood that the beatings would occur again when he woke up, with potentially lethal consequences. The fact that in order to recognize legitimate defense there should be a "state of present danger" and the victim should have "no chance to escape" had always worked, in these cases, to exclude female self-defense because women might have run away when the state of ill-treatment was not in progress. Often, indeed, women received an increase in their sentences for premeditation. However, this interpretation did not consider the different level of physical strength that makes it difficult for the woman to mount an immediate reaction to a dangerous state and does not consider the effects of the development of the battered woman syndrome. For this reason, the judges decided to adjust the test of a "reasonable person under all circumstances" so as to include the situation of a woman being constantly beaten and not of the "ordinary man."[60]

The reasonable black person test was used in a few cases in which the courts have accepted the "black rage defense"[61] (Harris 1997). The expression indicates the state caused by the constant fearful awe instilled in African Americans, especially in the 1960s, of becoming targets of violent actions by the white population. In the case of a young black boy who had killed a white boy after the latter's group of friends had threatened him, the prosecution argued that the reaction had been disproportionate. But according to the defense, any average black person could reasonably believe that the conduct of the group, if not stopped, could result in his death, especially as the Ku Klux Klan was active in the area. The young man obtained the application of the justification of self-defense. Also in this case the agent model had been identified as a reasonable black boy in that particular social context.

This digression is intended to highlight how the reasonable (cultural) person standard is part of a wider process leading to the specification and the individualization of the demands of justice.

For the purposes of this work, the reasonable (cultural) person standard is particularly useful to draw a line between what is cultural and what is, instead, based on the character, temperament or biography of the subject.

The third requirement that was found in the hundreds of judgments in which American judges have addressed the evaluation of a cultural factor is the evaluation of the amount of time the claimant has resided in the host culture (also *infra* in the UK, sec. 7). The determination of this factor is considered for all activities particularly reprehensible. In this case, the protection the judge may grant does

60 *State v. Norman*, 89 N.C. App. 384, 366 S.E.2d 586, 1988 N.C. App. 262. The opinion acquitted Judy Norman for having killed her husband after years of abuse, thus recognizing a gender prejudice in the concept of "reasonable behavior" that influences the perceptions of what is a legitimate defense (Dalton, Schneider 2001: 717).

61 The black rage defense is a legal strategy centered on racial oppression experienced by the accused. It is an attempt to explain to the judge and jury how the context working on the defendant has contributed to the crime. This standard was historically applied during the period of struggles for civil rights of African-Americans when it operated as a mitigating circumstance or as an exclusion of punishment. The most well known case in which it was used is *U.S. v. Steven Robinson*, 1971, subsequently described.

not derive from the fact that the cultural conduct has a recognized value, but rather from a purely anthropological consideration: the subject could not see other ways, so it was basically impossible for him to act otherwise (enculturation).

One case in which the judge resorted to the time factor is that of Mr. Phoung Le,[62] a Vietnamese immigrant who, upon seeing his wife's application for asylum rejected, grabbed a pen and paper and wrote a letter in which he referred to the Virginia Tech massacre in 2007, threatened to cut off the head of the official who had evaluated the request for asylum and then to commit suicide. The letter arrived stained with blood. Accused of threat by correspondence, Phoung Le's defense claimed that his intent was not to threaten, but to insult. He therefore called a cultural expert, Dr. Leung, a psychologist who studies the effects of cultural difference on immigrants. Dr. Leung, according to the judge, made "three salient statements." The first is the clarification that the phrase "cut his head" as used idiomatically in the Vietnamese language expresses an insult and not an actual threat. The second explains that the act of sealing the letter with blood is a traditional Vietnamese custom which has the effect of attesting to the truth of the document, not of intimidating or any other motive. The third explanation is based on the fact that a lack of English and knowledge of American culture prevented Mr. Phoung Le from appreciating that his statements could result in another individual's feeling of being threatened. The judge observed that these statements left two details unexplained: the reference to the Virginia Tech massacre and the fact that Mr. Phoung Le was resident in the US since 1998 and could, therefore, be aware of the local culture and communication codes. In doubt, however, the court allowed the appeal and granted a new trial.

6.3 The cultural argument in civil litigation: the topos *of the reasonable (cultural) person*

The United States' long tradition as a multicultural country records a widespread cultural argument used not only in criminal law, but also in civil law (Dundes Renteln 2009b). Also within this field, the phenomenon has a history.

In 1963, a sixteen year-old girl, Ruth Friedman, went on a trip with nineteen year-old Jack Katz on Bellayare mountain, in the State of New York.[63] The two had bought a return ticket for the cable car to the summit. After the picnic they returned to the station, which was deserted, but found the cable car still functioning. Jack and Ruth jumped in a cable car for two people, but a few minutes after their departure the cable car stopped working and the two found themselves in mid-air, eight meters above the ground. It was getting dark. After calling in vain for help for a quarter of an hour, Ruth Friedman opened her seat belt and jumped out of the cable car. Completely bloody and having suffered multiple injuries, she returned to the departure station where, however, the phone was not working; she then walked to the arrival station, where the staff unblocked the cable car and administered first aid.

62 *United States of America v. Phuoung Nguyen Le*, Criminal No. 3:08cr516, U.S. District Court for the Eastern District of Virginia, Richmond Division, Sept. 14, 2009, Lexis 83933.

63 *Friedman v. State*, 282 New York State, 2d 858 (1967).

The State of New York, which ran the park, claimed not to have done anything to the youth as it was she herself who caused her injuries through her negligent behavior, which greatly aggravated the incident's consequences. The girl acted recklessly and jumped without waiting for someone at the departure station to notice that the cable car was still occupied. What – asked the state – motivated her to undertake such an unreasonable gesture?

Ruth Friedman testified at trial that she could not be alone after sunset with a man. Ruth is, in fact, an Orthodox Jew. At the trial an expert witness of Hebrew law, Rabbi Stahl, explains that in the *Shulhan Arukh* (a sector of Jewish law) there is a rule, that of *Jichud*, which absolutely prohibits to a woman to be with a man in a place that is not accessible by a third person after sunset. Violating the *Jichud* would be a huge shame that would ruin not only the reputation of a young woman, but also that of her parents. According to the rabbi, "a girl who had been trained in a 100% orthodox [sic] home, as Miss Friedman was, might go even to the lengths of jumping to her death to avoid violation of the *Jichud*."

The judge offers us, in this case, the rule on how to define the group to impute the practice, because the complexity of the case lies in the fact that the *Jichud* is not followed by all Jews. In that sense, applying the standard of the reasonable Jewish person does not dictate that another Jewish teenager in the same condition would have jumped as Ruth did. But the judge ruled: "the point is not whether Rabbi Stahl gave us an absolutely correct interpretation of Hebrew law . . . but, whether there is a branch of Judaism which believes in this interpretation; and, whether Miss Friedman is a member of this group." The term of reference, therefore, can also be a cultural sub-group. Two implied investigations emerge from this statement: to check if there is a group that actually supports the practice, and to verify that the subject belongs to that group (judges, at the comparative level, do not always pay attention to this dual objective and subjective connection).

In the resolution of the case, it is interesting to note the judge's efforts to find a behavioral equivalent in maintaining that any teenager, belonging to any culture, might have acted similarly under the same circumstances.

In the words of the judge:

> In the first instance, it does not require much imagination or experience to determine that a lightly dressed 16-year-old city girl might become hysterical at the prospect of spending a night on a mountainside, suspended in the air and with no apparent reason to hope for rescue until the next morning. Secondly, we must add to the fact of expectable hysteria, the moral compulsion this young lady believed she was under, not to spend a night alone with a man.

Summing up, the culture of Ruth Friedman "increased the hysteria we believe a young girl might well experience regardless of faith." A cultural equivalent of the coincidence of reaction is an element that, when present, may exert a strong influence.[64] Incidentally, one will notice how clumsily this judge also becomes a sociologist of his own culture, showing himself immersed in a 1960s' vision of women as fragile subjects and easy prey to hysterics.

The case was decided in favor of Friedman. The State of New York was ordered to pay the girl the sum of $35,000 and $2,231 to her father addressed as medical expenses, very large sums at the time.

Another case of cultural argument used in civil proceedings concerns the death of a young Egyptian man in a plane crash.[65] His parents asked for the payment of insurance compensation taking into account the particular cultural profiles of the case: in fact, in the Egyptian tradition, the eldest son is responsible for taking care of his parents in old age. The damage that resulted from the parents' loss of their son also had to predict the loss of assistance (Dundes Renteln 2009b). In this case, the court has proved sensitive to the demands of the part and measured the compensation on the basis of the cultural factor.

Another number of civil cases regards dietary practices.

A first case concerns a Hindu citizen who entered a restaurant of the food chain Taco Bell and ordered a bean burrito.[66] Mistaken, the cashier served him a beef burrito. Realizing the error only after tasting the meat, the customer filed a complaint for damages: the consumption of bovine meat, in fact, is prohibited in the Hindu culture and religion, because the cow is a sacred animal. The lack of clear explanatory signs on the menu and the distraction of the cashier traumatized the subject.

An analogous case occurred to several Hindu customers at the McDonald's chain in 2001.[67] The company at the time aromatized its fries with a spray of beef meat. One of the Hindu customers filed a complaint claiming that every morning, the idea of having ingested fries with meat made him retch and that in his mind there was always the idea of having committed a terrible sin. McDonald's, while denying having ever said that their French fries were "vegetarian," answered the writ of summons by paying $4,000 to each of the eleven people involved and donating $10 million to an association that dealt with promoting Hindu

64 See, on this point, the "theory of cultural convergence," according to which "cultural defense claims of minority and immigrant defendants are more likely to receive accommodation when there is convergence between their cultural norms and American cultural norms . . . including retrograde racist and sexist norms" (Lee 2007: 911). The author presents an analysis of cases employing the cultural defense successfully (jealous husbands murdering their wives, women in crisis over cheating husbands killing their children) and of those cases in which the defense did not prevail (manifestations of intimate affection by parties toward children) and demonstrates that the first coincide with visions of the world, of gender roles, of family which are acceptable also in American culture.

65 *In Re Air Crash Near Nantucket Island, Massachusetts*, 462 F. Supp. 2d 360 (2006).

66 Out-of Court Settlement *Hindu v. Taco Bell*, 1999.

67 Out-of Court Settlement *Hindu v. McDonald's*, 2001.

culture and representing Hindu immigrants, creating a center for food information on their menus and publishing an official apology on their website (Nafziger, Kirkwood Paterson, Dundes Renteln 2010: 73).

6.4 The cultural argument rejected: the topoi *of falsity, inconsistency and criminalization in one's homeland*

The appeal to culture risks becoming a strategic reference, used as a pretext to justify conduct that, in reality, even the minority group would denounce. Beside a passive attitude, in certain cases, in which judges uncritically accept the idea of being faced with a culture by the mere fact that the party is a foreigner, there are cases in which US courts have made a more rigorous verification to validate the cultural claim.

In a first group of cases the anthropologist judge notices that he is faced with a false cultural practice, invented *ad hoc* by the defense. These cases tend to lack the objective requirement (description of the cultural practice) *a priori.*

A second group encompasses cases where the cultural practice exists, but is not consistently practiced by the subject and, more generally, not fully linked to his or her personal identity. These cases, once the objective part of the declaration is satisfied, reveal some deficiencies from the point of view of the subjective factor (is the subject sincere?).

In a third group of cases the judge points out that the practice actually exists but cannot be recognized because it is also sanctioned by other legal systems or because it is a result of a political regime (and not of culture).

1) *The practice is false or nonexistent.* Among the cases in which an anthropologist judge has unveiled the untruthfulness of a practice is that of a Ukrainian couple arrested following reports from a photography studio that they had developed two photographic films of a naked girl. The couple defended themselves on the grounds that in Ukraine it was a cultural practice to photograph naked children. But the testimony of many Ukrainian citizens at the trial served to uncover that "nude photographs of seven- to eight-year-old children in Ukraine is not common;" the court rejected the cultural argument because the alleged practice was false.[68]

The judge refused to apply the cultural argument also in a case of domestic violence between a Native American woman and her daughter.[69] The latter had been heavily beaten by her mother and social services had arranged the procedure for the termination of parental rights. According to the Indian Child Welfare Act (ICWA) of 1978, the standard for termination is "evidence

68 *State of Washington, v. Nadezhda Pesotskiy,* No. 52502-6-I, Court of Appeals of Washington, Division One, 2004 Wash. App. Lexis 2317, October 11, 2004.

69 *Marcia V., Appellant v. State of Alaska, Office of Children's Services, Appellee,* Supreme Court of Alaska, No. S-13065, 201 P.3d 496, Jan. 21, 2009.

beyond a reasonable doubt, including testimony of qualified expert witnesses, that the continued custody of the child by the parent or Indian custodian is likely to result in serious emotional or physical damage to the child."[70] The mother contested that the social worker expert who decided the termination of her parental rights knew nothing about Native culture. The Supreme Court of Alaska, having decided to hear the case, noted that in this case "the basis for termination is unrelated to Native culture" and that "ICWA does not require testimony from an expert in Native culture to terminate parental rights when there is clear evidence of physical neglect" and affirms the previous decision in favor of foster care.

A substantial number of cases in this group occurs in asylum applications, which are often based on invented or distorted cultural practices in order to demonstrate a dangerous situation.

In the *Kalhili* case,[71] a Jordanian citizen applied for asylum on the basis of the risk of an honor killing by his first wife's clan due to the fact that he had divorced her and married another woman. The judge rejected the request on the ground that the practice of the murder of honor in Jordan applies only to women and does not extend to men.

In a very similar case, involving Mr. Al-Wawi,[72] a Jordanian citizen who had an extramarital affair with a woman and applied for asylum to avoid risking an honor killing, the judge provided ulterior arguments: in addition to the fact that "the alien had offered no objective evidence that the cultural practice of 'honor killing' extended to men," he "was never threatened directly, and . . . had failed to corroborate the existence of a threat." The alleged abstract existence of the practice (objective factors) should, according to the court, relate to the personal history of each individual (subjective factor).

2) *Inconsistency; practices irrelevant to the identity of the subject.* The second group of cases in which US courts rejected the cultural argument concerns, as mentioned above, cases in which the cultural practice exists, but nevertheless does not deserve protection because it does not fully link to the identity of the subject; for example, he does not practice it consistently or because, in that particular case, it was not the determining factor of his action. Unlike the Canadian cultural test, which is focused on the objective element and does not research how culture is embodied in the individual personal identity (a profile which is,

70 In the case of *Steven H. v. Arizona Dept. of Economic Security*, 218 Ariz. 566, August 19, 2008, one reads that Congress imposed this measure "to prevent state courts from too readily approving dependency dispositions that remove Indian children from their parents or native communities." For these reasons, "in many ICWA cases, expert testimony may be necessary to educate a court about tribal customs and childrearing practices to diminish any risk of cultural bias."

71 *Hamdi Al Khalili v. Eric H. Holder, Jr., Attorney General of the United States*, U.S. Ct. App. 6th Cir., Feb. 27, 2009.

72 *Mohammed Sulliman Al Wawi, Petitioner, V. John Ashcroft, Attorney General, Respondent*, No. 02-4292, United States Court of Appeals for the Sixth Circuit, 91 Fed. Appx. 493; 2004 U.S. App. Lexis 5382, March 18, 2004.

however, found in the Canadian religious test, *supra* 5.2), the cultural argument as used in United States reveals a strong attention to subjective elements in both the religious test and that of the cultural defense.

So, when Omar Abdelwahab, employed as a concierge, sued his employer, Jackson State University, accusing it of refusing him an exemption from night shifts in order to perform the night prayers as required by Muslim *Sura*, the judge did not dispute the existence of the practice invoked (objective element), but rather made a reference to the consistency of the subject in following his beliefs (subjective element). For three years Abdelwahab Omar had, in fact, performed his night shifts, giving up the prayer and only thereafter making his belated, pretentious and ultimately unacceptable demand: he had demonstrated neither sincerity nor an unreserved commitment to the practice.[73]

Another case inconsistently referencing religious practices is that of a Liberian citizen who introduced monkey meat into the US in violation of an international convention on the protection of endangered animal species at risk of extinction.[74] The judge heard evidence intended to show that the

> Bushmeat is sacred to us because it is of the free wild animals of our homeland, and these animals are gifts from God and filled with spiritual power. When we eat bushmeat, we get closer to God and we take in that spiritual power to our bodies. This is something our forefathers did, it is something we learned as children, and it is part of our treasured relationship with God as African Christians.

The American anthropologist judge accepts any practice, if it falls into a widely understood religious scheme, welcoming them "with the perspective of the 'other'" – but in this case the judge considered that the religious claim was "purely pretextual." In fact, during the trial the woman tried to deny that she was importing meat, which only shows how the woman was aware of the illegality of her conduct. In addition, the court suspected that this, rather than for religious reasons, happened for secular reasons: the consumption of meat in certain festivities. In this case, the distinction between culture and religion in the legal system revealed its difference in terms of legal consequences (*supra* sec. 2).

Another case of discrepancy between the test's objective and subjective element concerned a citizen of Ghana,[75] Mr. Mamah who, after confessing to a crime, intended to retract his statements and not to use them at the trial on the grounds that these were untrue because he, scared that the police would torture

73 This case, in truth, could be discussible on the merit as one could object that perhaps Mr. Abdelwahab has so far avoided raising the question for fear of being deported.

74 *United States of America v. Mamie Manneh,* 06 Cr 248 (RJD), United States District Court for the Eastern District of New York, 645 F. Supp. 2d 98; 2008 U.S. Dist. Lexis 105209, December 31, 2008.

75 *U.S. v. Abdul Raimi Mamah,* U.S. Ct. App. 7th Cir., No. 02-2931 (June 11, 2003).

him, confessed falsely. This seemingly inexplicable behavior stemmed from his cultural background. To prove it, the Ghanaian citizen had requested that the court of first instance hear the testimony of a sociologist and anthropologist, who related a study of false confessions made under contexts of psychological pressure favored by certain interrogatory techniques: "[Expert witnesses] were to testify that behaviors adopted by Ghanaians in response to living under a military regime could lead them to make false confessions when confronted by law enforcement authorities," for fear of violence by the latter.

The judge of first instance used three arguments to reject the request.

First, he noted that none of the experts "was a clinical psychologist qualified to assess Mamah's susceptibility to the interrogation techniques used by the FBI agents."

Second, he noted concerns about the testimony of the anthropologist as "Mamah had been living in the United States since 1984, more than enough time to have learned the difference between Ghanaian and American law-enforcement practices."

In the third place, the court of first instance rejected the merely abstract cultural claim: "Mamah claimed that he had been detained and beaten while still living in Ghana . . . but the court noted, Mamah had not accused the FBI agents of engaging in tactics similar to those purportedly common in Ghana."

The Court of Appeal confirmed this interpretation, in particular excluding the testimony of the anthropologist for these reasons:

> Dr. Pellow's expertise is limited to the cultural practices of Ghanaian nationals living in Ghana; she has no basis for extrapolating this conclusion to Mamah, a Ghanaian expatriot. Had she offered an empirical study demonstrating that Ghanaian ex-patriots who have lived in the United States for more than ten years are unusually likely to give false confessions, then perhaps she could have established this link. But Dr. Pellow did not have at her disposal sufficient facts and data to support the proposition that Mamah's cultural background might have induced him to give a false confession.

The problem raised by the court opens a reflection, that here we can only mention, on the difficulty of an anthropological reconstruction of behaviors when they occur outside the semiotic system in which the individual would naturally operate. This difficulty has led, in the United States, to the emergence of another type of defense, the cross-cultural defense, a sort of borderline issue between the cultural and the psychological argument, which is based on the shock and the difficulties of adaptation that a subject "transplanted" in another context meets. While the cultural defense is based on the anthropological consideration that a person holds a certain behavior because he is following a cultural practice, the cross-cultural defense is based on the psychological consideration that a person holds a certain behavior because he is located in a context of cultural transition which implies the loss of the landmarks of his identity membership, creating a kind of psychological weakness.[76] The cross-cultural defense is not generally accommodated.

Another example that excludes the cultural argument appears when the appeal to culture is correct, but is not linked to the motivations that, in that particular case, prompted the subject to act. The existence of a cultural belief does not always represent the motive of a crime. Such is the case of a murder committed by a member of the Laotian community in the United States.[77] The defense argued that the subject had killed while convinced of being under a spell of black magic effected by the victim fifteen months before, claiming that his mental state at the time of the shooting was enough to warrant the subsumption of the crime to the less severe second-degree murder (manslaughter) charge instead of first degree murder. Convicted of the most serious cases of murder, the accused appealed, arguing that the judge had failed to instruct the jury on his defensive theory:

> A cultural anthropologist testified about commonly held Laotian beliefs in black magic. According to the anthropologist, a majority of people in Laos still believe black magic exists, and many of those who migrate to the United States retain their belief that sorcerers can use bad spirits with black magic. These sorcerers can use black magic to put a spell on someone by giving the person a liquid or by obtaining a personal item, such as hair or clothing. If the victim of the black magic is unable to get relief from the spell, he or she might die. It is also a commonly held belief that a sorcerer can kill the victim through use of a spell.

76 One case in which this was used as a defense is *Quang Ngoc Bui v. State*, 717 So. 2d 6 (1997), Ala. Crim. App. Lexis 276. Mr. Bui, estranged from his wife, killed their three children. The defense used two arguments: insanity and the cross-cultural defense. In the words of the court: "Witnesses testified that Bui had not come to the United States voluntarily and that he missed his family in Vietnam. These witnesses also described a change in Bui's behavior several weeks before the murders: just days before the murders, Bui had watched a movie about Vietnam that had depressed him. On the night the children were killed, Bui told Jeannie Bui (his wife) over the phone that he was going to take the children to Vietnam with him." Through this process two experts were heard, including Dr. Tulao, chosen for "a good knowledge of the oriental culture [sic]" who testified how Bui spoke of his family in Vietnam and denied that his children were dead. According to the psychologist, the defendant was suffering from an acute psychotic reaction that rendered him incapable of appreciating the consequences of his actions. Another cultural expert, Dr. Cao explained the differences between American culture and Vietnamese culture. "Dr. Cao explained that in Vietnam, if a man's wife was running around on him, it would be a 'loss of face.' Had Bui been in Vietnam, he would have returned Jeannie Bui to her family to 'save face.' Dr. Cao also testified that since Bui was living in the United States, the only way Bui felt he could 'save face' was by killing himself and his children." This case demonstrates the problems of weighing the behaviors of subjects outside of their cultural context. The inference that the cultural expert deduced is not, in my view, so certain. The culturally obliged behavior is to send the wife back to her family. An insertion into another cultural context generates diverse and contrasting sentiments, but it is difficult to deduce the compulsion to murder one's children as a culturally necessitated consequence. Actually, we could say that here we are out of the paradigm of culture as Mr. Bui committed a behavior that is not common within his culture.

77 *Bounnhong Douangpangna v. Mike Knowles, Warden*, 2007 U.S. Dist. Lexis 25833, No. Civ. S-01-0764 Geb JFM P., U.S. District Court for the Eastern District of California, April 5, 2007.

However, the judge observed that, even if this practice exists, it has nothing to do with the actual case which looks like a jealous murder:

> [Petitioner]'s conduct during the shooting suggested that he, not the victim, was the aggressor. By his own admission, he went to the neighborhood to meet the victim. Eyewitnesses observed him stop his truck, chase the victim, and ignore pleas to stop. They saw the victim running away and attempting to retreat into the apartment. Even if the jury accepted [petitioner]'s testimony that he was under a black magic spell, the evidence that he was in fear of impending death was slim. [Petitioner] sought out Loommany and the victim even though he was aware of the restraining order against him. Moreover, his conduct following the shooting was inconsistent with his cultural defense. He fled the scene, buried the gun, and spent the night with friends, but never mentioned he shot the victim because he was under a black magic spell.

The lack of connection between the abstract cultural beliefs and *quaestio* controversy proves, once again, crucial to reject the argument.

3) ***Practices consequent to political regimes or subject to legal sanction in the country of origin.*** The third group of cases where the US judge rejected the argument concerns cultural practices that are apparently cultural, but are, in fact, an expression of political regimes or which were cultural, but are now condemned in the country of origin.

The distinction between culture and the political system was developed to resolve the case of a Senegalese citizen who had applied for asylum in the US after undergoing confinement for several months in a Senegalese government prison.[78] The subject "likens his confinement in the government-run jail to slavery, and points to materials indicating that enslavement of African 'Black Maurs' by upper-class Arab-Berber 'White Maurs' has deep roots in Mauritanian history and may still be practiced in some isolated areas." The judge, whilst recognizing the truth of this practice, sees no connection with the present case: "There is no evidence of any relevant connection between the government's confinement of some southern Mauritanians like the petitioner during the crisis surrounding and following their expulsion to Senegal in 1989–1991 and the cultural practice of Black Maur slavery." The court essentially identified the mass arrest episode as political, not cultural and, for this reason, unlikely to be perpetuated in the future. Since the political crisis had long ended, so that the same Senegalese government had invited its citizens to return home, there were no conditions for granting asylum. Moreover, this cultural practice affects remote rural areas and cannot have a connection with the biography and the identity of the applicant who lives in the city of Kaedi, one of the largest urban centers of the country.

78 *Issa Diakhite v. Alberto R. Gonzales, Attorney General of the United States*, 165 Fed. Apps. 636; 2006 U.S. App. Lexis 2747, U.S. Ct. App. 10th Cir., 2006.

More problematic is the case of Gomis,[79] a Senegalese citizen who applied for asylum citing the risk of incurring the practice of female circumcision. The judge began his anthropologist job this time by relying on a report drawn up in 2001 on the dissemination of the practice in Senegal and rejected the asylum application, citing the changes that had occurred in Senegal regarding this practice: it was now prohibited by the law, which provides penalties of up to five years in prison for those who practice it; the ethnic group that allegedly threatened Gomis usually performed the ritual in the period before puberty (while Gomis was an adult woman); and in urban areas infibulation was disappearing. Based on these premises, the judge confirmed the refusal to grant asylum. But a dissenting judge called the decision a major denial of justice. In his view, in fact, the majority of the court failed to consider the specific concrete situation of Gomis who introduced evidence showing that after she fled to the US, her father wrote her letters promising to use all means necessary to bring her back to Senegal and go through with the circumcision and marriage before his death. The dissenting judge also draws attention to the fact that the law against female circumcision is not effective in Senegal because of popular opposition to its application. In this case, the importance of personal history, beyond the history of the group to which the claimant belongs, and the attention to the effectiveness of laws rather than mere reference to legal forms, are items that should have been assessed.

7 English jurisprudence: the *topos* of time

England is one of the first democracies that developed a multicultural case law, with origins dating back to 1960 (Poulter 1986, 1998; Woodman 2009). Doctrinal exercises made by English judges are also heterogeneous, yet present a recurring theme: the evaluation of time spent in the host culture.

In the case of a West Indian parent accused for the second time of maltreatment, and who defended himself on the grounds that his intent was to provide his son with discipline methods that are culturally accepted in the West Indies, the judge observed:[80]

> There can be no doubt that once in this country, this country's laws must apply; and there can be no doubt that, according to the law of this country, the chastisement given to this boy was excessive and the assault complained of was proved. Nevertheless, had this been a first offence, and had there been some real reason for thinking that the appellant either did not understand what the standards in this country were or was having difficulty in adjusting himself, the Court would no doubt have taken that into account and given it such consideration as it could. The really outstanding fact in this case is that this is not the first offence.

79 *Francoise Anate Gomis v. Eric H. Holder, Jr., Attorney General of the United States*, 571 F.3d 353; U.S. App. Lexis 14606, U.S. Ct. App. 4th Cir., 2009.

80 *R. v. Derriviere* [1969], 53 Criminal Appeal Reports 637.

A similar argument was used in the case of a Pakistani father charged with the attempted kidnapping of his daughter who tried to avoid an arranged marriage. The judge observed that according to the accused's conception of his cultural and religious traditions, his conduct was not particularly unfair. Nevertheless the father was sentenced with the argument that he has resided in the new country long enough to know that his conduct was improper according to the English legal system.[81]

The time factor is also used to resolve the case of a Nigerian mother emigrated to London and accused of injury to her two children aged nine and fourteen years after she made ritual marks on their face with a boxcutter (scarification), perpetuating a rite of passage in the Yoruba community.[82] The children, however, had shown pride and consent to the practice. The judge, taking into account that the woman had no idea that she had violated English law, dropped all charges. Thus he concluded with a sort of judicial warning:

> you and others who come to this country must realize that the law must be respected. It cannot be questioned further, that other crimes of this type that intend to fulfill tribal traditions of Nigeria and other parts of Africa will only result in a conviction.

Because this is a test case, the judge declares he will work with the utmost indulgence. But no one else should expect to receive mitigation as other immigrants are now warned.

The *topos* of time of residence present in the English approach raises several issues. On the one hand, it introduces a dynamic element in the evaluation of the cultural factor because it admits the possibility of change and thus breaks the cultural determinism that often seems to underlie the arguments of anthropologist judges. The subject can change his or her identity and behavior, and in fact is required to do so once she chooses to live in England. On the other hand, the result of this argumentative approach is that the cultural exception is permissible only on a temporary basis, in cases where the person could not see any other path of action.

In fact, things are not exactly so. The English experience has been, for some time, one of the most open towards recognition. Just think of the law exempting Sikhs from the obligation to wear motorcycle helmets (Crash Helmets Religious Exemption Act 1976) and helmets at the workplace (Employment Act 1989) to enable them to keep their turbans. The time factor therefore acquires relevance in hard cases, while in other cases cultural difference is accepted on a permanent basis.

The English experience is emblematic because it represents an attempt to rationalize the cultural argument used by the courts, offering them some guidelines. In 1994, the courts of England and Wales received a manual to help them in proceedings in which one or more of the parties were ethnic minorities. The

81 *R. v. Ghulam Rasool* [1991], 12 Criminal Appeal Reports (S) 771.
82 *R. v. Adesanya* [1974], The Times 16, 17 July.

Handbook on Ethnic Minority Issues,[83] strongly solicited by the judicial body, was presented as a kind of anthropological guide that provided judges with "methodological" tips on how to approach a multicultural conflict and "cognitive tools" directed at individual cultures. The *Handbook* was reissued in 1999 as the *Equal Treatment Bench Book*, and was updated again in 2013 and 2015.

8 Italian jurisprudence

8.1 Culture as a custom: the topos *of legal pluralism*

In Italy, the use of the cultural argument appears in the judgments of some lower courts as early as 1990, with a subsequent progressive intensification (Bernardi 2006, 2010; Grandi 2009; Basile 2010; De Maglie 2010). In the absence of clear constitutional or legislative foundations for the recognition of culture,[84] its first uses were heterogeneous and contradictory (Bernardi 2007). Even today there are still uncertainties on how to classify the Italian model (Galli 2006; Allievi 2010): assimilationist (De Maglie 2010: 35–72), multicultural (Caponio 2013) or in an intermediate position (Fornasari 2008: 183). It passes from cases in which the cultural argument is raised to reduce the subjective ingredient of the offense[85] or – more rarely – in which the same argument is used to exclude the

83 The Judicial Studies Board, *Handbook on Ethnic Minority Issues*, June 1994, distributed by the *Judicial Studies Board*, London, a sort of center for the study of the bench which updated it in 1999 as *Equal Treatment Bench Book* www.casas.org.uk/papers/pdfpapers/ETbenchbook1999.pdf. Among the opinions which underlie this study, the Lord Chancellor in 1993 had written: "we ought to be taking whatever steps are practicable to enable every judge to feel confident when they are handling cases involving Hindus and Sikhs or Muslims, for example, or black Africans or black Caribbeans, that they are not causing offence through ignorance, that they are not causing injustice through misunderstandings and that they are not treating black people differently from the way they treat white people, perhaps without being aware of it." The handbook thus explains its aim: "A multifaith, multicultural, multiracial society makes special demands on its judges. It poses challenges in court that require an immediate, well-informed response as soon as they arise . . . it also requires of its judges a much deeper understanding of the characteristics of the different people who come before the courts."

84 The Italian Constitution does not contain the recognition of cultural rights as a broad category, mentioning only "the right of linguistic minorities" (art. 6) – identified by law no. 482/1999 in 13 linguistic groups which belong to specific Italian regions – and "freedom of religion" (art. 19). The only reference to culture is in art. 9: "The Republic promotes the development of culture and scientific and technical research," that could be subject to an "evolutive interpretation" which might include the development of the culture of migrants, but no judge has so far tried to use the Constitution as a foundation for cultural rights. Neither have judges directly used art. 27 of 1966 ICCPR as a foundation of cultural rights.

85 Such is the case of the full acquittal decided by the Juvenile Trial Court of Turin (Tribunale dei minori di Torino), July 17th, 1997 on an excision practiced on a Nigerian child who was brought to Nigeria by her parents to perform the ritual. Upon their return to Italy they were denounced by doctors who visited the child for extremely harmful wounds. According to the Court parents had submitted "the daughter to a practice of female genital mutilation fully accepted in the local traditions (and apparently by the legislation) of their country." For this reason the parents could not be sentenced. Decisions like this led the Legislature to intervene, by creating the autonomous crime of female genital mutilation in art. 583bis of the criminal code introduced by law 9 January 2006, no. 7.

illegality of behavior,[86] to still others in which it was, by contrast, used as an aggravating factor.[87]

In time, however, the Supreme Court of Cassation seems to have provided some hint to the lower fact-finders courts, with a series of decisions from which it is possible to extrapolate an "Italian model" of multicultural conflict resolution. As happens in almost all legal systems, this model also has a judicial origin, being the result of a purely jurisprudential reconstruction accomplished in the near silence of the legislature and still under development.

The reasoning of the Italian anthropologist judge may be summarized as follows:

1) *Cultural influence in the very broad sense.* The first element required is that the person's behavior be culturally motivated. Potentially, any cultural influence might be relevant to the court because the assessment of what is or is not culture is carried out according to very broad criteria, unlike in other systems which require that a very precise cultural practice be identified (Canada *supra* sec. 5).
2) *Culture as customary norm.* The behavior of the migrant is legally framed as a customary rule. The Italian Supreme Court reads multicultural conflicts as an expression of the phenomenon of normative pluralism and treats culture as a "web of rules" (Kroeber, Kluckhohn 1952: 95–104; Pigliaru 1959; Pospisil 1967, 1971), as folk law (Dundes Renteln, Dundes 1994). This locates the Italian model outside of the theory of culture as a fundamental right or a human right as opposed to what happens in other jurisdictions (Canada *supra* sec. 5; international order *supra* sec. 4; Appendix: the status of culture in constitutions); rather, the Italian

86 This is the case of the decision that excluded the crime of unlawful carrying of arms by the Sikh who donned a ritual knife, by the Criminal Trial Court of Cremona (Tribunale penale di Cremona), February 19th, 2009 (*infra* sec. 8.2).

87 As in the case of the two Pakistani citizens accused of violent sexual assault, who defended themselves with the argument that they were rendered incapable of understanding the wrongfulness of their actions by the fact that in Pakistan women are treated as objects and that rape is not considered a serious crime there. The lawyer asked the judge to reduce the penalty according to art. 133, sec 2.4 of criminal code which impose to the judge to consider the "individual, familiar, and social conditions of life" of the delinquent. The judge of the preliminary hearing (Giudice dell'Udienza preliminare) GUP Bologna November 16th, 2009 (unpublished, reported by Desi 2007) countered that "the criterion fixed within art. 133 works toward the exactly opposite valuation, inasmuch as it indicated that the worse the individual, familiar, and social conditions are – reflecting a system of values antithetical to those which inspired the penal law – the more severe the sanction should be." For this reason the judge applied an aggravating factor. Note how, in this case, the judge "fell" into a panculturalist fallacy (Chap 3 sec. 6 and 10), instead of saying, more correctly, that Pakistani culture does not actually justify sexual violence and that, therefore, we are not confronted with a culturally motivated crime, but in fact just a common crime. The premises of these arguments are, therefore, flawed and could be avoided through the first question of the cultural test proposed in this book (Chap. 4 sec. 5).

Supreme Court considers the cultural practice as, indeed, a custom, an external source of law placed in a certain position within the system of sources. Therefore the migrant is not seen as entitled to a right to exert his/her culture but as trapped in a normative dilemma (Sellin 1938), between two conflicting norms: the one belonging to his original "web of rules" and the new Italian one.

3) *Fundamental rights as a limit to culture.* The judge is called upon to play the role of "mediator" between the cultural system to which the migrant belongs and the Italian legal system: the Italian Supreme Court accepts the importance of culture and in a significant decision (op. 1520/2008, Chap. 1 sec. 2.1), also identifies the foundation of this constitutional relevance in the "principle of the personalization of the sentence, established in opinion 253/2003 of the Constitutional Court." However – says the Supreme Court – the role of "mediator" of the judge can only take place when the culturally motivated behavior does not affect constitutional values incorporated into the criminal law.

The broader Italian approach in the identification of culture has consequences worth noting. It is not required, in fact, that the court identify a specific practice, describe it or show that it has peculiar features as compared to other similar practices present in all cultural systems; neither is any proof of the historical roots of the practice required. It is not even necessary to assess the level of obligation that the practice may have within a group, or to pay attention to the identification of the characteristics of the group which the individual belongs to. However, all these requirements, as we have already seen, are found in other systems (Canada and US *supra* sec. 5 and 6).

The Italian case law does not limit *a priori* the recognition of any behavior that appears even remotely due to cultural influence. Although there is no explicit constitutional or legislative recognition in Italy of cultural factors, the presence of this concept, understood in a very broad sense, is able to activate the judicial reflection, to introduce an element of the case that must be assessed. But this triggers a paradox. Against this extremely broad view of what is culture, the Italian law circumscribes much more than other legal systems recognize. If the door is wide open – and thus questionable – in describing what is cultural, this closes drastically when "cultural" behavior must be protected. But it should be stated that this restriction often refers to conduct which, in reality, is not cultural. The Italian courts, in fact, generally tend to accept the narratives of the defense by the mere fact of being faced with a stranger. They extend, in substance, sometimes with guilty approximation, sometimes with the best intentions of showing an anthropological sensitivity to the stranger, a "culturalist fallacy" veering toward panculturalism (Chap. 3 sec. 10).

As has been seen (Chap. 1 sec. 2.1), the Supreme Court has presupposed that beating a wife who refused the "marital debt" was a Moroccan practice, without questioning whether the practice really exists in Morocco. Theft[88] or begging (Chap. 1 sec. 3.1) have been qualified as cultural behaviors when committed by Roma. Other jurisdictions, where the assessment of what is or is not culture is subjected to the most rigorous standards, narrow the space of behaviors readable under the species of culture. In the spectrum between Italy, which has no boundaries, and Canada, which makes it almost impossible to recognize any cultural practice (sec. 5.1), the legal system should find an intermediate solution to guide the court: it is critical that judges know when to evoke culture, and when not to (Chap. 4 sec. 5.1–2).

This situation, in Italy, is closely related to the absence of specific rules to guide the cultural argument. It is usually the role of the lawyer to raise the cultural exception. The problem is not seen as a technical one for which the court must seek the support of an anthropologist or other members of the minority in question. Indeed, the possibility of resorting to anthropological expertise could even be considered precluded by art. 220 Code of criminal procedure, which establishes a ban on "criminological" expertise to avoid any bio-psychological determinism by the judge.[89] However, even without the help of a technician, the judge who would follow an established set of investigations (Chap. 4 sec. 5.1–3) would sometimes avail himself of such expertise, or even with the simple testimony of members of the minority, to reconstruct whether the cultural exception has an objective foundation, or is only being used strategically by the defendant.

The second item that characterizes the Italian model, as listed at the beginning of the section, is the fact that in Italy judges began their anthropological field work by traversing the terrain of the sources of law (culture as a custom) and not because they were faced with a clash of rights (i.e., cultural vs other constitutional rights) to balance. The status of cultural behavior is always that of a tradition, a custom, a habit – never of a right. While the UN Human Rights Committee uses art. 27 of the 1966 ICCPR, which codifies the right to culture (*supra* sec. 4); while the Canadian courts when faced with cultural exceptions must ascertain the existence of the cultural rights of indigenous peoples protected by art. 35 of the Constitution (*supra* sec. 5); a similar argument has never been made for the construction of cultural behavior in Italy. The Italian Supreme Court of Cassation made no attempt to conceptualize the idea that protecting the immigrant culture is indirectly protecting a constitutional right. This is certainly a consequence of the silence of the 1948 Italian Constitution

88 Trial Court of Trieste (Tribunale penale di Trieste) February 22nd, 2011 which recognized mitigating circumstances to Roma fathers who induced their children to steal, reversed by Court of Cassation (Corte di Cassazione) July 16th, 2013, no. 43412.

89 Criminological expertise was common in Italy during the fascist period (1922–1945) when the attitude to crime was attributed both to biological features (eg. the shape of the cranium, the length of the mandible) and to psychological tropes (Lombroso 1876). Art. 220 has long excluded reference to anthropological expertise until recently when, against this interpretation, it has been said: "cultural expertise is *not* a criminological expertise, in that it does not objectify the personality of the defendant, his tendencies or his psychological qualities" and can, therefore, be performed (De Maglie 2010: 157).

which recognizes only the freedom of religion (art. 19) and linguistic rights of national minorities (art. 6) and not a right to culture. This is also a consequence of the status of obligations under international law: whereas international treaties are compulsory for the signing state, they are not directly binding for the citizens until the Legislature implements them. As a consequence, art. 27 of the ICCPR alone is not sufficient to found a solid base for a right to culture in Italy. In fact, although Italy signed the ICCPR, only with a Multicultural Act by the Legislature or an explicit recognition of a right to culture in the Constitution would the judges feel comfortable classifying culture as a right.

Moreover, art. 22 of the Charter of Fundamental Rights of the European Union, which states "The Union shall respect cultural, religious and linguistic diversity," is not directly usable either with a view to founding a right to culture, as it applies to states only when they are implementing European Union (EU) law, and not on matters (such as criminal law) over which the EU has no normative power as clarified by the Italian Constitutional Court in op. 80/2011.

Things are probably primed to change with the entrance in the judiciary of new judges trained in the age of human rights multilevel protection. In 2015 the Supreme Court quoted as directly binding for Italy the 19 October 1996 Hague Convention on Jurisdiction, Applicable Law, Recognition, Enforcement and Cooperation in Respect to Parental Responsibility and Measures for the Protection of Children (art. 3 lett. b and art. 33), thus allowing a Moroccan child "adopted" by his uncle using ***kafalah*** to join him in Italy. The Supreme Court, in fact, invalidated the refusal of the visa by the Italian Consulate in Casablanca which used the argument that with ***kafalah*** no family bonds are created.

Although not recognized as a right and occupying the last level in the pyramid of legal sources, culture finds a value and is part of the balancing of rights/ interests. That is well gathered by analyzing the third element of the Italian model: its limits. On this point, there is an element of opacity: cultural tradition must not be contrary to law – as the Supreme Court affirms several times – but it is not perfectly clear whether the violation of law includes only the Constitution and the criminal law that protects constitutional rights or, vice versa, regards every other source of written law.

On the one hand, the latter view seems accredited by the following statement of the Supreme Court which, faced with a case of Roma begging who defended herself with the argument that Roma beg in compliance of a cultural tradition, even seems to predict that only ***secundum legem*** cultural practices are eligible:

> a custom can have a justifying value . . . only when it is recalled by a law . . . Even an allogeneic people like the gypsies, once established in Italian territory, must comply with the existing legal order rules in this area; and cannot rely on their traditional uses to discriminate behaviors that are prohibited by criminal laws, except in cases where these uses are called, and then legitimized, by territorial [Italian] laws.[90]

90 Supreme Court of Cassation (Corte di Cassazione) sec. III penal, 2841/2007, case Djordjevic.

On the other hand, in most occasions, the Supreme Court seems to reinforce the position of cultural practices, elevating them above other customs,[91] as when they declare that the tradition can be accepted until it begins to clash with "the cardinal rules of the Italian order,"[92] its "criminal rules" or its "fundamental rights."[93]

Perhaps the decision to clarify the issue is op. 22700 of 29 May 2009 which resolved a case of family maltreatment defended with the argument that child-beating in Moroccan culture is accepted. The court observed:

> the ethical-social traditions of those who are present in the territory of the State, of an essentially customary nature although of an undisputed cultural value, can not be practiced outside the ambit of the criminal law. The principle assumes particular moral and social value once – as in this case – the criminal protection concerns matters of constitutional significance, such as the family, that the fundamental law of the state recognizes as "natural society", based on the moral and legal equality of the spouses (art. 29 Const.). That equality is therefore a guaranteed value, intrinsically involved in a legal system focused on the dignity of the human person and aimed to respect the irrepressible rights he enjoys.

When addressing "the undisputed cultural value" of immigrant traditions, the Supreme Court seems to elevate them above the normal customs, establishing only the "criminal law" and "matters of constitutional significance" as limits.

In another decision,[94] similar to what may be seen in the reasoning of the European Court of Human Rights in *Lautsi vs Italy* 2010 (the crucifix case) and

91 Eg. Italy has a rich regional set of laws that regard the common use of lands which, being at the bottom of the pyramid of the sources of law, can be repealed at any moment if a written law establishes otherwise.

92 Supreme Court of Cassation (Corte di Cassazione) sec. VI penal, 1520/2008, case Kassam (analyzed in Chap. 1 sec. 2.1).

93 Supreme Court of Cassation (Corte di Cassazione) sec. VI penal, September 2008, no. 44516, case V.M., known as the begging case (analyzed in Chap. 1 sec. 3.1). See also the case of *Nasri*, a Tunisian accused of maltreating and injuring his wife. The Trial Court of Udine (Tribunale di Udine), November 21st, 2002, as reported in *Rivista italiana di medicina legale*, 2003, 704 et seq. observes: "the agent cannot invoke a defense based on a different conception of familial roles and of the powers of the patriarch in his own country of origin, when this irreparably collides with the principles of the Italian legal system, based on the equal dignity of spouses and on the accord over choices of how to conduct the family." The use of the adverb "irreparably" suggests that the conflict should be resolved in favor of the Italian law only if a principle of constitutional strength is at stake.

94 Supreme Court of Cassation (Corte di Cassazione), 48272/2009, regarding a case of maltreatment inflicted by a father from Morocco on his child (Pedullà 2009). Refusing the cultural defense, the Court affirms: "regarding the socio-cultural difference of the defendant it cannot be considered as there are at play fundamental values of the [Italian] legal system (consecrated in the principles of articles 2, 3, 30 and 32 of the Constitution). Those principles are part of the visible and consolidated ethical-cultural heritage of the nation and of the supranational context in which Italy is inserted and, as such, are not susceptible to derogations by subjects who live and work in our territory and are therefore subject to the Italian penal law. Neither it is possible to recognize an excusable ignorance of the law/*ignorantia legis* in this case."

S.A.S vs France 2014 (the *burqa* case) (*infra* sec. 10), the court develops, next to the limit of constitutional principles, a kind of counter-cultural argument, rejecting those traditions that seek to compromise the "consolidated ethical and cultural heritage" of Italy.

The perception that the practice has in Italian culture also operated in a case which has as its protagonist a Nigerian mother accused of inflicting injuries because she circumcised her child without resorting to a doctor; the child, experiencing massive bleeding, had to be admitted to hospital care in a serious condition.[95] This case leads us into one of the most modern multicultural conflicts: the acceptability of male circumcision, an issue which has been reopened by the decision of the Court of Cologne, in June 2012 (*infra* sec. 9 and Chap. 4 sec. 6) and by the Parliamentary Assembly of the Council of Europe with the non-binding Resolution in 2013 (Foblets 2016: 133) and that in Italy has been resolved in convoluted fashion in favor of its legitimacy when practiced by a Jewish *mohel* or by a doctor.

In 2007, the court of first instance in Padua noted that not all interventions harmful to physical integrity are *per se* punished. For example, it is not the case with cosmetic surgery and, as a good anthropologist, the court identifies a possible cultural equivalent (Chap. 4 sec. 5.9)[96] – explaining that male circumcision is admissible to ensure the psycho-relational balance of the subject. So, the court observes:

> Accepting a notion of health understood as achieving the fullest possible integration between physical and mental well-being, the ritual circumcision may seem addressed to reach a higher state of health, through a bodily form which corresponds to the idea of physical perfection and psychological satisfaction of the individual, as a result of conforming to his ethnic or cultural identity. This explanation is often used . . . to justify, under the ethical profile, the fact that the circumcision act is practiced by a physician in the absence of a pathology.

The judge cites the opinion delivered by the Italian National Bioethics Committee on 25 September 1998. The Committee has expressed its acceptance

95 Trial Court of Padua (Tribunale di Padova), November 9th, 2007. The decision was pronounced as unauthorized exercise of the medical profession, as the child required immediate medical intervention from the circumcision applied by an acquaintance of his mother.

96 Thus reads the judgment: "The full legitimacy of the cosmetic surgery is now generally recognized as surpassing the restrictive interpretations of art. 5 civil code (acts of disposition of one's own body) that would have limited the surgical activity to those interventions that, in a comparative evaluation of the advantages and risks, become finalized to the betterment of the physical conditions of the patient. The way forward is that which broadens the concept of health, a recognized and guaranteed right of the Constitution (art. 32), not circumscribing it to only physical integrity, but also to psychic well-being, thus requiring an evaluation of the person in all his components, even of his psychic and relational equilibrium in general. Health is a state of complete physical, mental and social well-being. Broadening the concept of 'health', also that of 'therapy' broadens. Therefore, the interventions over one's own body to acquire a major confidence in itself as well as in the relationship with others can be permitted."

of male circumcision, by introducing a policy of damage measured by the "capability of the body to carry out the activity for which it is responsible." Given that sexual activity, in the case of male circumcision, is not compromised, while in the case of female genital mutilation the sexual organ functions are severely affected, the Committee has considered it possible to differentiate between the two practices by allowing the first and repressing the second.

At this point, the judge gives his opinion as to why practices similar in content (cosmetic surgery, female circumcision, male circumcision) are governed differently under the legal system:

> beyond a purely objective notion of the concept of health, in order to determine which actions can help to ensure or improve the social-psychological well-being of the individual, the inquiry has to follow a historically relativistic criterion, necessarily depending on the degree of acceptance that a given practice has in a social context. Although it was emphasized that male circumcision still determines the mental and physical integrity violation of a subject that typically, due to tender age, is unable to express an effective consent (it is the parents who decide, in the exercise of their *droit*-duty to educate the child according to the principles of their culture), it appears difficult to dispute that, since it is devoid of physical, psychological and symbolic negative connotations typical of female genital mutilation, and probably also for the influence of Judaism, it has long been widely accepted by Western culture.

Despite this abstract theoretical defense of male circumcision, the trial court sentenced the Nigerian mother because she practiced surgery without resorting to a doctor thus contributing to "unlawful practice of the medical profession" crime, punishable by art. 348 of the Italian criminal code. On appeal,[97] the sentence was confirmed with a opinion focused on the fact that the woman, who was Catholic, had not performed "a ritual of the religious faith professed, but a conduct in use in their communities (the Nigerian Catholic);" because it is her "culture" and not her religion which motivated her, she could not invoke the exercise of the right to freely practice her faith as exempting circumstance. The woman was ordered to pay compensation for moral damages, for "the suffering caused to the infant after surgery and subsequent complications."

The Supreme Court,[98] conversely, set aside the decision because the Nigerian mother committed an excusable – because it was inevitable – *error iuris*. In the words of the Supreme Court:

> The offense under art. 348 pen. cod. shall be punished by way of fraud, consisting in awareness and willingness to participate in the performance of

97 Court of Appeal of Venice (Corte d'Appello di Venezia), October 12th, 2009.

98 Supreme Court of Cassation (Corte di Cassazione), sec. VI penal, November 24th, 2011, n. 43646 (Pusateri 2012).

> an act of unlawful practice of the medical profession . . . The tenuousness of the connection that a person of African ethnicity, recently migrated to Italy and not been yet integrated into our social fabric, encounters with respect to our legal system is undeniable. This situation cannot prejudice this person who, having a cultural heritage alien to the Western civilization, is in an objectively difficult condition in understanding values and prohibitions unknown to her.

Conscience goes missing, and the act does not constitute an offense.

Beyond this peculiar and exceptional case in which *ignorantia legis excusat*, the Italian solution to the conflict that revolves around circumcision is based on an assessment of how circumcision is performed. The Supreme Court cites the fact that the Jewish community "entrusts this task to the *mohel*, who is usually a doctor or at least a person skilled in the practice of circumcision and related rituals." This is an argument that focuses, therefore, on the risk of current and concrete harm to the child. Conversely, as we will soon see, the Cologne Court in 2012 understood differently the "damage" which revolves around the practice, considering the permanent transformation of the genitals as harm (*infra* sec. 9).

8.2 Religion as a fundamental right: the topoi *of security and of Western values*

The Italian legal system is no exception to the trend described that provides legal systems with different tools depending on whether culture or religion is at stake (*supra* sec. 2). In fact, in the latter case, Italian judges frame their reasoning under the constitutional "freedom of religion" right protected in art. 19 of the Italian Constitution, using classic "balancing rights" techniques (Veronesi 2012).

Cases evidencing the *topoi* Italian courts have used when faced with a religious conflict show a heterogeneity of solutions but a common starting point based on the possibility of using religion as a fundamental right.[99]

In a case concerning a Rastafarian practitioner found with a high quantity of marijuana for personal use, the accused defended himself by claiming that marijuana is the sacred herb for the Rastafarians who smoke different amounts to connect with the divine. The Supreme Court[100] overturned the conviction on the grounds that the practice is "suggested" by the Rastafarian religion. This decision extends protection to an optional religious practice, showing great favor towards the protection of religion.

99 As proof of the strength of freedom of religion, see the case decided by the Criminal Court of Appeal of Cagliari (Corte di Assise di Cagliari) with an opinion of December 13th, 1982 in reference to two parents, Jehovah's Witnesses, accused of homicide by omission of their child for whom they refused to allow a blood transfusion. The parents were condemned, but with a less severe penalty for reason of the religious motives behind their conduct.

100 Supreme Court of Cassation (Corte di Cassazione), sec. VI penal, 923/2008.

A second case is that of a woman who attended the trial of a close relative while wearing the *burqa*. After initially imposing an administrative penalty, the appellate judge[101] annulled it, explaining:

> With reference to the "veil that covers the face", or in particular to the *burqa*, it is a use which is not generally intended to prevent recognition, but is rather implementing a tradition of certain peoples and cultures. Art. 5 of Law no. 152/1975 allows in our legal system that a person may wear a veil for religious or cultural reasons; public safety needs are met by the ban on the use at events and the requirement for such persons to undergo the identification and removal of the veil, where necessary to that end.

This judgment adopts an indifferent stance to the religious or cultural practice, demonstrating the similar nature of the problems posed by the two conflicts.

A third case, concerning the *kirpan* wore by Sikhs, reveals a change in the Supreme Court's attitude with respect to religion. Until 2016 trial and appellate courts used to acquit Sikhs denounced for carrying the long curved knife. Due to its religious nature, the practice of wearing the *kirpan* was not confined to the mere status of customary source but received the benefit of significant constitutional provisions (Provera 2010).[102] With judgments 24739/2016, 25163/2016 and

101 Council of the State-Administrative High Court (Consiglio di Stato), sec. VI, June 19th, 2008, no. 3076. The administrative penalty was imposed on the basis of art. 5, Law no. 52/1975, a law enacted to respond to the terrorism of the Red Brigade and of Fascist groups operating in Italy during the 1970s. The provision establishes that "it is forbidden to participate in public meetings . . . having the face fully covered or partially covered."

102 Trial Court of Cremona (Tribunale penale di Cremona), February 19th, 2009, no. 15 decided the case of Mr. Singh, an Indian citizen and member of the Sikh religion, reported for carrying illegal weapons while shopping in a supermarket in Cremona. The man, in fact, wore, along with the traditional clothes and turban, the *kirpan*. The judge, carefully investigating the nature of the practice, used this argument: "in accordance with what is given to know from the documents produced by the defense and the facts known to the public, it should be noted that according to this Indian religion, founded after the mid 1400s, there is only one God, who teaches his followers to reach 'absolute bliss' along five stages. The symbols of religion are: the *Khanda*, symbol of the *Khalsa*, that is the Sikh community, which consists of a central sword (symbol of faith in God) and two crossed swords (symbol of spiritual and temporal power); the *Khanga* (comb), a symbol of the care and cleaning of the person as a creature of God; the *Kirpan* (dagger), a symbol of resistance to evil; the *Kara* (metal bracelet that recalls the principle of non-stealing and also has a balancing function of the body's iron) as a sign of unity with God and, finally, the beard and uncut hair, a sign of acceptance of God's will, as it follows the natural will of God. In particular, the *kirpan*, as well as the turban, should always be carried by the follower of the Sikh religion. And this, mind you, is also expressly confirmed, in a similar case, by the Consulate General of India (see the certificate of 21 June 2001, produced by the defense, which indicates how the Indian Sikh is 'forced', and not, mind you, just facultized, 'for religious reasons to always carry a turban and *kirpan* (small dagger) as required by Sikhism'." After these assessments the judge concluded: "if these are the motivational coordinates which guided the conduct of the accused, it must then be inevitably recognized that they find sound legal support, as objectively placed within the protection of freedom of religion. This is a legal protection of great significance, as it is assured, in all its possible ramifications, both by art. 18 of the Universal Declaration of Human Rights of 10 December 1948, by art. 9 of Law 4 August 1955, n. 848, ratifying the Convention for the Protection of Human Rights and Fundamental Freedoms, and by art. 19 [freedom of religion] of our Constitution."

24084/2017 the Italian Supreme Court abruptly changed this trend. In the latter case, the Appellate Court of Mantua tried to treat religion as a cultural custom stating that: "the religious habits are a mere custom of the culture to which the defendant belongs and cannot abrogate a criminal norm enacted with the aim of protecting public security." The defendant asked to the Supreme Court to invalidate the judgment, claiming that he had the protection of art. 19 Const. and the wearing of the ***kirpan*** fell within his freedom of religion, but the Supreme Court, in op. 24084/2017, stated that the prohibition of the ***kirpan*** struck a correct balance between religion and security. While at first the decision seems a normal exercise of balancing rights, together with the security argument, the Supreme Court also makes the assertion that migrants should conform to the values of the host culture:

> in a multiethnic society, the cohabitation between people of different ethnicities necessarily requires the identification of a common nucleus which both immigrants and members of the hosting society must recognize. If integration does not impose the abandonment of the culture of origin, according to art. 2 Const., which encourages social pluralism, the unsurpassable limit is represented by the respect of human rights and of the legal civilization (*civiltà giuridica*) of the hosting society. Therefore it is an essential duty of the immigrant to conform his/her values to those of the Western world, in which he/she freely chose to live, as well as to verify the compatibility of his/her behaviors with the principles that rule it and their legality . . . The multiethnic society is a necessity, but it cannot bring to the formation of cultural archipelagos conflicting with each other depending on the cultures which form them. Against this scenario stands the cultural and legal homogeneity of our country that sees in public security a good to protect and, to this aim, prohibits to bring weapons and objects capable to offend.

The judgment's reasoning fails on several points.

First of all the identification of the ***kirpan*** with a weapon reveals a lack of cultural translation (Chap. 4 sec. 5.9) and acceptance of the other's point of view (Chap. 4 sec. 4). In fact, for a Sikh the ***kirpan*** is no longer a weapon and cannot be used to harm others.[103] It is a protection against spiritual evils only, a mere symbol.

Second, the idea that migrants freely choose to leave their countries ignores that the majority of so called "economic migrants" are actually "climate migrants,"[104]

103 As a matter of historical fact, the tradition of wearing the ***kirpan*** originated in a different political context in the fifteenth century, when the forebears of modern Sikhs armed themselves to fight Muslims. Yet Sikhs today point out that when that religious war ended, the ***kirpan***'s function changed to that of a religious symbol, and in fact today Sikhs are absolutely forbidden by their religion to use the object as a weapon, even to defend themselves. For them, banning the ***kirpan*** as a potential weapon which might be used to hurt someone is analogous to forcing a Christian to remove a life-size cross they may have erected as an expression of their own faith, on the far-fetched theory that they may actually try to crucify someone on it. Although it is true that in India some incidents happened with people using the ***kirpan*** as a weapon, no similar incidents have occurred in Italy.

104 The expression was created by Lester Brown in 1976 (Brown, McGrath, Stokes 1976).

"colonial migrants"[105] and are pushed to leave their countries for complex reasons that range from colonial and neocolonial exploitation to climate change (Morrissey 2009; Piguet, Pécoud, de Guchteneire 2011) that have significantly debited the moral accounts of the Western world (Roberts, Parks 2009).

Third, the evocation of a compact and unified system of "values of the Western world" or the "cultural and legal homogeneity of our country" is not factually correct; in fact, many other Western democracies, such as Canada, admit the *kirpan*, and in Italy public opinion is split between those who want to permit its adornment and those who do not.

In my opinion, a better reasoning would have been to admit what I think is the true reason behind this decision: public shock and outcry in response to images of ISIS extremists decapitating Western victims. The abrupt change made in 2016 by the Supreme Court has its roots in a shift in the social perception of the *kirpan*. The images shown on television and on the internet of large scimitars violently used created a sort of social panic that brought more people to denounce Sikhs, who are often mistaken for Muslims. As luggage left alone in the airports may now spark panics due to still-fresh memories of terrorist attacks, so does the appearance of a *kirpan* in public. In my opinion, especially in the absence of any attempts toward violence by anyone misusing this religious symbol, the freedom of religion should prevail because this is a truly certain "Western value" which is, in a hierarchical scale, superior to security. But given that the Supreme Court considered the social panic important and invoked the right to security, it would have been better to admit that in this historical moment, given the political context, the *kirpan* is not perceived anymore by the Italians as a religious symbol, but as a potential source of violence. So due to this exceptional circumstance, our value of freedom of religion must be temporarily balanced with security. Instead, the Court chose to build the conflict as an irreconcilable antagonism between the Western world and Sikhism, upsetting the Sikh community and obscuring from Italians the betrayal of their own cherished values, of which freedom of religion is one of the pillars.

In conclusion, the Italian model, as outlined by the Supreme Court, is characterized by the conceptualization of religion as a right and culture as a source of law/tradition. The latter has reduced axiological recognition, but not so much reduced as to expel it from the balance. It is, in fact, a valuable habit that pushes the judge to the role of mediator to decide in favor of the minority if its practices do not result in the breach of particularly meaningful standards. In the assessment of someone else's practice, the Italian model sometimes also takes into account the way the practice is perceived in Italian customs and history. An honest admission that the court is located within and must take into account the social context in which the conflict derives shows that a conflict is always a relationship that involves and affects the majority (Chap. 4 sec. 5.11).

105 "Climate change is environmental colonialism at its fullest development – its ultimate scale – with far-reaching social and cultural implications. Climate change is the result of global processes that were neither caused nor can be mitigated by the inhabitants of the majority of climate-sensitive world regions now experiencing the most unprecedented change" (Crate, Nuttall 2016: 11).

That said, the character in the making of Italian argument also shows how, depending on the judge, different elements are taken into account to resolve a multicultural controversy: some judges are more willing to recognize only mandatory practices, while others are open to recognize any cultural practice provided that no criminal laws are violated; sometimes the judge examines whether the practice is reasonably shared within the group, and sometimes only investigates the influence on the individual defendant regardless of whether the practice is contested within the same group. The scenario could leave any jurist disoriented and wanting to recover their footing. Also for this reason, the adoption of a comparative view and the search for a common matrix to follow may prove indispensable. The heterogeneity in decisions, in fact, can become prejudicial to legal certainty, predictability and the rule of law.

9 German jurisprudence: the *topoi* of harm and consent

Defined as a multiculturalism of "detached tolerance" (Cerrina Feroni 2008), in Germany there is no officially defined cultural argument or any constitutional recognition of culture (Schönwälder 2000), but "the attitudes, values and beliefs" of cultural minorities are "occasionally considered" (Maier 2009).

German courts often respond with a cultural counter-argument, as is clear from the decision of the German Supreme Court, January 28, 2004, which put an end to a wavering attitude towards honor killings:

> the standard for determining a motive has to be extrapolated from the values and ideas of the German community in accordance with the law of the place where the accused is a resident and of the courts that adjudicate them, and not the values of an ethnic community that does not consider itself fully bound to the ethical and juridical values of the German legal community.

Notice how this standard, which appeals to the *lex loci*, is the opposite of what the very first Australian anthropologist judges had suggested coining, since 1950: the culturally situated agent model (Chap. 1 sec. 4.1), still used today in the United States (in the form of the "reasonable cultural person" test analyzed above in sec. 6.1 and 6.2). As the aim of this work is to reconstruct the *topoi*, the absolutely relevant elements, the fixed points of legal reasoning around multicultural conflict, these divergences reveal that still no consensus exists in the community of comparative interpreters on when to apply the *lex loci* and when to apply the *lex personae* (Parolari 2016) – that is, if the values of the host or the hosted culture should be the first to be considered. Again the German case law reveals the same heterogeneity in addressing the issue of multicultural conflicts as registered elsewhere (Luther 2006).[106]

106 The Constitutional Court of Germany has addressed the issue of the Islamic headscarf by confirming its legitimacy in BVerfGE 108, 282, September 24th, 2003.

Other criteria to assess a multicultural conflict emerge from German doctrine: the criterion of harm, and especially physical harm, and that of the consent of the recipient of a cultural practice. These constitute the principal judicial reasons of the opinion of 25 June 2012, delivered by the Cologne Court of Appeals regarding male circumcision. In that decision, the judge said that circumcision violates "the fundamental right of children to physical integrity." Although this decision was struck down a few months later by an intervention of the Legislature, which affirmed the legitimacy of male circumcision for religious reasons, the legal arguments raised therein are relevant indicators of the standards anthropologist judges try to elaborate. Furthermore, it opened a debate, which is not yet closed. In fact, despite the legislative permission, the Parliamentary Assembly of the Council of Europe, through the non-binding Resolution in 2013, invited the states to consider the prohibition of the practice (Foblets 2016: 133).

The Cologne court evaluates the fact that circumcision has a religious nature and is mandatory and effects a balance, which does not say that religious freedom succumbs entirely to the right to physical integrity of the child, but states that: "the religious freedom of parents and their right to educate their children is not unacceptably compromised by the fact that they are obliged to wait until such time as the child can decide for himself whether to be circumcised." In this way, the judge introduces another element in the evaluation of multicultural conflict: the attention to the point of view and the consent of the recipient of the practice: "The child's body is irreparably and permanently changed by circumcision. This modification is contrary to the interests of the child to decide later on his religious beliefs." The combination of these elements – that there is a mandatory religious practice, but that it could be achieved later in time; and that there is an irreversible violation of physical integrity for which the victim does not express consent – compels the judge to prohibit the circumcision of minors.

The resonance that this decision brings at the comparative level where, conversely, the question of religious circumcision seemed until recently peaceful in the sense of its admissibility, is a test of the "globalism" of the debate on multicultural conflicts. The German decision served also to detonate conflicts internal to Western societies, like the one under way in the United States where circumcision is a widespread practice among all citizens including non-Jews: three-quarters of US adults are circumcised because until 1970 the practice was as common as vaccination and every year the procedure is performed on over one million, or 55 percent, of newborn boys. It is, in the United States as well as in Australia and New Zealand, a non-religious practice, but a health-related and cultural one: circumcision began to be practiced to discourage masturbation, to reduce urinary infection or prevent cancer and the spread of HIV. Since 1999, however, medical guidelines have said that the health reasons behind circumcision were not enough to make it routine, suggesting to discourage recourse to the practice, but leaving parents the choice. Many US activists have launched campaigns against circumcision, clashing with the fact that circumcision has become part of the normal way that many Americans perceive the body, so even today, in the US the most widespread parental motivation behind continuing the practice is to make their son the same as everyone else so he will not be ridiculed for the different appearance of his penis. These brief parentheses are useful for comparing the grounds that support behavior and their logical weight. Could the fact that the motivation for Jewish and Muslim circumcision is religious while in the US the motive is health and culture allow a diversified response among legal systems? What weight should be given when the practice may be mandatory and essential to make the group what it is?

Among the counter-arguments that the Jewish community in Germany has raised with regard to the decision of the Cologne court, several *topoi* recurring in multicultural discourses emerge: the essentiality of the practice, its historicity, consensus, legality, the diffusion of its recognition. Dieter Graumann, head of the Jewish Central Committee in Germany, in a critique of the judgment of Cologne noted that "circumcision of newborn children is a fixed part of the Jewish religion and has been practiced around the world for centuries. This religious right is respected in every country in the world." In evoking that which is a "fixed part," the Jewish position seems to acquire greater value than, for example, US circumcision that, at the moment when the medical community denies it has a preventive function of disease, becomes a matter of mere preference for parents. But the comparison between these two different meanings once again presents the question of whether the essential nature that circumcision holds for Jews is enough to justify exceeding the harm to the child. That damage appears, in fact, a Rubicon within many cultural arguments.

But even here further questions are posed: How is damage measured? For the Cologne court the criterion is the "irreversible change to physical integrity," which much be prevented in the absence of consent. Different indeed was the position of the Italian Supreme Court in 2011 (*supra* sec. 8.1) that circumcision is permissible because it "does not cause an irreversible impairment and does not significantly change the mode of being of the individual in terms of weakening functional integrity or relationship life skills." Still before, in 1998, the Italian National Committee for Bioethics issued an opinion of 1998 stating that there is no harm if there is "no distorted capability of the body to carry out the activity for which it is responsible" (*supra* sec. 8.1). Basically as the activity of the penis is reproduction, which is not impaired by circumcision, the Committee for Bioethics permitted it. The Italian is a more circumscribed criterion, which *a priori* does not close the doors to practices which involve permanent mutilations of a body part if its function remains intact. However, even this criterion, in hindsight, does not solve all problems. In fact, what if – as is precisely the case of circumcision – the organ's function is not compromised, but will take place in a different way? In this case – some say – with less physical pleasure, because circumcision removes the most heavily engorged portion of the penis which, if present, produces a more intense sexual experience (Chap. 4 sec. 6). Should it be scientifically demonstrated that male circumcision impairs masturbation and diminishes sexual pleasure, a new right – sexual freedom – would enter in the debate reinforcing the reasons for its prohibition.

The positions of the German case law in respect to circumcision show that the composition of multicultural reconciliation is an ongoing process, which remains potentially "open" to review and rethinking, encouraged also by comparative literature allowing one to put together major elements to illuminate each case. The rethinking of circumcision also shows a "vortex effect" that the debate about certain practices can engender: it is, in fact, very likely that the changing perceptions around circumcision now registered in Germany and the US are a result of extensive discussions held around female genital mutilation that, almost inevitably, have called into question by analogy and comparison a number of practices which usually involve physical alterations: not only male circumcision, but also breast surgery on minors, facial scarifications or piercings in the ears of infants. Comparing solutions provided for various multicultural conflicts can help in the process of defining new ways of being together: it could be that for centuries no one in the West saw circumcision as a mutilation due to familiarity with the Jewish religion. The debate over female genital mutilation has produced a disturbing effect that has pierced the veil of practices so far accepted; the comparison with the other has moved and challenged us. In this context, it becomes important for the judge to refine his dialectical instruments to research the similarities and differences in related cases.

10 The jurisprudence of the European Court of Human Rights: the *topoi* of diversity as a public value and of the impact on the majority

The European Convention on Human Rights, signed by the forty-seven states which belong to the Council of Europe, reflects the different legal treatment of religion and culture. Freedom of religion is, in fact, recognized by art. 9, but there is no trace of a right to culture, given the fact that in 1950, when the Convention was adopted in Rome, the debate on those rights was not settled.

Notwithstanding that the European Convention on Human Rights does not contain any reference to a right to culture or cultural identity, the European Court of Human Rights (ECHR, Strasbourg Court) has used art. 8 (right to respect for private and family life) to protect some practices. Articles 9 and 10 have been also used to this end (Palermo, Toggenburg 2003).

Across some cases involving both the Roma (the largest trans-European cultural minority, present in all member states) and Sami people (the only European indigenous population), it is possible to extrapolate the following conditions under which culture can be protected under art. 8 of the Convention:

1) *Essentiality.* The practice must be essential and characteristic of the group.
2) *Traditional nature.* The practice must have a historic root and not be modern.
3) *Diversity as a public value.* The cultural practice must be protected not only in order to safeguard the interests of the minorities themselves but to preserve a cultural diversity that has value for the entire society, including the majority.

4) *Graduation.* It is possible to distinguish quantitatively between "alteration" and total "destruction" of a cultural practice or of a culture itself.[107] Behaviors that compress, without totally destroying a cultural space, can be accepted.

The first three elements of this kind of embryonic cultural test are present in the case of Ms. Chapman,[108] a Roma woman who claimed the right to install her caravan on a piece of land which she had purchased in a rural region of the United Kingdom. The woman traveled for part of the year, but to allow her children to attend school she chose a partially sedentary life. Not wanting to station her two Roma caravans in camps within areas imbued with violence, Ms. Chapman asked to be allowed to safeguard her Roma identity by installing the trailer on her property, though this contradicted a declaration of special landscape value of the area.

The European Court of Human Rights recognized at the outset that the woman had an abstract "right to nomadism" connected to her Roma cultural identity and protected as part of her "right to private life" by art. 8 of the Convention. The most significant element of the decision is the fact that the reasons for protection are not exclusively centered on the minority. The Court, in fact, proposes diversity as a public value and seems to open the door to overcoming the conceptualization of recognition in order to protect a minority, in favor of diversity as a new, more inclusive value. Thus a new *topos* emerges, previously unknown to doctrines of multicultural conflict:

> There is an international consensus between the States of the Council of Europe recognizing the special needs of minorities and an obligation to protect their security, identity and lifestyle . . . not only in order to safeguard the interests of the minorities themselves but to preserve a cultural diversity that has value for the entire community.

This argument attempts to capture the most valuable aspects of diversity by opening the door to a new perception of the role of culture in the democratic public sphere.[109] If the constitutional tradition generally recognizes a need to

107 *G. and E. v. Norway*, Appl. n. 9278/81 e 9415/81, decision from October 3rd, 1983 by the then European Commission for Human Rights, that protected the legitimacy of the construction of a dam in an area where the Sami pastured their reindeer, hunted and fished. The Commission recognized that the construction of the dam undermined their rights under art. 8 of the European Convention on Human Rights, but ruled that this was justified both as it was undertaken for the good of the entire Norwegian community and that it affected a small portion of land of that remaining to the Sami, such that their style of life would not be irredeemably compromised. It used a type of evaluation also present in the UN Human Rights Committee (*supra* sec. 4).

108 *Chapman v. the United Kingdom*, ECHR, 27238/95, Jan. 18th, 2001.

109 Silvia Niccolai (2007) observes, in more general terms: there is "a school of thought which has looked at differences in terms of inequality, that is as problems of disadvantage, of injustice, and thus as situations to remove or remediate." According to this school "equality is the point of equilibrium beyond which there exists only the risk of falling into new discriminations" (Niccolai 2007: 475). The author observes, however, that this setting "has been intensely contested by those who, within feminist thought in particular, have noticed how, in this way, differences are denied any value and meaning, being deprived of their transformative virtues, their capability to put in discussion a given and consolidated order" (Niccolai 2007: 487).

protect culture with anti-discriminatory action, the introduction of a new narrative that assigns a positive value to cultural diversity itself has a disruptive capacity as it transforms the "recognition" from being a "favor" that a majority grants to minorities to an element vital for the whole democracy, and for the society at large (Courtois 2008).

The spread of identity and cultural language has brought the majority to adopt a new cultural frame. Culture within the law loses its connotation as a call for a protective mechanism to shield discriminated minorities. It becomes extended to all subjects, even to those belonging to the majority, as in fact also happened in the case of *Lautsi v. Italy*, decided on 22 March 2011 regarding the exposition of the crucifix in the Italian public schools. At the challenge of Mrs. Lautsi who claimed that the exposition of the crucifix favored one religion over others, Italy answered saying that the Christian cross was not a religious symbol, but rather part of the Italian culture.[110] The European Court, on this occasion, acknowledged that "the decision of whether or not to perpetuate a tradition falls, in principle, within the margin of appreciation of the State"[111] (sec. 68).

The attention to the view of the majority is an important *topos* also in another case decided by the European Court of Human Rights: *S.A.S. vs France*, 2014 concerning the use of the *burqa* which was prohibited by French law. Despite the fact that the European consensus is against banning the *burqa* (only two states, France and Belgium, out of forty-seven, prohibit it), the European Court stated that the French law did not infringe any right of the Convention and the decision should be left to the margin of appreciation of France as the presence of the *burqa* touched supreme values of the French such as "living together" (*vivre ensamble*), derived from the constitutional principle of brotherhood (*fraternitè*).

Although I personally disagree with both the solutions given in the crucifix and *burqa* cases,[112] they reveal interesting attentions to the perception of the majority, introducing a strong relational element in the multicultural conflict. The *topos* about the impact that a cultural practice has on the majority of people should be taken into account (Chap. 4 sec. 5.11); if not, we risk locking the conflict into mere ascertainment of objective elements, eliminating the dialogical part of the law.

In summary, the embryonic model extractable from the Strasbourg jurisprudence is characterized by the application of certain conditions so that the

110 Administrative Trial Court (Tribunale amministrativo regionale-TAR) Veneto, March 22nd, 2005, no. 1110 and Council of the State-Administrative High Court (Consiglio di Stato), February 13th, 2008, no. 556. On the hardly-convincing nature of the cultural argument on the part of Italian administrative judges see Croce (2009) and Bin, Brunelli, Pugiotto, Veronesi (2004).

111 The ECHR clarified that "a reference to a tradition cannot relieve a contracting state from its duty to respect the rights and freedoms protected under the Convention." In the case of the crucifix that violation was not given, the same being considered by the European Court "a passive religious symbol" incapable of effecting any proselytism.

112 I would have permitted the crucifix in school on the condition that other religious symbols could also be displayed on the classroom wall to guarantee the equal status of all the religions in Italy (Ruggiu 2013). I am against the prohibition of wearing the *burqa* because it is inherent not only to freedom of religion, but also to freedom of dress, and I see in the removal of dresses a sort of neo-colonial intent from Western states to "undress" migrants, similar to that described with respect to Algerian women (Fanon 1965; Bourdieu 1960).

minority cultural practice can be recognized, and it takes into account whether any essential values of the majority are compromised. It confirms a recurrent *topos*: culture cannot violate any rights or fundamental freedoms; but it also introduces a new *topos*: cultural diversity is a public good that benefits not only the minority, but indeed the whole society.

11 From culture to gender: the *topos* of female equality

Since the publication of Susan Okin's "Is Multiculturalism Bad for Women?" (Okin 1999), the category of gender has appeared to be in potential conflict with that of culture. In fact, Okin questioned the "progressive" nature of multiculturalism with the main argument that most cultural practices were, in fact, patriarchal practices. The well-known debate between feminism and multiculturalism (Hirschmann 1998; Cohen, Toward, Nussbaum 1999; Kukathas 2001; Shachar 2001; Volpp 2001; Song 2005, 2007; Eisenberg 2007; Hoffman 2009) which erupted after that work still challenges scholars, penetrating judicial discourse to the point that we can say that today gender equality has become one of the fixed points (*topoi*) or standards against which to measure the recognition of cultural claims. When faced with a cultural practice that involves women, judges ask themselves whether there are gender issues to be taken into account. In a nutshell, the "anthropologist judge" is turning into a "feminist judge." It is not only that gender is weighted as more important when balancing cultural rights with women's rights. Often the mere presence of a gender dimension of the controversy brings the judge to completely de-culturalize the claim. In criminal law "cultural crimes" thus transform into "gender crimes." In civil law the recognition of patriarchal cultures is considered discriminatory.

The shift is recent, and it is happening across several multicultural conflicts. The strongest example is FGM. When the first cases of FGM began to appear, judges tended to act as anthropologists, giving much consideration to the practice's cultural dimension. Sometimes they acquitted the parents, and they almost always mitigated their sentence.[113] In Italy, the Legislature took action against this judicial trend, which was considered too mild and too oblivious of the oppression of women that FGM implied. Italian Law no. 7/2006 introduced a new crime to section 583 *bis* of the criminal code.[114] This section sentences people carrying out any kind of FGM to six to twelve years' imprisonment, and to the loss of parental rights. The high penalty is justified because the law is

113 See the Italian case of the Juvenile Court of Turin (Tribunale dei minori di Torino), July 17th, 1997.

114 After this law only one case of FGM was discussed in courts: it regarded the practice of *aruè*, a small puncture made on the clotorides of a Nigerian baby which did not produce any permanent damage. After the condemnation of the Trial Court of Verona (Tribunale di Verona) April 14th, 2010 motivated by the fact that art. 583 *bis* was meant to criminalize any form of FGM, the Court of Appeal of Venice (Corte d'Appello di Venezia) November 23th, 2012, n. 1485 reversed, motivating that art. 583 *bis* required the intention of sexual control which was absent in this case, as the *aruè* was lacking any permanent harm.

protecting a new constitutional interest: women's dignity.[115] The UN Resolution adopted on 20 December 2012,[116] which contains a blanket ban of any kind of FGM, confirmed the emergence of this new value. In fact, it based this ban on two arguments: the "gender/patriarchal argument" according to which any FGM is an oppressive practice against women and girls; and the "harm argument," according to which FGM causes irreversible and irreparable harm to a woman's health, both physically and psychologically. The Resolution never mentions FGM as a cultural practice, but rather defines it as a "harmful practice" five times, and a form of gender "violence" nine times.

After this change, Italian Courts, in the context of evaluating asylum claims for refugee status, started to recognize that FGMs are "acts of persecution for belonging to a social group"[117] and are "inflicted on girls and women as they are of the female sex, to assert power over them and to control their sexuality. Therefore the practice is part of a broader model of discrimination against girls and women."[118] Using this argument, the courts recognize the right to obtain asylum according to the 1951 Geneva Convention.

A second clear emergence of the gender discourse over cultural recognition regards honor killing of women. When, between 1980 and 1990, judges in the US began to raise the cultural defense, there were several cases in which culture was used in order to mitigate the punishment for honor killings. The most famous case[119] is that of Dong Lu Chen, a Chinese man who killed his wife following his discovery of her infidelity. Mr. Chen was sentenced to only five years' probation as the judge decided to take into account the cultural explanation provided by an anthropologist, Dr. Pasternak, heard as an expert witness in Chinese culture during the trial. Dr. Pasternak explained the strong blow to honor caused by a woman's infidelity. Judgments like this were sharply criticized,[120] and scholarship analyzed the differences "on whether to analyse 'honour crimes' as gender-based violence, or as cultural tradition" (Coomaraswamy 2005; Sen 2005). Some scholars clearly supported the theory that honor killings were not cultural crimes but gender crimes (Reddy 2008). This debate diffused the jurisprudence. Despite the cultural dimension often invoked by lawyers, Italian judges have tended to deny the existence of any cultural reason for honor killings, and to follow another classification instead: the patriarchal one. The most famous honor killing case decided in Italy confirms this. The Hina Saleem

115 Also the European Court of Human Rights reads FGM under gender in *Emily Collins and Ashley Akaziebie v. Sweden*, n. 23944/05, 8 March 2007.

116 A/Res/67/146, Intensifying global efforts for the elimination of female genital mutilation, adopted by the 67th Section of the General Assembly.

117 Trial Court of Cagliari (Tribunale di Cagliari) Order April 3rd, 2013.

118 Court of Appeal of Catania (Corte d'appello di Catania), op. November 27th, 2012.

119 *The People v. Chen*, N.Y. Sup. Ct. December 2nd, 1988.

120 On the other side, there were also cases in which honor was not used against the woman as in *The People v. Metallides* (1974). Mr. Metallides killed his daughter's rapist, and his defense was based on the Greek rule of revenge: "The law of the old country (Greece) is that you do not wait for the police if your daughter has been raped." This reasoning seems to be incorporated in the patriarchal protection of the woman.

case was decided by all the three levels of jurisdiction (trial court, court of appeal and Supreme Court of Cassation) by denying the cultural defense as the father was a patriarchal father (*padre-padrone*) who wanted to exercise authority over his daughter (Chap. 1 sec. 2.1). Those judgements encouraged the reading of Hina Saleem's death not as an "Islamic killing" due to Pakistani culture, but as a "patriarchal killing" (Dominijanni 2006).

In a similar matter, the Venetian Court of Appeals,[121] faced with a father who killed his daughter because she had started a relationship with a man other than he who had been promised in marriage, observes:

> this is the issue of a person of the Muslim culture who, under the pretext of an apparent legitimacy deriving from the Islamic religion, adheres to models of life in which there is a difference in treatment between men and women, the latter being by custom, according to archaic rules, subject to the arbitrary will of a tribal patriarchal family that keeps her as property and does not consider her as a person. This situation is, however, now increasingly rare in moderate Islamic environments such as Morocco, as there is a slow process of Westernization, also aided by the mass media that tend to globalization. A Moroccan national, after spending several years in our country [Italy], despite having maintained links with his country of origin, is thus quite capable, while retaining his own culture and their origins, to understand the crucial importance, in a civilized country, of certain fundamental rights of the human person. In this context his violent reaction becomes not the expression of an archaic culture, but a punitive spirit towards the victim, whose insubordination he does not tolerate.

This is true – the judge goes on to say – "even from the perspective of a Moroccan citizen" under the reasonable cultural person standard, and of "any citizen of any nationality and culture."

The emergence of the category of gender crime finds expression at the legislative level where Italian law October 15, 2013, no. 119, "Norms against gender violence" establishes as an autonomous category of murder: "femicide," with aggravating circumstances. With this law, the Legislature confronted the problem of the high rate of women killed by their partners in Italy.

International law established that women's rights prevail over honor and culture in general with the 2011 Istanbul Convention[122] (Parolari 2014; Scudieri 2018).

121 Court of Appeal of Venice (Corte d'Appello di Venezia), January 9th, 2006.

122 Council of Europe Convention on Preventing and Combating Violence Against Women and Domestic Violence, Istanbul, April 12th, 2011, art. 42 "Unacceptable justifications for crimes, including crimes committed in the name of so-called 'honour': 1. Parties shall take the necessary legislative or other measures to ensure that, in criminal proceedings initiated following the commission of any of the acts of violence covered by the scope of this Convention, culture, custom, religion, tradition or so-called 'honour' shall not be regarded as justification for such acts. This covers, in particular, claims that the victim has transgressed cultural, religious, social or traditional norms or customs of appropriate behaviour. 2 Parties shall take the necessary legislative or other measures to ensure that incitement by any person of a child to commit any of the acts referred to in paragraph 1 shall not diminish the criminal liability of that person for the acts committed."

Another controversial cultural practice has been read through the lens of gender instead of through that of culture: polygamy. From the comparative standpoint, a judgment that shows the gender dimension involved in polygamy is the decision rendered by the Supreme Court of British Columbia in 2011[123] (Spigno 2012; Federico 2010). Called upon to ascertain whether the clause of British Columbia's criminal code denying the possibility of polygamy was contrary to the Canadian Charter of freedom and rights, the judge stated that polygamy is a practice harmful to women:

> I have concluded that this case is essentially about harm; more specifically, Parliament's reasoned apprehension of harm arising out of the practice of polygamy. This includes harm to women, to children, to society and to the institution of monogamous marriage.

The harm to women is specified by the judge as follows:

> Women in polygamous relationships are at an elevated risk of physical and psychological harm. They face higher rates of domestic violence and abuse, including sexual abuse. Competition for material and emotional access to a shared husband can lead to fractious co-wife relationships. These factors contribute to the higher rates of depressive disorders and other mental health issues that women in polygamous relationships face. They have more children, are more likely to die in childbirth and live shorter lives than their monogamous counterparts. They tend to have less autonomy, and report higher rates of marital dissatisfaction and lower levels of self-esteem. They also fare worse economically, as resources may be inequitably divided or simply insufficient.

The pattern of the Court's reasoning is similar to the other cases: a predominant classification of the practice as patriarchal and oppressive towards women, which prevails over its cultural or religious dimension.

When gender is involved, even freedom of religion, to which in general is granted a special favour, surrenders. In Italy the religious argument was not enough to win even a mitigating factor in the case of a Jehovah's Witness, having forcefully imposed his faith onto his wife. The defense of the husband alleged that his religion is "characterized by a spousal relationship based on male supremacy," therefore for him the behavior "was normal, given this religious vision of life." The Italian Supreme Court[124] rejected the defense, specifying that "imposing onto others of one's religious beliefs" constitutes abuse in the family, in accordance with art. 572 criminal code. The issue of equality between man and woman is confirmed as a non-negotiable value, even in the face of the religious argument.

The comparative nature of the phenomenon emerges also in the UK, where the gender argument was used to reject the request of a Pakistani man to use

123 *Reference re: Section 293 of the Criminal Code of Canada* [2011] BCSC 1588.

124 Supreme Court of Cassation (Corte di Cassazione), sec. VI penal, 64/2010.

Pakistan's laws to dispose his divorce.[125] In explaining why this was not possible, the judge writes:

> I would therefore be approving both racial and gender discrimination, which is something that no judge of this country would be prepared to do . . . Why do I say that it would amount potentially to gender discrimination? There is no expert evidence before me about the position in Pakistan but it is reasonably clear from what I have been shown that the rights granted to men in Pakistan to secure divorces pursuant to the laws of that country are different from the rights granted to women and that it is more onerous for a woman to secure a divorce in Pakistan than it is for a man.

Because this decision regrettably lacks any clear cultural evidence, it is evocative of the fact that the mere fear that a concession may impair gender equality, even if not proven, can lead to a rejection of the cultural argument.

Another multicultural conflict in which the gender discourse and the idea of protecting women from the patriarchal structure have been strongly present regards the ***burqa***; in this case, however, the gender argument has not prevailed. The most recent authoritative ruling on this in Europe has been the European Court of Human Rights judgment of July 1, 2014, *S.A.S. v. France.*

The ECHR rejected the argument made by the French government based on the idea that "wearing of the full-face veil by certain women shocked the majority of the French population because it infringed upon the principle of gender equality as generally accepted in France" (par. 119).

The ECHR used two arguments to reject the French position on this point. First, it recognized the agency of women. According to the Court: "a State Party cannot invoke gender equality in order to ban a practice that is defended by women – such as the applicant" (par. 119). Second, it stated that gender equality should not be measured using French parameters, but, to the contrary, should be measured by opening the concept to cultural relativism:

> The Court is aware that the clothing in question is perceived as strange by many of those who observe it. It would point out, however, that it is the expression of a cultural identity which contributes to the pluralism that is inherent in democracy. It notes in this connection the variability of the notions of virtuousness and decency that are applied to the uncovering of the human body. Moreover, it does not have any evidence capable of leading it to consider that women who wear the full-face veil seek to express a form of contempt against those they encounter or otherwise to offend against the dignity of others.

The reader may recall (***supra*** sec. 10) that the ECHR confirmed the validity of the French ban with respect to the Convention using the argument of

125 *B v L* [2016] EWFC 67 (20 October 2016), England and Wales Family Court Decisions (High Court Judges), Birmingham.

"coexistence (*vivre ensamble*)" but refused the gender argument along with the security argument, the human dignity argument, and the secularity/*laicitè*[126] of the state argument. At the present moment, with the exception of France, Austria and Belgium, all remaining forty-four states of the Council of Europe grant protection to the *burqa* through judges who apply either the cultural or the religious defense.

Those trends registered at a comparative judicial level reveal the sharing of a common value that can find, as we will see, reflection in the cultural test (Chap. 4 sec. 5.12).

12 Toward a common Western legal tradition on the resolution of multicultural conflicts?

The analysis carried out in these two chapters reveals how any theory of multicultural conflict resolution cannot overlook the judicial dimension. By judicial dimension, I mean both the concrete case by case nature that the issues on multiculturalism involve as well as the fact that they have been addressed according to the "thinking problematically" approach (eg. the judge finds the solution inductively from the peculiarity of each case) and not according to the "thinking systematically" approach (eg. the judge finds the solution deductively from a pre-established law) (Viehweg 1962: 38), often encouraged also by the lack of standardization. Thinking "for problems," and therefore also "for attempts" which are subject to revision and which may pave the way for new solutions, may reveal more convincing and safer alternatives.

Do the many arguments that courts have developed over the decades reveal the existence of a common Western legal tradition; do they provide an *idem sentire*? Is it plausible to argue that a multicultural jurisprudential law exists which would represent a reference point for regulating the issue of multicultural conflicts and provide them with the stability that is lacking today? Through the *topoi* produced by judges, can one find the first steps of a dialectical reasoning on how to solve multicultural conflicts?

At first glance, the divergent features seem to overcome the recurring ones.

Divergent, first of all, are the markers of what the judge considers "culture" (see also Chap. 3). Sometimes any behavior may be classified as culture by the mere fact that a minority group engages in it, as in Italy or Germany (*supra* sec. 8 and 9), without considering the presence of similar behaviors within the same host culture and without careful consideration of what the minority considers truly "cultural." In other jurisdictions, conversely, culture must withstand close scrutiny, as is the case in Canada, by conditions for the recognition of a cultural practice that appear almost too rigid and formalistic (*supra* sec. 5).

126 I do not dwell, in this work, with this "grand argument" against the veil. I want only to mention that the appeal to secularism, especially in the extreme form that it has assumed in France, risks the transformation of an important constitutional principle in a cultural counter-argument brandished without any attempt of understanding the others' points of view. Also in respect to supreme principles such as secularism, multiculturalism demands a lenient approach and constitutional flexibility.

There are several consequences that judges derive from the fact of being faced with a cultural practice. Often the heterogeneity that dominates this profile is present even within the same system. For example, there were some judges for whom the word culture has operated in a formulaic way, seeming to justify any behavior. Other judges instead are likely to recognize the cultural value, but only up to the point where it does not infringe on the fundamental rights of all. Still others recognize it, but only as a transitional measure in the sense that the subject will only be excused the first time. Others totally ignore the cultural argument or even consider it an aggravating factor.

There are several ways in which the judge operates as an anthropologist: in some jurisdictions he normally uses the aid of a cultural expert; in others, like the Italian one, conversely, the judge evaluates the cultural element independently.

Faced with this diversity of models one could raise the question of whether it is appropriate to maintain the current existing diversification between states rather than to suggest a common pattern. This is especially true when diversity is not simply the result of an occasionalism due to the novelty of the subject, but is rather influenced by specific historical or political reasons. The Canadian model reflects, as seen, a specific political situation at a moment which distinguished between indigenous peoples and immigrants, and between religion and culture. Similarly, we have seen how important is the context in which judges intervene in cases where the court has enforced its role as an anthropologist with the intention to protect a vulnerable group such as the Roma in Italy or Jews in Quebec.

One could even raise the doubt that it is impossible to compare *topoi* developed in Protestant countries with *topoi* developed in Catholic countries, to find commonalities between common law and civil law systems, not to mention the non-Western sphere accepting Western *topoi* (De Roover, Claerhout, Balagangadhara 2011; Shah 2015b).

Though these considerations are surely to be taken into account, *topica* tradition suggests a common reflection on the way to resolve multicultural conflicts to arouse a circulation of experience, find the most persuasive reasonings and increase the interpretative horizon of the law.

Alternatively, if the analysis carried out shows too many differences in how to resolve conflicts, it still permits the identification of some common elements. Perhaps the evidence would not support the argument that there is already a common Western legal tradition, but at least there is proof of the fact that the doctrinal thinking of far-flung judges registers several points of convergence.

The request for a detailed description of the practice is present in Canada, the US and the UN Human Rights' Committee; the assessment on the compulsory nature of the practice is performed almost everywhere, and it is brought to its highest level in Canada which even requires that the practice be essential to the survival of the cultural group. The historical origin of the practice requirement is present in Canadian and in ECHR case law. The sincerity and consistency of the subject requirement is present in England and the United States. Whether the group is discriminated against or has endured historical injustice is also a factor often mentioned by both the Canadian courts and the Italian ones. The physical damage and the residence time in the host culture requirements are found in Germany, England and Italy.

The data emerging from the comparison allow one also to reason on the traceability of a map of the rights or principles that judges consider more or less negotiable. For example, it can certainly be said that life, physical integrity (Kymlicka, Lernestedt, Matravers 2014) and gender equality are principles/values before which the cultural argument almost always succumbs.

The doctrinal solutions given by Western judges in the last sixty years allow, therefore, to identify – not to accept uncritically, but at least to begin a reflection on – the elements to which the anthropologist judges give the most importance.

I believe today it is possible to gather together all these commonalities in a cultural test that can be used comparatively as a common reference to resolve multicultural conflict (Chap. 4). As I will try to demonstrate, the test is not an uncritical legal transplant (Watson 1993; Legrand 1997) from North America to Europe, but rather emerges from a dialectical process which has comparison at its core (Menski 2006).

Before elaborating this encompassing tool, it is important to deepen the analysis of the use of culture by Western judges.

If in these first two chapters we have focused on a descriptive analysis of the phenomena for which judges use the cultural argument, now is the time to critically investigate such use. To do this, I will analyze some of the main ideas developed in cultural anthropology, which are then, in the form of clichés, spent heavily within the legal discourse. The connection with anthropology is revealed as essential for deconstructive analysis, because it allows us to record how judges in their decisions reflect the different anthropological conceptions of culture – some outdated – and to prepare the groundwork for prescriptive analysis and proposals. Anthropological knowledge can, in fact, help us recognize the concepts of culture embodied by the law, signal which of them are outdated, and which are the more persuasive to build a "*métis Dike*" (Ricca 2008), a multicultural justice.

Part II

Deconstructive analysis

A critical reading of culture

3 Concepts of culture in anthropology and judicial reasoning

1 Deconstructive analysis of the concept of culture

"Comparable in explanatory importance to the idea of gravity in physics, disease in medicine, and evolution in biology," (Shweder 2001: 3151) the concept of culture has, in recent decades, imposed itself as the main lens for reading social interactions, surpassing both economy and class in the social sciences (Martìn Alcoff 2003). And it has been the discipline of anthropology that has given the greatest contribution to its theorization.

As a relatively young social science compared to far more consolidated disciplines (including the law), anthropology has nevertheless imbued the Western mind with its discoveries. The distillate, quintessential thought of anthropology is the realization that beings become human beings in quite different ways and that, wherever there exist common structures, they assume such a diverse phenomenology as to make it almost impossible to speak of only one humanity. This awareness has changed the prevailing common sense and, consequentially, the idea of justice and the interpretative horizon of the law, calling the latter to new assessments as it faces more and more frequent cultural contacts.

In 1952 a famous anthropological study collected one hundred and fifty-eight definitions of culture (Kroeber, Kluckhohn 1952: 77–143).[1] The number has at

1 The authors sort the collected one hundred and fifty-eight definitions into six macro-group categories, respectively: descriptive definitions "with emphasis on enumeration of content, usually influenced by Tylor" (Kroeber, Kluckhohn 1952: 81–88) who listed the compositive element of culture (eg. art, beliefs, law, morals etc.); historical definitions "with emphasis on social heritage and tradition" according to which culture is something inherited by the past (89–94); normative definitions with "emphasis on rule or way" and "on ideals or values" in which culture appears to be a net of rules, often sanctioned, that govern human behavior more or less bindingly (95–104); psychological definitions with "emphasis on adjustment," in which culture is seen "as a problem-solving device," or as an habit learned within the group, or as sublimation of impulses (107–117); structural definitions with "emphasis on the patterning or organization of culture" (118–124); genetic definitions "that focus upon the question: how has culture come to be?" that define culture as product or artifact, ideas, symbols (125–140). The authors of this catalogue proceed to offer a synthetic definition: "culture consists of patterns, explicit and implicit, of and for behavior acquired and transmitted by symbols, constituting the distinctive achievement of human groups, including their embodiments in articrafts; the essential core of culture consists of traditional (i.e. historically derived and selected) ideas and especially their attached values; culture systems may, on the other hand, be considered as

least tripled since (Hylland Eriksen 2004; Moore, Sanders 2006; Moore 2009). The definitional problem that has so troubled anthropology (Bidney 1944) is reflected also in judicial reasoning, where there is no unitary concept of culture (Appendices: the status of culture in constitutions and the status of culture internationally). But this is not an insurmountable epistemological problem; indeed it may be not a problem at all. It would probably be unfair to expect to see used, in legal interpretation, a homogeneous use of the concept. The law absorbs the definitions that circulate in society today, and these are by no means unique, since the concept of culture has been disputed from the moment in which the first theories were formulated in the nineteenth century.

Rather than trying to pin down a concept in constant transformation by seeking a legal definition of culture, it appears more useful to acknowledge that we are facing a "contested concept," (Gallie 1956) whose legal uses are diverse, thus revealing the different underlying implications to some use over another. The ideas of culture that a judge takes as a reference of his own reasoning, in fact sometimes even unknowingly, are indicators of the way in which we build our rapport with each other and with diversity.

In this chapter, therefore, I will provide an overview of some of the most significant cultural concepts that have been incorporated into legal reasoning in the presence of a multicultural conflict. The analysis will be conducted with the interdisciplinary approach that will lead to building a parallel between anthropology and law, pointing out how the many ideas of culture present in anthropology – and diffused in the social *idem sentire* – are used in legal reasoning. I will try to perform an operation of descriptive and, simultaneously, deconstructive meta-legal analysis. In fact, this part of the research uses also a post-modern[2] approach designed to bring to light the different "discourses" or "narrations" on culture

product of action, on the other as conditioning elements of further action" (357). The research is predated by *Mirror for Man* (Kluckhohn 1944) that had already provided a rich list of definitions of culture, seen as: "the total way of life of a people;" "the social legacy the individual acquires from his group;" "a way of thinking, feeling and believing;" "an abstraction from behavior;" "a theory on the part of the anthropologist about the way in which a group of people in fact behave;" a "store-house of pooled learning;" "a set of standardized orientation to recurrent problems;" "learned behavior;" a mechanism for the normative regulation of behavior; "a set of techniques for adjusting both to the external environment and to other men;" "a precipitate of history." On the interactions between the concept of culture and that of society see Kroeber (1952: 118–120).

2 The term "post-modernism" is defined in multiple ways, from the very first definition (Lyotard 1979), synthesizable in the idea that post-modernism is the end of all meta-narrations, grand-theories and ideologies which supported modernity. In the present work, I will use the concept of post-modernism as the philosophical movement aimed to reconstruct the discourses that mature within a society in order to historicize and deconstruct them. The advent of post-structuralism and post-modernism has destroyed the methodological certainties of all the social sciences, pushing them to research, not any more facts or certain structures – as happened, in the case of the law, with the jurisprudence of concepts, with normative ontologism and, in the case of anthropology, with structuralism – but rather the discourses and narrations in which the same social sciences find themselves immersed. On the influx of post-modernism on the juridical method see Volpe (2000) and Orestano (1989: 333) who observes: "the loss of the mystique of each 'ontologism' marks a new way to think among many jurists and marks the entry into a new historical dimension: to wit, 'post-modernism'."

that have developed in anthropology and law and then to compare them, highlight their historicity and subject them to a process of "deconstruction"[3] to reveal the structures of power that the various narrations may trace. I will question, therefore, when the uses that the anthropologist judge makes of certain ideas of culture correspond to a hegemonic discourse: When does culture operate as a "dispositive" of power (Foucault 2002) instead of a liberating concept that tends toward the recognition of neglected groups in the public sphere? When does culture operate as a new substitute for race (Balibar 1991; Crenshaw, Gotanda, Peller, Thomas 1995; Song 2009; Lentin, Titley 2011)?[4]

The "cultural discourse" that emerges from anthropology and from jurisprudence will be deconstructed for eventual modification, replacing some of its elements with others better able to activate a closer relationship with the other. This analysis will, in fact, be used to propose a recovery of the role of law and its weak critical gaze toward questionable cultural ideas that circulate in the social sphere and which the law seems to absorb passively by osmosis. It is time that the law speak with its own language and cease to be dictated by uncritically assimilated conceptions which may no longer be suitable to produce reasonable accommodation to contemporary multicultural encounters.

The investigation that follows will take us on a journey through the progressive elaboration of the concept of culture in anthropology from its beginnings until today.

2 Culture as *artifact*: reification, synecdoche and metonymy in judicial reasoning – the veil and the crucifix

Anthropology is a discipline founded with roots in colonialism and born from the first interest of Europeans towards the objects of colonial discoveries. In its early days, c. 1800, anthropology was concentrated on analyses of the artifacts of the people that the explorers, who later became settlers, brought to Europe from newly discovered lands.

Rivers of objects, removed from their cultural context, flooded nineteenth century Europe to become fetishes of a world perceived ambivalently: as less evolved on the one hand (according to attitudes defined as evolutionism, primitivism or allochronism); and on the other with an exotic charm of a primitive golden age, in which the "noble savage" could escape the discontents of civilization (exoticism). The lives of these objects (Appadurai 1988) changed and whatever the everyday or spiritual uses associated in cultural systems from which they came, they became objects of curiosity, disgust, fear, desire, collection, fascination or art in the

3 As deconstruction can be intended as "a strategy for revealing the underlayers of meanings in a text that were suppressed" (Appignanesi, Garrat 2003: 80).

4 "Culture is an anodyne representation of race, which is a historically constituted relation of organized inequality, domination and subordination. To speak blandly of a plurality of cultures in coexistence is to obscure the historic dominance of one of them, that of Anglo-Britain, and an array of continuing social effects that are not mainly 'cultural'" (Mulhern 2009: 43).

markets of Europe. One thing was certain: the idea of culture tended to coincide with those objects (Fabian 2007).

This aspect is clearly viewable in early anthropology museums (Stocking 1985; Kotler, Kotler, Kotler 2008): long files of clothes, masks, bows and arrows, canoes fill the display cases, ordered according to a perspective that ignores the context of use, transformed spoils almost totally released from the people to which they belonged.

After the first classificatory, and almost fetishistic, enthusiasm for objects arriving *en masse* from the New World or the African and Asian Colonies, the first anthropologists realized how these objects came from contexts where they assumed diverse lives and meanings, and how important it was for anthropologists to personally immerse themselves in such situations. William Rivers, Franz Boas, Bronislaw Malinowski and other founders of anthropology decided to go and stay for years with the peoples whom they planned to study, no longer content with the second-hand information that, from the beginnings of the discipline, were provided by settlers, explorers or missionaries. Participant observation, also known as field work, ethnography[5] or ethnographic research methodology became what distinguishes anthropology from other social sciences, and remains the north star of the discipline today, even after deep transformations.

Through anthropology, the method of participant observation changed the ways these objects came to be viewed. It consents to discover that every object has a definite link with the wider context of signs to which it belongs. Thus was born the concept of a cultural system and it was central to overcoming the initial material and reifying approach (Honneth 1992, 2005; Coombe 1995; Niccolai 2007). The transition to the cultural system successively brought anthropological holism, a method which arose in the context of structuralism, which tended to read every single phenomenon as connected to another and culture not as a sum of practices, but as a coherent system, serving a function. It passes, thus, from a sectorial vision – of culture as a set of objects or practices – to a holistic vision – of culture as a unit that surrounds and shapes the individual in all his manifestations of life. Translated legally, we could speak of an idea of culture as a system of rules, a web of norms, a kind of legal system, which shapes social life.

The holistic vision applies to the individual material objects, both in themselves and in relation to other "cultural products" such as individual behaviors previously considered removed from the context. Instead of looking at them with fascination or horror, anthropologists try to insert them into the broader

5 "If you want to understand what a science is, you should look in the first instance not at its theories or findings . . . you should look at what the practitioners of it do. In anthropology, or anyway social anthropology, what the practitioners do is ethnography" (Geertz 1973b: 5); "From one point of view, that of the textbook, doing ethnography is establishing rapport, selecting informants, transcribing texts, taking genealogies, mapping fields, keeping a diary, and so on;" it is doing "thick description," that is a description that assigns each human behavior in the web of meanings in which it is understood (Geertz 1973b: 6). Ethnography is for the anthropologist what laboratory research is for the biologist (Monaghan, Just 2000: 13). This methodological aspect of anthropology arouses diverse interrogatives with regard to training of judges and even the legislature. Since for judges a field observation is not possible, the law could obviate this with a greater activity of junction with anthropology.

horizon of meaning in which they mature. Culture ceases to be decomposed into several compartments, studied separately. As we shall see, holism and the idea of the "cultural system" should command more attention in legal reasoning, as it is often misled by undue attention to individual practices interpreted out of the whole cultural system. For this reason the cultural test I propose requires the judge to connect the practice to the wider cultural web of significances (Chap. 4 sec. 5.3).

An even more radical approach against the first reifying attitudes of anthropology is to refuse objects completely. People, individuals with their own ability to act (agency as opposed to the inevitability of enculturation[6]), have become the center of attention for anthropologists (Keane 2003) – no longer only material culture or artifacts. Even the concept of a cultural system is now deconstructed by anthropologists: the agency of individuals who, according to the previous ordering logic, remained "coherent" has become unstable, mutable (Leach 1954; Thornton 1988). The field observation practiced in anthropology reveals that human life does not respond to rigid organizational rules, which as such precludes the unexpected. Even in the most consolidated cultures, on the contrary, the unexpected appears the rule that nurtures or moves life's experiences. The idea of a "cultural system," in fact, tends to be substituted with that of "contextualism." Anthropology still considers the context as fundamental: each phenomenon as an object or a practice cannot be fully understood without examining its relationship dynamic with other phenomena. Contextualization is an integral part of the anthropological method, but without ideals of coherence and fixity as it used to have (Hylland Eriksen 2004: 38–41).

Tensions inside anthropology, between culture as artifact, holistic system, or agency of the subject, are reflected almost as a mirror image in the law, both at the level of constitutional texts (Appendix: the status of culture in constitutions) and of judicial reasoning.

The tendency to focus attention on objects brings three closely intertwined phenomena to jurisprudence: the reification that is the transformation of a cultural element, from a living and changing entity to something static and fixed; the creation of argument by synecdoche – namely the exchange of a part of a culture for all; and the creation of argumentative metonymies which reverse the relation between cultural cause and effect.

These phenomena emerge in the jurisprudence of symbols. Conflicts over religious or cultural symbols are, in most cases, the expression of an attitude to select

6 In reality classical anthropology is in part misunderstood in respect to the concept of enculturation. It does not negate the autonomy of the individual: "culture provides the raw material of which the individual makes his life. If it is meager, the individual suffers; if it is rich, the individual has the chance to rise to his opportunity" (Benedict 1934: 251–252). Moving from this consideration, Ruth Benedict questions the traditional concept of mental insanity as a pathology: "abnormals are those who are not supported by the institutions of their civilization. They are the exceptions who have not easily taken the traditional forms of their cultures . . . The issue in psychiatry has been too often confused by starting from a fixed list of symptoms instead of from the study of those whose characteristic reactions are denied validity in their society" (Benedict 1934: 258)

"one thing" and build the conflict around it. The synecdoches develop in this way: lawyers begin to consider a part, an object of a culture, as the whole. This part may be treated as one of those artifacts that so attracted the first anthropologists: as something devoid of life, that cannot be understood in its fullness because it is not inserted in the environment from which it draws meaning, divorced from it, extracted to be read in another system of signs.

Western debate thinks of the Islamic headscarf as a symbol of gender oppression (Chap. 2 sec. 11). As if totally focused and bewitched by this cultural object, jurists have spilled rivers of ink, entrenching argument either for or against its use. The part – the veil – becomes the object through which we read the whole thing – Islamic culture/religion – and, in particular, gender relations within that culture/religion. But to say that the role of men and women in Islam is embodied by the veil seems too oversimplified: it is a synecdoche, in fact, that may be effective as a figure of speech, but does not help to find a plausible solution to the conflict. Furthermore, the use of an object can often transcend its original meaning: for instance, the veil in Turkey comes to be a vindication of women's political ideals – not just religious identity, but also political opposition was represented by the veil – for which assessments such as those of the European Court of Human Rights (ECHR),[7] which approved the prohibition in the name of the "the principle of secularism" addressed by Turkey, disregard the multiple meanings that the veil can have. The reasons for wearing the *burqa* may be varied (Niccolai 2005). The symbol, whatever it is, is dropped into a context where it changes meaning. In this sense, it would be appropriate to de-reify these conflicts of "things" and relocate both the veil and the *burqa* within the more dynamic right to self expression.[8]

Thus synecdoche may easily switch to another fallacy, a type of metonymy confusing the cause for the effect. The fallacious approach is most visible in the moment when it becomes established that removing the object (the veil, presented as the cause of gender oppression) also removes the effect (gender oppression). In reality, the artifact – the veil – even supposing that its function is to oppress women, is a consequence rather than a cause of gender oppression. Removing it, the conflict generally persists intact. Investment into the object does not solve the gender problem at all: if anything, it makes it invisible. The practical result is even counterproductive because the "battle" waged by the West in favor of women will be considered terminated once women win the freedom to dress without the *burqa* or veil. Thus the far more effective policies – integration of migrant women in workplaces, social services which are culturally sensitive, gender-oriented education – to encourage the removal of the really oppressive causes can be postponed.

Focusing on the veil and making it the exclusive subject of legal experience, or investing it as the dividing line between Islam and the West, leads to a series

7 *Leyla Sahin v. Turkey* (Application no. 44774/98) 10 November 2005, ECHR Grand Chamber.

8 "Why is it oppressive to wear a head scarf but liberating to wear a miniskirt? The crux of explanation lies in the assumptions each side makes about the women involved in their ability to make choices . . . many of these Muslims sisters have thought seriously about the issue of covering their heads" (Al Hibri Azizah 1999: 46).

of cascading failures. Not only the one just shown – to obscure the "true" conflict, thus impeding the address of energies in more fruitful directions to remove it – but also to overstate the role of an object read through the lens of Western cultural system, something very similar to what happened to the early anthropologists encountering artifacts for the first time.

The West reads the veil within its system of meanings and gives the only meaning it knows, without making any effort to read through another cultural system. This effect can be avoided by inserting in the cultural test, as will be proposed at the end of this work, an element to guide the judge in reading the object through interpretations which takes in another's cultural system (Chap. 4 sec. 5.3). Once such a holistic inclusion is applied, the veil will no longer be left alone to speak without verifying the overall role that women occupy within Islam.

A similar reifying, synecdochic and metonymic effect is realized in the conflict that has arisen around the symbol of the crucifix in Italy. By law, all Italian schools must expose a crucifix; this norm was contested in 2005 by Mrs. Lautsi, a Swedish citizen, who complained of the violation of her freedom to educate her children in a secular way. The Italian administrative Court[9] (upheld by the ECHR[10]) rejected her request, saying that the crucifix is not a religious symbol but rather an emblem of Italian culture:

> it is clear that in Italy, the crucifix is capable of expressing, in a symbolic way, the religious origin of values of tolerance, solidarity, personal enhancement and rejection of any discrimination . . . that characterize Italian civilization. These values that have permeated the traditions, ways of life and culture of the Italian people . . . underlie and emerge from the fundamental rules of our constitution . . . The crucifix is designed to underpin the principles guarded by the same Constitution.

Just as the veil or *burqa* become the sum of all gender oppression, the crucifix is presented by the Italian judges as the sum of all positive constitutional values. A bit too much is being asked of these objects, which, in hindsight, do not have any proper meaning other than the use that the agency of the subject makes for them.

In conclusion, just as anthropology has had to elaborate the participatory observation method to break the spell that objects exercised, in the same way jurists should strive to insert the various symbols or objects of a conflict within the cultural system to which they belong. If a cultural test is to activate a relation, it should operate as, at some point, anthropologists did, leading the judge inside others' systems of interpretation to see the object through others' cultural lenses. I designed two prongs of the proposed cultural test, to place the individual practice within the group's broader web of significances (Chap. 4 sec. 5.3) and to find

9 Council of the State-Administrative High Court (Consiglio di Stato), February 13th, 2008, no. 556.

10 *Lautsi v. Italy and others*, ECHR, 30814/06, 22 March 2011.

a "cultural equivalent," a similar or analogous practice within the majority culture (Chap. 4 sec. 5.9), to assist judges through this process.

3 Culture as *the evolution of civilization*: primitivism and the judge faced with the "time factor"

The first complete conceptualization that anthropology made of culture bears the name of "cultural evolutionism." Evolutionary theory has its roots in the legacies of scientific positivism and colonialism. Positivism tended to read human history as a series of evolutionary stages that marked the spacing from a primitive stage of backwardness to an ever-greater progress. Colonialism was a political project aimed at spreading such progress among "less civilized" peoples.

Early anthropologists studied the communities with which they came in contact as if they were living fossils of the first human evolutionary phases and as if Western society represents the highest development in the history of mankind. According to this concept, cultures are located in different time scales. There are more advanced and less advanced cultures, primitive cultures and more developed cultures.

This Darwinian conception is present in one of the first definitions of culture, provided by Edward Tylor, that "culture or civilization" (the terms were often confused at that time) is "an accumulation of human accomplishments" consisting of "that complex whole which includes knowledge, belief, art, morals, law, customs and any other capacity or habit acquired by man as a member of a group" (Tylor 1871: 5; Kroeber 1952: 118–120). Not surprisingly, the works of Tylor, as well as those of other anthropologists of the period, aimed to investigate the origin of an institution (eg. marriage, kinship) to evidence the evolution of society from the most basic to the most complex. The chronological scansion often, however, became a value judgment: what came first was less elaborate, less complex, even less evolved.

In this phase, primitivism had a precise negative connotation. The exo-European cultures, in fact, were not perceived as having equal value, but placed on a lower evolutionary scale.

At the beginning of the discipline, anthropology's subjects of study were the so-called primitive cultures identified in simple human groups, technologically undeveloped: "people who have never learned to adapt nature to their needs, but rather have adapted themselves to the rigors of their wilderness environment" (Birket-Smith 1963: cover).

Within anthropology, the primitivist orientation was slowly deconstructed to reveal the structures of power that it implies, in its own language. The word primitive, for example, is based on development elements that are limited to technical evolution, neglecting the spiritual and using, therefore, a prism of observation that suits Western cultures (Davis 2002). Not coincidentally, these are seen as very little evolved from so-called primitive peoples or traditional cultures also in other respects: the ability to communicate with the spirit world, inner awareness, environmentally sustainable economies and so on (Nader 2015).

Another point of criticism was that to define a people as primitive means giving a misleading representation of the factor of time. In particular, anthropologists have focused on two phenomena: that of the so-called "ethnographic present" and that of "allochronism."

The first term refers to an attitude to crystallize the other in a time that always remains equal to itself. This attitude appears in a series of classics of anthropology in which, after a period of ethnographic fieldwork, researchers provided a guide to cultural groups that were presented isolated spatially and temporally, almost frozen in time and without attention to the changes that groups had gone through.[11]

Allochronism means the process of placing the other in another (*allos* in Greek) time (*cronos* in Greek), diachronically distant or synchronically retreated (Fabian 1983). Such a placement in another time generally implies a relationship of power as the other culture is placed in an implicitly lower time scale. But even if this were not so and if, as happens in exoticism, the value judgment is positive, it would in any case be a distortion. The construction of the other tends to occur in a space and time different from the one in which the anthropologist lives and especially takes away the fact that the group lives in the present and in such time continuously rewrites the symbols of the past.

If the evolutionist ideology might appear until recently a phenomenon to be archived in the history of anthropological thought, it should be noted that the very same issues of multiculturalism have led to a comeback:

> relatively few anthropologists would actually describe themselves as cultural developmentalists. Nevertheless, that stance is far more common in anthropology than many admit, especially when the topic concerns gender relations and family life practices, for example, polygamy, *purdah* [a practice prohibiting men from seeing women], arranged marriages, bride-prices, female circumcision, and the association of femininity with domesticity and the production of children.
> (Shweder 2001: 3155)

A return of the evolutionist stance is recorded also in other social sciences such as economics or political science (Huntington 1996; Harrison, Huntington 2000).

Trends inside anthropology in relation to the time in which to place the other are echoed by judicial reasoning. There are several "evolutionist" attitudes into which judges may fall.

The first is a form of diachronic allochronism, which consists in recognizing as "cultural" only those practices which arose in a certain historical time.

The second is a form of primitivism, which consists of attributing a barbarian and atavistic character to the practices of the minority.

11 The classic by Raymond Firth, *We, the Tikopia* (Firth 2004), published in 1936, is a fictionalized research that crystallized the Tikopia in the first years of anthropological study. When Firth returned to study them he, for example, neglects the fact that half were already converted to Christianity (Monaghan, Just 2000: 25–26).

Regarding the first attitude, the most striking example is the Canadian cultural test forged in relation to indigenous peoples (Chap. 2 sec. 5.1), requesting that the origin of the claimed cultural practice remain in times earlier than contact with Europeans. The pre-contact test is a symptom of how the other exists only in the past. The judge does not appear to find relevant whether the customs of the most recent individual native tribes are now essential to the survival of the group and to its sense of identity, but only considers the moment of contact with Europeans, thus freezing the cultural system of indigenous peoples in that moment.

The deconstruction of this argumentative choice allows one to bring to light the possible power structures that lie behind the pre-contact test.

A possible reading is that behind this test crouches the specter of cultural genocide: what should be saved is the primitive world that existed before the arrival of settlers who brought devastation. The test serves to remedy an injustice, an injustice found in the past, on very precise dates, shaped by the destructive force of the advancing settlers. It is no coincidence that the date from which the practice must be assessed changes, as seen (Chap. 2 sec. 5.1), depending on the westward advance of the colonial border.

Another reading is that the judge falls into a kind of anthropological romance: contact with the Europeans is the watershed, as if the indigenous people came then into a new era, modernity, where the ability to develop their own cultural choices vanishes; the practices that will emerge from this point forward are not worthy of protection.

Other explanations see in the pre-contact requirement a stratagem to restrict the claims of the natives to the period before they lost political sovereignty, reiterating, in this way, that sovereignty has now passed definitively to the Canadian state.

All these reasons leave unsated the search for a solution of coexistence. Native peoples, in fact, exist in the present, in contemporary Canada.

The second evolutionary/primitivist attitude reveals, as mentioned, when the judges make judgments of backwardness of a particular culture. Various judgments of the Italian Supreme Court of Cassation contain manifestly primitivist language.

In the *Bajrami* case,[12] faced with an immigrant from Albania charged with mistreatment towards his wife and children, the judge heard a defense urging him to consider that "the concept of family life and of the power due to the head of the family" could have "set a kind of consent (from the victim) relevant according to art. 50[13] of the criminal code to exclude culpability of the defendant." The Supreme Court says that these arguments are

> absolutely at odds with the rules on which the Italian legal order is based which constitute one insurmountable barrier against the introduction – *de iure* or

12 Supreme Court of Cassation (Corte di Cassazione), sec. VI penal, November 24th, 1999, no. 3398. The principle was reaffirmed by Court of Cassation (Corte di Cassazione), sec. VI penal, January 8th, 2003, no. 55, in the case of a Moroccan man who had beaten his wife and fractured her hand.

13 Art. 50 "he is not culpable whom who does violate or put at risk a right of an other person with his or her consent."

> *de facto* – in the civil society of customs, practices, traditions, which seem "barbaric" faced with the results obtained over the centuries to affirm the inviolable rights of the person . . . The barbarization of the law and jurisprudence, which is claimed by invoking the provision contained in art. 50 of the criminal code when we are faced with conduct prejudicial to the physical integrity, to the personality of the individual, to the family community . . . apodictically supposed to be legitimate in other systems . . . find an insurmountable obstacle in the legal rules (if not in the social consciousness) that presides over the present legal framework.

In the case of *Bel Baida*,[14] where a Moroccan father was denounced for involving his minor son in itinerant unlicensed trade activities, the cultural defense – which explained how in all the Maghreb area it is perfectly normal for a child to contribute to family support, as well as to conduct sales activities of objects in the absence of any authorization – was rejected by the Italian Supreme Court with this argument: "a culture backward and insensitive to the enhancement and protection of childhood must give way."

In the already examined opinion 1520/2008, the traditional customs of Morocco are qualified as "unhistorical" (Chap. 1 sec. 2.1).

In another decision, faced with the case of Mohammad Lhasni, who killed his daughter Kaputar because she had an affair with a man other than her betrothed, and asked by the defense to evaluate "the atavistic and socio-cultural values . . . the strong and extreme sense of family" of the accused as a mitigating factor, the judge replied that "in a civilized country some fundamental rights of the human person, such as self-determination, are irrepressible"[15] and found for aggravating factors based on the defendant's motives.

Also the Venice Court of Appeal, called upon to judge an honor killing in 2006 is found to say that a conception of the submissive woman is disappearing in Morocco "as there is a slow process of Westernization, also aided by the mass media that tend to globalization," implying that it is the West that "liberates" Morocco from patriarchal archaic rules (Chap. 2 sec. 11).

The phenomenon is common at the comparative level. In the case of a Nepalese citizen, arrested in the United States and accused of having imported heroin, the judge writes in his decision that Pemba Rita Sherpa was born in "a small and rather primitive village in Nepal" and he was a "relatively unsophisticated man . . . from a relatively unsophisticated culture, who had never been in the narcotics trade or had any connection to it."[16]

14 Supreme Court of Cassation (Corte di Cassazione), sec. VI penal, January 30th, 2007, no. 3419 (Zanchetta 2007).

15 Trial Court of Padua (Tribunale di Padova), June 9th, 2005, no. 446. The decision was confirmed by the Court of Appeal of Venice (Corte d'Appello di Venezia) January 9th, 2006, and by the Supreme Court of Cassation (Corte di Cassazione) June 14th, 2006, no. 20393. The first two decisions are reviewed in *Diritto, Immigrazione e Cittadinanza*, no. 1/2009, 199 and 202 et seq.

16 *U.S. v. Sherpa* 110 F.3d 656 (1996), adding that "Sherpa was culturally sheltered in such a way as to prevent his awareness of the questionable nature of his task."

The other culture, in the terminology above is, therefore, presented by the judges as "anti-historical," "ancestral," "barbaric," "uncivilized," "unevolved," "unsophisticated." These traces of primitivism in their reasoning elicit a reflection on how the judge should relate with respect to the time factor.

In general, that the judge expresses temporal judgments on the "backwardness" of a custom is perfectly plausible: it is the role of the judge to assure the development of society conforming to constitutional principles. One cannot, therefore, forbid that the judge in any case make judgments about the "backwardness" of a practice, in the name of a politically correct attitude or inspired by the most intransigent anthropological relativism.

The colonial complex that weighs on the West should not inhibit the expression of judgments that may put parts of a culture "on trial." It is indeed appropriate that the judge seeks to guard the future and to suggest that what is practiced, even from ancestral times, can be subject to discussion and eventually to change. Just as it is important to observe the practice through the eyes of the other in order "to transcend the limitations of our positional perspectives" (Sen 2009: 155), it may also be important that the other knows what reactions his behaviors provoke in a cultural system that does not appertain to them.

The judge, therefore, who attempts to make a finding on the times, on the evolution of a society, in some way drives it, becoming one of the promoters of change. But there are some conditions to be met to ensure that the judgment does not accentuate the divisions and gaps with that culture.

First, it is essential to curate the language of decisions and to avoid derogatory expressions such as those just now recorded. Expressions like "barbaric customs" evoke an us (civilized country) and them (barbarian) dynamic that is questionable even *a priori*. For example, to identify the other as primitive because they do not respect women risks to create blindness to discriminatory and patriarchal practices that take place in the same culture of the judge (Nader 1989;[17] Mancini 2012). The problem of gender violence encroaches transversely across all cultures, from the Arabic to the northern European. The investigation by the court should be made with a high degree of bilateralism. The judge must "remember" (Giuliani 1984), in his opinions, what happened in his culture and what is still happening.

Second, it is critical that the court view the other as capable of agency, a subject who can operate here and now, with whom a dialogue can be established in the present, who is not fixed and crystallized into an immutable past. For example, in very few of the decisions catalogued in the course of this research are there cases in which the court notes that, in reality, the cultural practice in question, although it exists, is disputed and is not unanimous in the same community to which the claimant belongs or there have been legal reforms that now reshape family relationships or gender. This profile would allow, instead of rejecting the practice because an archaic past contrasts with the modern present of the majority, to point out that a transformation, a before and an after, begins to manifest

17 Nader (1989: 324) observes how: "images of women in other cultures act as a control to women in one's own society."

itself within that culture, to take note that this is a controversial practice in the same group and, therefore, to look at this group as a present reality, alive, moving instead of frozen in time.

In conclusion, there are some attitudes with respect to time that definitely should be removed from legal argument (such as the Canadian pre-contact test), while others are potentially eligible and able to introduce transformative effects in society, but only if carried out without an imperialist attitude and when adequately justified and inserted into relational argument. I designed two prongs of the proposed cultural test to inquire whether the practice is broadly shared within the identified group or disputed within it (Chap. 4 sec. 5.5), and to search for a "cultural equivalent" (Chap. 4 sec. 5.9) to assist with this process.

4 Culture as *exoticism*: the irresistible charm of the "different" on the judge

If the evolutionary conceptions of culture have led to the construction of a primitive "other" set in a time from which the West has advanced, it should not be omitted that theories of evolution have also produced another, clear and opposite attitude: exoticism. It is rooted in the myth of the "noble savage" (Ellington 2001). The discomfort of civilizations that live in the West has, at one point, led to precisely discern in primitive societies a possible existential response, a place back in time, untouched by modernity, to find shelter in the tempest of existence; a spatial or temporal dimension to be protected in all its authenticity. And anthropology was quick to buy into the myth.

Despite a visible difference in values, exoticism produces effects similar to those produced by primitivism: it is a process that removes the other and prevents seeing him in the present, in connection with the majority *hic et nunc*.

Anthropology has indeed professed, as it consolidated as a scientific discipline, a neutral attitude, trying to refrain from both judgments of contempt and of elation when studying cultures; however, romanticism and exoticism have inevitably influenced scholars.

Often there are even minority groups which endorse exotic representations. In these cases, in which culture resembles something nostalgic to be recovered, primitivism can become a counter-discourse that minorities practice with the dominant culture in a conscious way. The so-called primitive cultures are claiming, for example, to be able to establish a better relationship with the environment, to have more established human relations, to be more advanced in search of wisdom, spiritual peace, to have more inclusive legal forms,[18] a higher quality of life and so on. The value judgment is thus reversed: regaining possession of the negative representation, groups transform it and put it back in the public sphere with a positive charge. Also anthropology has redressed old

18 On this last profile note how many indigenous peoples adopt the consensus method to arrive at a decision, therefore refusing to decide without the unanimity of the group, as they consider the rule of the majority to be less evolved.

primitivist paradigms in exoticism: in the Declarations of Barbados in 1971 and 1977 emerge a clear criticism of the paradigms of modernity and progress, and suggestions of the indigenous life as "an alternative of civilization."

Despite these cases where primitive speech is narrated by the same group as their own choice, normally it acts as an instrument of false representation of the other that can prove fatal in framing a multicultural conflict.

To analyze how the legal argument incorporates the idea of exoticism leads, first, to consider that for some judges the very fact of confronting a stranger produces an exotic effect.

Subtle linguistic clues detect it. The Italian Supreme Court speaks, in op. 1520/2008 (the *Kassam* case, Chap. 1 sec. 2.1) for instance, of the "evocative profile of cultural crimes," as if there was something charming about domestic violence committed for cultural reasons. A trace of exoticism is, in some ways, also found in the judgment 44516/2008 on *manghel* (Chap. 1 sec. 3.1). The fact that begging is practiced by the Roma works to rob it of its character as a social practice, a result of an economic distress, as it would have been classified if the beggar had been an Italian, deprived of the cloak of culture.

But the legal system, among those analyzed, where the strongest exoticist attitude appears is Canada. The request, in their cultural test, that the practice be "distinctive" (integral to a distinctive culture) constitutes the best evidence. Using this element, in fact, the judge can deny the "cultural" nature of all practices that are identical to those of other cultures, which do not feature in any "exotic" way the culture of the natives. Turning to an overview of the practices that have been recognized (or not) in Canada, the overall picture clearly works in favor of practices with an exotic flavor. Very evocative is, on this point, the lawsuit filed by the Canadian government for violation of criminal laws on gambling against native tribes that opened casinos on their reservations (*R. v. Pamajewon* 1996, Chap. 2 sec. 5.1). Although sometimes the court had said that a practice could also evolve with modern means, and despite that the tribe had proved that gambling (in the form of card games) was also practiced before the arrival of settlers, the request was rejected. The judge reasoned by saying that the practice was non-essential to the cultural survival of the group, but perhaps the opening of a casino does not offer a sufficiently distinct/exotic character to be recognized. Only if the other remains a "noble savage" in his culture can he be considered worthy of protection, while if he is trying to thrive in the present or escape poverty this cannot be recognized.

The requirement that the practice be distinctive turned out in some cases to be so formalistic and extreme that, over the years, the cultural test forged in 1996 has restated some of its parts to temper the excessive "exoticism" claim. A decision that revised the testing scheme was *Regina v. Sappier*[19] (Charlton 2007–2008). The case involved two indigenous persons who cut wood in a forest without authorization. The government believed that the cutting and the use of wood was not "essential and integral to a distinctive culture" because any community of human beings near a forest could have found recourse there. On that

19 *R. v. Sappier*, [2006] 2 S.C.R. 686.

occasion, the Supreme Court loosened the meaning of the character "distinctive practice" and recognized the existence of the aboriginal right to timber used "within the community" for building houses and making objects, and to support a group distinct from the rest of Canadians. If the natives had cut wood to sell it would have remained outside the protection of the test, but when they used it within their own group, the requirement should be assessed with less rigidity.

Exoticism and primitivism conspire, then, to narrow down which cultures can be recognized, bringing the judges, often, to conceptions of the "cultural" that are not persuasive.

5 Culture as *relativism*: the abandonment of reasoning in *modus iuridicus* in favor of *modus anthropologicus*

Whereas the first steps of anthropology were characterized by a materialistic approach and value judgments intrinsic to both variants of evolutionism – primitivism and exoticism – as well as by forms of emotional involvement – romantic idealizations or a sense of horror by anthropologists against groups that they studied (Malinowski 1989) – with the consolidation of the discipline these approaches give way to what will become the heart of anthropological reasoning: relativism.

According to Franz Boas (1930, 1938), culture is not so much "an accumulation of human accomplishments" achieved by different human groups, but rather consists of "cultural" lenses (the "native point of view" of Malinowski 1922) that, once worn by the different processes of socialization, lead human groups to see the world in diverse ways: culture embraces all manifestations of social behavior of a community, the reactions of individuals as conditioned by the group customs in which they live and the product of human activities as conditioned by these customs. This definition deviates from that provided by cultural evolutionism mainly for two reasons. First, because it abandons the idea of culture as a "milestone" or "progressive accumulation" of achievements in favor of equality of all cultures, not distinguishing between more evolved or not. Second, because it claims that culture is something that is socially acquired and totally free, therefore, of biological profiles.

From this moment anthropology also assumed a very specific role in the social sciences as a discipline at the forefront against racism and colonialist ideologies that tried to theoretically justify the political superiority of some human groups (Bidney 1968; Stocking 1968; Hatch 1983; Spiro 1986). Anthropology became the science that, once it established the biological unity of the species *homo sapiens* and therefore the identity of his genetic inheritance, reveals and studies the diversity of social inheritance: humans are biologically equal, races do not exist; only cultural differences exist (UNESCO 1968).

This aspect is also central in the definition of culture proposed by Bronislaw Malinowski who observes how man varies in two aspects: physical fitness and social heritage or culture, and this social legacy, usually called culture in modern anthropology, is the key concept of the social sciences. Culture is defined by Malinowski as the cumulative creation of man (Malinowski 1937: 621, 645) but without any evolutionist connotations, only to contrast it to the cumulative creation that nature performs, for example, with mutations of the gene in the context of biological evolution.

In 1934 Ruth Benedict brought Boas' model to an extreme, saying that ends and means "in one society cannot be judged in terms of those of another society, because essentially they are incommensurable" (Benedict 1934: 223). Even practices such as cannibalism or magic find significance when placed in a certain system of meanings, with their own full internal logic and even producing effects in reality (De Martino 2004). Anthropology expresses, as well, an unconditional respect for any cultural system. For Benedict, in fact, all cultures propose equally valid patterns of life and cannot be judged, because each human being is, in some way, an adaptive response to historical or natural conditions in which she is called to live. In studies by two other founders of relativism, Margaret Mead (1928) and Melville Jean Herskovits (1950), this approach is further loaded with value structures: a relativistic approach, according to these authors, produces tolerance.

Anthropological relativism is essentially based on two pillars. The first consists of cultural particularism: culture being an adaptive response of man to his environment, every human group has developed different answers so it is impossible to speak of an abstract humanity. The second pillar is the idea that all behavior has its explanation in the system in which it takes place, so the external judgment is flawed as the cultural systems are incommensurable, relying on different adaptive premises. The task of anthropology, in this context, cannot be one to judge, but simply to penetrate as much as possible into the other's cultural system to describe it with the other's perspective.

Anthropological relativism reached its climax in the debate on the adoption of the Universal Declaration of Human Rights of 1948, when anthropologists participated with the document to oppose the universalist language therein adopted (American Anthropological Association 1947; Engle 2001). The motivation was the consideration that the concept of human rights was not universal, but was rather a purely Western product (Dundes Renteln 1988, 1990).

The relativistic attitude has been, even within anthropology, subjected to criticism and currently, at least in part, scaled down. The main criticism is that according to relativism, culture is the structure within which personalities are formed. The processes by which the individual is socialized into a culture (enculturation) appear irreversible. This seems to imply a subject substantially deprived of agency, but it is well known how even a single individual has been able to shake and crack entire cultural systems: just think of Franca Viola, the first Italian woman to refuse, in 1965, the shotgun wedding that would have paid off the crime of sexual violence perpetuated against her, pursuant to then art. 544 of the criminal code;[20] or Rosa Parks, who in 1955 in the US put into question the practice that forbade African Americans to sit in the bus seats reserved for whites,

20 As at that time rape was a crime "against public morals" and not "against the person," and the wedding (*matrimonio riparatore*) that the rapist wanted to contract with the victim would have extinguished the crime. Art. 544 was repealed by law no. 442/1981.

to mention only two of the best known examples of individuals who have challenged and subverted established cultural systems.

Anthropological relativism has influenced judicial reasoning particularly at the dawn of the use the cultural argument, when judges were ready to recognize a cultural mitigating factor based on the mere fact that people see the world differently.

This clearly emerges in the words of the US judge in the *Chen* case (Chap. 2 sec. 11).[21] Mr. Chen killed his wife with a hammer after discovering her infidelity. He was a native of China and his lawyer had evoked a cultural defense. After listening to an expert in Chinese culture, the anthropologist Dr. Pasternak, the court accepts the defense's argument:

> were this crime committed by the defendant as someone who was born and raised in America, or born elsewhere but primarily raised in America, even in the Chinese American community, the Court would have been constrained to find the defendant guilty of murder in the first degree. But, this court cannot ignore the testimony, the very cogent forceful testimony of Doctor Pasternak, who is, perhaps, the greatest expert in America on China and interfamilial relationships.

Dr. Pasternak had stated in his report that "in general terms . . . one can expect that a Chinese would react in those circumstances in the most volatile and violent way, utterly different from a subject belonging to our society;" his reaction, therefore, would be immeasurable compared to the standard of the average American husband which was the original point of comparison proposed by the judge. From the testimony of the anthropologist the judge obtained an absolute determinism: Mr. Chen could not have acted otherwise. The man was convicted of second-degree murder, a lesser charge, and served no prison sentence, but rather only five years of probation. Decisions of this kind revealed a total subservience to the depositions of the consulted anthropologists, an almost total renunciation of addressing the dispute with tools of legal reasoning and a passive surrender to relativism.

Another case decided in Italy[22] reveals a similar attitude. The facts regard a young Moroccan woman beaten by family members for having met a boy: after her affair was discovered she threatened suicide, but the family tied her hands and beat her as punishment. In affirming that the father was not guilty for the crime of maltreatment, the Court of Appeal points out:

> It is true that it is contrary to the sense of affection and humanity, especially that which should inspire family relationships, to beat a girl who threatened suicide, but it is likely that in that family, as is clear from the evidence taken, there were norms inspired by ironclad hierarchical relationships, the violation

21 *People v. Dong Lu Chen*, No. 87–7774, N.Y. Sup. Ct. Dec. 2, 1988.

22 Court of Appeals of Bologna (Corte d'appello di Bologna) October 6th, 2006, no. 2433 and confirmed by the Supreme Court of Cassation (Corte di Cassazione), sec. V penal, August 2nd, 2007, no. 31510.

> of which would result in an exemplary sanction that could not be left out even in the face of attempted self-harm.

The Italian Supreme Court affirmed the decision, saying that it is not convinced of "the proof of only three episodes (of beating) in the life of E., moreover all motivated from a daughter's behavior deemed unfair and therefore not expressing the necessary requirement of oppression and contempt (from the side of the father)."

With these arguments, in some way, it seems that the court may accept the point of view of the father with a relativistic attitude. This is rare in the Italian Supreme Court, which generally neglects the recognition of culture in lieu of women's rights.

Another case in which judges had adopted a relativistic stand is the matter of circumcision decided in Italy between 2007 and 2011 (Chap. 2 sec. 8.1). The op. 43646/2011 of the Supreme Court, which acquitted the accused of the offense of conspiring to malpractice in the medical profession, says:

> A multi-ethnic society, which more or less consciously accepts multiculturalism, cannot ignore a certain amount of cultural relativism, which allows it to look at other cultures without judging them according to their own parameters. It follows that the approach to this delicate matter [of circumcision], for its ethical and legal implications that are relevant, must be guided by a prudent and enlightened interpretation of the reference standards, without undervaluing the peculiar position of the person involved in the incriminated ritual act.

In other cases the relativist attitude was rejected in Italy, in the name of a universalism of values. Thus was the motive in the case of two Roma parents accused of abuse in the family for having left their children to theft and truancy: while the defense appealed to the "different cultural background of the accused" to support the absence of a "subjective ingredient" of the offense, the court replied that the non-value of such conduct "is, or at least should be, universally perceived, regardless of ethnicity, contrasting with natural criteria, even before legal, peaceful coexistence between humans."[23]

If relativism may have a value in a descriptive discipline like anthropology, it is not well adapted to a prescriptive discipline like the law. The law should resolve conflicts between interests that have to meet and enter into a relationship. Anthropology can grasp the culture in full and in "isolation;" the law may, however, want to encourage a miscegenation, almost inevitable in a pluralistic society. If anthropology can afford a judgment of incommensurability between cultures, the law is, by contrast, justly called to measure them, to break the lack of communication between different systems of meaning, to translate them;

23 Trial Court of Turin (Tribunale di Torino), October 21st, 2002. Other parts of the work address the critique of the premise which in part moved the judge, namely the fact that theft and school truancy are cultural practices.

and cannot, in order to produce an equitable solution to the dispute, take a relativistic attitude when social coexistence could be impaired. To sum up, the judge in multicultural society should be an anthropologist, but primarily a judge.

6 Culture as an attribute that only *the other* has: the "culturalization" of foreigners

The emancipatory scope, compared to evolutionary theories, that relativism has surely had cannot conceal the fact that anthropology still remains a discipline that perpetuated, even unconsciously, a construction of the discourse of the other which tends to reaffirm his separation from the West (Asad 1973; Hymes 1974: 29). The path of this discipline to free itself from its colonial DNA was still long and the founders of relativism had only taken the first steps.

This aspect of the other-separation found reflection in the division between the social sciences: anthropology – the science of culture *par excellence* – studied the so-called primitive cultures, while other emerging social sciences, such as psychology or sociology, took care of the study of Western society.

The moment of symbolic break with this approach can be identified in the publication, in 1956, of what became a classic of anthropology: "Body rituals among the Nacirema." In this essay, the anthropologist Horace Miner (1956) describes the population of the "Nacirema" using the tools of ethnographic description.

The anthropologist describes various magical rituals and observes that when Nacirema perceive themselves as ugly, they undergo several mutilations to change their breasts, nose, etc.

The ethnographic analysis of the other is complete and plausible, until, reading backwards "Nacirema," it turns out that the description, in fact, concerned the "American."

The condemnation of this article is sarcastic and double-edged. On the one hand, the author wants to show how ethnographic language distances the other and places him in an unreal time and space (Clifford 1988; Said 1989), so that when the same language is used to describe the same culture to which the anthropologist belongs it produces an effect of estrangement, plausibly similar to how it would affect groups which are the object of ethnographic description. On the other hand, the author wants to address an implicit complaint that anthropology has refused to apply its tools to the study of Western civilization.

Anthropology has now extended its subject of study to many aspects of the operation of the post-industrial society, with methods which even today continue to strongly characterize this discipline: field research, ethnographic interviews, participant observation.

The difficulty that anthropology has encountered in reading Western society as culturally connoted assumes two aspects in legal argument.

The first is the tendency of lawyers to culturalize any conduct by foreigners, often "blaming culture for bad behavior" (Volpp 2000).

The second is that behaviors of the majority culture are explained by the judge with the tools of psychology or investigations into their economic and social reasons, but never with culture (Damian 2008).

The first phenomenon is present, in marked measure, between the Italian courts where a whole range of common crimes were covered with the cultural label on the sole ground that they were made by foreigners. This has been accentuated by the fact that in Italy there is not a clear obligation for the court to determine in detail whether they are facing a cultural behavior and to accurately describe the cultural practice (Chap. 4 sec. 5.2). As evidence of this, note how in op. 31510/2007, the Supreme Court does not even care to describe the accused's country of origin, instead speaking generally of "Islamic Culture" (case of the girl beaten by her father described *supra*, sec. 5). Faced with this attitude, several minorities have "returned to sender" the cultural mantle graced to certain behaviors, denying it at the root: recall the case of Roma *manghel* (the begging case, Chap. 1 sec. 3.1) or filicide in Pakistan (*Saleem*, Chap. 1 sec. 2.1).

The second attitude is clearly visible by comparing closely related behaviors among minority and majority which nonetheless are explained with completely different categories. Think of the phenomenon of violence against women. If it is true that Pakistan has a high number of female murders for reasons of honor, it is equally true that Italy and broader Europe know hundreds of cases of women killed by their partners. In the first case jurisprudence has, with some exceptions, framed a cultural practice of "honor killing." Conversely, when an Italian, Norwegian or German kills his wife in a fit of jealousy, no judge evokes the Italian, Norwegian or German culture.[24]

It would be more egalitarian if the judge were also to use the cultural frame for his own culture, when appropriate.

The risk of blindly labeling the other with culture can be mitigated by introducing the request to find a cultural equivalent present in the majority culture (Chap. 4 sec. 5.9). The judge who faces a multicultural conflict must be asked to act as a double-anthropologist: for another's culture, but also that of the majority.

7 Culture as *interpretation* and *translation*: the search for the "cultural equivalent" in the host culture

The object (culture), method (participant observation) and guiding principle (relativism) of anthropology entered a new phase in the first half of the twentieth century with structuralism. This philosophical movement, born within linguistics and then spread to many other social sciences, is based on the idea that reality is a structure, a complex set of relationships making up systems, without which the individual units cannot be understood, nor function. The study of such a structure, often concealed within the immediately perceptible forms, became the target also of anthropologists who began to research the invariants of "cultural

24 Even scholarship, when it seeks an anthropological approach and seeks to contextually study the concept of honor in the Arab and Western culture, for example, stops the investigation of Western culture after the duels of the 1800s (Cohan 2010).

structures" beneath variables that produce such a vast amount of cultural systems. With Marcel Mauss (1990) and Claude Lévi-Strauss (1969), anthropology goes in search of the universal structures of the gift and kinship.

The heritage of structuralism was overwhelmed by post-structuralism and post-modernism: these movements of thought put into question the actual existence of a structure, arguing that in fact there is nothing ontologically underlying social phenomena, but that "everything is speech," narration. It becomes essential, in this sense, to deconstruct the discourses and the language in which we are immersed to be able to break free from the power relations, which they express and make them producers of new meanings.

Another fundamental revolution within anthropological thought develops as a result of the spread of hermeneutic theory (Mootz 2010b). Hermeneutics moves from being the "art of reading and comprehending sacred, legal and literary texts" to become a seminal twenty-first century philosophy. Philosophical hermeneutics or hermeneutical philosophy "does not mean interpretation of philosophical texts, but access to a different theoretical dimension, in which interpretation becomes the fundamental question of philosophy." We assist in this way to a "universalization and radicalization of hermeneutics, pushed from the purely epistemological to the ontological plane" that can be summarized in the thought of Heidegger for whom "to exist is to interpret" (Benedetti 2010: 4).[25]

On this philosophical humus, Clifford Geertz (1973a, 1983) elaborates an idea of culture that marks a revolution analogous to that of relativism introduced by Franz Boas and Ruth Benedict: culture is no longer looked upon as a set of objects, practices, behaviors, *formae mentis*, but as "a web of significances" (Geertz 1973a: 5),[26] a semiotic space which can be navigated by those who fully master its rules of interpretation, having been socialized in this web.

A central element of the interpretive theory invests the role of anthropology as a science capable of navigating these networks of meaning. Geertz calls into question the pretense of objectivity of ethnographic observation: "what we call our data are really our own constructions of other people's constructions of what they and their compatriots are up to" (Geertz 1973a: 9).[27] Thus is born interpretive anthropology.

25 The author observes how: "the thought of the past century has been pinned on language. Linguistics, Semiology, Structuralism, new rhetoric, logical neo-positivism, the analysis of language, and hermeneutics, that has assumed such a pervasive dimension that contemporary thought is said to be characterized by a hermeneutic *koinè* . . . Even philosophy of law and positivist jurisprudence could not remain insensible to this intense cultural climate, with the result of new studies in the structure of juridical discourse within all its various forms. There is a critical revision of the syllogistic logic . . . there are researches into juridical arguments . . . But overall there is a change of orientation by the jurist, that has exalted the importance of the case law, with their rationales."

26 "The concept of culture I espouse . . . is essentially a semiotic one. Believing, with Max Weber, that man is an animal suspended in webs of significance he himself has spun, I take culture to be those webs, and the analysis of it to be therefore not an experimental science in search of law but an interpretive one in search of meaning."

27 The author adds that "descriptions of Berber, Jewish, or French culture" are not themselves Berber, Jewish or French people but rather are anthropological interpretations "because it is, in fact, anthropologists who profess them" (15).

In this context, every ethnographic assertion is disputable, is something built as a result of an interpretation. This awareness has provoked an anthropological reflection on the authority process and how the mere fact of using writing alters reality, which will be reprised by James Clifford and George Marcus (1986).

Reading cultures as webs of significances, we deviate permanently from the idea of the artifact and we are invited to read a behavior, an object, a mentality through the eyes of the other, not to make it operate in our semiotic web, but in theirs. In this theory of culture, the conflicts that arise in the context of multiculturalism are nothing but conflicts over meanings that we can solve by reciprocally learning the codes of communication.

The concept of culture as an interpretation returns to legal reasoning under various guises.

First, whenever judges or parties strive to find a "cultural equivalent" and then translate the other's cultural practice by finding a locus of meaning similar to what it would assume within the majority's system of signs. Interpreting is premised on recognizing that communication can take place in another's semiotic space and, starting from this premise, draw bridges of communication between the two spaces. Note the reasoning of the Canadian judge in the *Multani* case, which resolved the controversy of a Sikh boy who wanted wear the *kirpan* as part of his school uniform.[28] To the argument that the ritual knife could be a danger to other children because it was a weapon, the judge observes: "there are many objects in schools that could be used to commit violent acts and that are much more easily obtained by students, such as scissors, pencils and baseball bats." The fact that those objects are read by everyone in that web of significances not as weapons but as learning and recreational supplies, is analogous to the perception that the *kirpan* has for Sikhs, who are in fact authorized by the court to be able to bring them to school. But notice how the anthropological attitude is tempered by the pragmatic attitude of the law: the judge required that the *kirpan* remain sealed in its sheath.

Another example of culture as interpretation and translation is found in several decisions of Italian anthropologist judges who recognized that the Moroccan *kafalah* has effects similar to the institution of adoption for the purposes of familial reunification. In 2015 the Italian Supreme Court recognized the right of an uncle, Mr. Hassan El Assani who was the *kafil* on his brother's son, to reunite with his nephew.[29] The child was stopped in Casablanca as the Italian Consulate refused to release the visa, claiming that the *kafalah* was not enough to produce a family bond and that, admitting him would have been cheating the rules of adoption. The Supreme Court annulled the administrative prohibition, stating

28 *Multani v. Commission Scolaire Marguerite-Bourgeoys* (2006), 1 S.C.R. 256.

29 Italian Supreme Court (Cassazione) sec. I, civil, 2nd February, 2015, no. 1843. Even before, the Court of Appeal of Turin (Corte di Appello di Torino) decreed May 30th, 2007 in *Diritto, Immigrazione e Cittadinanza*, no. 1/2008, 191, 196, that: "this institution of Islamic law having the characteristic of indefinite duration . . . approximates the institution of adoption better than what happened with the family foster care, that has an essentially temporary nurturing nature."

that "*kafalah* realizes, in the best interest of the child, his protection in a cultural context different from the Italian one."

Another case that reflects an idea of interpretative culture is when judges (as seen in Chap. 2 sec. 7, especially in England) consider how long an immigrant has been a resident. In this way, they make implicit reference to the ability of people to understand what kinds of interpretations prevail in a given semiotic space, to learn how to move within the web of meanings, and to change their interpretative horizons.

The idea of culture as translation and interpretation is, in my opinion, crucial to elaborating a persuasive and understandable judicial solution to a multicultural conflict, and it will be incorporated in the cultural test proposed at the end of this book as a prong aimed at finding a cultural equivalent in the host culture (Chap. 4 sec. 5.9).

8 Culture as *authenticity*: the judge in search of "pure" cultures

The concept of authenticity was born in anthropological studies (Herzfeld 1987), as well as in other social sciences (Fisher 1992; Bramadat 2005b), with the advent of globalization – although some tracks can be found since the beginning of the discipline if one considers the goals of many anthropologists who went to live between colonized peoples specifically to collect customs and traditions before the colonization process blotted them out or altered their cultural production mechanisms.

Authenticity is a response to the fact that many groups suffered cultural genocide, and that through recovering traditions in their original forms they may heal the trauma. As some cultural processes were not physiological but pathological, the law is required to remedy an injustice (Fisher 1992; Appiah 2005). In the very idea of cultural rights, there is a factor of "protection" of something vulnerable. The way in which the cultural discourse enters the legal horizon was affected deeply by the post-colonial condition. It is, therefore, this shadow of injustice some cultures have suffered that keeps authenticity alive as an anthropological and legal value. At the same time, when authenticity comes into play in multicultural conflict resolution, it does not always produce a persuasive effect.

The authenticity paradigm finds many echoes in the law, both in constitutional texts, with the emergence of the categories of ancestral or historical rights, and in judicial opinion, where authenticity assumes two different profiles: diachronic and synchronic.

To have authenticity in a diachronic sense is when the judge thinks that only behavior that is rooted in the past and that recurs in the same cultural form is fit for and worthy of protection. The judges who appear more alert to this type of assessment are Canadian. In the case of the Mohawk who claimed the right to move freely along the Canada–United States border, the court consulted archaeologists to reconstruct exactly what kind of routes the Mohawk traversed before contact with Europeans: only if the Mohawk retraces the route faithfully to the past can he obtain protection (Chap. 2 sec. 5.1). As already noted, in this way, the practice of crossing the border is not permitted to controversially interact with other interests but must remain frozen in the past.

Diachronic authenticity presents several problematic aspects. I mention two in particular. The idea of culture as authenticity transferred to law fails to give voice to lifestyle choices that move on the border between two cultures. The cultural test forged to request the individual to keep a total adherence to all the elements of a fixed and static culture does not hold up to the recompositions and "contaminations" which cultures will naturally encounter.[30] Another problem with diachronic authenticity is that when the loss of authenticity is a consequence of colonialism, the refusal to recognize the other because they are no longer authentic risks perpetuating forms of neo-colonialism: the groups are punished and denied recognition for being culturally genocided.

Authenticity acquires relevance in the law also in a synchronic sense – that is when the judge measures the practice held by the subject on the basis of its compliance with the manner in which this is normally put in place by the group. According to this standard, if the subject diverges even partly from the practice, he could not find protection.

Whereas the diachronic authenticity is no longer scientifically supported in anthropology (except as a counter-discourse against the dispossession that globalization carries) following the demonstration that cultures are not fixed and immutable but evolve over time, synchronic authenticity could, conversely, be a reference point for the law to avoid "do-it-yourself" cultures or religions. Those who claim an important practice for their own personal identity should have a justification in the fact that this practice is shared by a group. On this point, as we have seen, the American model, with the culturally reasonable person test, introduced a form of connection between individual behavior and the authenticity of the group. This work attempts to bring anthropological knowledge into dialogue with the law in articulating the authenticity paradigm with the test prong by asking how the reasonable person in a similar cultural situation would act in the same circumstances (Chap. 4 sec. 5.7).

Alternatively, in cases not about culture but religion, the law differs largely from the authenticist paradigm. For example, in carrying out the sincerity test in both Canada and the United States to assess the recognition of religious practices, the sincerity of the subject prevails over the authenticity of a religion (Chap. 2 sec. 5.2 and 6.1). Another proof of the favor that the present legal order concedes to religion and denies to culture.

30 What happened with the Canadian pre-contact test is emblematic. In *R. v. Powley* (2003), 2 S.C.R. 207, the Canadian Supreme Court had to waive the requirement that the practice be strictly pre-contact to affirm that the test also applies to the culture of the Métis, a minority born from the unions of indigenous women with French settlers. This minority, which is recognized in sec. 35 Const. 1982 as one of three official aboriginal minorities, was in danger of losing protection because the pre-contact element required by the test excluded the whole group which, by definition, is entirely post-contact. With the exception of the Métis, however, the element that requires that the practice originated before contact with Europeans continues to be used and considered mandatory in Canada.

9 Culture as *creolization*: judicial recognition of cultural transformations

If the advent of globalization has accentuated the authenticity paradigm it has, at the same time, put it in crisis, by giving rise to cultural processes in which contamination, mixing and creolization (hybridization) have become the rule (Yastrzhembskiy 2013: 449). The object of the study of anthropology is thus changed: no longer small and potentially isolated communities, but groups that move between webs of meanings and that, in more or less traumatic ways, mix, become fluid and elaborate strategies to adapt (Breidenbach, Zukrigl 1998). These processes have had profound consequences in anthropological thought: if in principle it was studying "culture," then moved on to "cultures," perceived as separate units of human diversity, today it focuses on the study of "cultural processes." The idea of cultural process expresses a reality in transformation and departs from the static idea of culture in two ways: one objective, one subjective. Objectively, cultures are not something fixed in time. Subjectively, they are not external forces that shape individuals who belong to it. The idea of a cultural process, in fact, places at its center not culture as an entity with its own life, but rather the individual. To meet or clash are not cultures, but people (Aime 2004). This view, therefore, reiterates the agency of the subject, who can become an active protagonist of her own culture.

In the previous section we analyzed some attitudes of the courts inspired by the idea that only cultural behaviors that are pure and in accordance with the past can find recognition. However, the law has also absorbed the idea that cultures are, in fact, processes, flows.

Let's follow the reasoning of one judge in a case, which incorporates the idea of culture as creolization.

We are in Texas, in 2009.[31] A family changes residence and wants to move to Needville. When beginning to enroll their five-year-old child in the local school, the parents are notified that, according to the school rules, students must wear their hair short. The child's father is Native American and explains to the school authorities that for Indians, hair is an integral part of the spirit, which can only be cut in case of crucial events of existence (bereavement, an initiation etc.) as it marks a person's presence on this earth: outside of these circumstances the "loss of hair equated to loss of a body part."

The judge, by adopting the Indian perspective – for which clothing or long hair are no mere look, but imbued with a spiritual meaning – agrees that the practice of wearing long hair qualifies as religious. In fact, the first requirement of the US religious tests (Chap. 2 sec. 6.1) evaluates the concept of religion in the broadest terms that fully allow inclusion of the native religion.

But at this point, problems arise. For the US religious test requires that the father actually and sincerely practiced the native religion. And, in the course of that determination, the court is faced with a human biography that took place

31 *A.A. v. Needville Independent School District*, U.S. District Court for the Southern district of Texas, Houston division, civil action n. H-08-2934, January 20, 2009.

among the insignia of hybridization, through a path of interruptions, expulsions and rapprochements from the original cultural group.

The school, for example, observes that the father of the child has been brought up as a Christian and how for many years he practiced as a Methodist and, therefore, cannot be considered a true member of the native religion, which he joined as an adult.

The school also observes that the practice of keeping long hair is not an expression of the group to which the father belongs. In fact, he is a member of a "bald tribe."

However, this court adopts the idea of creolization. The cultural expert who is heard at the trial explains how cultures evolve and how the native identity is no longer exclusively allocated in single tribes: "as a result of losing contact with their original tribe, many younger generations of Indians have adopted one sense of 'Indianness'. Often, Pan-Indianism is based on images of Plains Indians, wearing long hair in braids, or sometimes free-flowing." This new collective identity expresses a resistance to the process of colonization and is, therefore, necessarily "post-contact." For many Indians the two identities (of their original tribe and Pan-Indianist) coexist, while for others – whose groups are culturally missing or extremely weak – there exists only that last, contemporary matrix.

Because of this framework provided by the anthropologist, the court decides in favor of the child and allows him to be able to wear long hair.

Another example of the judicial recognition of creolization is the affirmation of the cultural assimilation defense, as a cause of justification or mitigating circumstance to reduce the penalties for deported immigrants who remain within the United States, adducing, on this point, that they have already assimilated into the culture (Porto 2005).

10 *Panculturalism*: "blaming culture for bad behavior" in judicial reasoning

Panculturalism (from the Greek *pan* which means all) is that attitude that sees a form of culture in any way of life and an expression of culture in any behavior. The effect of panculturalism is that every aspect of social life can be read *sub specie* of culture. Everything is potentially "absorbable" in that category: thus one speaks of urban cultures (to explain phenomena such as squatters or rappers), black culture, gay culture, queer culture, transsexual culture or the culture of the deaf, blind, disabled, or feminine communities (Gutmann 2003); such appellations are extended even to sports culture, yoga culture, vegan culture and so on. In this way the concept of culture expands its borders, but also loses, in some way, its epistemological utility.

Anthropology carefully sets borders to the concept of culture: even when it defines it as "a way of life" it requires some minimum standard for practices, such as to be shared among a group or be recurrent and not occasional.

The law may fall into a panculturalist attitude when it begins to classify any behavior as "cultural" for the simple fact that it has been committed by a foreigner.

Among the "lists" that scholarship, and in particular criminal law, has traced for culturally oriented acts are found as follows:

> violence in the family: mistreatment and kidnapping to the detriment of family members; kidnappings of young women aiming to impose an arranged marriage; suppression of family members who rebel against the rules and the code of ethics of the family of origin . . . Crimes of enslavement. Crimes against sexual freedom: sexual abuse of underage girls; sexual abuse of older women . . . Failure to provide compulsory education. International terrorism offenses.
> (Basile 2010: 165–237)

The list is full of stereotypes, and shows an uncritical adherence, by the judges, to the use of the cultural category (Viganò 2011). These catalogs, if deconstructed, reveal that in several cases the culturalization of a behavior is disputable (Chap. 4 sec. 5.1) as they blame culture for bad behavior (Volpp 2000) or the culturalization is rooted in the Western Christian experience of a group, as in the case of the Indian caste system (Jalki, Pathan, Shah 2017).

11 Culture as *ethnosphere*: cultural diversity as a value for the whole society

In the itinerary to trace parallels between the ideas of culture developed in anthropology and the way in which these "return" in the law, another stage leads us to the concept of the ethnosphere.[32]

Coined on the matrix of the concept of the biosphere, the ethnosphere presupposes that the preservation of a distinct cultural unit is a value in itself. Ethnodiversity deserves protection similar to biodiversity since, just as one guarantees the possibility of genetic exchange, so does the other keep cultural possibilities alive. Based on this premise, many anthropologists have raised the alarm about the risks of the reduction of cultural diversity in the world, phenomena which in the long run will produce a restriction of horizons and possibilities of life choices for how to be human.[33]

What in anthropological relativism was a neutral attitude, based simply on the descriptive finding that, from a biological identity, people become human beings in socially diverse ways, this attitude has become charged with a value dimension because these ways are at risk.

Such views supported within anthropology return to the legal universe through the emergence of what could be described as a new constitutional principle: cultural diversity (Parolari 2016), understood as a public good to be

32 "Just as there is a biological web of life, there is also a cultural and spiritual web of life – what we at the *National Geographic* have taken to calling the 'ethnosphere.' It's really the sum total of all the thoughts, beliefs, myths, and institutions brought into being by the human imagination" (Davis 2002).

33 "When asked the meaning of being human, all the diverse cultures of the world respond with 10,000 different voices. Distinct cultures represent unique visions of life itself, morally inspired and inherently right. And those different voices become part of the overall repertoire of humanity for coping with challenges confronting us in the future . . . As we drift toward a blandly amorphous, generic world, as cultures disappear and life becomes more uniform, we as a people and a species, and Earth itself, will be deeply impoverished" (Davis 2002). Concerning "vanishing cultures" see also Yastrzhembskiy (2013).

protected and, in some jurisdictions, even one of the founding principles of democracy. This reading marks a radical new way to perceive cultural diversity: not only as an advantage to be accorded to the minority, but also as a situation of value for the majority.

The presence of such a perception is gathered in the thirty constitutions that, at the present moment, recognize multiculturalism (Appendix: the status of culture in constitutions) and in the UNESCO Universal Declaration on Cultural Diversity of 2001 which reads: "cultural diversity is as necessary for humankind as biodiversity is for nature" (art. 1).

Given the presence of the concept of the ethnosphere in legal texts, it should be noted that among the research reviewed, the reason that judges give to recognize the cultural validity of the argument is almost never the perception of cultural diversity as a public good, but rather anthropological conviction that the person acted under an irrepressible cultural input that mitigates his culpability or the need to take into account the point of view of others.

However, there are a few decisions in which the judge seems to shift from this approach, to move towards a value adhesion to the concept of cultural diversity. In addition to the *Chapman* case, in which the European Court of Human Rights states that the protection of minorities has a value for the whole society (Chap. 2 sec. 6), there is also the *Multami* case, decided by the Canadian Supreme Court in 2006 to address the request to include the Sikh *kirpan* in school uniform, which describes multiculturalism as "part of the democratic principles" (Chap. 2 sec. 5.2).

12 *Turning away* from culture in anthropology: the crisis of multiculturalism in the law

It is not just a certain "syndrome of the crises" diffused a little through all disciplines that has caused the appearance in the anthropological debate of ideas such as: "against culture" (Abu-Lughod 1991),[34] "beyond culture" (Gupta, Ferguson 1992), "rethinking culture" (Bohannan 1973), "rewriting culture" (Watson 1991) or "the end of anthropology" (Comaroff 2010). The concept of culture has long been subjected to a critical process (Hobsbwam, Ranger 1983; Trouillot 1991; Fabietti 1995; Remotti 1996; Brubaker, Cooper 2000):

> two broad and intersecting sources of unease infuse anthropology beginning in the mid-1970s, and become broadly recognized by the end of the twentieth century: a gradual rejection of a unitary notion of culture and the growing concern about how anthropological paradigms and frameworks shape or distort understanding the social experiences of others.
>
> (Moore 2009: 290)

34 The solution that Abu-Lughod suggests is what she calls the "ethnography of the particular" that is a way of performing ethnography based on the particularities of the subject, without any pretense of extrapolating generalizations.

From the beginnings of the discipline up to structuralism, culture was seen as having a superorganic nature, an autonomous ontological entity with its own rules, which transcended the individuals who composed it. In the critiques that developed since 1970, the concept began to be considered lacking of real substance, as cultures do not exist as systems in their own right, but live embodied in individual subjects (Hylland Eriksen 2004: 86). Even the idea of a cultural system as a whole is called into question as it does not take into account the differences within the group (Sapir 1968), and the fact that the groups are sub-divisible in so many ways (Sen 2006). Not to mention the complaints against processes of artificial creation, of the invention of culture (Anderson 1983; Hobsbwam, Ranger 1984; McCrone, Morris, Kiely 1995; Abu-Laban, Gabriel 2002).

But the decisive blow against the concept of culture has come from postmodernism (Rabinow 1986). The attention to the power structures that lie behind social constructs and discourses drove anthropologists to question whether the concept of culture is not, in fact, an imperialist product, created in a given place and time by the precise structures which serve power. Structures of Western powers, for which culture appears as a new "social" device with which to perceive the other, substitutes for race but plays, in sweeter terms, the same building effect of any artificial alterity (Winant 2004; Lentin, Titley 2011: 62–69). But there are also structures of power internal to individual groups: since often what is seen as culture is actually how an elite group defines it and how the law recognizes it is likely to be, therefore, the validation of the choices of such elites (Eisenberg, Spinner-Halev 2005; Mulhern 2009: 41).

Another attack on the idea of culture comes not from theory but from a situation of fact: globalization (Tucci 2004). Concepts like cosmopolitanism, deterritorialization, transnationalism and creolization highlight a reality that appears inexplicable by resort to such a concept as culture (Hannerz 1992, 1996).[35] When contacts become so strong, as happened in the context of globalization, they call into question the very idea of whether the cultural units which meet each other even exist: in fact, through the encounter they dissolve (Brettel 2006; Robins 2006). This has led some anthropologists to suggest abandoning the very concept of culture as a surpassed categorical armamentarium and have thus introduced a certain cultural nihilism into the discipline.

35 Hannerz (1996) observes that it is uncertain if globalization will produce "less culture or more" (23) and that even in the global world the concept of culture "can be kept genuinely useful" (43). See also the observations of Appadurai (1991): "the landscapes of group identity – the ethnoscapes – around the world are no longer familiar anthropological objects, insofar as groups are no longer tightly territorialized, spatially bounded, historically unself-conscious, or culturally homogenous" (191); "tourists, immigrants, refugees, exiles, guest-workers, and other moving groups and persons constitute an essential feature of the world" (192). "A central challenge for current anthropology is to study the cosmopolitan cultural forms of the contemporary world" – a task which seems impossible without studying the "transnational cultural flows" that reframe "the link between space, stability, and cultural reproduction. There is an urgent need to focus on the cultural dynamics of what is now called ***deterritorialization***. This term applies not only to obvious examples such as transnational corporations and money markets, but also to ethnic groups, sectarian movements, and political formations, which increasingly operate in ways that transcend specific territorial boundaries and identities" (192).

Anthropological nihilism seems to not have had a particular impact on the case law. It suffices to chart the dates of the cases examined in this study to see how use of the cultural argument has grown. However, it would be impossible to deny that the last fifteen years have been characterized by a crisis of legal literature which seems to evoke a kind of swan song of multiculturalism (Parekh 2000; Kelly 2002; Baubock 2003; Phillips 2007; Welsh 2008; Barry 2009; Bertossi 2010; Christensen 2012; Taras 2013; Malik 2015).

A series of political events produced its delegitimization: the New York attack on the World Trade Center's Towers on 11 September 2001,[36] the murder of Theo Van Gogh in the Netherlands in 2004, the terrorist attacks on 11 March 2005 in Madrid and 7 July 2005 in London, the affair of the twelve Muhammad cartoons published in the Danish newspaper *Jyllands-Posten* in 2005, the violent reactions to the film *The Innocence of Muslims* in 2012, a series of declarations by political leaders – David Cameron (Mahamdallie 2011), Josè Manuel Barroso,[37] Angela Merkel[38] – proclaiming the failing of multicultural policies; the massacre at Charlie Hebdo in Paris on 7 January 2015 and at Bataclan Paris on 13 November 2015; the bombing of Bruxelles airport and other institutions on 22 March 2016.

But these are not only the contingencies of the moment. At the doctrinal level, even Will Kymlicka (2007) has had a "multicultural crisis," saying – almost as an abjuration – that what looked like a globalizable model actually was based on Canadian specificity and was not, therefore, exportable in tense situations like those caused by migration in Europe.

Despite this political and doctrinal context, it cannot be said that the questions of multiculturalism have all been answered and that we can go back as if the questions raised in the last sixty years had not changed the legal horizon and even concepts of law (eg. the new category of cultural rights, the cultural defense). A dry return to the pre-multicultural period is unlikely and what is recorded in the courts – but also in social services, municipalities, public offices, schools – proves it handily. The need for a theoretical construction of diversity remains, therefore, within the agenda of the law (Haddock, Sutch 2003; Modood 2007).

The swan song, if anything, can refer to a certain way of understanding multiculturalism that has, in recent years, overlooked the fact that every cultural conflict is a relation. In this respect, the idea of interculturalism may better evoke the idea of a dialogue between cultures. It is just as important that the law allow intersectional lessons, which invite readings of behavior using several categories: culture, class, race, gender. With respect to this last category, for instance, feminists have staged a "classificatory fight" with anthropology in order to add or substitute the frame of patriarchy for culture.

36 Modood (2011) reports "the beginning of the end" on the publication of the *Satanic Verses* by Salman Rushdie in 1989.

37 In the discourse held at Strasbourg on February 15th, 2005 when he was president of the European Commission.

38 "Multiculturalism has failed" www.repubblica.it/esteri/2010/10/16/news/merkel_modello_multiculturale-8138678/

13 Culture as *patriarchy*: the feminist objection to culture – the shifting from "culturally motivated crimes" to "gender crimes" in the law

A major critique which has put concepts of culture and of multiculturalism in crisis comes from feminism, which has raised the possibility that what we call "culture" is, instead, "patriarchy"[39] and has launched a battle to de-culturalize many customs to re-read them using feminist terms: female genital mutilation, forms of domestic violence inflicted as a direct consequence of the disobedience to the orders of the husband or father, honor killings, arranged marriages, polygamy, the wearing of traditional garments such as the *hijab*, the *niqab*, the *chador* or the *burqa*, the dowry in family law, divorce rules, the *purdah*, and so on.

The theoretical reflection on the borders that can be traced between the two concepts of culture and patriarchy can be synthesized into two opposite positions.

A first position is sustained mainly within anthropology, which holds that the claim of feminism to deculturalize gender practices is not solid, and insists on the cultural classification of the above-mentioned behaviors; patriarchy is a Western concept inapplicable to other cultures that must been understood through their own lenses (Fox-Genovese 1982; Strathern 1984). Even feminist anthropology has been skeptical about the possibility to use patriarchy as an all-encompassing concept present in each culture, preferring more neutral terms such as "gender system" (Rubin 1975).

A second position, inspired by the radical feminist panpatriarchal attitude, which became widespread in the 1970s, is at the opposite extreme. This position is based on the assumption that every society is built on a symbolic order, or a political contract that embodies patriarchy (Pateman 1988) in such a way that the majority if not all the behaviors towards women are oppressive. Patriarchy is considered the longest-lasting global system of inequality and privilege in history, in continuous existence since 3000 B.C. or perhaps even longer, that started to be challenged radically with the second wave of feminism but still persists, both in industrialized and in traditional societies.[40]

Far from being a pure academic exercise of classification, the choice of under which label to classify cultural practices involving women may have a huge impact

39 According to a neutral definition, patriarchy is a family system based on the "Rule of the father," in which fathers or father-figures hold authority over women and children. Feminism broadened this definition by looking at patriarchy as a system of familial, social, political and legal power that makes men prevail over women (Walby 1990).

40 In general, Western societies recognize, at most, the persistence of circumscribed "legacies" of the patriarchal system: sexism, male chauvinism, the wage gap between men and women, and paternalism. Conversely, it is believed that patriarchy survives in the form of systematic oppression of women in many "traditional" cultures that, with emigration to Europe and more generally to the West, carry with them gender relations rooted in this logic. One proof often adduced to this dichotomy is that the Western legal systems have been almost all amended by anti-patriarchal legislation (apart from a few residuals such as the laws on surname transmission), while other legal systems still permit strong discriminations.

upon their judicial and legislative regulation. In fact, the legal scenario is the opposite, as culture is generally perceived as endowed of some value to be protected within the constitutional states, while on the contrary, patriarchy as gender oppression is strongly opposed. Think on the different framing that can be given to female genital mutilation: one of the many anthropological readings is that it is a kind of aesthetic plastic surgery: a way through which women beautify themselves (Yastrzhembskiy 2013: 63). But after the 2012 UN Resolution it was prohibited as gender violence.

Multicultural jurisprudence shows an ambivalent position toward patriarchy (see Chap. 2 sec. 11). The concept is sometimes blurred with the concept of culture, or complementary to it and supports the concession of mitigating factors (as seen in the *Pusceddu* case, Chap. 1 sec. 2.2); other times it acquires an autonomous dimension, that leads the judge to re-write the conflict as a "gender crime" or "patriarchal crime," depriving it of any excuse (as seen in the *Saleem* case, Chap. 1 sec. 1.2), and even implying an increase in punishment (as seen in the FGM treatment in Italy with law 7/2006, Chap. 2 sec. 11). This trend, as shown, is consolidating.

In my opinion, a synthesis of the present positions can be formed through a unified theory of patriarchy and culture that invites the judge to examine a behavior under both categories before reaching a conclusion.[41] Let's take arranged marriage as an example: using patriarchy, it appears to be an oppressive practice, which subordinates the will of young women and men to their parents; but under the lenses of culture, other elements emerge.

First, there are some logical and persuasive elements in delegating the choice of one's spouse to persons who know very well what is good for their sons and daughters and who would never harm them. Particularly in a context of an enlarged family where a bad choice of the partner can affect many more persons than in a nuclear family, the idea of involving other persons – themselves affected by the decisions – may appear reasonable.

Second, the idea of love is not necessarily based on the principle "I love you therefore I marry you," but can be based on the opposite: "I married you therefore I love you" (Fromm 1956).

Third, by looking through the other's cultural lenses it is possible to see that those who practice arranged marriage consider the romantic system of choice as totally irrational as the supposed free choice is actually under the influence of strong passions.[42] This criticism is today proven by science that compares the effect of falling in love to drugs (eg. dopamine stimulated by cocaine). In this sense, no free and rational choice is practiced by Westerners either.

41 When "gender and culture are theorized as distinct this does not help the cause for women" (Phillips 2003: 531).

42 "The choice of a girl just come from the nursery, and desirous by nature to get a husband, in an affair on which the happiness of her whole life depends, can neither deserve that respect nor consideration which is due to the choice of her parents, who have profited by experience, and are not blinded by passion," quoted in Nader (2015: 275).

Fourth, it is important to note that the value of choice is itself a cultural creation which is not present in other webs of meaning that consider the needs of the community over one's egotistic interests.

The analogy drawn between the two practices of selecting one's own partner (passion choice/decision of the parents) does not lead to condemn arranged marriages *per se* as merely patriarchal, as some persuasive cultural elements in them, excluding the case of violent imposition, may be taken into account.

Given its constitutional protections, freedom of religion seems immune to the anti-patriarchal attack that culture is facing. My suggestion is that religion should also be included in this unified theory and cross-checked under patriarchy. Although religion is recognized in many states as an autonomous legal system,[43] the pervasiveness of the anti-patriarchal argument should not halt its scrutiny at the practices of any creed. Think only for a moment on the absence from the public debate on multicultural conflicts of this religious practice: the exclusion of women from access to the priesthood in the Catholic and many other cults. It seems to me a double standard that female circumcision is prohibited in the name of gender, while oppressive practices such as the exclusion of women from the clergy, involving a strong component of human experience – is not spirituality as important as sexuality? – are not questioned.

The importance of gender in the current debate is addressed in the test proposed at the conclusion of this work by including the question: Does the practice perpetuate patriarchy? (Chap. 4 sec. 5.12). This question is crucial to shed light on possible patriarchal dimensions of the practice without blurring its cultural components.

14 Relevance of the concept of culture and endorsement of a new relation between law and anthropology

If the concept of culture has been ever-changing almost from the moment in which it was drafted, the nihilistic temptation, seeking to deny its epistemological utility, is surely strong. If what is culture is uncertain even to anthropology, is it appropriate to include this within the conceptual universe of the law? Is there not a risk of finding a useless tool, if not a misleading one?

Despite all this, the law and the constitutional law in particular cannot fail to address the issue by taking refuge behind epistemological inconsistency. To abandon this concept would mean to abandon many demands of justice, presented to the law by anthropology and its new way of conceiving human beings honed by its fights against colonial oppression.

The jurisprudential framework which emerges is varied, but it is possible to find some constants that reveal the formation of shared, fixed points on how to

43 For instance, in Italy, religious rules are protected as autonomous legal systems as they are covered by art. 7 of the Italian Constitution which states that "The State and the Catholic Church are, each within its own order, independent and sovereign."

utilize the concept of culture. Although many jurisprudential responses are the result of the contingent history of the individual jurisdictions in which they were produced, confronted with the comparative method, they reveal fragments of a larger cultural discourse. Rather than leave the discourse to internal national developments deprived of poles, it is possible to assemble the comparative constants in order to help judges and legislatures to develop a more informed discourse (Chap. 2 sec. 12).

Moreover, the critiques of the concept of culture relate to a certain way of understanding it and do not preclude, perhaps, a recodification with other characteristics.

An attempt to actualize the concept appears in the fact that it has become the axis of new disciplines (Ahmed, Shore 1995; Brumann 1999; Giglioli, Ravaioli 2004), supplementary and partly competitive with anthropology. Consider cultural studies (Sarat, Simon 2003). These also make culture the principal object of investigation, but radically change the method, replacing ethnographic participatory observation – which today is a cornerstone of anthropology even when studying Western civilization – with the deconstruction techniques of Derrida, the structuralists (De Sausurre, Lévi-Strauss, Barthes) and post-structuralists (Foucault, Bourdieu), and the Gramscian concept of hegemony, which is extended from hegemony within capitalism to other structures of power/subordination. In particular, cultural studies pay great attention to cultural narratives, those discourses produced by the dominant group to describe another group that, across their diverse narratives, is placed in the position of oppression or subjugation, even if only symbolically (Geller, Stockett 2006).

Also centered primarily around the concept of culture are post-colonial studies that question how the construction of the other proceeds and, again in the wake of a deconstructive approach, analyze the microforces of power this supports (Said 1993). Post-colonial studies are very careful to denounce as post-colonial some choices which are currently steeped in colonial legacies and perpetuate, in some way, oppressive practices.

These ferments reveal that "there is a reason why the social sciences and politics look to anthropology for a concept of culture that is more useful, and not for other concepts" (Shweder 2001: 3157).[44]

Those described in this chapter are some of the main concepts of culture that coexist, often in contradictory fashion, in the current historical moment, and that, not surprisingly, are borne out both in anthropology and in law. This analysis

44 The author suggests, in one view, a "light" definition of culture: one that "does not imply the absence of debate, contestation, or dispute among members of a group. Nor does it necessarily imply the existence of within-group homogeneity in knowledge, belief, or practice . . . Not everything has to be shared for a 'culture' to exist. Members of a cultural community do not always agree about this or that, but they do take an interest in each other's ideas about what is true, good, beautiful, and efficient because those ideas (and related practices) have a bearing on the perpetuation of their way of life, and what they share is that collective inheritance" (Shweder 2001: 3157).

reconstructs fragments (because the debate is fragmented[45]) of the discourse around culture and allows some reflection on the role of law within this discourse: Is the law an active protagonist or, rather, a passive recipient?

As the analysis has brought to light, often ideas of culture pass through the legal universe into forms of clichés, in rather unconscious ways. Sometimes this happens because of the lack of training of the judge to work in multicultural contexts. Sometimes this is because the support of the cultural expert, donning the mantle of technicality, leads the judge to abdicate ***modus iuridicus***, and to seek a ***modus anthropologicus*** instead.

The ideas of culture and of human being elaborated within anthropology have altered the sense of justice and insinuated doubts and upheavals in the legal experience. In this sense the values of coexistence have changed, partly in the sense to recognize this alterity, and in some cases even to consider it as a source of mutual enrichment. From this exchange, however, it remains to consider that law and anthropology have profoundly different evaluative spaces and social tasks.

On this basis, it is possible to advance some observations on the relationship between the two disciplines in the near future.

As is known, the relationship between anthropology and law dates back in time and each has given rise to its own cross-discipline: law and anthropology and the anthropology of law, in the Anglo-Saxon world (Donovan, Edwin Anderson III 2003; Freeman, Napier 2009): *l'anthropologie juridique*, in France; *l'antropologia giuridica* in Italy (Sacco 2007). Many of the early anthropologists had legal training and, from the start, the contacts were innumerable. If, on the one hand, anthropology has attempted to anthropologize law, making it one of the many cultural products of a given society, on the other hand, the law has provided anthropology with many categories of analysis: folk law, *vendetta*, normative pluralism, dispute resolution etc.

However, this encounter has long remained, somehow, an intellectual exercise, a fruitful exchange, but confined within the walls of the academy. Currently, there is the need of a new interaction. In multicultural societies, in particular through the involvement of anthropologists invited by judges to witness in trials, a need to switch from "law and anthropology" to the "law through anthropology" and to use the tools of anthropology to not only study the law, but also forge practical tools and more effective frames for a full understanding of multicultural conflicts is emerging.

Beyond the anthropological investigation of legal categories, beyond the search for other forms of juridicity in non-Western societies, all of which are domains that have been widely explored, this work hopes that the dialogue between law

45 In the economy of the present work I could not give account of every movement that has surrounded the concept of culture. Among the most important that I have not considered, cultural materialism merits mention, a theory that sees culture as an adaptive strategy with which humanity resolve material problems (Harris 1968, 1979). Neither have I mentioned the fact that an early phase of anthropology was characterized by the study of the reasons of cultural variances: anthropologists were divided between diffusionists and the supporters of the theory of casual convergence (Kuper 1996).

and anthropology may renew along this front. It is hoped that the interaction between the two disciplines bring about the elaboration of a cultural test that can be operatively used in conflict resolution and includes the greater presence of anthropologists in the processes, to assist the judge in the work of interpretation and translation of other webs of significance (Chap. 4).

The endorsement of a renewed encounter between law and anthropology does not mean passive internalization by the law of the concepts of anthropology, but it does mean putting the two disciplines in a dialectical relationship, without excluding that at some point their paths may diverge.

The assessment by anthropology of cultural elements, in fact, differs in respect to the dimension, the weight and the questions it raises in the law. Anthropology, with a few exceptions (evolutionism, exoticism and the ethnosphere), does not assign either a positive or a negative value to the diversity of the other. It simply takes note.

If the anthropological experience is essentially descriptive, legal experience is in its essence an ethical experience, aimed to seek the rule of the case and to ensure social coexistence. Unlike anthropology, law proposes accommodations, seeks mediation and contact points between cultures. Also, unlike anthropology for which the question of the correctness of the solution remains silent, and for which the incommensurability of cultures can sometimes be total, the law has to resolve cases that in some way call into question the sense of justice of a society and that often cannot admit a solution of mutual coexistence in two separate spheres. The problem with the court arises from the fact that this sense of justice cannot be what existed before contact with each other. It has changed and it is problematized, partly because the other does not perceive certain behaviors as unjust, and partly because that behavior reveals the injustice of some of the host culture's practices (Chap. 4 sec. 5.9).

Another strong difference between the anthropological experience and the legal experience consists in the different approaches to the interference factor. The anthropologist studying a culture has no power to change its symbolic mechanisms and practices, or to affect the intergenerational transmission of values and beliefs, and anthropology does not claim any transformative instance of the culture which it examines. And not just because it is a descriptive science, but because the anthropologist's method and *forma mentis* translates into a full adherence to the point of view of others.[46] Conversely, the law is in constant transformative tension with society. The judge, but more generally anyone involved in legal experience, is immersed in a tension that requires the search for more just and reasonable rules in that historical moment, is in an impasse of arguments and reasons from which she must choose, is in a rapport that looks to the future. The argument "it is of another culture" has a vital importance for anthropology, for which, in some way, it represents a point of no return: beyond this threshold everything that happens should be explained with different eyes,

46 Actually anthropology has had an opposite attitude, a conservative one, protective of cultures as they are.

and all judgment suspended. But the law, conversely, cannot stop there. In this sense, many *topoi* and cultural tests examined appear deficient in a relational part and clip the wings of legal experience. Even the most sophisticated test does not include questions that are at the heart of legal experience: what will happen in the future? Recognizing this practice, how does the law contribute to future coexistence? In what way does this decision bring together, or rather, risk separating the two cultural worlds?

Can the differences between the two disciplines be so radical that the law cannot cross the impervious paths of culture? Must it proceed self-sufficiently and develop its own idea of culture and make its own autonomous cultural discourse? It is neither necessary, nor desirable. The law cannot disregard the knowledge that anthropology has achieved and substitute its own. At the same time, it should also go further. If the argument "it is of another culture, you cannot see everything that you think you see" proves to be a powerful reason for judges, this argument is not persuasive in its relativistic nakedness: it must be enriched and integrated.

The law cannot stop at the fact that the other is different. The law's response to Kimura, who sacrifices her children because she is unable to perceive them as something else and cannot leave them alone in this world, can neither be one of mute horror nor a resigned acceptance that Kimura thinks that way and never will think differently. Legal experience is a comparative experience of reasons: reasons not necessarily already contained in the law in itself, reasons that change historically, some to disappear forever, others to resurface like an underground river elsewhere, and others to appear suddenly, illuminating *ex novo* the horizon of law. It becomes, for example, essential that the person belonging to another culture cannot by that fact alone make resort to an anthropological justification, but must present convincing reasons (Chap. 4 sec. 5.13).

In this different view of functions and benefits of the two sciences in question, the cultural test proposed in the next chapter is designed both to incorporate anthropological knowledge in judicial reasoning and to highlight the dimension of dialogical relations, through which the law tries to pursue the encounter.

Part III

Prescriptive analysis

A proposal of a cultural test

4 A test as contribution to the resolution of multicultural conflicts

1 Cultural tests in scholarship

The idea of criteria for ordering the recognition of the cultural element has been explored more carefully in the scholarship of recent years.

Alison Dundes Renteln has been a pioneer in this path. A principal supporter of the official recognition of the cultural defense in the United States[1] and elsewhere[2] (Dundes Renteln 2011), this scholar suggested a test as a legal tool, consisting of the following questions (Dundes Renteln 2004: 207):

1 Is the litigant a member of the ethnic group?
2 Does the group have such a tradition?
3 Was the litigant influenced by the tradition when he or she acted?

This argumentative scansion has the merit of uniting both objective and subjective assessments and urging the judge to reflect on the culturality of a case. At the same time, Renteln's test does not disregard the relational part of the controversy. In fact, although not explicitly integrated in the test, her reasoning aims to incorporate the point of view of the victim by asking, if all other prongs of the test are answered in the affirmative: Is the practice irreparably harmful? (Dundes Renteln 2004: 208). In this way the task of the judge is not exclusively that of an anthropologist going in search of the cultural dimension of behavior, but remains that of a judge going in search of the rule of the individual case, of a fair solution which would make coexistence possible, balancing the different interests involved in the

1 Dundes Renteln (2002: 199) theorizes a "right to the cultural defense" as a *species* of the broader *genus* of cultural rights and notes: "there has not been any serious attempt to connect the right to culture to the cultural defense, though it is precisely in cases involving the cultural defense that individuals seek to protect ome of their cultural rights."

2 In fact, the cultural defense could be invoked also in case of cultural crimes committed by Westerners abroad, see Dundes Renteln (2009a) who reports: the case of kisses on the cheek between Richard Gere and a Bollywood actress, that has provoked criticism for obscene acts within Indian public opinion; cases of crimes connected to the consumption of drugs or violations of certain codes of dress or behavior, as in the case of a couple caught kissing on a Dubai beach and accused of committing "sex outside of marriage" because their kisses between the unwed couple were regarded as sexual acts. The couple risked two years in prison, but later the charges were settled with fines.

dispute. In this test the word "culture" does not work as a magic formula that, once pronounced, produces predetermined consequences. In fact, a positive response to the three first questions of the test does not imply that the court must necessarily take account of cultural factors. The author is, in the first place, concerned that the culturality of a behavior be ignored *a priori*, causing a slanted representation of the other. Once the judge has a clear cultural framework, he must still proceed to a balancing that, according to the author, should be maximally inspired to favor toward cultural recognition, but still subject to the irreparable harm condition. Renteln's position can be summarized as: culture is a way of life, which should have the right to be represented in courts; but the existence of culture does not imply an obligation toward recognition, as a way of life which operates against coexistence cannot be recognized (Dundes Renteln 2002, 2010b).

Also in the Canadian academy there have been proposals for a standardized resolution of cultural conflicts. Avigail Eisenberg (2009: 12) suggests a "regulatory" framework to resolve multicultural conflicts based on the assessment of three conditions:

1 *Jeopardy condition* – "important and otherwise unrealizable dimensions of a group's or individual's identity will be severely jeopardized in the absence of granting the claim."
2 *Validation condition* – "the practice is suitably validated through legitimate processes internal to the community and, where relevant, between communities."
3 *Safeguard condition* – "the claim, if protected, will not place people at risk of serious harm."

The guidelines suggested by Eisenberg pay attention to the conditions to possibly refuse to grant a cultural practice and, in all other cases, the author opts for an openness towards recognition.

Also the Italian criminal law scholarship has expressed the need to govern the use of the cultural argument. According to Cristina De Maglie (2010: 253–260), we should incorporate into Italian law a "narrow concept of culturally motivated crime," in the presence of which a "cause of non-punishment" operates. This would be a very limited notion, based on what the author calls "three degrees of verification":

1 *Cultural motivation*: the finding that the crime is an expression of a cultural practice.
2 *Coincidence of reaction*: the finding of a similar pattern between the behavior of the defendant and what could have been committed by any reasonable person belonging to her group.
3 *Distinctiveness between cultures*: the finding of a cultural peculiarity between the country of origin and the host country and the exclusion from recognition of behaviors that are common to both groups or universally spread.

Fabio Basile (2017: 131–133) identifies "three variables" – also defined as "test" by the scholar (Basile 2017: 134) – that should guide the assessment of culturally motivated crimes:

1. *Offensiveness of the conduct* (livello di offensività del fatto commesso). The judge should ascertain: the kind of "juridical interest or right" (*bene giuridico*) prejudiced by the conduct; its rank within the legal system (eg. constitutional, fundamental right); the level of danger, if the offensiveness is concrete (there is an actual victim) or potential (i.e. there is a general risk that the *kirpan* or the *burqa* may be used to commit violent acts).
2. *The features of the cultural norm* (natura della norma culturale). The judge should ascertain whether the cultural norm is: a religious norm (in this case the freedom of religion might justify the behavior); a juridical norm (*norma positivizzata*) in the migrant's legal system; a compulsory norm; a norm which is unequivocally shared by the minority group or, on the contrary, contested by part of the same group.
3. *Personal background of the offender* (biografia del soggetto agente). The judge should ascertain the immigrant's level of integration in the host country; the immigrant's level of adherence to/compliance with the cultural norm. Alongside the period of stable residence in the host country it is important to understand if there is an *ignorantia legis* that might be excusable.

According to Fabio Basile, Italian judges are already intuitively applying this three-step test in their rulings (Basile 2017: 132–135).

The conditions suggested reflect *topoi* that are forming as part of a common Western legal tradition to resolve multicultural conflicts.[3]

Moving again from the consideration that "courts have not used a systematic approach" (Dore 2016: 551) to solve multicultural conflicts, Isaak I. Dore identifies twelve conditions that should be respected to provide a cultural defense and that at the same time represent limits to it. Those conditions are (Dore 2016: 552):

1. Genuine membership in a native class
2. Motivation on the part of the defendant by a cultural belief system
3. Innocent nature of defendant's conduct
4. Uniform acceptance of such conduct by the native class of culture
5. The absence of victim harm
6. The lack of violence
7. The lack of intent
8. Absence of culpable mental state
9. Absence of extraneous proof of blameworthiness
10. Lack of moral turpitude
11. Legislative intent regarding unanticipated cases, and
12. In sexual cases, absence of sexual gratification

3 In the Italian criminal law academy also Ubertis (2011: 1134) proposes two dimensions of cultural investigation: "when there is a significant nexus between the charge and the original culture of the accused, one should admit testimony of the components of the minority to which he belongs and opinions of anthropologists or ethnologists on the existence and on the content of the allegedly cultural behavior (the objective profile of the question). After this, the effective adoption by the defendant of the declared system of values should be verified, across depositions of his family or acquaintances or production of documents concerning, for example, his scholastic course or his work activity (subjective profile)."

The author observes how "under the twelve guidelines, the cultural defense would not be available for conduct such as female genital mutilation (FGM), honor killings, homicide for loss of face, marriage by capture" and he points out the importance of protecting the "core values of the host culture" (Dore 2016: 551).[4]

All works cited express, with different sensitivity, a common need: to find some certainty, some fixed points, to approach a multicultural conflict. My proposal is to further detail the logical steps suggested by integrating them with the *topoi* emerging from comparative Western jurisprudence and with anthropological knowledge to present a fully satisfactory guide that the judge and the lawyer can follow to avoid cultural misinterpretation. The test about to be proposed seeks to summarize those that appear in the current historical moment, the points of consensus on how to frame multicultural conflicts on the jurisprudential level – derived from a common legal tradition slowly forming – as well as to improve some aspects of the academic tests by seeking a more discursive approach toward the other. In fact, to fully maximize the role of law and judge, my test adds to the objective and subjective assessments a final relational assessment aimed to enhance the function of the law as a tool to guarantee social coexistence.

2 An overview of the structure of the proposed test

The test that is suggested here gathers in a single instrument the most compelling issues that have emerged in Western jurisdictions, but also introduces some new questions to expand the legal experience and to arrive at a solution of maximally inclusive and relational coexistence. It could represent, for the judge who wants to build a culturally sensitive opinion, a tool to follow to give even greater legitimacy to his reasoning. The development of an argument that rests on a shared experience on a comparative level may indeed prove more persuasive.

The proposed test has a complex structure. It consists of thirteen logical argumentative and cognitive steps that the court should traverse before arriving at the solution to any multicultural conflict:

1 Does the matter adjudicated fall within the *category of culture*?
2 *Describe* the cultural practice and the group.
3 *Relate* and *link* the practice to the wider cultural *web of significances*.
4 Is the practice *essential* (to the group's survival), *compulsory* or *optional*?
5 Is the practice *shared* or *contested* within the group?
6 Is the group *vulnerable* within a society? Is it discriminated against?
7 How would a *reasonable person in that group* behave in the same circumstances?
8 Is the subject *sincere*?

4 Dore (2016: 551) observes that a cultural defense "is not, however, a license to unbridled freedoms that threaten core values of the host culture. It is of course a truism that such core values differ from culture to culture, but at some point such relativity of values, while conceded, must of necessity engage in line drawing to prevent the destruction of the social fabric of the host culture."

9 Is there a *cultural equivalent*, a similar or comparable practice, in the majority culture?
10 Is the practice *harmful*? Is the harm irreparable?
11 What is the *impact* of the practice on the fundamental rights, culture and value system of the *majority*?
12 Does the practice perpetuate *patriarchy*?
13 What *value* does the minority ascribe to the practice at issue? Does this value reflect the choice of a *meaningful life*?

In the lexical formulation of the test the term "culture" prevails, but the test is also applicable to religious conflicts based on a broad conception of multicultural conflict beyond the traditional and, in my opinion, outdated distinction between religion and culture (Chap. 2 sec. 2).

These questions, intertwined with and complementing each other, can be grouped into a triadic structure comprising the objective, subjective and relational parts of the test:

1 *Objective evaluation.* The first group of questions (#1–6) aims to investigate the conditions for the recognition of a cultural practice by examining its objective characteristics. The judge is called to adopt the perspective of the other in reading a certain fact, and to question if indeed the category of culture is effectively usable; once it is established that the court is not faced with behavior that can be explained in terms of psycho-pathology, social class or individual personality, the judge must wade into the description of the practice and then place it in the broader symbolic system of the culture; thus the judge is called upon to assess how a given cultural group considers the practice at issue – for example, whether it is mandatory, and how essential it may be to the survival and self-definition of the group. In this part of the test, the focus is on culture as a system of meanings that are investigated by the court regardless of their incarnation in the person at issue. If some of the cultural tests examined (Chap. 2 sec. 4 and 5.1) stop at this objective stage of the assessment, in the course of research carried out it seemed of great utility what happens in the Canadian and US religious tests (Chap. 2 sec. 5.2 and 6.1) which add also an investigation of the degree of internalization of the practice in the individual belonging to the group.
2 *Subjective evaluation.* The second set of questions in the proposed test (#7–8), therefore, focuses on the relationship between culture and its concrete expressions in different personal identities. This concrete subjective part comes in two questions: How would a reasonable person in that group behave in the same circumstances? And is the protagonist of the event sincere, honest and consistent in claiming the cultural practice? This subjective investigation is needed to verify that the litigants are not using cultural argument as a mere tactical tool, and to give the judge a more accurate measure of the interests involved in the dispute. It could, in fact, be the case that the cultural practice actually exists and is perhaps even mandatory for the group, but it is not so crucial to the identity of that particular individual.

3 *Relational evaluation.* The test is completed with a relational assessment of the conflict (questions #9–13). The fact that the objective (there is a cultural practice, with some level of obligation) and subjective (the person sincerely adheres to that practice, which is a constituent part of his/her identity) requirements are met does not mean that the legal response must be recognition. There is, in fact, the need to consider cultural needs compared with those of others, in this case, the society of the majority. Indeed, judges already balance the different needs at stake, but this balancing activity often is not spelled out in a transparent manner, resulting in formalistic reasoning (*Thomas* case, Chap. 1 sec. 4.2). A test that is limited to the mere objective and subjective assessment betrays the specificities of law as a science of social conflict settlement.

The relational part of the test suggests that there are, therefore, some new elements, or elements present only occasionally in other jurisdictions, which appear crucial to understanding a case. In particular, I refer to the search, by the court, for a cultural equivalent within the semiotic system of the majority group in which the court operates. It is, as we shall see, an element that has never been formalized into an existing test, but it has appeared in some decisions, often as an argument presented by the parties in order to better explain to the judge the meaning and significance of a practice.

One of the *topoi* (the fixed points on which there is agreement), this time not novel but consolidated in the approach to the resolution of multicultural conflicts at the comparative level, is the criterion that the practice cause harm to others, which was thus included in the proposed test, with one caveat that we will soon see.

Another *topos* that is emerging in the most recent jurisprudence regards the gender dimension of a multicultural conflict that leads some judges to refuse cultural recognition when the practice is deemed an expression of patriarchy. Since gender equality and the defeat of the patriarchal system are core values of international law around which states converge, I deemed it important to insert it in the test, with the caveat that it is important that the investigation on patriarchal practices not exclude the cultural dimension, but rather see the affected women as agents in deciding whether the practice actually impairs their freedom, in order to avoid the imperialistic imposition of what is oppressive towards women decided by the West or by men (Chap. 3 sec. 13).

The test ends with the demand that the minority adduce good reasons for preservation of a cultural practice. In this way, the minority is not statically secluded in its cultural space, but is rather called to controvert and to defend its practice in the public sphere. The evaluation of these reasons is made from the point of view of an impartial, potentially culturally neutral, spectator.

This third relational dimension of the test originates from an awareness that is itself anthropological: the ability to change one's behavior, transformation through contact with other interpretive horizons, that anthropology has discovered and conceptualized in contemporary definitions of culture (Chap. 3 sec. 9).

3 *Topoi* not included: antiquity of the practice, distinctiveness, time of residence

I have deliberately not inserted into the test certain types of conditions, even if they recur in different resolution models of the examined cultural conflicts: i.e. the antiquity of the practice, the need to be "distinctive" (both described in Chap. 2 sec. 5.1), and the factor of residence time within the host culture (Chap. 2 sec. 7). These conditions raise issues which suggest to leave them out of the test.

It is important to consider that, if a practice has arisen in a certain historical period, judgments may risk the allochronism (*allos*-other and *cronos*-time, in Greek) already examined by deconstructing the concept of culture (Chap. 3 sec. 3).

The choice to exclude from the test any analysis of the "distinctive" character of the practice may appear more controversial. This requirement, in fact, may allow the judge to realize that many cultural practices that she thinks exist only in other semiotic systems emerge, in fact, even in her own. Consider the murders of women who do not conform to the standards of conduct imposed by patriarchal contexts (Chap. 1 sec. 1.2). The "distinctive culture test" used for instance in Canada would imply that honor killings do not differ from femicides: they are the same fact (the murder of a woman) due to the same cause (she resisted men) and with the same aim (assert control over her). However, it seems to me that to pretend that the practice is distinctive in order to be able to give it recognition risks to deny *a priori* the cultural nature of a behavior for the mere fact that it is diffuse. Returning to the first case to open this work (Chap. 1 sec. 1.1): if it is true that infanticide occurs around the world, it is equally true that the peculiarities of Japanese culture made the *Kimura* case a different one than that of the mother who kills her son because she suffered from post-partum depression or other reasons. It is, therefore, possible that outwardly identical practices have profoundly distinctive cultural values.

Also excluded from the test is the *topos* relative to the time of residence within the host culture, widespread in English jurisprudence and often used in Italy. This criterion may seem valuable because it goes beyond the idea of enculturation – that once born in a cultural context the subject is shaped by it forever – but embraces, rather, the idea that the identity of each individual can change according to the context into which she comes into contact during the various stages of life (creolization examined at Chap. 3 sec. 9). While consistent with the most modern identity and anthropological theories, the residence time should not be, in my opinion, regarded – as it implies that cultural recognition is limited to an initial and transitional phase. Its use is appropriate to the purpose of establishing guilt, but to add it in a stable manner in a test would mean that everyone, after a certain period, would be required to assimilate. It seemed to me also that the finality that this element pursues in other systems is usually satisfied in the relational part of the test, where the encounter produces mutual transformation. For instance, question 13 of the test, which inquires into the good and beneficial reasons to continue the practice, implies that if the reasons the minority adduce to preserve the practice are valuable, the majority can even adopt the practice and be transformed.

4 The premise of the test: to take the other's perspective

There is a prerequisite without which neither any cultural argument nor any other sophisticated form of test may even be considered: this is the reading of the object of the controversy through the perspective of the party who is the bearer of another worldview.

This premise is indispensable in that, otherwise, it would be impossible to understand the cultural dimension underlying the dispute: the fact may appear as a common behavior; the problem of seeking new answers of justice could not even arise.

The anthropological spirit that permeates the contemporary mentality has prompted judges to read the world, as do the subjects who present themselves to demand justice. This has made possible the raising of the cultural argument and its subsequent elaborations.

The Italian Supreme Court of Cassation in its judgment on circumcision in 43646/2011 (Chap. 2 sec. 3.1) takes note of the two different perspectives with which circumcision is read: that of Western medicine, for which the practice violates the principle of ***primum non nocere***, and that of Jewish thought, in which it is an initiation to join the chosen people.[5] The case must be resolved with other people's cultural lenses and with these the court came to declare the practice's admissibility.

The request not to build a public work in native ancestral territory may appear a mere matter of property unless the cultural component were brought to light, which is derived from the fact that, for the natives, the earth is a spiritual being, with its own life. But the premise for the application of this reasoning is that the judge read the case ***sub specie*** culture, as did the Inter-American Court of Human Rights in a 2001 judgment:

> For indigenous communities, relations to the land are not merely a matter of possession and production but a material and spiritual element which they must fully enjoy, in order to preserve their cultural legacy and transmit it to future generations . . . the close ties of indigenous people with the land must be recognized and understood as the fundamental basis of their cultures, their spiritual life, their integrity, and their economic survival.[6]

5 In the words of the Court: "This is perceived by a western doctor as a genital mutilation for the child and an evident violation of the fundamental commandment that should inspire sanitary activity: ***primum non nocere*** ["first do no harm"] . . . This perception, however, is not, in itself, decisive for the solution of the question brought to the attention of this Court, as it does not account for the complex, connected problem of the reasons and of the strong symbolic meaning that the practice of ritual circumcision has in certain contexts. The significance that this practice has for the members of a specific religious belief, that is indeed shared between two monotheist religions – Judaism and Islam – in fact, cannot be omitted."

6 ***The Mayagna (Sumo) Awas Tingni Community v. Nicaragua***, Inter-American Court Decision, August 31, 2001. The judge adds: "Among indigenous peoples there is a communitarian tradition regarding a communal form of collective property of the land, in the sense that ownership of the land is not centered on an individual but rather on the group and its community" (sec. 149).

Another significant example of the ability to wear the cultural lenses of the other is found around the issue of salmon fishing and its significance in indigenous communities. The Canadian Supreme Court has stated that:

> Fishing rights are not traditional property rights. They are rights held by a collective and are in keeping with the culture and existence of that group. Courts must be careful to avoid the application of traditional common law concepts of property as they develop their understanding of the *sui generis* nature of aboriginal rights. While it is impossible to give an easy definition of fishing rights, it is crucial to be sensitive to the aboriginal perspective itself on the meaning of the rights at stake.

Quoting the anthropologist called to testify, the Court notes that salmon fishing has not only a nutritive function, but is also

> an important part in the system of beliefs of the Salish people, and in their ceremonies. The salmon were held to be a race of beings that had, in "mythical times," established a bond with human beings requiring the salmon to come each year to give their bodies to the humans who, in turn, treated them with respect shown by performance of the proper ritual. Toward the salmon, as toward other creatures, there was an attitude of caution and respect which resulted in effective conservation of the various species.[7]

Even a practice that in the cultural system of the judge could easily be classified as "superstition" receives, by adopting the point of view of others, a recognition equal to any other religious conviction.

The adoption of the other's perspective (Newman 2007), more and more diffuse on the comparative level, was achieved through progressive pragmatic exercises:[8] it debunks the allegations that courts are inevitably contaminated by an ethnocentric perspective. In fact, the judge is not impermeable and, if put in the conditions to discover them, is then able to take other perspectives (Connolly 1988).[9] Today, in general, the prospect of another's point of view is undertaken at the request of the defense asking for a cultural exception. But if the defense is not sensitive to these issues or does not consider them strategically applicable (eg. because if a cultural motive were admitted, the judge might regard the offence as premeditated or

7 This is reported as the testimony of Doctor Suttles in *R. v. Sparrow*, (1990) 1 S.C.R. 1075, already cited (Chap. 1 sec. 5.1).

8 Miller (1998) reveals the difficulty that the Native Americans encountered within claims of protection of a sacred site for the fact that the judge could not accept their proofs based on oral legends. See how only a few years after in *Delgammuukw v. British Columbia* (1997) 3 S.C.R. 1010 the Canadian Supreme Court instead accepted oral proofs.

9 Connolly (1988) observes that the success of confronting a cultural question depends on some "epistemological conditions" (191) such as the presence of cultural interpreters that provide the judge with the capacity to translate and explain the practice, and a prior intercultural formation of the judge (204–205).

committed under an aggravating circumstance), it is possible that these would be ignored. Therefore it is desirable to form a greater awareness in judges that the presence of culturally different subjects may involve a different reading of their behavior.

In synthesis, the attention to others' points of view will become the starting point of each cultural test; it is actually the *conditio sine qua non* without which it is impossible to proceed. Only once she has adopted this perspective and begun to wear these cultural lenses can the judge (or the legislature if the debate takes place in other places of the public sphere) begin its cognitive-argumentative process.

5 The test

Below I explain the proposed cultural test, with which judges could proceed to the framing of multicultural conflicts (and also religious conflicts). The three parts and the thirteen questions of which the instrument is composed have not each in themselves any decisive value, but are designed to be mutually interconnected, as issues that illuminate the case one after the other, allowing a full vision which likely, as the test progresses, will move to new assessments. This test could be a guiding tool for the court, but any legislature, lawyer or any person acting in the public or even private sphere (employers, businesses, condominiums) who is facing a multicultural conflict may find recourse in it.

5.1 Does the matter adjudicated fall within the category of culture?

The first element of the test is to ask whether the judge is really faced with a behavior or vision of the world readable *sub specie* of culture. Numerous behaviors currently classified as cultural should, in hindsight, be de-culturalized.[10]

Below we will examine how claims of domestic violence, prostitution of minors, sexual violence, begging and, in some cases, even the *burqa* (when imposed by political regimes) and honor killings (for trivial reasons) are erroneously considered as cultural practices.

To decide, therefore, whether the case is readable *sub specie* of culture, the court may proceed to some certifications: the fact that the practice is understood as such in the semantic space to be culture or, *vice versa*, is perceived as a pathological event, the imposition of ephemeral political regimes or reactions against traumatic alterations in economics or the social fabric.

In the first place, it serves to certify, therefore, whether that behavior is part of a "shared" system of beliefs and is actually recognized as cultural according to a non-external, intra-group qualification. In this context I suggest to adopt a logic of self-qualification by the group of what is cultural.

In the *Kimura* case (Chap. 1 sec. 1.1), effectively the group of her provenance condoned her behavior, but not all other practices are granted the same

10 In this sense, the Italian Supreme Court of Cassation (Cassazione) sec. III penal, January 29th 2015, no. 14960.

treatment. A survey on Sardinia would have allowed the judge in the *Pusceddu* case (Chap. 1 sec. 2.2) to understand that this practice is not at all considered to be part of Sardinian culture. One might ask as well: Do all Muslims kill their daughters who want to embrace a Western lifestyle? Or do all Moroccans beat their wives? Or, rather, is this behavior usually criticized within these "webs of meaning?"

A second tool that the judge should use to ascertain the culturality of a behavior is to investigate if it is a consequence of policies imposed by totalitarian political regimes. This type of assessment can significantly illuminate the cultural conflict that arises around the *burqa*. To dress in that garment, in fact, is revealed in Afghanistan and other Islamic theocracies as a recent practice, which has replaced the common veil and that was imposed by the political regime of the Taliban. Aware of this, the judge could weigh differently, as less relevant, the claim to wear it than to wear other types of Islamic veils. In fact, if the *burqa* can actually be considered a cultural practice dating back in some rural areas, its generalization appears the result of the Taliban's political regime, opposed by the people themselves.

The same could be said for child marriages in Iran. The Iranian Parliament is still debating the 2012 repeal of the latest limit (thirteen for girls, fifteen for boys). The reason given by the proponents for the repeal is that the presence of the limit would be "anti-Islamic." In reality, as progressive Iranian doctrine has noted, there is nothing Islamic, and thus indirectly anti-Islamic, either in the first or in the new law. It is manipulation of religion undertaken by the conservative fringes of power (Engineer 2012).

To find a parallel, it would be like saying that certain attitudes imposed by fascism in Italy between 1922 and 1945 – the cult of the body, the cult of the race, the Roman salute, the prohibition of weddings with Jews – were part of the Italian culture. To contextualize the behavior in time, in history and in politics could provide significant arguments for assessing whether it has a cultural nature.

In the third place, the judge could investigate if the behavior developed as a consequence of a traumatic alteration of the economics or of the social fabric. For example, before the collapse of the economy based on traditional circus activities, horse breeding and processing of copper, the Roma and Sinti were not in fact "begging cultures" (Chap. 1 sec. 3.1). Begging appeared, therefore, not as an expression of that culture, but as a consequence of the collapse of the same, due to external factors: industrialization, urbanization, the increasing difficulty of practicing nomadism (Simoni 2009; Ruggiu 2016). In this case the Italian Supreme Court has constructed the narrative as a multicultural conflict, although on the cultural nature of *manghel* there is a disagreement that comes primarily from the same group to which the practice is attributed. The fact that, in this case, it was the Roma defense that proposed *manghel* as a cultural practice does not release the court from its responsibility.

Through this first survey, a sort of "test within a test" that seeks to govern one of the most complex certifications, many behaviors are deculturalized or otherwise lose their exclusive cultural dimension.

As already underlined, the task of the cultural test proposed here is not only to resolve the conflict, but also to produce convincing judgments. An example of judicial argument demonstrates that to fulfill this first requirement of the test – to question the cultural nature of the behavior – the judge would have produced a more persuasive argument. In February 2012, Israel's Supreme Court declared unconstitutional the exemption of Orthodox Jews from military service as being contrary to the principle of equality among Israelis: the choices afforded by the law "are not available to young people who are not Ultra-Orthodox," reasoned the Court.[11] Utilizing the principle of equality, the judgment seemed to question the whole multicultural *acquis*, which falls within the idea that the principle of equality is not in and of itself violated if it accords preferential treatment to minorities to protect practices related to cultural or religious identity (*contra* Barry 2001). In reality, if the Supreme Court had applied a cultural test containing this first assessment on the actual cultural or religious nature of the practice, it could then be argued that there is no cultural or religious precept that prevents the ultra-Orthodox from performing military service; we are not, in fact, faced with a religious practice, but a concession explained by the political context of 1970, with a particularly vulnerable situation experienced at that time by the ultra-Orthodox minority. It was a political decision of the then-Prime Minister Ben Gurion to give the ultra-Orthodox Jews that exemption to permit their community to survive and flourish again. Since there is no religious prohibition in regard to military service, an ultra-Orthodox Jew can remain Orthodox while performing it. But this argument rests in the shadow of judgments which seem, instead, to use the principle of equality as a barrier to religious differences.

The first question in the test could be deemed banal and naïve, as it seems obvious that the use of the cultural defense should occur when and only when culture is at stake. Nevertheless, the several erroneous classifications realized by judges on the comparative level, and the ongoing phenomenon of "blaming culture for bad behavior" (Volpp 2000), suggest that this question become the very first step that judges ask when facing immigrants or national minorities. Otherwise, rather than interrupt the culturalist narrative presented (sometimes strategically) by the defense, the courts will keep following it and then demolish it with the appeal to fundamental rights. But without resorting to the mantra of human rights, the judge already at the first question in the test could close the issue, thus sparing the stereotyping effects on immigrants and minorities.

5.2 Describe *the cultural practice and the group*

Once satisfied that the cultural category is usable, a second task of the judge should be to "describe" the practice or the vision of the other world in its details.

11 *Ressler v. The Knesset [the Parliament]*, February 21, 2012, with which the Israeli Supreme Court declared unconstitutional the law no. 5762/2002, known as "The service deferral law." An official summary of the opinion in English is available at http://michaeldorf.org/IsraelSupCtMilitaryServiceCase.htm.

As has already been observed, some judges have imposed, as the test requirement, the individuation of a single cultural practice, deeming insufficient the mere offer of the argument that "I have so acted because it is my culture," or "my culture led me to do this." In particular, the Canadian Supreme Court (Chap. 2 sec. 5.1) has stated that a generic reference to culture is not sufficient, but rather it is always necessary to confront its specific manifestation and has inserted the description of the practice as part of the cultural test since 1996. Identification requirements of a practice also appear in the US religious test (Chap. 2 sec. 6.1) and the jurisprudence of the UN Human Rights Committee (Chap. 2 sec. 4).

The detailed description of a concrete practice serves to satisfy the requirement of the obligation for the judgment to state reasons for the sentence; to avoid inferences derived from a generic reference to culture *tout court*; and to accurately identify those matters that concern the conflict (the controversial *quaestio decidendi*) and, therefore, what is to be accommodated.

To say "culture moved the subject to this behavior" cannot in itself satisfy judicial obligations. It might, at first sight, appear that the court need not go further and that it is enough to bring a new, "anthropologized" Western common sense which modifies the sense of justice. But with a clearer view, a judgment that limits itself to that general reference is lacking. The aforementioned formula, in fact, is an empty container which needs to be filled with substance. In order to submit the validity of the judge's reasoning to public opinion, it must be clear what kind of behavior is in question, what interests the parties claim, and what part of that most vast universe which is a cultural system is at stake in that case.

In this respect, some judgments leave a deafening silence. Even the Italian system is devoid of this requirement, and, not surprisingly, has seen questionable pronouncements: not so much in the judge's reasoning (which is often convincing) as at the level of the grounds. Taking again the begging case decided by the Italian Supreme Court of Cassation in 2008, the obligation to describe in detail the practice would have helped against the stigmatization of Roma behavior, by pushing the judge to identify the correct cultural practices at stake such as the relation between mother and child, and the idea of childhood.[12]

12 In spite of the fact that begging is not a cultural practice in itself, it involves and is connected to other Roma cultural practices. In my opinion, a more careful judge interested in the cultural argument should have given attention to these cultural practices – more shared, and not contested among the Roma such as: 1) Roma women are not used to being separated from their children (as observed by the Assemblée Générale des Roms de Bruxelles in 2007, "there are several reasons why certain parents prefer to take their children to the streets instead of sending them to school: the main cause is social exclusion and poverty," but it is also important to consider that: "culturally, the ties between the mother and the child are quite close: children in Romania do not go to school before the age of seven. Consequently, to separate from one's children when they are still small may be seen as a form of abandonment"); 2) In every Roma group, children are involved in adult activities, without this being seen as a form of exploitation; 3) The concept of time among the Roma is different. They in general may prefer begging to other kinds of more disciplined jobs, but again, this is not to say that begging belongs to their culture. It is an adaptive economic strategy that fits with their conception of time (Ruggiu 2016: 47).

Vice versa, in cases where the courts have delved deeply into the description of the practice, the judgment allows a full understanding of the behavior.

In this sense, it reconfirms the importance of a test that delineates a logical process and that imposes on a court certain clarifying passages.

To focus on the practice means also to individuate its scope and then grasp the differences or similarities with other cultural practices of the majority, in a dialectic process, and to avoid misunderstandings about the exact identification of the object to accommodate. Otherwise, the matter over which the parties controvert remains obfuscated. An example may help to clarify the problem. "School truancy" is frequently cited among culturally motivated behaviors. The case of a Muslim parent who, in England, did not want to send his daughter to school because the class was mixed was, for example, presented as if the Islamic culture in its practices mandated a prohibition against going to school. Similarly, it is often said that the Roma do not send their children to school "because of culture." But in these two cases, focusing more closely on the cultural practice, it can be observed that this is not in itself about "not going to school;" this behavior has nothing to do with culture, but is rather the result of other cultural attitudes. In the case of the Muslim parent, the cultural practice is the "separation between men and women;" in the case of Roma, a different perception of infancy and, in particular, the fact that parents consider children "too small to separate from the family" until they are seven years old. The exact description allows, first, to avoid representing certain groups as being culturally averse to education and, second, to open the door to a more effective accommodation, aimed at promoting the conditions under which these groups can send their children to school. How far such accommodations can go will be discussed at the end of the test; by now it can be anticipated that if the groups seek to maintain the practices that express ways of life equally endowed with meaning and value, the law should seek some accommodation, as happened in the US in connection with a partial exemption from mandatory public education for Amish children (*infra* sec. 5.13). Perhaps, then, one could not reasonably claim to create female-only classes to allow a school climate more suited to the young Muslim girl, but one could consider, at least temporarily, to accept different ages at which children gain access to schools to accommodate Roma needs.

This second question of the test consents to expunge those practices which are invented without any historical basis (such as the prohibition of singing in front of the Wailing Wall in Jerusalem that some ultra-Orthodox rabbis tried to impose on women, considering female singing a sexual siren call) or are simply the result of a tightening of existing rules, but reinterpreted in a rigid way (the request, again of some ultra-Orthodox Jews, that whole districts – including non-Jews – refrain from driving on *shabbat*[13]).

It is likewise appropriate that, in their holdings, judges identify more specifically the group to which the practice should be attributed. On this point the case

13 The Hebrew *shabbat* can be validly observed simply if the individual people abstain from the activities of work, without necessarily imposing the abstention on others (Gavison 2005).

law has nearly unanimously recognized that the concept of the group does not coincide with that of the nation and that even subgroups can find recognition. The identification of the group is important because it helps the judge in the process of understanding the culturality of the practice and permits judgments that do not attribute practices indiscriminately. For example, honor killings cannot be considered a Pakistani practice *tout court*, but they can be attributed to specific rural areas, to specific groups.

One problem which arises with the identification of the boundaries of a group is addressed by US jurisprudence concerning persons outside the group who wish to adopt its practices and customs. Anthropology has discussed the question of whether it is possible to "become" Arab, indigenous or Italian; and post-identity studies claim that identities are not fixed properties, and therefore it is perfectly possible to change one's cultural identity and adopt another. A court in Utah[14] faced the case of Mr. Samuel Wilgus, who "although not of Native-American ancestry . . . has practiced a Native-American religion for a number of years." Mr. Wilgus, so reads the judgment, was raised in a Baptist church, but while living among the Paiute his "spiritual practices and beliefs evolved" enough to push him to seek a spiritual master among the Native American Church: "so sincere was Mr. Wilgus's commitment to his new faith" that his teacher "presented him with a large eagle feather . . . to recognize his progress in his religious training." Similar gifts were also offered by the other members of the tribe. Possession of eagle feathers is, however, forbidden in the United States under the Bald and Golden Eagle Protection Act of 1962, drawing an exception only for the benefit of recognized Indian tribes who use eagle feathers within the scope of prayer, so when Mr. Wilgus was found carrying the feathers he was arrested. Applying the religious test (Chap. 2 sec. 6.1), the anthropologist judge acknowledged that theoretically the right to hold feathers falls under religious freedom. However, in this case, the judge considered that there was a compelling interest of the government to set limits by choosing to exclude non-native people, because the eagles are in limited number and not everyone can dispose of them. Although the decision was not favorable to the accused, it is indicative of the fact that one could potentially recognize all persons who consistently and sincerely adhere to a particular religion/culture as entitled to cultural recognition.

5.3 Relate *and* link *the practice to the wider cultural* web of significances

The various test steps should complement one another, like spotlights that, one after the other, illuminate the case, enabling readings from a plurality of points of view, each in a tension to seek a new rule of coexistence, of a "re-signification of citizenship" (Bascherini 2007: 346) to give new horizons of meaning other than that which each side had when the conflict began. In this optic, the description of the practice risks revealing a suffocating element of the test if, once she has identified the singular

14 *United States v. Wilgus*, 606 F. Supp. 2d 1308 (2009).

cultural expression, the judge does not proceed to insert it into the larger semiotic system in which it originated. Only by following this two-way approach – which first details the single practice and then brings it within the cultural system – can one avoid a number of risks associated with the ambiguity that the concept of culture brings into being. This test question is, in fact, to trace a difference between those behaviors which simply happen within a community and actual culture. Culture presents an internal normative aspect, as it is given by a set of rules created by the group (that are not always reflected in the life of the individual, who might be "deviant"). This "web of rules," according to a vision of normative pluralism, arrives to form a legal system and, as in any legal system, so also in a cultural system the single units should be consistent with each other and the whole.

A first example reveals the importance of inserting every single practice in the vaster cultural horizon of a group: the courts have often attributed to Muslim countries the cultural practice of "beating one's wife" (Chap. 1 sec. 2.1). In reality, this is not a consequence of this cultural vision. In fact, the cultural system of Islam provides that the woman has a different role from man, but no less worthy. The fact that the woman's business is primarily in the private sphere is consistent with this "cultural system," but it provides no license for women to be beaten, raped or even killed.

Otherwise we should say that homophobic murders are the result of Italian or American culture, or that people kill homosexuals as a result of homophobic Western culture. The facts might even support the conclusion, but only within a panculturalist view (Chap. 3 sec. 10). In a more limited connotation of culture, the fact that the killing of gay people is not a consistent practice with the overall Italian and American cultural system, which recognizes sexual freedom, decreases the possibility of advancing a cultural argument.

As well as to reinforce the judge in tracing the stakes between what is culture and what is not (an operation already begun with the first question in the test, *supra* 5.1), the investigation of the cultural system serves also to correct any "errors" that the judge may have made in responding to the identification of the practice. During the description of the single behavioral practice it is easier for the court to incur a reified synedochical (mistaking the part for the whole) or metonymic (mistaking the cause for the effect) approach to culture. Often, judges identify an action and a behavior, and then trace an equivalence between that and the culture of the group *de qua*. Giving relevance to concrete fixtures of a certain culture – as if they were the artifacts that so fascinated the first anthropologists – the judge does not realize that the behavior is not the true cultural practice, but rather that the same behavior evidences a worldview that indeed is part of that culture. It also happens that the behavior itself can have odious results, but if the judge is able to penetrate deeper within the cultural system, maybe she can bring forth a worldview that is more understandable, and that can even teach us something.

Let us consider three Roma behaviors commonly considered unsuitable for accomodation, to examine in what way the relationship between individual behaviors and cultural systems may form: Roma women bring their children to beg; they do not send them to school or proceed to send them out until they are eight or ten years old; they are not very attentive in the personal care of the child, often leaving them dirty and badly dressed. The judge, faced with these behaviors, has different paths: to declare them consequences of economic and social difficulties, thus denying the cultural matrix and closing the test with its first question; to declare that there are three practices (begging, truancy, not washing) of that culture that we need not "tolerate" (depending on how these cultural practices violate the "superior" rights); or to dig deeper into the overall cultural system of the Roma to investigate the positions of these alleged cultural practices. If he chooses this course, the judge will find a concept of care and the mother–child relationship that could form the matrix, the true cultural essence of all these behaviors (Ruggiu 2016). To find that a Roma mother brings the child begging not because *manghel* is a cultural practice, but because Roma mothers bring their children with them everywhere, tending not to separate from them (hence also the reluctance in sending them to kindergarten), so if the cultural transformations impose on them to beg, they will carry their children to work; to discover a conception of childhood in which the child participates in the life of their elders, but always within the community's supervision, and is considered too small to face the world alone, at least up to seven years; to discover a cultural system in which perhaps the attention to hygienic care of the child is less than that of the majority, but it is compensated by other forms of affection, so much so that to Roma mothers some practices of the Italian or French mothers (eg. to let their children sleep alone since infancy) appear to be maltreatment or signs of detachment.

When this work of uncovering the layers, the deconstruction of synecdoche, to go to the heart of culture is completed, many "practices" that seem aberrant acquire more meaning.

To draw a close link between a practice and the overall cultural system proves an essential element of any culturally oriented argument because without it, the case is likely to remain obscured.

5.4 *Is the practice* essential *(to the group's survival)*, compulsory *or* optional?

The "objective" test part should also include a determination of the level of importance that the practice plays within its cultural system, measured along dual axes: whether the practice is "essential" and whether it is "compulsory" or merely "optional." While the two terms *essential* and *compulsory* are often used interchangeably, they actually have some important nuances. The judgment of essentiality implies the identification of those practices without which the group would be doomed to cultural extinction. A practice is essential or *integral* (some jurisdictions prefer this term) when it defines the community, without which the group would not qualify as such. *Vice versa*, the requisite of compulsoriness mandates the recognition of all those practices which are felt as binding within the group, although not necessarily decisive to its cultural survival.

This assessment has been stated in various ways in the examined legal systems. Its extremes range from the Canadian model that, in its cultural test, requires that the practice be "essential" for the cultural survival of the group, to the US model which gives importance to the compulsoriness of the practice while remaining open to subjective aspects or balancing factors, to the Italian model that does not make any kind of assessment on compulsoriness, thus potentially leaving the door open to all cultural practices, even the merely facultative (op. 923/2008 permitting marijuana smoking even if only optional for Rastafarians, Chap. 2 sec. 8.1). In this work we have concentrated on the analysis of the use of the cultural argument in the West, but the pervasiveness of the requirement of essentiality or obligation also extends beyond these boundaries.[15] The element of the compulsoriness of a practice is perhaps the most prevalent of the arguments used by judges, in the sense that, even when not stabilized in a test, it was found frequently in all the examined experiences. This is explained by the circumstance that one of the most convincing philosophical justifications for recognition is that culture should be recognized as a constituent part of the identity of a group or an individual (Taylor 1989). If to suppress the exercise of a behavior does not affect the hard nucleus of that identity, there may be more reasons to refuse recognition.[16]

Part of the legal and anthropological literature criticizes the essential and compulsory requirement for the diverse risks connected to it.

The first criticism alleges it to be an impossible task, especially in reference to the requirement of essentiality (Modood 1998; Narayan 1998; Kompridis 2005). Which practices can be said to be essential? Which are not? Each is part of a complex cultural system and this complexity can result in poor attribution of essentiality (or none at all). The idea of culture as a holistic system and not as an accumulation of single juxtaposed practices would seem to oppose this test element (Chap. 3 sec. 2). A review of practices that the Canadian Supreme Court considered essential to an indigenous group finds: fishing for salmon and the performance of rituals such as the lighting of fires in the woods. Among those not essential: the dance of the spirits, the sale of salmon, commercial nomadism and gambling. We have seen, however, how these classifications, as well as being questionable on the merits, were mostly used in lieu of other factors not made explicit in the controversy. But even if it were possible to identify the practices of each culture without which it would not exist, other problems would arise.

15 In India, for example, the Supreme Court (*State of Gujarat v. Mirzapur Moti Kureshi Kasab Jammat and others* Appeals no. 4937–4940, 1998) has certified the essentiality of the practice in a dispute between Muslims, who proceeded to sacrifice cows for the feast of Bakr Id, and an Indian state that, responding to strong Hindu feelings that the cows were sacred, had passed a law which forbade their killing. The Supreme Court, observing that essential religious practices were protected by art. 25 of the Constitution, upheld the sacredness of cows for Hinduism but not the obligation to sacrifice cows for Islamic feasts. The reasoning adopted by the Supreme Court is, in truth, overly formalistic, residing in the fact that the obligation is not written in the Koran. In reality, as was noted, with the exception of some religions like the Jehovah's Witnesses, the criterion of literal interpretation of sacred texts is not sufficient to stabilize the essentiality or compulsoriness of a practice. I think a better argument would have been that while Muslims can still celebrate the feast without sacrificing a cow, the Hindu faith is clearly compromised by permitting their sacrifice (Yldirim 2004).

16 *Vice versa*, adhering to the constitutional model of diversity as a public good opens the door also for recognition of non-essential or non-compulsory practices.

Admitting that the observance of the Sabbath is essential and integral to Judaism, what to do with practices related to it such as the *eruv* (Chap. 2 sec. 5.2)? It is a practice strongly "welded" to the Sabbath, but for which there is no mention in the Bible, as it was born later in order to temper the severity of the Sabbath. The essentiality problem not only works against the judge who has to surgically excise other cultures, but also poses a problem for minorities likely to be crystallized in the past: How to assess the fact that the Amish, whose essential trait could arise in the desire to preserve a way of life of the nineteenth century, want to adopt electricity, or that Roma nomadism (treated often as essential and integral to their culture) wish to become sedentary? Do these changes mean that the group is no longer what it is, thus freeing the majority of recognition obligations?

Then there is always, in the background, the issue of who decides: Can elites or the majority of a group decide "politically" on the essentiality of practices that "specialists" do not credit? What happens when a symbol, like the crucifix in Italian schools, is required by law while not existing as dogma and not considered compulsory by the Catholic Church? Or, conversely, when the *burqa* is meant to be worn as an essential part of the definition of oneself regardless of the opinions of imams or Islamic experts which affirm that only the veil which covers the hair is essential for Islam?

The essentiality or not to the survival of the group, other than resulting in a complex element to be ascertained, does not take into account the subjective elements of identification. Not everyone feels Italian, Sardinian, Pakistani or indigenous for the same reasons (Cohen 1996).

A second criticism concerns the requisite of compulsoriness. Since the values of coexistence are changing and cultural diversity is emerging as a new democratic principle, it appears possible, indeed desirable, to give importance to others' practices, even if they are not mandatory. Perhaps the construction of a minaret is not mandatory to allow Muslim prayer, but can its presence be prohibited for this reason (Baraggia 2010)?

In this sense, the Italian approach, which agrees to give relevance to any cultural practice as long as does not violate other fundamental rights, is preferable to those that impose basic essentiality/compulsoriness requirements in order to proceed to recognition, thus restricting the number of accepted practices. The introduction of these requirements would exclude a number of practices that, although purely optional and not critical to the group's survival, could easily find space and acceptance by the majority and be a fount of pluralism's enrichment.

Despite the grounds of those reflections, it is still true that the compulsoriness assessment can play a very important role to reach a fair settlement of the dispute. The fact that a cultural or religious practice is merely optional and collateral to the semiotic system, in fact, has a weight in the balance. It is an intuitive criterion, basically common sense, which facilitates pondering the balance of interests at stake; not surprisingly it is a *topos* found in almost all jurisdictions. Consider the utility that this element could have in resolving some conflicts. While wearing the Islamic veil can be considered as a practice directly related to Islam accompanied by a certain obligation (although not absolute because it cannot be said that those who take it off cease at that moment to be a Muslim), the same cannot be said of the so-called practice of displaying crucifixes in public spaces in Italy. There is no obligation or dogma that requires it, and from here one could furnish an argument for removal. Requests to move the public holiday from Sunday in predominantly Catholic or Christian societies, however, may not be accepted because it would interfere with a practice, going to Mass on Sundays, that is in fact mandatory for the Catholic religion.

For these reasons it was decided to include such a determination in the test in its three versions, albeit without attributing any absolute value, since even non-essential and non-compulsory practices can, in principle, find protection; and conversely, even essential or mandatory practices could be found not to satisfy the other test inquiries. In any case, the completion of this determination could help the judge to truly understand the extent of the interests at stake and to prepare more congruent opinions.

5.5 Is the practice shared *or* contested *within the group?*

As cultures, but also religions, are dynamic processes, it can be the case that behaviors which historically have been obligatory have progressively become the object of inner-cultural dispute: they have begun to be questioned and in certain sectors of the group their intergenerational transmission may interrupt or develop into an opposite behavior. The controversial nature of a practice can attenuate the force of the cultural defense.

As seen in the first element of the test (*supra* 5.1), the lack of demonstration that a practice is shared within the group can even be used to exclude its cultural nature. In this part of the test, this requirement refers to practices that certainly have long been part of the culture, but are now undergoing an internal process of contestation.

The inquiry that the judge should undertake to respond to this test question might start with an analysis of how the official legal system treats the practice: there may be a relevant indicator, for example, whether the conduct is criminalized and what is the established penalty. The fact that many African states have prohibited infibulation or have inserted specific constitutional clauses in favor of culture, but subject to the limits of human rights,[17] for example, is significant as a change in perception, just as the 2004 reform of family law in Morocco could be considered

17 Ghana Constitution 1992, art. 26: "(1) Every person is entitled to enjoy, practise, profess, maintain and promote any culture, language, tradition or religion subject to the provisions of this Constitution. (2) All customary practices which dehumanise or are injurious to the physical and mental well-being of a person are prohibited;" Niger Constitution 1999, art. 14: "Each person shall have a right to the free development of his personality in its material, intellectual and spiritual, cultural and religious dimensions as long as he does not violate the right of others, does not infringe on constitutional order, legal order or morality;" Rwanda Constitution 2003, art. 51: "The State has the duty to safeguard and to promote national values based on cultural traditions and practices so long as they do not conflict with human rights, public order and good morals." Similar provisions in Seychelles Constitution 1993, art. 39, and in South Africa Constitution 1996, art. 30.

a valid argument for ignoring recognition of certain oppressive family practices (Chap. 1 sec. 2.1). Conversely, as seen in the *Kimura* case, that the *Oyaku Shinju* is a crime in Japan, but is considered "involuntary manslaughter" and punished with a lenient penalty, reveals how there is still a degree of social consensus on the practice (Chap. 1 sec. 1.1).

Sometimes, however, it may not be enough to check the given law. Especially in despotic regimes, indeed, the criminal justice system may reflect a resurgence of already abandoned practices (think of the penalty of stoning, re-introduced in Iran in 1983, only to be abandoned again in 2012). In these cases, the judge may make an assessment of its anthro/political nature to understand how much the practice may be obsolete and how much of its revival is the result of a forced political regime and not a real change of shared values.

The investigation of the consensus of the group on the practice appears, albeit not systematically, in several judgments at the comparative level. At times this results in problematic outcomes, as in the case of the Nigerian mother (Chap. 2 sec. 7) who had practiced ritual scarifications on the faces of her children, already able to understand and consenting. The anthropological survey presented at trial showed that indeed the practice existed among the group to which the woman belonged, but that it had fallen into disuse in recent decades: the woman had emigrated from Nigeria to the UK some time before and, ignoring the transformation that occurred in her homeland, she thought to put into place a living practice. In these cases, it will be the subjective part of the test to offer the woman support: the fact that she sincerely believes she perpetuates a practice, not knowing that it is contested by the same group, should be taken into account (as indeed was done).

This requirement of the test, which Avigail Eisenberg calls the "validation condition" consisting of the fact that the cultural practice has been validated through a process of legitimation internal to the community (Eisenberg 2009: 12), appears useful also to avoid elites taking control over a group and representing their culture according to their interests.

In general, in situations where the practice is not followed unanimously by the whole group, or even within the part in question, the solution need not necessarily be the lack of recognition. As we shall see, a subjective assessment may serve in tests to understand the importance that a concrete practice has for the person who practices it.

5.6 Is the group **vulnerable** *within a society? Is it* **discriminated** *against?*

One of the constitutional and philosophical justifications that underlie cultural recognition is the fact that the minority has been or is a victim of injustice (Young 1990). This powerful discourse operates in the background of both the provision of cultural rights and the choice of which minorities to protect at the constitutional level. It, moreover, indirectly conditions jurisprudence where numerous cases of judgments designed to protect an endangered minority have been registered. This is clearly evident, often by the admission of post-colonialist judges in the cases of indigenous peoples. But not only, as shown in the case of the Roma in

Italy (with the Supreme Court declaring that one should not "criminalize" their lifestyle, Chap. 1 sec. 3.1, keeping in mind the process of stigmatization that the group suffers) or of the Jews in Quebec (Chap. 2 sec. 5.2).

This work adheres to the thesis of a constitutional foundation of culture based on the idea of diversity as an integral part of pluralism and as beneficial for the entire society. In this sense the criterion of discrimination need not be absolute, and even minorities who do not face discrimination could aspire to gain recognition within the test. However, this question may help the judge in the complex tasks of measuring the reasons for or against a practice. Provided that it is not conclusive – but none of the single questions proposed in the test are – to assess the presence of discrimination can tip the scales towards accommodation. It is, in fact, important if the minority is in a state of social vulnerability, to understand the likely effects of the decision. It needs, in particular, to prevent the kind of recognition that, although made with the best intentions, yet harbors a consequence that is prejudicial to the same minority or obscures a perception, interiorized by the same court, of lesser social dignity for the minority. As we will soon see (*infra* sec. 5.13), the US Supreme Court has granted an exemption of two years of compulsory high school attendance for Amish boys. In this case, the court must be certain that the exemption is not accorded to those children because it recognizes a value of lesser dignity than children of the majority, but rather because it recognizes that they have a different system of education, which in any case will provide them with the tools for a happy and meaningful life. Similarly, different policies in regard of Roma children, belonging to a minority highly discriminated against in almost all European societies (Tavani 2012), can be motivated by their situation of discrimination and their different lifestyle, but will, in fact, serve to remove this injustice and not to consolidate it.

Similarly, before reaching a decision, the courts must ask themselves whether to mitigate the punishments for parents who infibulated their daughter is not in fact to express a judgment of lesser value toward the dignity and health of that child (Chap. 2 sec. 8.1); or reducing the penalty of the Sardinian man who tortured his Lithuanian partner is not, behind the cultural argument, perpetuating latent forms of contempt or disregard for "non-German" groups (Chap. 1 sec. 2.2). Even when it is certain that the use of the cultural argument is made with the best intentions toward the minority, it must still be considered whether it diverts attention away from far more effective policies. In this sense, perhaps, to affirm that a Roma child can beg because it is culture among Roma disregards problems of poverty that the state should confront with more incisive measures of redistributive justice intervention (Young 2000; Fraser, Honneth 2003; Banting, Kymlicka 2006).

Once sure that none of these attitudes is present, the judge (or legislature) may well use cultural recognition as an anti-discriminatory practice both in the sense of permitting the group to engage in their own practices, but also in the sense of giving them more presence, even if merely symbolic, in the public space.

The logical process of the test has so far analyzed objective behavior from a plurality of perspectives: how the behavior is interpreted in its own culture, which contents it presents, how to insert it in a wider system of meanings, how obligatory and shared the practice may be within the group, and to what extent the latter may suffer discrimination.

Some of the examined cultural tests, in particular the Canadian one, stop at this level of analysis. Even in Italy the jurisprudence mainly focuses, often loosely, on objective profiles. Conversely, other tests introduce a subjective dimension that, in hindsight, may be essential to unravel the controversy. The presence of this additional dimension corresponds to the fact that cultures are no longer perceived, as at the beginning of the anthropological thought, as reified; and that a stronger focus is given to "lived culture" (Chap. 3 sec. 2).

A test to guide multicultural conflicts cannot stop at an objective assessment, but should also provide for an accurate subjective analysis.

5.7 *How would* a reasonable person in that group *behave in the same circumstances?*

A key finding that the judge must assess is whether the behavior is average, normally retained by the subjects of that culture. This implies to identify, from a subjective point of view, how a reasonable person in that group would behave in the same circumstances: in fact, the agent model (*homo eiusdem condicionis et professionis*) should be identified not with the standards of the majority, but with that of the minority.

This assessment is not consolidated explicitly in any of the tests examined in this work, but it emerges as an argument in the Australian case law since 1950 (Chap. 1 sec. 4.1) and is quite recurrent within the cultural defenses of the United States (Chap. 2 sec. 6.2 and 6.3). In this system, the new awareness about the fallacy of the myth of the neutral, liberal individual has determined the contextualization of establishing the reasonable behavior (the reasonable man under all circumstances) to the canon of the culturally situated individual. Even the Italian criminal law doctrine has theorized that the ascertainment of the "coincidence of reaction" (De Maglie 2010: 31) between the defendant and the average person of his/her group is an important element for cultural recognition. The Italian jurisprudence has used it several times. Saying that the killing of his daughter Hina by Mohammed Saleem "appeared devoid of proportion . . . to the same Pakistani community," the judge implicitly says that a reasonable Pakistani father, an average Pakistani man would not kill his daughter for cohabiting unmarried with an Italian man (Chap. 1 sec. 1.2). But if this type of assessment is not proceduralized, the judge might perform it only occasionally – as demonstrated again by the Italian model – where at other times, the judge assumes that behavior is readable as cultural merely because it happens (Chap. 1 sec. 2.1). The importance of a test that constitutes a fixed course for the judge and that renders explicit all the conditions for cultural recognition reveals its utility also at this juncture.

Other than to understand the level of influence that cultural background may have had on the person, the application of the "reasonable cultural person" standard serves to prospect other ways in which the people involved in the dispute could have acted. We try to retrace, in the light of this test element, the case of Indian dancers who kidnapped their companion, subjecting him to beatings and forced fasting in order to force him to become a dancer of the dance of the spirits (Chap. 1 sec. 4.2). If the Canadian Supreme Court had foreseen in its tests a finding of a "reasonable indigenous dancer," one might have to ask: Would any indigenous dancer, overlooking the clear and obvious protests of their companion, really behave that way? Is it part of a fairly common behavior, given the fact that now the indigenous communities do not live completely separate from the majority, to ignore the protests of Thomas? Conversely, as seen, the Court decided to condemn the dancers on the grounds that the practice is not essential to the survival of the cultural group. Same result but very different, much more incomprehensible and rockier arguments.

Proceeding to the subjective analysis of the test, one passes by assessments of the reasonable person of that culture, in ever more concrete assessments which focus on the incarnations that particular cultures take within specific individuals. The reasonable cultural person standard, in fact, is an element to ascertain, but, in the spirit of the proposed test, it is illuminated through other, successive assessments.

5.8 Is the subject sincere?

A central element in some tests examined in the second chapter, in particular the Canadian and US religious tests (Chap. 2 sec. 5.2 and 6.1), is the evaluation of how immersed the subject may be in their own culture or religion and how it has contributed to mold his personal identity. The connection between the cultural system and personal identity is crucial because cultures do not live as a reality in their own right, separate and independent from the members that make them up (Abu-Lughod 1991; Cohen 1996). The cultural practice, therefore, must be connected to the identity of the subject in the controversy, in that it must be constitutive of his way of seeing the world. From the analyzed cases emerge several items that the court may assess to test the subject's sincerity, among which is the coherence of her behavior in other spheres of her life and the kind of sacrifices that the individual is or was willing to face to remain loyal to the practice claimed (eg. the dismissal of the Seventh-Day Adventist women or the Native American boy, respectively, for refusing to work on Saturday and cut his hair, Chap. 2 sec. 6.1 and Chap. 3 sec. 9).

The subjective assessment appears an effective instrument for reasonable accommodation of any conflict that brings to the test aspects of the concrete case that the objective part of the test may not fully appreciate. For example, the fact that a practice is mandatory and essential in one culture does not mean necessarily that the person who controverts considers it such; as well as, on the contrary, it could happen that an optional practice becomes foundational to the identity of a subject. In the case of Mr. Anselem, the Orthodox Jew building his *succah* for nine days a year on the terrace and disturbing the aesthetics of the condominium, the test elements analyzed so far would probably have held against recognition: the construction of a private *succah* is not a mandatory practice and a reasonable average Jewish person cannot expect to have his own *succah* in an urban environment when he is able to pray in a shared *succah*. However, in this case the arrangement is possible, according to the court, because there is a strong sincerity and a subjective way of living that faith (Mr. Amselem is a fervent believer) combined with the fact that the building remains standing only nine days a year and does not bear a serious harm to other residents (Chap. 2 sec. 5.2).

Alongside the objective test on the cultural practice, a subjective part presents the advantage of creating a dialectic between culture and its embodiments, that is crucial for the law asked to look for new rules of coexistence not only between abstract cultures but also between concrete individuals.

5.9 *Is there a* **cultural equivalent,** *a similar or comparable practice, in the majority culture?*

The objective and subjective parts of the test incorporate into multicultural judicial reasoning some of the more innovative theoretical achievements of anthropology and identity theory (Giddens 1991). However, they are not yet sufficient to found a persuasive legal approach to culture.

Anthropology has revolutionized the Western idea of being human and contributed to a change in the sense of justice being more sensitive to diversity, but on the point of response to cultural conflicts the consequence of this approach may be to permanently render them intact, insoluble. The positive response to these questions of the test would impose, according to anthropology, recognition and closure of the other in an impenetrable cultural space.

The law cannot stop at this: it has its own specificity as a discipline called to define the rules of coexistence, which it should bring out using its own argumentative logic, a controversial logic, which cannot be merely anthropological.[18]

In this sense, once the presence of objective and subjective elements of the practice are ascertained, one cannot assume that any party is authorized to conserve them without putting the matter into dialectic with contrary interests, in dialogue with the new cultural system in which he attempts to act. As with internal pluralism, so also with the multicultural: to permit the controversial logic which is typical of the law to fully express it is necessary to relate the two "webs of meaning" that are in dispute. By reducing the test to the mere objective finding (Canadian model), one risks creating an overly abstract test; by giving preference to the subjective element (the US model), one risks to accentuate an individualistic matrix. In any case, to stop at this stage of inquiry – especially at the objective – is to put cultural recognition into a mathematical logic, as the Canadian cultural test well revealed: if the minority meets certain requirements, recognition is guaranteed, no matter any future relation which may be exacerbated by this recognition; if, instead, the practice does not respect the requisites predetermined by the majority, recognition is denied, although perhaps the majority could accept

18 Alternatively, the same anthropologist has passed from statically photographing cultures, conceived as separate systems, to the study of the dynamics and interaction between cultures, thus discovering that cultural identities transform and merge. Significantly, in the lexicon of jurisprudence and other social sciences the term "multiculturalism" is more often connected with the term "interculturalism," proving that multiculturalism remains incomprehensible and opposed to a free and open society, serving instead a segregationist dimension (Ricca 2008).

the practice with a minimum of effort and indeed could have been also enriched by the additional diversity fed into society (Chap. 2 sec. 5.1).

Conversely, introducing a comparison of interests creates a test that allows both parties/cultures in the dispute to be visible, also in the opinion, along with their arguments and to reach solutions that provide a bridge for future coexistence.

The judge, the legislator, the public or private institution which is faced with multicultural conflicts is called, therefore, to enter into a further phase of the evaluation, which I call "relational." The final steps of the test proposed are designed to move the cultural practice from its isolation and to read it in relation to the context in which it operates.

To this end, a step that the judge should take is to find a cultural equivalent, a *secundum comparationis*, a similar and comparable practice within the culture of the majority to which the judge belongs, that can elucidate other people's practices and present them in a more comprehensible language. As the judge acts between two distinct semiotic systems, the practice must be "translated" (Ricca 2008; Benedetti 2010[19]).

As shown, the search for the "cultural equivalent" is not a necessary step in any of the tests examined. However, one can find its embryonic traces in different judgments. In general, the "cultural equivalent" is presented by the party requesting the cultural exception in an effort to tell the judge why that behavior is worthy of protection. Consider some cultural equivalents emerging from procedural depositions of Native Americans who were challenging the construction of public works in their ancestral territories: "we go to all of the sacred mountains for protection. We go on a pilgrimage similar to Muslims going to Mecca;" "Considering the mountain 'like family,' the Navajo greet the Peaks daily with prayer songs;" "The mother of humanity, called the Changing Woman and compared by one witness to the Virgin Mary, resided on the Peaks."[20]

In the case of the child which the school forced to cut his braids (Chap. 3 sec. 9), the father specifies that as a "Cherokee Indian descent, (he) followed a religious tenet dictating that his hair was 'a sense organ' and that loss of hair equated to loss of a body part."[21]

This translation work, which at the moment is occasionally carried out by the parties, could be made by the court, possibly with the mediation of the cultural group members or of the cultural expert,[22] but with a definitely more active role:

19 In the new discipline "juridical translation," the translator must not remain faithful to the letter, but to the sense: "translation constitutes a capstone of the vast subject of interpretation. It becomes, therefore, exactly located along the horizon of hermeneutics" (Benedetti 2010: 3).

20 *Navajo Nation vs United States Forest service*, United States Court of Appeals for the Ninth Circuit, 479 F.3d 1024; 2007 U.S. App. Lexis 5710; 37 elr 20062.

21 *A.A. v. Needville Independent School District*, U.S. District Court for the Southern District of Texas, Houston Division, Civil Action no. H-08-2934, January 20th, 2009.

22 Although it is not an official part of ethnography, anthropology often recurs to cultural equivalents when explaining a practice with the intention to better explain to the reader the exact meaning of it: "the African cattle-breeders eat beef very rarely, because their cattle are their very welfare but also a symbol of social status and a vital investment for hard times – something like a bank account for Europeans" (Yastrzhembskiy 2013: 206).

the judge knows the culture to which he belongs, can analyze the practices, highlight the elements of similarity or discrepancy with those of the minority group, and construct a judgment in dialogue between the two cultures, which in the work of translation shed light on one another.

In particular, there are three advantages in the judgment's enunciation of the cultural equivalent.

First, it is a tool that manages to make the allogenic (foreign: from *allos*-other, and *geno*, birth, in Greek) practice more understandable to the judge's audience.

Second, it is a tool that allows the detection of the presence of any double standard in the treatment of the allogenic practice with respect to other similar practices freely performed by the majority.

Third, the cultural equivalent problematizes the validity of the cultural system of the majority, in two ways: it can reveal to the majority that it has similar "horrifying" practices to those performed by the minority, thus pushing the same majority to change them; or the majority may realize that the practice of the minority has a better meaning and value than its own symmetrically identified practices; thus the comparison may regenerate the majority's universe of signs (Niccolai 2007: 485).

a) Translate the practice. The first advantage that the cultural equivalent identification produces, as mentioned, is to ensure a correct translation: "all good translation seeks to reproduce the structure of an alien discourse within the translator's own language" (Asad 1986: 156). Translation brings the allogenic practice closer, so that we can perceive its exact scope with our own language.[23] So, if the judge explains that forcing a Muslim woman to go to work without the veil can amount to a woman of the majority being asked to go to work in a bathing suit, the case will "come closer" and it would become clear what it is at play before balancing reasons. Conversely, if it turns out that wearing the Islamic headscarf or not is like asking a Western woman to decide whether to wear any ornaments in her hair, surely the reasons for Muslim women – in the presence of other competing interests – should acquiesce. Since the interpretive community is not always able to wear the cultural lenses of the other as an anthropologist can do, it should be up to the judge, in the judgment, to provide us with these lenses and the quickest way is just to show us the behavior correspondence in our own cultural system.[24]

When there are no comparison terms among the meanings that a sign (object or behavior) assumes within the semiotic systems of the minority and the majority,

23 "We need to anthropologize the West: show how exotic its constitution of reality has been; emphasize those domains most taken for granted as universal (this includes epistemology and economics); make them seem as historically peculiar as possible" (Rabinow 1986: 241).

24 Obviously this does not eliminate the risks of each process of translation: "the process of 'cultural translation' is inevitably enmeshed in conditions of power" (Asad 1986: 163). In this sense, the limit of anthropology, once it becomes ethnography, is that anthropologists must explore "the inequality of languages . . . in order to determine how far they go in defining the possibilities and the limits of effective translation" (Asad 1986: 164). Despite this risk, in my opinion, the judge cannot avoid trying the translation.

often the case remains unintelligible: the judge does not understand the exact interests at stake and thinks toward a disproportionate resolution of a conflict.

Finding a cultural equivalent brings the practice of the other closer to the judge's hearing also because it shows that to accord protection to it means simply to confirm, under other forms, an analog conviction of the majority. One sees, for example, what emerges in the case of the request for two years partial exemption for Amish children[25] from obligatory school attendance by the choice of the Supreme Court of the United States to act as double-anthropologist and to seek a cultural equivalent:

> this case involves the fundamental interest of parents, as contrasted with that of the State, to guide the religious future and education of their children. The history and culture of Western civilization reflect a strong tradition of parental concern for the nurture and upbringing of their children. This primary role of the parents in the upbringing of their children is now established beyond debate as an enduring American tradition.

The judge, belonging to a culture like the United States where there is the possibility that children could study at home, is saying that the request of the Amish is not tied to any tradition distant in time, but rather one which coincides with a similar idea shared by the majority. This argument constitutes one of the foundations of the decision in favor of the Amish request.

Sometimes, the cultural equivalent or *secundum comparationis* could result in a practice historically existent, but disappeared in the majority's cultural assets; or that persists, but it is accompanied by a strong reproof and is no longer tolerated. Think of *delitto d'onore* (honor killing/crime of passion) which was partially justified in Italy until 1981.[26] This practice may be considered persistent as femicide, which is punished with more rigor since law no. 119/2013. Even in these cases, the anthropologist judge or legislator could better bring the two cultures into dialogue by evoking the past "cultural equivalent," and explaining better – instead of the reductive argument "your barbarian customs" – the transformation that has taken place, long ago, in the majority culture, thus offering a transformative input to the same minority.

b) Avoid double standards. Besides translating and bringing external cultural practices closer to the majority's system of meanings, a second advantage of the cultural equivalent can be, as mentioned, to highlight instances of discrimination. On this point is significant a case resolved by the Supreme Court of the

25 *Wisconsin v. Yoder et al.*, 406 U.S. 205 (1972). The Amish are a minority who live a pre-modern lifestyle. The case was resolved by permitting the children to retire from superior school, avoiding two years of obligatory instruction.

26 Crime of passion, *delitto d'onore*, was regulated by art. 587 criminal code before the abrogation worked by law no. 442 of August 5, 1981: "Whoever causes the death of the spouse, daughter or sister, in a context in which an illegitimate carnal relation has been discovered and in that state of rage determined to be an offense to his honor or that of his family, is punished with imprisonment for 3 to 7 years."

United States, which saw the faithful of the Santeria religion appeal an order of the City of Hialeah, Florida, which forbade the sacrifice of animals.[27] Two aims underlying the ban and declared in the ordinances were: to prevent animal cruelty and to pursue public health. But since the animal sacrifices were made for ritual purposes and propitiatory in the Santeria religion, the applicants claimed that the measure violated their religious freedom enshrined in the US Constitution. The Supreme Court identified the cultural equivalent of "animal sacrifice" in all other forms of "killings of animals" that are fully accepted in the majority culture and disposed the case as one of discrimination. To this end, it points out that neither the State of Florida or the City of Hialeah have ever maintained a general prohibition against killing animals, but only prohibiting their sacrifice, considering it different from other forms of killings that, conversely, are fully permitted by law. The Court, acting as an anthropologist and researching the significant differences accorded by the culture to the same behaviors, notes critically: "according to the City of Hialeah it is self-evident that killing animals for food is important;" that the elimination of insects with pesticides, also a form of killing, is "obviously justified" and that euthanasia of excess animals "makes sense" but "this *ipse dixit* does not explain why the religion (Santeria) alone must bear the weight of the ban, while many of these secular killings do not fall in the interest of the City to prevent the cruel treatment of animals."

The Supreme Court also confronts the question around the second purpose of the ordinance: to prevent animal sacrifices to ensure public health. Again, the anthropologist judge finds a *secundum comparationis* within the majority culture, in the "hunt" and observes that the City "does not prohibit the hunters to bring home their game, nor rule what they must do after their activities:" no health care precaution around the game that will be consumed within the city, though it may potentially cause illnesses, is observed, yet this practice is not discussed.

Using the cited cultural equivalents and finding similar practices treated differently in the absence of a compelling state interest, the US Supreme Court attests to the presence of discrimination against Santeria and annuls the prohibition of making animal sacrifices.

c) Problematizing the cultural horizon of the majority. Besides allowing a full understanding of another's cultural practice and revealing the presence of discrimination, the *secundum comparationis* is a harbinger of a third virtue: acting as a

27 *Church of the Lukumi Babalu Aye, Inc. v. City of Hialeah*, 508 U.S. 520 (1993). Santeria originates in the nineteenth century, as the consequence of a massive importation of slaves who brought the Yoruba religion from West Africa to Cuba. It presents a syncretism between elements of African animist religions and Catholicism. Santeria, in fact, means "the way of the saints." Across the iconography of saints, members of the religion also adore spirits called *orishas*. The essential nucleus of the religion is the nurture of the personal relationship with the *orishas* and one of the ways is the sacrifice of animals like chickens, ducks, pigeons, pigs, goats, sheep and turtles. The animals are killed by slicing their throats and normally the animal is eaten, except for cases in which the sacrifice is performed on occasions of death or for the cure of a disease. The religion, prohibited in Cuba and practiced in secret, arrived in south Florida with the exile of diverse Cubans. At the time of the decision there were around fifty thousand adherents to the religion in the state.

mirror, it problematizes the cultural system of the majority allowing, in turn, a transformation, a widening of "interpretative horizon" (Glendon 2006). In the process of translating others' practices into a cultural equivalent, the judge could come to discover that even in his culture there are equally questionable practices. The comparison with the other might unravel identical power structures, identical "dispositives" *a là* Foucault, within the majority. One of the thorniest hard cases posed by multiculturalism can serve as an example: What kind of cultural equivalent of the judge could find for infibulation? Are there similar practices, qualified as "female genital mutilation" in the culture of the majority? At first sight this appears to be an immeasurable behavior, but in hindsight plastic surgery, especially on sexually connoted body parts such as the breast, the hymen, the gluteus lends itself, at least, a primary point of comparison: just as female circumcision is a ritual of initiation without which women would risk social exclusion to the point that it can not enter into marriage, in the same way for Western women to rebuild the breast can become an essential element of self-perception, or can serve to increase self-esteem and to be accepted socially, by promoting the search for romantic partners. In both cases, the family may support the practice: complacent Western mothers and fathers often accompany their underage daughters to undergo the rite of pain, which may irreversibly alter the breast's physical integrity, impairing breastfeeding, but that promises a future in the body at last socially accepted. In both cases the construction of this body seems to be the result of a typically patriarchal design that normativizes beauty and characteristics of the sexually appreciable body.

From this comparison,[28] also the society that is judging the practice of infibulation is pushed to question reflexively upon itself (Gilman 1999): Under what conditions is plastic surgery acceptable? To what idea of the body do women correspond? Why is it also possible for minors? The way the practice of plastic surgery is perceived is, as noted, plural and controversial in Western culture.[29] Those who support it appeal to the values of free personal choice, or of psycho-physical equilibrium, as did the Italian Trial Court of Padua in 2007 (Chap. 2 sec. 8.1). But there is a second orientation that criticizes this practice as an expression of an objectification of women, designed to accommodate male tastes. Infibulation and breast surgery are revealed, adhering to such a reading, both to be practices related to patriarchy (*infra* sec. 5.12).

Through the search for a cultural equivalent, which is nothing more than a translation, the interpretative horizon would become common and this commonality could start to challenge and change it. This would have an immediate impact on the level of the opinion and the level of perception of the conflict in the public sphere. Instead of falling into primitivism (Chap. 3 sec. 3) reading female circumcision as a typical and retrograde element of traditional cultures,

28 "In all Western countries there are many necessary aesthetic surgical interventions on the face and on the body of the person, even minors, to keep them presentable in the culturally dominant canons: consider tatoos, piercings, the use of prostheses on the cheekbones or breast, on operations to reduce or enlarge the lips or nose and of liposuction" (De Maglie 2010: 49).

29 See the debate against surgery to correct the intersex or hermaphrodites (Chase 2002).

the judge (or the legislator) would reveal a common feature around a vision of a woman's body that needs to be rethought, with much more relational and discursive outcomes.

Another example that reveals the reflexivity which can carry the search for a cultural equivalent in the majority is the practice that tends to create places and times of life to separate men and women such as *purdah*, a very strict rule that forbids men from seeing women, or the practice of separate school classes for boys and girls.

Through *secundum comparationis* emerges that the separation between men and women persists in many areas of Western culture, such as in bathrooms or in the locker room: the other's vision remands to us, as in a mirror, ourselves; it brings into question the similarities of our attitudes with those of the other which may seem oppressive. In this sense, the fact of having separate bathrooms can arouse analogous questions in the majority: What is behind the cultural practice? A mere hygienic rule? An innuendo to the possible danger for women to suffer violence which keep them subtly immersed in patriarchal power relations? Or do we face a rule that helps normativize gender, to make people remember the binarism of the sexes? The research for a cultural equivalent shows that if Western men and women interact now in all spheres, that of the body is still subject to separation. Again, think of the specific clothing stores, the gender-specific beauty rituals of the female and male body, separate male and female prisons and sports. Asking "what is our *purdah*?" and finding it in prisons which prevent men and women from meeting, could lead to a new constitutional conversation.

The same could happen to another very controversial cultural conflict: the marriage between children or between teenagers. If for children there may effectively be no cultural equivalent, when the person reaches twelve or thirteen years in some way the phenomenon encroaches on a custom that is also ours: Do not Western children begin having their first coupling life experiences, including sexual experiences, at this age? A courtship between two Western teenagers that begins at twelve years is not seen as something for which the people involved are not ready. And often the parents encourage their fifteen-year-old daughters to decide to have a sexual experience (inside or outside a lasting relationship) by accompanying them to the gynecologist to take the pill or guide them with advice. Basically in the West people do not marry so early, but they can start their sexual life early. This is not to defend the practice of marriages between children or teenagers, but only to invite a reflection on how the really controversial aspect of this is the lack of consent of minors (often such marriages are combined and imposed) and not the practice itself in which it is seen that, without wedlock, the experiences of married life and sexuality at that age are the same in the West. Even here to proceed for *generum proximum et diferentia specifica*, following the *ars dialectica* (dialectics) can lead to more relational and purposeful results.

A further face where the *secundum comparationis*/cultural equivalent pluralizes the interpretative horizon of the majority is achieved when the comparison shows an opposite practice of the majority to be put in discussion/relation with the other culture. For example, in the case of Roma women the cultural practice to focus on, as seen, is keeping the child with them until grown, which, as a chain of consequences, often produces children who are not sent to school or who follow the mother in almost all the activities she performs, including begging. Which Western cultural equivalent could the judge find in this case? He can find an opposite mirror, because, unlike the Roma culture, the families of the majority culture have established the practice of "sending their children to day care" since they are very small. Two practices – to always keep the children with them, or to send them to day care – basically neutral *per se*, but which, compared, illuminate each other by discursively pushing both the European majority and the Roma minority to reflect on their vision of childhood and the idea of raising children.[30]

Other examples related to the care of children show that the gaze of the other can change our perception. In several cultures, the Western practice of making children sleep in separate rooms from their parents or letting them cry before intervening is considered a form of abuse. In some cultures, such as the Swedish one, beating children is prohibited by the law and this can problematize the idea of discipline (Dundes Renteln 2010a) and the relationships between generations, bringing new horizons of sense.[31]

Another example of an enriching translation can be comparing repudiation with divorce. When repudiation can be done both by men and women with reciprocity there might be some positive aspects like the fact that it is quicker than divorce. In this way the majority can reflect on the religious roots of its own legal system (Shah 2015b): as the indissolubility of marriage is a Christian concept, the difficulties, costs and long waiting times to obtain a divorce can indirectly serve religious interests.

In conclusion, the judge should act as a double-anthropologist: toward another's culture, but also toward her own, trying to gain an anthropological approach to the meaning that the behavior of others would have in the web of significances of the majority. This activity could lead to a positive shift: a process of regeneration for the law. In fact, the point of view of the minority, projected on the majority through the mediation of the court, may be a moment of awareness of the majority cultural practices – in which they may be so steeped as not to perceive

30 To seek to understand others' cultural practices can be useful to diachronically retrace the different perceptions around a behavior developed within the majoritarian society. In this case, it becomes very important that judges remind the majority of its previous concept of care that, actually, was similar to that of the Roma: Western mothers were, until a few decades ago, the direct caregiver of the child and he used to go to day care not before the age of three. Without this reminder from the judge, it would be more difficult to understand the almost visceral Roma mother–child relationship, as today the majority tends to perceive as normal the fact that parents physically separate from their children for the greater part of the day.

31 See the case of an "Italian parent, on vacation in Stockholm, arrested by the police for mistreatment of a minor, and forced to spend many days under arrest pending the judgment." The father slapped his son's face and pleaded he had exercised the *ius corrigendi* accepted in the Italian legal system and culture (Gustafsson 2011). The case opened a debate within Italian public opinion on the legitimacy of child beating.

them as problematic – and their transformation. The arrival of the other is fundamental to regenerate the law for new interpretations, to help grasp other possible readings of reality, as well as to produce new legislation.[32]

5.10 *Is the practice* harmful? *Is the harm* irreparable?

The criterion of harm is, along with the requisite of the compulsoriness of the practice (*supra* sec. 5.4), one of the most widespread elements in the reasoning of anthropologist judges at the comparative level (Dundes Renteln 2004: 214–219; Caggia 2010: 101). Harm to fundamental rights such as life and physical integrity has become, in multicultural jurisprudence, one of the strongest limits to cultural defense.

I maintain that this is a crucial element in the evaluation that the judge conducts. However, I will touch on some important risks to be avoided in this part of the test.

The measurement of harm strongly risks becoming culturally characterized. The cultural practice of beating children as a way to educate them (*ius corrigendi*) is not perceived as harmful in Anglo-Saxon and Italian cultures, while in Sweden it is a crime (Levesque, 2000). In some African groups excision is invested with a positive initiatory, if not aesthetic, value among women who practice it (Obiora 2000) while it is considered an extreme form of harm in the West.

The criterion of harm easily lends itself to ethnocentric attitudes. For instance, it has constituted the jurisprudential lynchpin in decisions such as that on polygamy in British Columbia in 2011 (Chap. 2 sec. 11) or the *kirpan* in Italy in 2017 (Chap. 2 sec. 8.2), both banned because they appear "harmful" to the majority, while for the minority this reasoning is inconceivable.

To avoid those risks, all the factors today randomly used by judges to measure the severity of harm – irreversibility of the damage, capability of the body to perform its functions, consent of the recipient to the harm – that are grouped in this test, should be managed with a skilled anthropological sensitivity and integrated with an analysis on the possible good reasons for why the harm is caused.

a) *Irreversibility.* A first criterion to understand if the practice is harmful and at what level, is the permanent change in physical parts of the body it causes or "irreversibility." Applying this standard, the beating of children would be very different than, for example, genital mutilation. However, in my opinion, this criterion should be expanded as it does not consider the psychological consequences

32 A group could, in fact, pass years, centuries, without a thoughtful perspective on its own legal and cultural universe: To whom would come to mind that the plants and animals can be seen as relatives? Or that the term "Italian" could include not only citizens of a state called Italy, but also the plants, animals, ancestors and future generations, until happening upon the corresponding term "Haida," the native tribe of western Canada? The indigenous culture, not coincidentally, has exercised an influence on Western law, leading to the coining of two important legal categories: the rights of future generations and the rights of Nature.

that the practice may imply. In this sense, it is true that hitting a child cannot leave permanent physical damage, but it might leave damage on a psychic level. At the same time, the criterion of the irreversibility of the body change should not be decisive as not all cultural practices that leave permanent physical marks (scarification rituals, male circumcision, tattoos, cosmetic surgery) should, by that fact alone, be forbidden.

b) *Functionality.* A second criterion to measure if the practice is harmful was developed by the Italian National Bioethics Committee in 1998 and reaffirmed by the Italian Supreme Court in 2011 (Chap. 2 sec. 8.1), which looks not so much at the irreversibility of the alteration of physical integrity as to how the damage will affect the "feature" of the organ of the body, and its ability to perform the "function" for which it is naturally predisposed. Based on this distinction, the Italian Committee on Bioethics explained why FGM should be considered prohibited as radically alterating sexual activity, while, conversely, male circumcision could be considered admissible, as the function of the male genital organ (sexual activity and reproduction) is not compromised. Even this criterion is not, in my opinion, decisive. An intervention of plastic surgery of the breast, for example, may affect breastfeeding. The lost production of milk is three times higher in women who have an intervention of this type, so it can be said that even plastic surgery can block the function for which that part of the body is intended; but not for this reason alone should it be prohibited.

There may, however, be irreversible treatments that prevent the functionality of an organ that are nonetheless actually wanted by the subject who claims his freedom of choice. A movement born in the US, but that is echoed elsewhere, claims the possibility to disable a "healthy" part of the body, for example by requesting the amputation of a leg or an arm, or actions which deprive the person of their vision or hearing (Arfini 2010). At first considered a sexual pathology, the idea of the trans-able body (which moves from an able condition to a disability or other skills) is based on the assumption that the disability is possible to be assigned a value, as it allows the subject to perceive the world in a different way – hence the refusal of some blind or deaf persons to recover the functionality of their vision and hearing. Those who advance such claims challenge the cultural vision which privileges the healthy and functional body as only one normative and dominant model. The concept of disability is, according to these positions, relative. The human body is objectively bounded by functional limitations: it cannot fly, cannot jump over a certain distance, cannot stay awake at all hours and so on, but no one would have a thought of considering these characteristics a disability, because society constructs the social space and time adapting to them. Even the fact that a person cannot use his hands or his legs or cannot hear or see would not be a penalizing fact if society itself were not disabling.

c) *Consent.* For these reasons it seems to me that the two above-mentioned criteria should be integrated with the consent that the recipient of the harmful practice gives to it. There are, in hindsight, an infinite number of majoritarian practices which cause some form of damage, both to adults and to minors, for whom the criterion of consent is dispositive: drinking, smoking, taking the pill, using a cell phone or the computer, going through cosmetic surgery, eating processed food. To avoid double standards, similar "harmful" practices should be recognized also in the minorities if consensual: fasting, scarification of the face, sun dance and other painful rituals, while the lack of consent could be the criteria for prohibiting both female and male circumcision or intersex surgery on minors (Chase 2002).

d) *Purpose of the harm inflicted*. To conclude, the measure of the damage should not only focus on its severity and permanence, all of which are too culturally influenced, but on other aspects of the test such as the purpose of inflicting harm, its potential good reasons which, in fact, were applied even in the *Kimura* case (Chap. 1 sec. 1.1), the value that lies behind the harmful practice (*infra* 5.13) and the consent and freedom of those who receive it.

5.11 What is the impact of the practice on the fundamental rights, culture and value system of the majority?

> A conflict over "difference" is not a struggle of one minority for recognition in relation to other actors who are independent of, unaffected by and neutral with respect to the form of recognition that the minority seeks. Rather, a struggle for recognition of a minority always calls into question and (if successful) modifies, often in complex ways, the existing forms of reciprocal recognition of the other members (individuals, other minorities and majorities) of the larger system of government of which the minority is a member.
> (Tully 2007: 21–22)[33]

With these words, James Tully criticizes the monological approach (as opposed to dialogical) to the recognition of cultural factors in the public sphere, which concentrates all the focus of attention on the minority and its competing claims to those of the majority. In order to arrive at a fusion of horizons, multicultural conflict cannot be thought of as a relationship in which a minority begs the majority for recognition and to fix their conditions, or even furnish very strict rules for according it (as does the Canadian cultural test with

33 Tully (2007: 22) proceeds to observe that "No members (including parliaments, courts and states) are transcendent to the field of struggle . . . the number of other members affected are almost always more than one, so these struggles cannot, except in the most simplified cases, be conceptualized as two-member struggles between self and other, master and slave, bourgeois and proletarian, minority and majority, minority and the state, or individual and collective, as an older tradition of reflection on struggles over recognition from Kant and Hegel, Mill and Marx, to Sartre and Fanon, liberals and communitarians tended to assume. That is, struggles over recognition are relational and mutual rather than independent, and multiple rather than dyadic." In this frame one locates the problems of post-recognition, such as those of how to construct a judicial system that accords the respect of differences without shattering and undermining social cohesion.

the indigenous people), ignoring the impact that recognition can have on the overall rules of coexistence.[34]

When assessment of the conditions for recognition is based only on the objective or subjective part of the test, all the attention is directed toward the minority, without assessing what impact the practice has on the majority.

The relational part of the test proposes that reviewing questions should be implemented such as: How much is the fundamental rights system of the majority placed at risk by the acceptance of the practice? How essential and mandatory is it for the majority to inhibit that practice? Who bears the greater sacrifice if the practice is permitted or prohibited?

This type of evaluation that presupposes an "us" and "them" in dialectical confrontation appears the latent reason in many judgments, but it is almost never verbalized in an appropriate manner. In fact, when the judge tries to say that there are at stake important values of the majority he espouses, as a misguided anthropologist, a rough counter-cultural argument that sounds like: "if you have your culture, I have mine" or "when in Rome do as the Romans do."

Alternatively, to exclude that the minority can understand the majority point of view returns to the beginnings of anthropology when the incommensurability of cultural universes was assumed. Conversely, a product of a more modern anthropology is the fact that persons belonging to a culture can transform their behavior: enculturation is combined with agency. As the judge of the host culture is able to understand the other's point of view, so the subject who claims a minority practice can and should do so with respect to the needs

34 Tully (2007: 29) again: "The forms of recognition that individuals and groups struggle for are articulated, discussed, altered, reinterpreted and renegotiated in the course of the struggle. They do not pre-exist their articulation and negotiation in some unmediated or ascriptive pre-dialogue realm accessible by individuals. They are worked out in dialogical relations with others . . . For example, the self-understanding of men and women, Muslim and Christian, French and English and indigenous and non-indigenous have changed enormously over the last decades of conflict, negotiation and discussion . . . Thus our understanding of who we are, of the partners with whom we are constrained to cooperate, and hence the acceptable norms of mutual recognition change in the course of the dialogue. Accordingly, the members need to be in on the webs of interlocution of the struggle in order to go through these changes in self-understanding and other-understanding." What should be the role of the judge in this context is well expressed by Webber (2007: 67–100): "the judge must then attempt to construct a synthesis that speaks to the concerns of both parties – that constitutes a vision of justice based on a broader range of experience than that possessed by the judge at the beginning of the hearing" (98); "the dialogical construction of a societal conception of justice described here" diverges from "the theories of justice in syllogistic form traditionally presented in legal philosophy" (98); "legal reasoning is a perpetually critical and creative enterprise, in which (if we are doing our jobs) we are consistently broadening the range of experience on which our conceptions of justice are based, and in which we re-evaluate and remake both premises and conclusions to maintain the connection between our legal norms and our best conceptions of the social order" (98); "The test of an acceptable process cannot be full substantive agreement. It has to be something less, something that has to do with the opportunity for and the quality of one's participation in the decision, as well as confidence that the goal of the process is some conception of justice, not mere imposition" (99); at this aim the requirement is "that the judge accept the integrity of the contending visions (at least provisionally) and attempt to achieve a synthesis of them" (100).

of the majority. To negate, *a priori*, this possibility means, in some way, to entrap the other in immobilism.

Obviously, even the majority must have good reasons to keep their own practices in a multicultural context. Those reasons should be made explicit with detailed explanations and not with general arguments like saying – as did Italy with the crucifix (*Lautsi vs Italy*, ECHR, 2011) – simply that it is one's own culture or that the practice violates undefined "Western values" – as again Italy did in 2017 by prohibiting the *kirpan* (Chap. 2 sec. 8.2).

The conflict around the *burqa* is further illuminated by this question of the test: Which of the majority's values is, in fact, placed at risk by allowing women to wear it? The offense to gender equality that this "object" would cause has already been deconstructed and revealed to be inconsistent (Chap. 3 sec. 2; *infra* sec. 5.12); the value of safety does not seem expendable, at least until the *burqa* is actually used for criminal purposes; the argument that the *burqa* prevents the wearer to interact and to have social exchanges (*vivre ensemble*/living together) is also debatable as each of us has a right to be a stranger. By contrast, I agree with the thesis that to allow the wearing of such clothing is perfectly in line with one of the values of the Western majority: the freedom of expression and the basic, so far undisputed right, to wear what one wants. To look inside oneself is a good exercise also for the majority to understand that sometimes, when proposing the suppression of a cultural practice, it may thereby betray its own constitutional values.

One crucial *topos* for the majority is the protection of the rights of women. Being this value so quintessential, I considered it appropriate to make it explicit in autonomous form in the relational part of the test as every minority group which wants its customs recognized should relate with it.

5.12 *Does the practice perpetuate* patriarchy?

Both at doctrinal level – especially within feminist critiques of multiculturalism – and at jurisprudential level, "culture" tends to lose strength, along the axiological scale, when it undermines the principle of male–female equality. The 2011 Istanbul Convention and some constitutions have come to establish this hierarchy of values (eg. art. 35 of the Canadian Constitution,[35] art. 32 of the Ugandan Constitution[36]). It can, therefore, be said that there is a widespread consensus comparatively (Chap. 1 sec. 1.2 *Saleem* case and 2.1 *Kassam* case; Chap. 2 sec. 11), on the

35 After stating in subsection 1 "The existing aboriginal and treaty rights of the aboriginal peoples of Canada are hereby recognized and affirmed," subsection 4 of sec. 35 states: "Notwithstanding any other provision of this Act, the aboriginal and treaty rights referred to in subsection 1 are guaranteed equally to male and female persons."

36 Art. 32: "Affirmative action in favour of marginalised groups. 1. Notwithstanding anything in this Constitution, the State shall take affirmative action in favour of groups marginalised on the basis of gender, age, disability or any other reason created by history, tradition or custom, for the purpose of redressing imbalances which exist against them. 2 Laws, cultures, customs and traditions which are against the dignity, welfare or interest of women or any other marginalised group to which clause 1 relates or which undermine their status, are prohibited by this Constitution."

fact that feminine subjugation cannot be accepted even in the face of culture. This element has become one of the recurrent themes of judicial reasoning because gender equality is one of the values to which democracies aspire, at a level that the European Union considers that there is not democracy without it.

I have framed the question as "does the practice perpetuate patriarchy?" instead of as "is the practice oppressive to women?" or "is the practice against gender equality?" in order to avoid some limiting effect that the reference to gender can have, such as excluding children, and to create a common ground between us and the other that concentrates not on what can be different conceptions of the role of the women in a society, but on systems of power and domination.

Patriarchy is the most ancient system of inequality and privilege known in Western history, dating as far back as 3000 B.C. (Lerner 1986). Western legal systems began a process of de-patriarchalization in the nineteenth century which can be summarized in different stages: the extension of "right to vote" to women thus opening the political sphere to them (1800–1950); the liberation of the woman's body from the constraints of her family, by permitting abortion, divorce, sexual freedom and abolishing crimes like adultery, prostitution, passion crimes (1960–1970); and the "liberation" at work, fully guaranteeing access to professions and maternity leave rights (1980–1990). Nowadays, legal de-patriarchalization takes on new forms with the recognition of the autonomous category of women's rights at the international level, affirmative action (eg. quotas to enhance women political representation) and gendered law (eg. "gender crimes" such as stalking, femicide, FGM). Although Western societies are still imbued with "legacies" of the patriarchal system – sexism, male chauvinism, the wage gap between men and women, misogyny, paternalism – if judges validated gender relations rooted in a patriarchal logic, they would fail to reflect the present sense of justice. Judges have been faced with classification problems with respect to arranged marriages, female genital mutilation, forms of domestic violence inflicted as a direct consequence for disobeying the husband's or father's orders, honor killings and in the most recent years they have sometimes deculturalized some of these conducts and have read them only in the light of patriarchy (Ruggiu 2015).

There are some conditions that should be respected when using a patriarchal framing to forbid a cultural practice. They may be summarized as follows: 1) patriarchy should be used not as a restricted notion limited to women, but as indicating a more complex system of control including that of parents over children, older men over younger men and older women over younger women (Gruenbaum 2001: 41); 2) the law should reject an abstract notion of patriarchy which fails to recognize that women can bargain with it or adopt strategies of passive resistance, and thus ends up making their situation worse (Kandiyoti 1988); 3) the law should avoid concealing the majority's patriarchal practices by projecting patriarchy only upon the minority (Braunmühl 2012; Mancini 2012).

Applying a broad notion of patriarchy not limited to women, both female genital mutilation and male circumcision should be prohibited. According to the gender argument used both in Western states and by the 2012 UN Resolution Intensifying

Global Efforts for the Elimination of FGM, FGM is an oppressive practice of sexual control over girls, while male circumcision is an act of empowerment of the baby, who is then recognized as part of the community. Nevertheless, we have to consider that patriarchy is a very complex power structure that is not limited to control by men over women; one of its chief characteristics is the idea of the child as property. In this sense, male circumcision could also be read under the category of patriarchy: it may express the absolute control by the father over his son's body. The constitutional conversation over the prohibition of male circumcision is still going on, and several possibilities have been discussed – the choice criterion, the irreversible harm criterion, the religious criterion or the patriarchal criterion. All are debatable, but I think that the law should choose to avoid the present discriminatory treatment of similar facts. Were the law to consider adopting the patriarchal argument, I think both male and female genital alterations would be forbidden because, taken together, they are an expression of parental control over children.[37]

The second condition I would like to focus on is that of avoiding an abstract notion of patriarchy that keeps women from bargaining with it. Since patriarchy has a multiple and heterogeneous nature, Deniz Kandiyoti (1988: 274) attempted to oppose the ontological, "abstract notion of patriarchy encountered in contemporary feminist theory" with a more concrete vision of patriarchal phenomenology, in which "women strategize within a set of concrete constraints." In this context, according to this scholar, "different forms of patriarchy present women with distinct 'rules of the game' and call for different strategies to maximize security and optimize life options with varying potential for active or passive resistance in the face of oppression" (Kandiyoti 1988: 274). For this reason during the case of *S.A.S. v. France* decided on 1 July 2014, some feminist movements opposed to the French law banning the *burqa* stressed the following: even assuming that the *burqa* is a patriarchal practice, wearing a *burqa* can provide women with a certain degree of security and protection, and be the lesser evil in a context of broader oppression; for instance it gives women the possibility of leaving the home unaccompanied, something that might be prohibited if they were not allowed to wear it. The fact that many women defended it could be seen as a strategy of "bargaining with patriarchy." It is important to avoid an overly abstract vision of what is oppressive, depriving women themselves of the agency to negotiate their roles within their own culture. For the same reason, I would not support the prohibition of breast surgery, heels and pants just because they express a vision of the woman's body that corresponds to the "male symbolic order."

The third condition is that the appeal to patriarchy does not conceal patriarchal practice in a majority projecting patriarchy only on the minority. This risk was raised by Sarah Song (2007) who speaks of a "diversionary effect" and by Susanna Mancini (2012) with regard to the *burqa*, and it emerges, in my opinion,

37 I am open also to other solutions, on the ground of equal treatment. If the law were to choose the child's freedom of choice over his/her own body, any kind of genital alteration on male or female would be forbidden, even Jewish and Islamic circumcision. If the law were to consider the "harm" criterion and the functionality of the body, both male circumcision and the milder forms of FGM (now all forbidden by the 2012 UN resolution) would be admitted.

in the polygamy cases as well. In fact, in asserting that the practice is a patriarchal one, the majority assumes that its own marriage practices are not. In this way, using a gender argument, the judge reinforces an institution – monogamy – that feminism denounced as one of the main expressions of patriarchy.

Furthermore, classifying polygamy as gender oppression closes the door on a possible revolution in the conception of the modern family and of male/female relations to forms of polyamory.[38]

With the respect of these conditions, and with an anthropological sensitivity that can be increased by using the cultural equivalent (ninth question of the test *supra* sec. 5.9), the use of patriarchy to test the recognition may prove to be useful.

5.13 What value does the minority ascribe to the practice at issue? Does this value reflect the choice of a meaningful life?

The subject who appeals to their culture must bring explanations for which he is to conserve the practice, which serve both to convince the majority, and also to verify that the minority is aware and has chosen to continue the practice, after both an internal and external debate. Once established that the minority, including the most vulnerable groups within it, retains sufficiently good reasons to adhere to the practice, it must explain them to the majority.

The question that closes the test can, indeed, be subjected to various objections. With it, in fact, it seems that the court is called to move from a descriptive level to an evaluative plan on the capacity of a culture to produce lives with meaning and that will lead to happiness; but on what authority could the court perform an evaluation of this type, especially once it recognizes that the right to culture is internationally covered? Would not it be preferable to stop at the previous twelve "*de facto*" investigations instead of entering into a kind of "moralizing" attitude which analyzes the intrinsic validity of other cultural systems? The test began with the premise that culture is a constitutionally relevant factor, which has a value: this alone should suffice to exclude further investigations that would seem to demonstrate precisely what should, instead, be the premise of the entire discourse. Also, have not the "good reasons" to continue the practice already been ascertained by asking whether the practice is mandatory and shared, and whether the group faces discrimination (questions 4, 5 and 6)? Why must the group adduce further proof?

Notwithstanding these objections to keep in mind, I maintain that this last step should be inserted at the end in order to render the choice of the judge still "more comprehensible" and to implement the relational profiles of the settlement

38 Not to mention the hypocrisy of ignoring that from a cultural and anthropological point of view, Western societies already practice a sort of *de facto* polygamy: when the crime of adultery was decriminalized (in Italy, this took place with the Constitutional Court's judgment no. 126 of 1968), the behavior of having a lover during another relationship became legal. And the introduction of divorce was a way to legalize serial polygamy, which is to say not polygamy in a single setting, but over time.

of the conflict, thus offering to the majority an occasion to learn new ways to be human.

As seen, sometimes to demonstrate that one has good reasons to keep a cultural practice, it can be sufficient to show the cultural equivalent (*supra* sec. 5.9). Thus a Sikh has good reasons to wear the *kirpan* in the public sphere since for him the knife hanging from his neck has a protective meaning, comparable to that of a chain with the cross worn by a Christian – though with an even higher value, being an obligatory symbol – and it is absolutely not thought, within the interpretative horizon of Sikhism, as a weapon. In general, when one requests concession for cultural rights or prerogatives identical to those enjoyed by the majority, once the work of translation from one cultural system to another is accomplished, it is easier to accord recognition. This appears, in fact, constitutionally justifiable, according to the principle of equality. Obviously, when the contested cultural rights have some costs their effective protection can face difficulties: for example, the potential right to have educational programs that also treat the history of certain groups or courses in minority languages may be ineffective for lack of money to fund the teachers or the drafting of specific handbooks. However, conceptually, the provision of such protection does not raise any particular legal difficulties.

Some multicultural conflicts, however, are solvable not so much because of substantial equivalence, identifying one common reason that simply appears under different forms and cultural garments, but rather admitting the potential validity of both the incompatible reasons of the minority and the majority. The decisive criterion could be, in these cases, that the minority culture deserves recognition since it creates the possibility of choices to which one can assign value. From this point of view, if the minority proposes an idea of existence which serves to achieve a meaningful life (Rombinson 2007), even if totally removed from that of the majority, then their system should be accorded recognition.

In this regard, it is of interest to return to the case of the Amish who obtained an exemption from the full obligation of scholastic attendance in a ruling that takes great care within the relational profile of the argument.[39] Here's how the judge explains the Amish world view:

> Amish objection to formal education beyond the eighth grade is firmly grounded in these central religious concepts. They object to the high school, and higher education generally, because the values they teach are in marked variance with Amish values and the Amish way of life; they view secondary school education as an impermissible exposure of their children to a "worldly" influence in conflict with their beliefs. The high school tends to emphasize intellectual and scientific accomplishments, self-distinction, competitiveness, worldly success, and social life with other students. Amish society emphasizes informal "learning through doing;" a life of "goodness," rather than a life

39 *Wisconsin v. Yoder et al.*, 406 U.S. 205 (1972)

> of intellect; wisdom, rather than technical knowledge; community welfare, rather than competition; and separation from, rather than integration with, contemporary worldly society.

The judge in this opinion seeks to evidence that the way of life that the Amish intend to pursue is radically different from the American one, but not charged with less value. It is treated as a different value:

> The Amish alternative to formal secondary school education has enabled them to function effectively in their day-to-day life . . . and to survive and prosper in contemporary society as a separate, sharply identifiable and highly self-sufficient community for more than 200 years in this country.

The judge also hears from two cultural experts. Dr. Hostetler testifies that:

> compulsory high school attendance could not only result in great psychological harm to Amish children, because of the conflicts it would produce, but would also, in his opinion, ultimately result in the destruction of the Old Order Amish church community as it exists in the United States today.

Could this mere objective fact – that the practice that is being sought is essential to the survival of the group – dispose the case? In reality, this is an important element, but not decisive. The pivot of the decision is the assessment of the fact that the Amish want to keep an equally valid lifestyle. In other testimony, education expert Dr. Erikson shows, in fact, how the Amish can successfully prepare their children to be productive members of the Amish community, with an even better method than the mainstream American: "their system of learning through providing the skills directly relevant to their adult roles in the Amish community [is] as 'ideal,' and perhaps superior to ordinary high school education." This observation may open a discussion on the school system of the majority. The awareness that other educational systems exist and the fact that mainstream American culture is internally put under discussion makes this arrangement acceptable.

At this point of the analysis the judge will have all the elements of the controversy on the table, and can move forward to combine them and find a solution of the case that won't omit any part of the balancing attitude of the law.

6 How to use the test

An important point to clarify regards the use of the test and the weight to give to the single questions and to the tool as a whole. What happens when a practice meets every point of the test, except for a single question? Should one assume that the test is satisfied only if all the answers are positive, or only two thirds? Half?

In my opinion, each of the thirteen steps of the test must not be given a plenary value, but rather each should complement each other; only at the end of the test will there be a complete picture of the relevant dispute elements for its composition.

The absence of a lexical order, any hierarchy of importance between the test questions may be seen as its weak point. One could argue that when conceived in the flexible way suggested here, the test misses its function of being an effective operational tool in the hands of judges. Where resides the advantage of a test which is neither binding nor final? Or a test that does not choose in advance which element to give greater importance? With such a test, in fact, the conflict could remain unresolved. What happens, for example, if a practice is essential to the survival of the group, but at the same time causes harm? Or if a practice causes harm, but the "victim" consents?

Choosing not to insert any order of priority in the questions derives from the desire not to construct the test as a tool that mathematizes legal reasoning. Using a metaphor, it can be said that the test questions proposed are as different lighthouses that gradually light up, to illuminate the case from different points of view. Only once the case has been illuminated can one begin to look for a solution. In this sense, a sophisticated test, with many questions, is more appropriate to illuminate every element of the case. As the inquiry within the test progresses, there is a process of self-correction of some parts of the test that, if taken individually, would risk providing only a partial view. Had hierarchical order been inserted between the questions, the test could be solved simply with a single question: Does the practice cause harm? Or is there the consent of the recipient of the practice? But, in my view, this would leave in the dark many other issues.

7 The role of cultural expertise within the test

The presence of a test in which the court is called upon to verify, through a matrix of predetermined questions, the conditions under which to grant recognition to culture raises the question of how to get the cultural knowledge needed to answer the test, and once gathered, which weight to give to it. Especially in the first five questions of the test it is necessary, in fact, that the court has recourse to competent anthropological technical skills in order to identify exactly whether culture is invocable, the confines of the practice claimed, its obligatory nature and so on (questions 1–5). Cultural knowledge is necessary also to measure the "reasonable cultural person" behavior (question 7), and often to find a cultural equivalent (question 9).

The comparative survey reveals, at present, considerable heterogeneity regarding the subjects and the methods with which the court establishes the objective part of a cultural dispute and the weight judges give to the cultural expertise once acquired (Holden 2011).

The analysis shows great heterogeneity on the subjects to be consulted. It is possible to speak of a *summa divisio* between technical consultations, principally of anthropologists and other qualified experts on the one hand and members belonging directly to the culture in question acting as lay-witnesses on the other. Courts, in fact, have alternatively consulted: a variety of academic expertise on culture (eg. anthropologists, archaeologists, folklorists, psychologists, sociologists); a qualified representative of that culture (eg. embassies or consulates, political leaders of the communities, activists, rabbis or other religious leaders); testimonies of *quisque de populo* (lay people) belonging to that culture; or the accused or the defendant left alone speaking for themselves.

In respect to this utterly mixed picture it would, in my view, be appropriate for the consultation carried out by the judge to combine both a representative member of the minority and a cultural expert,[40] in the view of providing a balanced answer to the dilemma "who speaks for the minority?" and also in the view of providing the judge with the most complete picture of the cultural practice. In fact, the presence of a technical figure avoids, on the one hand, the risk of a strategically "invented" practice by the minority or, on the contrary, the adoption of a defensive attitude denying culturalism, perhaps to avoid further stereotypes of the group:[41] it is, therefore, a guarantee of neutrality and impartiality.[42] The presence of the consultation of persons who belong to the same minority (whether qualified representatives or *quisque de populo*) avoids, on the other hand, distortions that even an anthropologist may incur, as an outside observer projecting the gaze of "the other" onto the group.

Regarding the methods used by the judge to incorporate the cultural knowledge into the trial, they again are various.

40 There are also other crucial questions that the anthropologist judge should confront. As happens when the judge maintains that he is not faced with a behavior classifiable by anthropology, but rather is better served by the intervention of another discipline: psychology (Woo 2004). The difficulty to identify to which "expert" to appeal is one mirror of the competition between the various disciplines to explain human behavior, but also of the way in which one regards alterity. Depending on the discipline to which she may choose to appeal, the judge defines the idea of the other and contributes to the forging of the idea of culture. For instance, defensive lines oscillate between the use of the cultural argument and mental illness, a profile that emerges in glaring ways in the *Kimura* case with which this work opened. At times, attorneys and judges are not able to read a behavior as cultural and, utilizing the real behavioral schemas of our own culture, read it as a pathology of the psyche. At other times they follow the opposite approach, namely under the wave of the excess of culturalization of all that is done by foreigners, often use the category of culture to explain behavior considered insane in the immigrant culture.

41 As happened in the case, which occurred in Los Angeles in 1989, of two Cambodians who had killed a dog to eat it. Hearing the cries of the animal, the neighbors had denounced the deed to the police and the two were accused of maltreatment of animals; the two defended themselves by sustaining that in Cambodia the dog was considered an edible animal. But the leader of the United Cambodian Community, who spoke as a representative of the community, negated the culturality of the practice, observing: "while the eating of dogs is not uncommon in such countries as Korea, the Philippines and Vietnam, it was highly unusual in Cambodia until the 1970s, when people there were near starvation during the regime of Pol Pot. During the war, a lot of things happened and they ate anything to survive." The preoccupation of the leader of the community was that this fact projected a negative and excessively disproportionate image of the cultural differences (Haldane 1989; Nafziger, Kirkwood Paterson, Dundes Renteln 2010: 70–71).

42 On this point, in truth, given the fact that anthropologists are often "activists" of the protection of the cultures they study, the possibility that an ethical dilemma arises in the anthropologist called to witness knowing that what she says could prejudice that group cannot be neglected. In this case, in my view, the rule of scientific independence should prevail, with the possibility to renounce the appointment if this cannot be respected.

In many European states, several elements converge to push the judge to think that she can proceed as a solo anthropologist. Often, as in Italy, anthropology is not a profession organized in a state board from which the judge can select engineers, doctors, psychologists and other technical experts more established and recognized. Anthropology suffers also the prejudice in favor of "hard sciences," being a social science, and one of the youngest, so it happens that the judge neither thinks he needs to deepen the information brought by the lawyer. Judges tend to work alone also in contexts where there is a widespread knowledge of the groups, generally because they are national minorities and not "new" minorities such as immigrants.[43]

This solipsistic attitude, in my opinion, bears the risk of mistakes. The presence of a test like the one suggested in this work is aimed to reinforce the need of a cultural expertise: having to answer to many technical issues, either the judge is really an expert on that culture, or otherwise the external consultation becomes "a must." The presence of the test frees the judge from the effort of choosing what questions to ask to the expert: they are predetermined by the test. The judge may integrate them depending on the case, but she has already a working grid available.

The need of consulting a cultural expert to clarify the objective part of the test raises some practical issues: the lack of available experts on that specific group in the country, the time needed to release the cultural expertise, and its costs. Those practical problems can be addressed in several ways. A step to take could be to socialize anthropological knowledge. For instance, the creation of databases of cultural expertises already released could permit the judge to consult them, avoiding repetition of consultation in similar cases, thus saving time and money. Similarly, handbooks[44] and *vade mecum* previously prepared by anthropologists, which list cultural practices and explain them, could compensate the impossibility to consult an anthropologist because they are lacking in that country or due to economic restraints in the administration of justice.

In general, it would be opportune for multicultural societies to strengthen the anthropological formation of the courts, with appropriate university curricula and continuing education courses for judges.

Once permitted – preferably with a joint presence of a cultural expert and a member of the minority, and subsidiarily through handbooks and cultural expertises previously gathered – to enter into the trial, the anthropological knowledge begs the question of which weight the judge should give to it (Cassell 2009; French 2009; Holden 2011).

The entrance of the cultural expert in the process can be attributed to the greater chapter of the relationship between technical and legal assessments, between science and the law. Just as when faced with technical standards derived from medicine, engineering or psychology, the court risks losing its role in the

43 See the knowledge professed by the Italian courts for the practice of ***kafalah*** (Italian Supreme Court op. 2nd February, 2015, no. 1843, Chap. 3 sec. 7) or for Judaism (Chap. 2 sec. 8.1).

44 I am conscious that this tool may recall the old colonizers' report during imperialism, but I think that if built in a critical and conscious way this tool can satisfy the practical need to spread anthropological knowledge between judges, and to favor mutual understanding

dispute if it adopts an excessively deferential attitude toward science, so the use of the test could technicalize the concept of culture to the point of coercing significantly what the law has to say to reach a fair conflict resolution. The two moments of anthropological evaluation and legal assessment must not be the same, because they express two very distinct benefits: one to describe the other's point of view, and the other to promote coexistence. The resolution of a cultural conflict should not be given over to the hands of whatever cultural expert deemed most technically competent. Furthermore it should be noted that, in general, anthropologists are not comfortable in giving a solution to the case; not being jurists, they prefer to keep a descriptive attitude, leaving the final decision to the judge.

To avoid the envisaged risks, the test proposed in this work does not simply give prominence to mere ontological elements of culture; it also introduces a subjective and relational analysis. In this sense, after the judge has collected, including through the technical expert, evidence on the existence and characteristics of the cultural elements, he will be encouraged by the proceduralization of his argumentative reasoning given by the test (sec. 5.6–5.13), to make further investigations that best fit the reasoning accorded by ***modus iuridicus.***

8 The test's risks: technicality, formalism, bureaucratization, reductionism of reality

There are basically four objections to the use of a cultural test as judicial argumentation guiding tool: the first relates to the risk that it brings out the technical part of the anthropological evaluation to the detriment of the balancing attitude of the law; the second is that it becomes the means of a neo-positivism, which reproposes a formalistic idea of law as mathematic; the third is that the test may become a harbinger of dangerous bureaucracy, a straitjacket for the judge; the fourth objection is that the test results in a reductionism of reality as it limits the analysis to some elements of the dispute while excluding others (new *topoi*) which may in the future prove relevant to found a persuasive approach to culture.

a) Technicality. Regarding the first risk it has been already addressed *supra* sec. 7 when I showed how the judge may surrender in a passive way to cultural expertise instead of solving the case according to the balancing point of view of the law. The answer to avoid this risk is in the way in which I constructed the cultural test: it previously inserts in the judicial ascertainment precisely those elements which are characteristic of the balancing attitude of the law (questions 6–13) so the judge cannot limit her analysis to the technical knowledge of anthropology.

b) Formalism. More complex is the second critique advanceable against the test instrument: that it can become a mere mathematical rule, expression of a jurisprudential neo-positivism. According to this criticism, the test risks, in and of itself, to restrict action for courts when resolving disputes – to stifle legal experience. The latter has, as its essence, the controversial comparison of different reasoning and the search for a settlement that will restore the values of coexistence. If judges were required to apply a pre-established test every time they are confronted with a different culture, they would be trapped in those tracks, producing formalistic reasoning.

One example of this risk appears in the case of the indigenous dancer, Mr. Thomas, kidnapped and beaten by his companions to be initiated into the dance of the spirits (Chap. 1 sec. 4.2). The Canadian Supreme Court rejected the cultural defense because the dance of the spirits was not essential to the cultural survival of the group, as the cultural test required. The reasoning appears trapped inside the test, which operates as an abstract norm which prevents the emergence of other, more comprehensible reasons to justify, in this case, the impossibility of recognition. What makes that opinion extremely problematic is the question that the Court's reasoning immediately arouses: if the practice were indeed "essential," could the dancers then inflict such treatment on their companion?

Used in this way tests, indeed, appear to be inadequate tools, which block the practical reasoning of law.

Without the presence of the test, the Canadian Supreme Court could have relied on established judicial principles to arrive at solutions more in keeping with common sense: Mr. Thomas cannot be compelled by force to become a dancer of the dance of the spirits. Using the test, the Court avoids exposing the real reasons underlying the decision and also avoids a frank discussion with the indigenous minority.

If the reported case is illustrative of how criticism of neo-positivistic jurisprudence may prove founded, the problem, in my opinion, does not reside in the test tool in and of itself, but rather in how it is constructed and used. This work regards the test neither in a technocratic perspective, as a tool that allows the judge to access an anthropological wisdom to which to pay absolute deference, nor as a dogmatic tool from which to derive fixed consequences.

The test is not considered in this work as a good in itself. Existing tests are subjected to criticism and evaluated based on their ability to improve the legal experience (or, conversely, restrict it). This work rejects those tests which consider worthy of recognition only practices arising in a certain historical moment – when perhaps those arising after are much more understandable to the majority – or those tests offering an essentialist vision of culture crystallized over time. Similarly, it refuses those tests which are limited to merely ontologically ascertain the existence of a culture without looking at the incarnation it manifests in individuals or at the relational dynamics between the group and the majority. The test that I propose attempts to fill the gaps of existing tests in order to expand legal experience, allowing the consideration of new points of view, and pushing parties to demonstrate the reasonableness of the use of a cultural practice. The test, in this sense, is inserted into a vision of law as practical reason, based on experience not on mathematics; it should not be seen as a mathematical, formal grid, but as a matrix that accompanies the experience of the other. For this reason the test is not a good in itself, but becomes as such if it can be an instrument able to promote practical reasoning, *in primis* by making its exercise more sapient. The test aims to be, therefore, an argumentative technique, a guided tour for the judge, an itinerary that favors legal experience by seeking justice in each individual case in the overall equilibrium of constitutional principles.

c) Bureaucratization. Connected to formalism, a third criticism is that behind the test could arise a bureaucratic conception of jurisprudence: if the test is a procedural grid that the judge has to traverse before every multicultural conflict, its purpose seems to submit conflicts to an administrativist logic that is more typical of companies and corporations than of courts. Particularly in European legal systems, which are far from the tradition of the common law tests, and in which the "duty to motivate" every opinion is exerted with a certain discretionality in choosing the arguments, the test may appear a straitjacket for judicial reasoning.

I will answer this criticism by trying to show how the test is the result of a bottom-up approach, and is crucial to guarantee legal certainty.

First of all, it is important to consider that the test descends from previous pragmatic exercises made by judges when resolving cases which, through it, are simply brought to synthesis: it is a bottom-up tool, not imposed on judges bureaucratically from above, being the result of a "circulation" of models (Guazzarotti 2001: 5; Lollini 2007: 479–523). The enterprise undertaken in this book to firstly reconstruct the *topoi* inductively elaborated by judges and then to propose a unified tool to solve multicultural conflicts can be ascribed to the larger chapter of the proceduralization of the judicial argumentative *iter* that acquires ever-increasing urgency in studies on jurisprudence (Mengoni, Modugno, Rimoli 2003; Gallo 2005; Petrillo 2005; Picardi 2005; Sagnotti 2005). Especially in a context in which many new arguments which judges may use arise (eg. the cultural argument, the comparative argument, the anti-patriarchal argument), there is a need to bring more rigor to precedent, in order to avoid excessive differences between decisions.[45]

Indeed, it may appear pretentious to proceduralize new topics if even the most familiar arguments still have not been placed in order of priority and if even today the judges may alternatively resort to historical/originalist, literal/textualist or systematic interpretations within their broad discretion. However, as long as the judicial approach to the solution of multicultural conflict remains deprived of references, the risks of unpersuasive decisions increase. Even case by case reasoning needs elements of certainty and points of reference.

Far from an administrative logic based on a strict answering of the questions, the test that this book proposes is intended as a tool for taking a "dialectical syllogism."[46] A tool that, more than authoritatively reaching a truth, wants to persuade: it concretizes into an instrument what is born out of the life of the

45 Other authors radically criticize any creative attitude from the judges with the argument that they do not have legitimization and that they invade the task of the legislature (Bork 2002) or polemicize against the case by case approach, in favor of the generalization that guarantees the law (Schauer 2003).

46 Namely, a dialectical syllogism "acts decomposing and drawing consequences (and therefore is called a 'syllogism')", it "no longer ascertains that a proposition has the same value of truth as another . . . but rather ascertains whether a proposition . . . can be approved" (Cavalla 1992: 723).

cases, but also seeks to individuate those elements of stability emerging from an albeit embryonic common legal tradition. This dialectical, new-rhetorical approach avoids that the test become an "impossible legal transplant" (Legrand 1997) from North American legal systems to Europeans.

d) Reductionism. A further critique against a tool like the test is the risk of reductionism of reality. The idea of wanting to extrapolate a predetermined path for the judge may appear to restrain the immense complexity of the case to oversimplification. It seems to subordinate judicial prudence to predetermined assessments of the public interest and reduce other interests that may arise in the current dispute.

Although the test proposed is not the result of a mere academic aspiration, nor imposed by any legislature or bureaucracy, but rather arises from a synthesis of different legal traditions, it could, however, appear a meta-text which aspires to fossilize, to standardize future texts (judgments). Is the test, therefore, a naive attempt to tame a heterogeneous textuality (as expressed in comparative judgments), a sort of judicial or academic fantasy aspiring to catalogue and systematize where neither catalogues nor systems can exist?

This objection is crucial to clarify another aspect of how a cultural test should be viewed in the light of judicial argument. My answer to this criticism is that the test should be kept open to ongoing self-correction.

The steps, the type of research that a test must face are historically conditioned. The new cultural ideas that emerge and the questions of justice that illuminate the cases will modify the suggested test. It is, in fact, located in a lively, dynamic rapport with the case to which it is applied and should not block the work of the judge. It seeks to anticipate all the steps that should be addressed in the face of a cultural dispute, but obviously the last word – the search for justice – will also review the test, which may be modified by the complexity of individual cases and cultural dynamics. The test is open to ongoing self-correction as long as new *topoi* will emerge.[47]

With respect to the *Topica* tradition (Chap. 2 sec. 1), I think it can be argued that the individual parts of the test provide the function of *topoi*, being tools that serve the discussion of the problems of multiculturalism, tools extrapolated from the "fixed points" gleaned across the sharing at a comparative level. Through the fact that the *topoi* serve the discussion of the problems, they acquire a very particular importance: they "intervene (to solve the problem), and receive in turn their own sense from the problem" (Viehweg 1962: 38).[48] The individual parts of the test could be modified, as the *topoi* mentioned by Theodor Viehweg: "it is in fact in relation to the relevant problem that they (the *topoi*) appear to provide an understanding . . . They must be understood functionally, such as opportunities

47 I corrected the test myself from its 2012 Italian version by adding the question "does the practice perpetuate patriarchy?" after noticing how strongly the *topoi* of gender equality and of women's dignity were asserting themselves within judicial reasoning.

48 "In the varieties of the situations of individual cases there should be found . . . new indications to tentatively resolve the problem" (Viehweg 1962: 38)

for guidance and common threads of thought" (Viehweg 1962: 39)[49] that are flexible and can be adapted to the concrete problem to solve.

9 How to introduce the test into the legal systems

The introduction of the test into the legal system can follow three paths. One is that the legislature codify it; the other is that a Supreme Court may start to use it, influencing other judges; and a third path is the spontaneous adoption by judges, encouraged by judicial boards' guidelines.

Given the fact that the debate on multiculturalism has a highly political connotation at the moment, the most likely path is the third one. I personally think that it is also the least problematic.[50] An adoption by the legislature, similar to what happened with the US religious test codified in 1993 RFRA (Chap. 2 sec. 6.2), would make the test compulsory but would also fossilize its questions, blocking the process of ongoing self-correction and incorporation of further *topoi* developed at jurisprudential level.

The introduction by the Supreme Court would be ideal, as in this case the Supreme Court could adapt the test and change it with more flexibility; nevertheless this may be against the tradition of many European states where the idea of writing and motivating the judgment by answering fixed questions may be perceived as contrary to the task of the judge who wants to be left free in the application of the law. This research does not aim to view cultural tests as recipes to be imported uncritically into a legal system[51] nor as forms of tightening legal argumentation, but rather as guides to reasoning, as tools to order an argument and to ensure that the judge (or legislators) take into account all aspects that anthropology currently considers relevant in identifying cultural practices.[52] In a context in which the anthropological training of judges is lacking, this tool provides them with a set

49 In this sense, the *topoi* are "the subsidy for the discussion of problems" (Viehweg 1962: 35). The problematic thought "tends to escape the bonds" (57); "*Topica* gathers together the points of view and summarize them in catalogs that are not ruled by a deductive nexus and can therefore be easily enlarged and completed" (58–59).

50 With regards to Italy, Basile (2010: 466) maintains that it is not necessary to modify the Italian criminal code, which already contains provisions capable of regarding cultural factors as relevant.

51 Running the risks denounced by Cartabia (2009: 566): "the comparison can lose meaning if it becomes the vehicle for a mechanical imitation or for a blind importation of victorious cultural models . . . If, and only if, the comparison of the judicial experience does not recline in the imitation of the solutions, but penetrates at the more engaged level of the deciding reasons, can it become a formidable resource for a critical examination of the diverse traditions and for an enrichment of the reasons that sustain one or the other possible solutions." In this sense, "the comparison should never become a shortcut for juridical reasoning, nor a channel of slavish importation of solutions, but overall an opportunity for the enrichment of the argumentations, of the reasons, that cannot lead us to accept, or even refute uncritically, the judicial response tested in other parts of the world" (567).

52 As Mengoni (1996) observes, "to draw a more mature phase" of the theory of argumentation "one should elaborate a system of rules to evaluate the arguments." The test can be this system of rules within multicultural argumentation.

of questions to summarize the issues that cannot be overlooked in a multicultural conflict and the elements that can move the decision one way or another. Some of the cultural test steps are rather elementary (eg. the accurate description of the practice, sec. 5.2), but are still important to take because, if omitted (as, unfortunately, is currently the case in many jurisdictions), the judge may be immediately led astray towards a misunderstanding of the case. Given this function of the test, and the risks and problems described, I think that a spontaneous adoption of the test by judges is at the moment the best solution. This can be obtained either by a coordination of judges (and lawyers),[53] with the elaboration of a sort of soft-law instrument – handbook, guidelines, protocols – to be disseminated to each court by judicial boards. In those legal systems where the tradition of stating the opinion's reasoning does not allow the insertion of a rigid grid, the test may even remain external to the motivation of the judgment. This means that the judge is under no obligation to state the reasons of the case by answering the questions of the test, but can keep the test as an external tool enabling her to reach the solution.

10 Applying the test to concrete conflicts

Through applying the proposed test, many multicultural conflicts acquire another dimension.

A first group is deculturalized because it fails the very first question of the test: including abuse in the family, school truancy, begging, child prostitution, sexual violence as well as all "false cultural practices" strategically claimed by the defense: justified rape, protests because of "sinful" women's singing.

Other practices, although recognized in their cultural dimension, would not find recognition because they clash with limits (harm or patriarchy) perceived as crucial: honor killings, infibulation, excision, *ius corrigendi* on children exerted with physical punishment.

Other multicultural conflicts such as the veil, the *burqa* or the *kirpan*, pass all the test questions and should, in this sense, be made in favor of admissibility, without forgetting that the court, in its cautious assessment, may introduce requirements designed to accommodate the practice to the needs of the majority (i.e. the *burqa* should be removed for identification, the *kirpan* must be sealed when worn by children etc.).

To "test the test" here proposed, it may be useful to see it in action related to some concrete conflicts.

53 Similar to the one which is taking place in Italy with the creation of the Observatory on Justice, Transcultural Dialogues and International Protection in May 2017 by lawyers and judges. The Observatory has been created on a model forged in the 1990 by Judge Carlo Maria Verardi who had the idea of bringing judges and lawyers together to discuss new issues before the confrontational conflict between lawyer and judge in court. The Observatory is coordinated by myself, the Supreme Court Judge Giacinto Bisogni and Paola Lovati, lawyer from the forum of Milan, and is composed by an interdisciplinary group. One of the aims of the Observatory on cultural diversity is to "test the test" proposed in this book in the Italian civil courts and with lawyers.

As applied to male circumcision, the test could ascertain that: this is undoubtedly a religious/cultural practice (question 1), describable in all its features and ritualized (question 2), coherent with the overall cultural system which, in the case of the Jews, elucidates the idea of the chosen people (question 3); in the case of the US, it gives value to health and disease prevention. With regard to the fourth question in the test, while among Americans it is optional (the parents decide), circumcision has an essential nature for the Jewish community (a sign of the chosen people), and is also obligatory for the Muslim religion. It is a practice not contested by these two groups, while the element of contestation begins to appear in the US (question 5). The conservation of the practice could also find support in the sixth question in the test for the oppression that, in the past, the Jewish minorities have suffered, and this requisite may not apply to circumcision of majority Americans.

From the subjective point of view every average Jew would circumcise his son (question 7). The sincerity of the individual subject in the controversy should be assessed from time to time by the judge (question 8).

More complex appears the identification of a cultural equivalent in a European society that does not have body rituals practiced on babies (question 9). Maybe a cultural equivalent can be found in Christian baptism that has a corporeal dimension in the sense that the baby is washed by cold water. There have been complaints about the fact that the babies can get pneumonia because of this, which were solved with warming up the water.

The finding of harm is certainly one of the decisive elements (question 10). On this point, we can apply the Italian concept of harm which looks not to the "irreversibility" of the physical alteration, but to the alteration of the "function" for which that part of the body is composed. It will be important to clarify in this regard, with the help of medical science, whether it is true that circumcision, while not affecting sexual function, makes it less enjoyable. Relevant also could be the fact that circumcision could hinder masturbation, which is also an expression of sexual freedom.

The eleventh question in the test does not appear satisfied: circumcision has a major impact on the host culture used to the idea that people may make free decisions about their own bodies. Although, indeed, the reasoning of the Italian court appears to accept that the practice is not contested by the Italian majority (Chap. 2 sec. 8.1), it seems to me that the recent debate has called this into question. More problematic, however, is the argument (repealed by the legislature) of the German court according to which circumcision implicates a final choice of religious affiliation: by that argument, even the Christian baptism of infants should be prohibited.

The question of whether the practice perpetuates patriarchy does not favor its conservation: in fact, male circumcision is an expression of the control of the parents over the body of their child, and in this sense it is an expression of patriarchy (question 12).

Conversely the good reasons to continue the practice (question 13) that the minority adduces can be of varying intensity depending on more or less weight given by the group practicing circumcision: those of a majority Americans are given less force compared to those of Jews.

Given that the practice does not meet all the questions of the test, a reasonable accommodation might be to not prohibit the practice *tout court*, but rather to postpone the performance of the practice until the child can express consent (for fifteen years perhaps) and by conducting a debate even outside of the family (eg. at school), so that children can choose from different points of view.

Another case, which benefits from the test, is the case of a Muslim taxi driver of a Canadian company who refused to carry people with dogs, including blind persons. The case was resolved with the instrument of reasonable accommodation (Chap. 2 sec. 5.3), imposing on the blind customers to await another taxi that was to be called by the Muslim taxi driver, who in turn was obliged to wait until the client had boarded the second taxi. The accommodation reached is difficult to understand without more details that can be acquired applying the test. In light of the test that is proposed here, the mere fact of saying "in my culture this animal is impure" should not be enough to grant protection, but one should, for example, evaluate what exactly is the cultural practice: to not touch the dog or to not be in its vicinity, and if this is the case, at what distance (question 2)? Would religion or culture admit that an exception in case of contact with the impure animal occurs by a higher ethical reason like to serve a blind client on the same terms as all other customers (question 3)? Are there alternatives that the subject could put in place: for example, some rite of purification after coming into contact with the dog (question 3)? Is it treated as an existing practice, but the violation of which has a trivial and insignificant impact (question 4)? How would the average Muslim taxi driver behave, the reasonable person of his culture: Have the other Muslim taxi drivers of the company advanced or would they advance similar claims (question 7)? How sincere and consistent is the subject: Does he always stay away from dogs or claim this practice only at work (question 8)?

The explanation of potential equivalents to contact with dogs within the system of signs of the Muslim taxi driver is very important: Is asking a Muslim to pick up a dog like asking to get in the car with a rat or a snake, animals repellent for Canadians too (question 9)? In this case, perhaps one could ask the taxi driver to make an extra effort. Or does a Muslim who has contact with a dog commit a gross breach of religious rules such as to be considered a mortal sin in the Christian system of signs? In that case his claim should receive greater attention by the judge. It should be noted that the translation into another system of meanings of the presence of a dog on board does not necessarily imply that the interest of the person with disabilities to have a fast and efficient service, especially in cases of emergency, should be sacrificed to the interest of the Muslim not to come into contact with unclean animals, as the protection of the disabled may be part of the core value system of the majority (question 11). The scope of the question is helping the understanding of each other's reasons and the search for a satisfactory settlement for all.

Once all these questions are answered, one has the conditions to understand what kind of accommodation is possible. Depending on the characteristics of the practice, the arrangement may be to insert a glass partition in the cab so that the driver avoids any contact with the dog; or to allow the taxi driver to go to wash, or to perform the rites of the case, after giving the ride.

The test could also be applied to the practices of the majority which are disputed by minorities. Some have, for example, argued: that the Catholic communion can be considered a rite of cannibalism; that if male circumcision is prohibited by the lack of consent of the child the same reasoning should apply to baptism; that all Catholic religious symbols from any public space (eg. altars in public streets, crucifix in schools, Nativity scenes during Christmas in Catholic countries) should be removed; that traditional messages of "Merry Christmas" should be substituted with the more neutral "seasons greetings;" that if the prayer broadcast from the minarets may be "religious noise pollution," the same could be said of church bells.

In all these cited cases it is fundamental to appeal to the judicial dialectics and the emerging *topoi* incorporated into the test. In this sense the communion cannot be prohibited as an essential and integral practice of Catholics and does not cause harm, being the cannibalism merely symbolic; for baptism one might reply that religious affiliation is not irreversible, unlike male circumcision, as one could "unbaptize" with a declaration of apostasy that implies an exit from the church; for a Nativity scene the same reasoning of the judgment on the *succah* in Canada (Chap. 2 sec. 5.2) may be adopted, considering the structure acceptable because it is temporary; conversely, the removal of crucifixes from schools should be ordered as they are not obligatory, and their removal would not affect any essential Christian value; while more complex is the issue of religious/cultural noise pollution, which will require an activity of arrangement under conditions of equality (eg. with night bans both for the bells and for the calls to prayer from the minarets due to the harm caused to sleep which is connected to health).

For all types of multicultural conflict it is, likewise, fundamental to enhance the practical attitude of the law, which can manifest itself in the concrete way in which the judge finds accommodation. It will be remembered that in many cases examined in which courts decided in favor of the minority, the court established, however, the conditions that this must fulfill: the *succah* of Mr. Amselem could indeed be built, but must be temporary; the *kirpan* worn by the son of Mr. Multani could be part of the school uniform, but had to be sealed; infibulation cannot be performed in Ontario, but may be replaced by ritual incision. It is an attitude present in the measurement of many cultural conflicts, and that is surely to be valued because it helps to find mediations and to avoid the perception that a decision is skewed in favor of one party.

In conclusion, it emerges that the way judges articulate the reasons of their decisions can trigger important messages of coexistence, and to me it seems to emerge that the theory of balancing between competing fundamental rights should be accompanied by the tool of accommodation as a criterion to resolve multicultural conflicts. It should, finally, be reiterated that the solutions given to multicultural conflicts, including through the described tests, are not definitive and irreversible, but are part of an ongoing constitutional conversation and may be subsequently reviewed.

11 Re-reading the *Kimura* case

But anthropology would reply that there is a group of cases which still brings the law to an inevitable relativistic capitulation. What to do, in fact, when the law is faced with the dilemma of Fumiko Kimura (Chap. 1 sec. 1.1)?

Her case complies with, and indeed exceeds, nearly every test question.

The practice of *Oyaku Shinju* exists and has ancient origins. It is consistent with the whole Japanese cultural system and even compulsory. The standard of the "reasonable Japanese woman" confirms that Kimura's behavior is in keeping with the logic of that group that in fact arose to support her claim.

The criterion of irreparable harm could be the decisive key, but even this, by adopting the Japanese perspective, vacillates. Kimura was certain that to leave her children alive would cause them more damage. The reason that she brings is very strong: it is that of the good of her children. To take them with her is an act of love: the mother would be insane to leave them behind to survive in this world. The symbiotic relation she has with them implies the cultural equivalent in the majority society would be to condemn a pregnant mother who attempted suicide and survived of murder: Western societies would not condemn the potential mother in this case.[54]

Is it possible to admit that, in a case like this, there is no answer? That each of the parties remains immersed in the idea of "good reasons" and her own theory of what is a meaningful life?

In effect, neither these nor the criterion of damage were useful to the judge: Kimura was not condemned.

This raises new questions that become more urgent when we compare how multicultural jurisprudence solved other cases involving parents who kill their children. Why did the death of Kimura's children receive a lower sanction than that imposed for the murder of Hina Saleem (Chap. 1 sec. 1.2)? May there be an element of the culture of the majority for which, in some ways, it is easier to understand the gesture of a mother who kills her children, or which leads to think that a woman betrayed by her husband is in a very fragile situation which makes her more inclined to desperate acts, while the gesture of the father who kills his daughter for honor is seen as an expression of a patriarchal culture with which the West has no element of convergence (Lee 2007)? But if that were the case would not the same majority be perpetuating an oppressive discourse that promotes the image of the frail woman, more prone to despair? Can it be said that the gender argument (that it was patriarchy that killed Hina Saleem) is the real reason implicitly underlying the decision, even beyond physical damage? May it be that the fact that Fumiko Kimura attempted suicide while killing her children made her behavior in some way sacrificial, while the fact that the action of Mohammed Saleem was unidirectional renders the murder even more unacceptable? Certainly,

54 A brief and controversial experiment of charging pregnant mothers who took illegal drugs with "fetal assault" was not renewed in the U.S. state of Tennessee in spring of 2016 (Burke 2016).

in the various episodes reported, the concrete dimensions of the case and the different attitudes of the protagonists were taken into account. These were surely influenced by the historical/national context in which the courts were located: if the history of the United States were replete with murder-suicides between parents and children, just as Italy had a history of leniency for honor killings before 1981, perhaps the *Kimura* case would have been decided in a different way, to emphasize the impossibility of going back to the past. In any case, it cannot but be noted that the criterion of irreparable harm, the deprivation of life, does not always manage to be decisive.

The case which opens this work continues to interrogate us and seems to stand there, immovable, to sanction the revenge of anthropology on law, which tries but cannot find the just solution in the face of mammothly incommensurable semantics.

The conception of justice is shaken to its foundations by the irruption of "culture" on the legal horizon. So as we come to the end of our journey the test reappears as a naive scientistic attempt to bring order into something that, by definition, lacks it: human existence. Our legal experience continues to be troubled, surrounded by doubt.

How, then, to advance legal experience?

Perhaps the way is to begin a discourse with the other culture, with the concept of human dignity that underlies this; a discourse that questions us and the other, and which can regenerate both. It is important to admit that each party enters into dialogue with a bias (Gadamer 1960; LeBaron 2003).[55] But one must admit that to even enter this discourse can transform such prejudice. This point deserves attention: it is, in fact, crucial to identify the parts that need to enter the dialogue. The conversation should take place not only between the parties engaged in the proceedings; the participants in this discourse should be expanded.

In the case with which we opened this inquiry and which continues to speak while remaining unanswered, Kimura spoke. American society has spoken. Missing are the children. They might say whether they want to go dying with the mother

55 Recall how Gadamer (1960) highlighted that each interpreter in the community of dialoguers is not a *tabula rasa*, but comes with his own "pre-comprehension," his cultural *a priori* which are the result of stratified traditions. Nevertheless, "each individual is naturally induced to review his own perspective in the light of experience and of other points of view; for those who participate in an authentic dialogue can no longer be as before." The "other," therefore, is not considered either as "identical," nor as "inferior" but as the bearer of another "horizon" that is offered to the community of dialoguers. In this sense, I maintain that the expression "multicultural conflicts," used in this work to reflect the current language, would become substituted by the expression "multicultural encounters" or by a new definition of conflict, as for example that suggested by LeBaron (2003: 3): "an intriguing opportunity to learn and change." Turning to Gadamer, the author defends the space of "dialogue," criticizing the presumption of infallibility: human existence is a great hermeneutic circle which constantly gains "experience;" dialogue is the way to do "experience," that can be done only by those who are free to interpret the world and conscious of "how little one knows." The strength of the dialogue rests on the *primacy of the question*: the one who asks, advances doubt, puts in discussion given truths; he does not dispense certainty, but seeks a direction. The existential condition of "questioning" is that which symbolically marks the destiny of the individual as an "errant seeker," who does not attach to his identity but exposes himself to contaminations and denials.

or whether they want to immerse themselves in the flow of life. They could tell their mother that maybe they can endure even without her, that the world will take care of them and will provide them with many other mothers. The reasons of the children could be deemed the only real answer to the problem. Their absence raises the question of whether a cultural practice can ever be accepted which prevent its recipients from speaking.

Faced with this impasse of values and reasons, there could be introduced, in addition, an "impartial spectator," a third observer beyond the positions of American society, and of Kimura and her children. One should not, in fact, overlook the fact that the recipients of the practice, when they can express themselves, often can still validate harmful practices because they are immersed in the cultural schema. This impartial spectator could be a synthesis of the other cultures and the other jurists. A global community of interpreters of the sense of justice to be applied to the validity, the reasonableness, the persuasiveness of some practices. The pretext of Kimura, the fact that she assigns value to her gesture, should be validated by the community of impartial spectators in search of a consensus. The concourse of these "parties" in the conversation widens the horizon of interpretation. Kimura cannot stand alone to support her reasons. They must be confronted.

Only together with the other, in a process of mutual transformation can one emerge from vulnerability but also from asphyxia, the existential impasse which inevitably condemns us to our individual lives, our individual cultures.

On American culture, the *Kimura* case may have had the effect of piercing the veil of the insolubility of the mother–child relationship, to reflect on a sentiment – the interdependence between people – that an individualistic society has too often removed, as well as on the need to create support networks for maternity and immigrants: Kimura's solitude was, in fact, "intersectional" in the way it drove her to act as a woman, as a mother, as an immigrant. Still, the *Kimura* case has surely not changed, in American society, the value assigned to life.

And on Fumiko Kimura, which effects produced the discovery that children can be perceived in American and other cultures as something separate from herself? Perhaps the successive developments of this story reveal how the reasons of life may appear stronger. After the tragedy, Fumiko Kimura and her husband reunited and sought to have other children. The fact that the woman has not been sentenced to the death penalty has enabled her to reconstruct, at least in part, her existence. Her culture saved her life, but what has the culture with which she came in contact produced in her, what changes or confirmations of her convictions?

I wonder if, looking at the ocean, Fumiko Kimura still believes that she made the right choice, if she continues to curse the students who saved her and regrets not being far away with her two children; or whether she instead wishes that they were still here, with or without her.

Conclusions

In a scenario of theoretical and legislative difficulties, it is principally judges who take on the challenges of multiculturalism, giving life to a "multicultural jurisprudence" which, in this work, was taken as the starting point for the elaboration of a theory for the resolution of cultural conflicts.

This research has sought to reconstruct the requirements that judges consider most relevant to give recognition to culture and the argumentative techniques that have been used at the comparative level. The hundreds of rulings produced reveal an embryonic common legal tradition. This tradition is, in part, born from a dialogue between courts and a circulation of models, in part developed through autogenesis. In both circumstances, it reveals an analogy of themes, questions, requirements and sometimes also stereotypes and incongruences in the argumentative paths.

This jurisprudential material has been used as a basis for proposing a "systematized jurisprudential theory" of multicultural conflict resolution: a theory that is jurisprudential because it is based on the concrete solutions that the courts have developed over decades, "thinking on problems and not on systems" as well as elaborating *topoi*, the fixed points of a discourse; but that is also systematized because, instead of leaving the issues of multiculturalism to a case by case solution, it rather suggests an instrument, a logical argumentative process to follow whenever faced with a multicultural conflict: the cultural test. The theory that is proposed sees in the instrument of the "test" an attempt to clarify multicultural conflicts, to guide the court in its grounds, to guarantee a certainty at least on the steps to be clarified in addressing a cultural issue. The proposed test uses as a matrix the North American tests, liberated from their historical and political specificity, and compares them with the most persuasive requisites that the judges have required to grant recognition to culture in European legal systems.

The test could, indeed, appear far from jurisprudential tradition, as it is potentially a scientistic, mathematical instrument, fixing many varieties of experience in a predetermined grid. I have, in this sense, long questioned the advisability of its introduction. However, I found that the test can be an initial contribution to a persuasive approach to multicultural conflicts. Not a formula, then, but an attempt to be revised in future research and in future dispute resolution, to show courts, and all policy makers or social workers, how to seek better balance. The instrument of the test seeks also to satisfy the need for certainty, a stability which is an intimate need of the law and judicial experience.

In a moment when the courts or the legislature are called to respond to the new demands of justice which emerge in increasingly plural societies, to me it seemed important that they avail themselves, also, of basic anthropological tools. For this reason I wanted to retrace the history of the concept of culture that exerts a magnetism on the law, often inducing it to abdicate the peculiarities of its method of reasoning, to the benefit of anthropology, with its relativistic matrix. Too many times the judge has stopped, faced with the argument of "it is my culture," without asking, for example, "what culture?" – evolutionism, the primitivism of the early anthropologists or a hybridization of the latest? There are, in fact, concepts of culture that convey an image of the other now rejected by anthropology. The current times cannot exempt the judge from becoming aware of the multiple deconstructions which such a concept of culture has undergone: in some uses it is considered a fun-house mirror which justifies the absence of social policies and the distribution of wealth, or as a new tool of hegemony which gives power to the elites of a cultural group, or as a substitute for a new racism given the fact that through decisions hidden under the cloak of "it is their culture," the judge expresses actually a judgment of inferiority, of lesser dignity of the person who is the victim, to whom protection is denied.

An awareness of the many faces of culture, united together with the test, could be two useful tools to lighten the conceptual and argumentative baggage that the anthropologist judge must carry along, during his journey through the intricate routes of multiculturalism.

Appendices

The status of culture in constitutions[1]

Afghanistan 2004: art. 45 (national culture)

Albania 1998: preamble, articles 3, 8, 20 (cultural rights)

Algeria 1996 am. (amended) 2008: preamble, articles 8, 21 (national culture)

Andorra 1993: article 34 (national culture)

Angola 2010: articles 12, 87 (cultural rights)

Antigua and Barbuda 1981: no

Argentina 1994: art. 75 par. 17 (cultural rights) and par. 19 (multiculturalism)

Armenia 1995 am. 2005: articles 8.1, 11, 40, 41 (national culture)

Australia 1900: no

Austria 1929: art. 8 (regional culture)

Azerbaijan 1995/2009: articles 40, 44, 77 (cultural rights)

Bahamas 1973: no

Bahrain 2002: no

1 The research into the one hundred and ninety-four constitutions in the world was based on the following keywords: identity, culture (in the anthropological sense), multiculturalism, minority, diversity. In the legal language, the word "culture" currently takes on three different meanings: 1) Culture as specialized knowledge, falling within the "right to an education." 2) Culture as the intellectual and artistic life of the community, falling within the "right to a cultural life" and to "cultural development." 3) Culture in an anthropological sense, falling within the cultural rights of minorities, the promotion of cultural identity, the recognition of multiculturalism. As the term "cultural rights" often refers to concepts 1 and 2, I wish to clarify that in this research I restricted my analysis to the third meaning. The results show that forty-eight constitutions recognize cultural rights and thirty-five recognize multiculturalism. Culture is mentioned in many other contexts (such as the reference to national culture in more than fifty constitutions) but, all in all, we can say that fewer than half of the existing constitutions address the matter of cultural diversity.

Bangladesh 1972 am. 2004: no

Barbados 1996: no

Belarus 1996: articles 15, 16, 97 (other uses) art. 51 (national culture)

Belgium 1994/2008: art. 23 (cultural rights)

Belize 1981: preamble (national culture and indigenous)

Benin 1990: preamble, articles 10, 11 (cultural rights)

Bhutan 2008: articles 4, 8 (national culture)

Bolivia 1995: art. 171 (cultural rights)

Bosnia-Herzegovina 1995: no

Botswana 1966 am. 2002: no

Brazil 1988: articles 216, 221, 227, 242 (multiculturalism); art. 215 (cultural rights)

Brunei Darussalam 1959/1984: no

Bulgaria 1991: articles 6, 23, 54 (cultural rights)

Burkina Faso 1991 am. 2002: preamble, articles 18, 28 (cultural rights)

Burundi 2004: preamble (other uses)

Cambodia 1996: articles 35, 69 (national culture), art. 70 (other uses)

Cameroon 1972–2008: preamble (multiculturalism)

Canada 1982: articles 25, 35 (cultural rights); art. 27 (multiculturalism)

Cape Verde 1992: art. 7 (national culture)

Central Africa 2004: preamble (multiculturalism)

Chad 1996: preamble, articles 33, 34 (multiculturalism)

Chile 1980–2003: no

China 1982/2004: preamble, articles 4, 116, 119 (regional culture)

Columbia 1991: articles 2, 7, 8, 176 (multiculturalism)

Comoros (Union of the Comoros) 2009: article 32 (national culture)

Congo 2005: preamble, articles 1, 13, 46, 51 (multiculturalism)

Costa Rica 1949–1999: articles 76, 89 (other uses)

Croatia 1990: preamble, art. 15 (cultural rights)

Cuba 1976: art. 39 (other uses)

Cyprus 2004: art. 4 par. 3 (cultural rights)

Czech Republic 1992: preamble (other uses)

Denmark 1953: no

Djibouti 1992: art. 9 (other uses)

Dominica 1978: no

Dominican Republic 2002: no

East Timor 2002: no

Ecuador 1998: Preamble, articles 1, 23, 62, 49, 62–66, 84 (multiculturalism)

Egypt 1971 am. 2007: no

El Salvador 1983–2000: preamble, articles 53, 62 (other uses)

Emirates, United Arab 1971: no

Eritrea 1997: articles 9 (national culture), 19, 21 (other uses)

Estonia 1992–2005: preamble, articles 49, 50 (cultural rights)

Ethiopia 1995: preamble, art. 39, 41, 91 (cultural rights)

Fiji 1997: preamble (multiculturalism), articles 3, 6 (cultural rights), 34, 39 (other uses)

Finland 2000: articles 17, 121 (cultural rights)

France 1958: art. 2 (national culture)

Gabon 1991 am. 1997: art. 91 (national culture)

Gambia 1996: articles 32, 60 (multiculturalism)

Georgia 1995 am. 2010: articles 34, 38 (national culture)

Germany 1949: art. 29 (regional culture)

Ghana 1992: articles 26, 39 (cultural rights; national culture)

Greece 1975: no

Grenada 1973: no

Guatemala 1985–1993: articles 57–65 (national culture), 66 (indigenous identity) (cultural rights)

Guinea 2010: articles 1, 21 (cultural rights)

Guinea Bissau 1984: art. 17 (national culture)

Guinea Equatorial 1991 am. 1995: art. 4 (national culture)

Guyana 1980–1996: art. 35 (multiculturalism)

Haiti 1987: preamble, art. 215 (national culture)

Honduras 1985–2005: articles 173, 151 (national culture)

Hungary 1949, 2007: articles 32, 66, 68 (cultural rights)

Iceland 1944, am. 2013: no

India 1959 amended 2005: articles 29, 30, 51 (cultural rights)

Indonesia 1945 am. 2002: articles 28 I, 32 (cultural rights)

Iran 1979 amended 1989: art. 13 (cultural rights)

Iraq 2005: articles 2, 35 (national culture), 125 (cultural rights); preamble, art. 3 (multiculturalism)

Ireland 1937: articles 1, 2, 3 (national culture)

Israel: no written Constitution/basic law 1958 am. 2003, bill of rights 1992: no

Italy 1948 am. 2001: articles 6 (multiculturalism), 9 (other uses) (regions recognize cultural regional identity)

Ivory Coast 2000: preamble, art. 7 (other uses)

Jamaica 1962: no

Japan 1947: no

Jordan 1952: no

Kazakhstan 1995: no

Kenya 1963 am. 2008: no

Kiribati 1979: no

Korea North 1972 am. 2016: Chapter III articles 39, 40, 41 (other uses; socialist national culture)

Korea South 1948 am. 1987: no

Kosovo 2008: articles 57, 58, 59 (cultural rights)

Kuwait 1962: no

Kyrgyzstan 2010: no

Laos (Lao People's Democratic Republic) 1991 am. 2003: preamble (multiculturalism); articles 8, 16, 23, 35 (cultural rights)

Latvia 1922: art. 114 (multiculturalism)

Lebanon 1926: preamble (national culture)

Lesotho 1993 am. 1997: art. 35 (national culture)

Liberia 1984: art. 5 (national culture)

Libya 1969: no

Liechtenstein 1921: no

Lithuania 1992: preamble, art. 37 (multiculturalism)

Luxemburg 1868/2009: no

Macedonia 1991: articles 8, 48, amendment X (multiculturalism)

Madagascar 1998: preamble, art. 26 (national culture)

Malawi 1994–1999: articles 25, 12 par. 4 (cultural rights)

Malaysia 1957 am. 1994: art. 45 (other uses)

Maldives (Republic of Maldives) 1932 am. 2008: article 39 (cultural right); article 67 (national culture and implicit multiculturalism);

Mali 1991: preamble (multiculturalism)

Malta 1964: no

Marshall Islands 1979: preamble (national culture)

Mauritania 1991 am. 2006: no

Mauritius 1968 am. 2001: no

Mexico 1917–2001: art. 2 (multiculturalism)

Micronesia (Federated States of Micronesia) 1981: preamble, article 10 (multiculturalism)

Moldova 1994: art. 10 par. 1 (national culture), par. 2 and preamble (multiculturalism)

Monaco (Principality of Monaco) 1962: no

Mongolia 1992 am. 2000: preamble (national culture), art. 8 par. 2 (multiculturalism)

Montenegro 2007: articles 76, 77, 79, 80 (multiculturalism)

Morocco 1996: no

Mozambique: art. 53 (national culture)

Myanmar 2008: articles 1.3, 22, 365 (multiculturalism)

Namibia 1998: art. 19 (cultural rights)

Nauru 1968: no

Nepal 2003: articles 3, 17, 23, 33, 34, 35 (multiculturalism)

Netherlands 1983 am. 2002: no

New Zealand: no written Constitution

Nicaragua 1987–1995: articles 5, 89, 90, 91 (cultural rights)

Niger 1999: preamble, art. 14 (cultural rights)

Nigeria 1999: art. 21 (cultural rights)

Norway 1814 amended 2004: art. 110 (cultural rights)

Oman 1996: no

Pakistan 1973: art. 28 (cultural rights)

Palau 1979: preamble (national culture)

Palestine (State of Palestine) 2003: article 5 and article 41 (cultural rights)

Panama 1972–1994 (national culture): articles 76–86 (national culture), art. 86 (multiculturalism)

Papua New Guinea 1975: preamble, articles 9 (national culture), 2, 5 par. 3 (multiculturalism)

Paraguay 1992: articles 25, 63, 73, 77 (cultural rights); articles 62, 140 (multiculturalism)

Peru 1993, 2005: art. 2; (cultural rights); articles 17, 89 (multiculturalism)

Philippines 1987: section 2 section 17 (national culture); section 5(2) and section 22 (cultural rights)

Poland 1997: articles 6, 35, 73 (national culture)

Portugal 1976: art. 78 (national culture)

Qatar 2003: art. 24 (national culture)

Romania 1991: articles 6, 7 (cultural rights)

Russia 1993: articles 71, 74, 114 (national culture)

Rwanda 2003: preamble, art. 51 (cultural rights)

Saint Kitts Nevis 1983: art. 119 (other uses)

Saint Lucia 1978: no

Saint Vincent and Grenadines 1979: no

Samoa 1960: no

San Marino 1974 am. 2002: no

Sao Tome and Principe 1975 am. 1990: art. 2 (national culture)

Saudi Arabia 1992: preamble, art. 29 (national culture)

Senegal 2001–2008: preamble, art. 24 (cultural rights)

Serbia 2006: articles 1, 3, 5, 18, 14, 75, 76, 81, 89 (multiculturalism)

Seychelles 1993: art. 39 (cultural rights)

Sierra Leone 1991 am. 2001: art. 12 (national culture)

Singapore 1965: art. 69 (other uses)

Slovakia 1992/2006: preamble, articles 7, 43, 44 (national culture), 34, 104 (cultural rights)

Slovenia 1991, 2003: articles 5, 61, 64 (national culture)

Solomon Islands 1968: preamble (national culture)

Somalia 1979: art. 51 (national culture)

South Africa 1996: articles 30, 31, 183, 211, 235 (cultural rights and other uses)

Spain 1978: preamble, art. 143 (regional culture)

Sri Lanka 1978 am. 2010: articles 14, 27 (national culture)

Sudan 2005: articles 1, 4, 13, 47, 82, 156, 207 (multiculturalism)

Suriname 1987: no

Swaziland (Kingdom of Eswatini) 2005: articles 17, 60 (other uses)

Sweden 1974 am. 2002: art. 2 (other uses)

Switzerland 1998: articles 69, 70, 78, 93 (multiculturalism)

Syria 1973 am. 2000: art. 21 (national culture)

Taiwan 1947 am. 2005: art. 158 (national culture)

Tajikistan 1994 am. 2003: art. 40 (other uses)

Tanzania 1977 am. 1995: no

Thailand 2007: articles 66, 81 (cultural rights)

Togo 1992 am. 2002: art. 40 (national culture)

Tonga 1875: no

Trinidad and Tobago 1976/2000: no

Tunisia 1959 am. 2008: no

Turkey 1982 am. 2010: art. 25 (national culture)

Turkmenistan 1992 am. 2003: articles 10 (national culture), 36 (other uses)

Tuvalu 1986: articles 3, 6, 7, 10.3, 11, 29 (national culture)

Uganda 2005: articles III, XXIV, 32, 37 (multiculturalism); art. 36 (cultural rights)

Ukraine 1996–2010: articles 11, 12 (cultural rights)

United Kingdom: no written constitution

United States 1789 am. 1992: no

Uruguay 1996: no

Uzbekistan 1992: article 49 (national culture)

Vanuatu 1980: preamble, articles 7, 30 (multiculturalism)

Vatican (City of Vatican) 2000: no

Venezuela 1999: articles 15, 102, 121, 98–111, 119 (cultural rights)

Vietnam 1992: articles 5, 30, 75 (cultural rights)

Yemen 1994: art. 41 (other uses)

Zambia 1991: articles 112, 127 (other uses)

Zimbabwe 1979 am. 2009: no

The status of culture internationally[2]

Additional Protocol to the American Convention on Human Rights in the Area of Economic, Social and Cultural Rights (OAS – Organization of American States) 1986 art. 16 (other uses)

African Charter on Human and Peoples' Rights (African States) 1981: Preamble (cultural rights) art. 20.3; art. 22.1 (cultural development with due regard to identity); art. 29 (African cultural values)

ASEAN Human Rights Declaration (Association of South East Asian Nations) 2012: art. 7 (cultural background); art. 33 (cultural rights)

Asian Human Rights Charter (NGOs – people's charter) 1998: art. 2.2 (cultural traditions); art. 2.3. (cultural context); art. 3.3. (cultural oppression); art. 6. (cultural identity)

Charter for African Cultural Reinassance (African States) 2006: all relevant

Charter of Fundamental rights of the European Union (European Union) 2007: art. 22 (cultural diversity)

Convention on the Protection and Promotion of the Diversity of Cultural Expressions (UNESCO) 2005: all relevant (cultural diversity, cultural rights)

Convention on the right of the child (United Nations) 1989: art. 20, 29, 30 (cultural rights)

Declaration on the Rights of Indigenous Peoples (United Nations) 2007: all relevant

Declaration on the Rights of Persons Belonging to National or Ethnic, Religious and Linguistic Minorities (United Nations) 1992: all relevant

European Charter for Regional or Minority Languages (Council of Europe) 1992: all relevant

Final Declaration of the Regional Meeting for Asia of the World Conference on Human Rights–The Bangkok Declaration (1993): art. 11 (protection of linguistic and ethnic minorities)

Framework Convention for the Protection of National Minorities (Council of Europe) 1995: all relevant

International covenant of civil and political rights (United Nations) 1966: art. 27 (cultural rights)

International Covenant on Economic, Social and Cultural Rights (United Nations) 1966: art. 15 (other uses)

Universal Declaration on Cultural Diversity (UNESCO) 2001: all relevant (cultural diversity)

2 The research was made searching in the main international human right instruments the following keywords: identity, culture (in anthropological sense), multiculturalism, minority and diversity.

Table of judgments

Canada

Alberta v. Hutterian Brethren of Wilson Colony [2009] 2 S.C.R. 567 (refusal to have photographs taken, Hutterites)

Beckman v. Little Salmon/Carmacks First Nation, 2010 SCC 53, [2010] 3 S.C.R. 103 (agricultural land grant, Indigenous people)

Delgammuukw v. British Columbia [1997] 3 SCR 1010 (evidence in court in the case of oral tradition, Indigenous People)

Grand Chief Michael Mitchell, also known as Kanantakeron (Plaintiff) v. Canada (Minister of National Revenue – M.N.R.) [1997], Federal Court of Canada–Trial Division Ottawa Ontario (customs duties in ancestral territories, Indigenous People)

Haida Nation v. British Columbia (Minister of Forests) [2004] S.C.R. 511 (felling of forests in ancestral territories, Indigenous People)

Ktunaxa Nation v. British Columbia (Forests, Lands and Natural Resource Operations), 2017 SCC 54, [2017] 2 S.C.R. 386 (resort on the home of Grizzly Bear Spirit, Indigenous People)

Mikisew Cree First Nation v. Canada (Minister of Canadian Heritage), 2005 SCC 69, [2005] 3 S.C.R. 388 (road in traditional land, Indigenous People)

Minister of National Revenue v. Grand Chief Michael Mitchell [2001], 1 S.C.R. 911 (customs duties, Indigenous People)

Multani v. Commission scolaire Marguerite-Bourgeoys, [2006] 1 S.C.R. 256 (*kirpan*, ritual knife, in school uniform, Sikhs)

R. v. Pamajewon [1996] 2 S.C.R. 821 (gambling and casinos, Indigenous People)

R. v. Powley [2003] 2 S.C.R. 207 (Mixed-group recognition, Indigenous People)

R. v. Sappier [2006] 2 S.C.R. 686 (wood-cutting, Indigenous People)

R. v. Sparrow [1990] 1 S.C.R. 1075 (salmon fishing, Indigenous People)

R. v. Van Der Peet [1996] 2 S.C.R. 507 (sale of salmon, Indigenous People)

Reference re: Section 293 of the Criminal Code of Canada [2011] BCSC 1588 (polygamy, Mormons et al.)

Rosenberg v. City of Outremont [2001] Q.J. No. 2858; [2001] R.J.Q. 1556 (Quebec Sup. Ct). (*eruv*, placement of a series of overhead wires, Jews)

Syndicat Northcrest v. Amselem [2004] 2 S.C.R. 551 (*succah*, branch hut on the terrace, Jews)

Taku River Tlingit First Nation v. British Columbia (Project Assessment Director), [2004] 3 S.C.R. 550, 2004 SCC 74 (road in traditional territory, Indigenous People)

Thomas v. Norris, [1992] 2 C.N.R. 139 B.C.S.C. (Canadian Native Law Reporter-British Columbia Supreme Court), 139–163 (forced initiation to spirit dance, Indigenous People)

Tsilhqot'in Nation v. British Columbia, 2014 SCC 44, [2014] 2 S.C.R. 256 (logging in traditional land, Indigenous People)

Germany

BVerfGE 108, 282, 24 September 2003 (veil, Islam)

Supreme Court of Germany, 28 January 2004 (honor femicides, Pakistan)

Court of Bückeburg, op. 25 January 2006 (battering of wife, Sardinia)

Court of Appeal of Cologne 25 June 2012 (male circumcision, Jews)

Italy

Cassazione Sez. I civile, 2 February 2015, no. 1843 (***kafalah***, child entrusted to the uncle's care, Morocco)
Cassazione sez. I penale, 1 March 2016 no. 24739 (***kirpan***, ritual knife, Sikhs)
Cassazione sez. I penale, 14 June 2006, no. 20393 (honor killing/filicide, Lhasni case, Morocco)
Cassazione sez. I penale, 15 May 2017, no. 24084 (***kirpan***, ritual knife, Sikhs)
Cassazione sez. I penale, 18 February 2010, no. 6587 (honor killing/filicide, Saleem case, Pakistan)
Cassazione sez. I penale, 2 February 2016 no. 25163 (***kirpan***, ritual knife, Sikhs)
Cassazione sez. III penale, 25 January 2007 no. 2841 (***manghel***, the practice of begging, Roma people)
Cassazione sez. III penale, 29 January 2015, no. 14960 (family maltreatment, Morocco)
Cassazione sez. III penale, 29 January 2018, no. 29613 (kissing a son on his genitals/homage to the penis, Albania)
Cassazione sez. V penale, 16 July 2013, no. 43412 (theft, Roma people)
Cassazione sez. V penale, 2 August 2007, no. 31510 (child rearing, "Islamic culture")
Cassazione sez. V penale, 28 September 2012, no. 37638 (***manghel***, the practice of begging, Roma people)
Cassazione sez. VI penale 29 May 2009, no. 22700 (woman abuse, Morocco)
Cassazione sez. VI penale, 1520/2008 ("marital debt", Morocco)
Cassazione sez. VI penale, 17 September 2008, no. 44516 (***manghel***, the practice of begging, Roma people)
Cassazione sez. VI penale, 24 November 1999, no. 3398 (wife battering and child abuse, Albania)
Cassazione sez. VI penale, 24 November 2011, no. 43646 (male circumcision, Nigeria)
Cassazione sez. VI penale, 30 January 2007, no. 3419 (itinerant trade, Morocco)
Cassazione sez. VI penale, 64/2010 (the role of women, Jehovah's Witnesses)
Cassazione sez. VI penale, 8 January 2003, no. 55 (wife battering, Morocco)
Cassazione sez. VI penale, 923/2008 (use of marijuana, Rastafarians)
Cassazione sez. I penale, 48272/2009 (child rearing, Morocco)
Consiglio di Stato, 13 February 2008, no. 556 (crucifix in schools, Italy)
Consiglio di Stato, sez. VI, 19 June 2008, no. 3076 (***burqa***, Afghanistan)
Corte costituzionale sent. 16 December 1968, no. 126 (adultery by women, Italy)
Corte d'appello Bologna, 6 October 2006, no. 2433 (rearing of daughter, Morocco)
Corte d'appello Bologna, 19 April 2017 (kissing a son on his genitals/homage to the penis, Albania)
Corte d'appello Brescia, 5 December 2008 (honor killing/filicide, Saleem case, Pakistan)
Corte d'appello Catania, 27 November 2012 (asylum granted on the grounds of FGM, Nigeria)
Corte d'appello Venezia, 23 November 2012 (dep. 21 February 2013), no. 1485 (***Aruè***, mild form of FGM, Nigeria)
Corte d'appello Venezia, 12 October 2009 (male circumcision, Nigeria)
Corte d'appello Venezia, 9 January 2006 (honor killing/filicide, Lhasni case, Morocco)
Corte d'assise Cagliari, 13 December 1982 (blood transfusion, Jehovah's Witnesses)
Giudice Udienza Preliminare (GUP) Bologna, 16 November 2006 (rape, Pakistan)
Tribunale amministrativo regionale (TAR) Veneto, 22 March 2005, no. 1110 (crucifixes in schools, Italy)

Tribunale Brescia, 19 January 2008 (honor killing/filicide, Pakistan)
Tribunale Cagliari, Order 3 April 2013 (asylum granted on the grounds of FGM, Nigeria)
Tribunale Cremona, 19 February 2009, no. 15 (*kirpan*, ritual knife, Sikhs)
Tribunale dei minori Reggio Emilia, 21 November 2012 (kissing a son on his genitals/ homage to the penis, Albania)
Tribunale dei minori Torino, 17 July 1997 (FGM, Nigeria)
Tribunale Padova, 9 June 2005, no. 446 (honor killing/filicide, Lhasni case, Morocco)
Tribunale Padova, 9 November 2007 (male circumcision, Nigeria)
Tribunale Torino, 21 October 2002 (theft and violation of compulsory school attendance, Roma people)
Tribunale Trieste, 22 February 2011 (theft, Roma people)
Tribunale Udine, 21 November 2002 (wife battering, Tunisia)

United Kingdom

B v L [2016] EWFC 67 (20 October 2016), England and Wales Family Court Decisions (High Court Judges), Birmingham (divorce, Pakistan)
R. v. Derriviere [1969] 53 Criminal Appeal Reports 637 (child rearing, India)
R. v. Ghulam Rasool [1991] 12 Criminal Appeal Reports (S) 771 (arranged marriage, Pakistan)
R. v. Adesanya [1974] The Times 16, 17 July (scarification of face, Nigeria)

United States of America

A.A. v. Needville Indipendent School District, U.S. District Court for the Southern district of Texas, Houston division, civil action n. H-08-2934, January 20, 2009 (long hair, Native American)
Bounnhong Douangpangna v. Mike Knowles, Warden, 2007 U.S. Dist. Lexis 25833, No. Civ S-01-0764 Geb JFM P, United States district court for the eastern district of California, April 5, 2007 (murder caused by black magic, Laos)
Cheema v. Thompson, 61 F.3d 734, 9th Cir. August 1, (1995) (*kirpan*, ritual knife, in school uniform, Sikhs)
Church of the Lukumi Babalu Aye, Inc. v. City of Hialeah, 508 U.S. 520 (1993) (sacrifices of animals, Santeria)
City of Boerne, Texas v. P.F. Flores Archbishop of San Antonio, and United States, 521 U.S. 507, 1997 (expansion of a church, Catholics)
David M. Burks-Bey, v. Sally Stevenson, et al., 328 F. Supp. 2d 928, (2004), U.S. Dist., lexis 14483, United States district court for the Northern district of Indiana, South bend division, July 12, 2004 (prayers in prison, Moorish Science Temple of America)
Employment division, Human resources of Oregon v. Smith, [1990] 494 US 872 (*peyote* ritual smoking, Native American)
Francoise Anate Gomis, v. Eric H. Holder, Jr., Attorney General, 571 F.3d 353; U.S. App. Lexis 14606, United States Court of appeals for the fourth circuit, July 6, 2009 (female circumcision, Senegal)
Friedman v. State, 282 New York State, 2d 858 (1967) (*Yichud*, prohibition of seclusion in a private area after sunset for a woman and a man that are not married to each other, Jews)
Gonzalez v. O Centro Espìrita Benecifiente União do vegetal, 546 U.S. 418, (2006) (*ayahuasca* ritual drinking, Native American/Catholic)

Hamdi Al Khalili, v. Eric H. Holder, Jr., Attorney General of the United States, United States Court of appeals for the sixth circuit, February 27, 2009, Lexis 4023 (honor killing of a man, Jordan)

In Re air crash near Nantucket Island, Massachusetts, 462 F. Supp. 2d 360, (2006) U.S. Dist. (compensation for damages arising from firstborn son's death, Egypt)

In Re Jertrude O., 466 A.2d 885 (Md App 1983) (child rearing: children left alone, cupping-folk medicine, Republic of Central Africa)

In the Matter of Peter L. Jr., Christina L., Appellant v. James Krauskopf, as Commissioner of Social Services, Respondent, 92 A.D.2d 853; 460 N.Y.S.2d 578; 1983 N.Y. App. Div. LEXIS 17225 (mourning, Greece)

Issa Diakhite, v. Alberto R. Gonzales, Attorney General of the United States, 165 Fed. Appx. 636; 2006 U.S. App. Lexis 2747, United States Court of Appeals for the Tenth Circuit, February 2, 2006, Filed (slavery, Senegal)

Krasniqi v. Dallas Cty. Child Protective Services (1991) (genital touching as an expression of affection from parent to child, Albania)

Marcia V., Appellant v. State of Alaska, Office of Children's Services, Appellee, Supreme Court of Alaska, No. S-13065, 201 P.3d 496, Jan. 21, 2009 (child abuse, Native American)

Mohammed Sulliman Al Wawi, Petitioner, V. John Ashcroft, Attor-Ney General, Respondent, No. 02-4292, United States Court of Appeals for the Sixth Circuit, 91 Fed. Appx. 493; 2004 U.S. App. Lexis 5382, March 18, 2004 (honor killing of a man, Jordan)

Quang Ngoc Bui v. State, 717 So. 2d 6, (1997) Ala. Crim. App. Lexis 276 (murder, Vietnam)

Sherbert v. Verner, [1963] 374 U.S. 398 (keeping of Sabbath, Seventh-day Adventists)

State of Maine v. Mohammad Kargar, 679 A.2d 81, 1996 (kissing a son on his genitals, Afghanistan)

State of Washington, v. Nadezhda Pesotskiy, No. 52502-6-I, Court of Appeals of Washington, Division one, 2004 Wash. App. Lexis 2317, October 11, 2004 (pictures of naked girl, Ukraine)

State v. Norman, 89 N.C. App. 384, 366 S.E.2d 586, 1988 N.C. App. 262 (reasonable battered woman standard, US)

Steven H. v. Arizona Dept. of Economic Security, 218 Ariz. 566, 190 P.3d 180 Ariz., August 19, 2008 (children removed from their families, Native American)

The People v. Dong Lu Chen, No. 87-7774, N.Y. Sup. Ct. Dec. 2, (1988) (femicide due to jealousy, China)

The People v. Fumiko Kimura, n. A-091133, California Superior Court, 1985, unpublished (*oyaku shinju*, parent-child suicide-homicide, Japan)

The People v. José Luis Gonzalez et al., Court of appeal of California, Second appellate district, Division three, January 23, (2009) Lexis 537 (child abuse, Mexico)

The People v. Moua, No. 315972-0, Cal. Sup. Ct., (1985) (*zij poj niam*, wedding through kidnapping, Hmong)

The People v. Wu, 235 Cal. App. 3d 614, October 24 1991 (filicide, China)

Trujillo Garcia v. Rowland, U.S. 6199 (Dist. Ct., 1992); U.S. 30441 (App. Ct., 1993), 114 S Ct 2145; U.S. 4219 (Dist. Ct. 1994) (murder due to provocation, Mexico)

United States v. Abdul Raimi Mamah, United States Court of Appeals for the Seventh circuit, 332 F.3d 475 (2003) (false confessions due to fear of the Police, Ghana)

United States v. Ballard, 322 U.S. 78, 64 S. Ct. 882, 88 L. Ed. 1148 (1944) (definition of religion, I AM religious movement)

United States v. Mamie Manneh, 645 F. Supp. 2d 98, 2008 U.S. Dist. Lexis 105209, United states district court for the Eastern district of New York, December 31, 2008, Decided (transport of primate meat, Liberia)

United States v. Phuoung Nguyen Le, Criminal No. 3:08cr516, US District Court for the eastern district of Virginia, Richmond division, September 14, 2009, Lexis 83933 (insults or threats, Vietnam)

United States v. Sherpa 110 F.3d 656 (1996) (heroin importation, Nepal)

United States v. Steven Robinson, 1971 (black rage, African Americans)

United States v. Wilgus, 606 F. Supp. 2d 1308 (2009) (eagle feathers for prayers, Native American)

Wisconsin v. Yoder et al., 406 U.S. 205, (1972) (partial exemption from school attendance, Amish)

Out-of Court Settlement 1996, (child in pushchair left outside a restaurant, Denmark)

Out-of Court Settlement *Hindu v. McDonald's*, 2001 (beef-flavored crisps, India)

Out-of Court Settlement *Hindu v. Taco Bell*, 1999 (non-vegetarian sandwich, India)

Other states

Gadam v. R., 14 W.A.C.A. 442 (1954) Nigeria (murder of witches, Nigeria)

Philip Muswe s/o Musele v. R. 23 E.A.C.A. 622 (1956) Kenya (murder of witches, Kenya)

R. v. Mbombela, 1993 South Africa (murder of person mistaken for an evil creature, South Africa)

R. v. Muddarubba [1956] NTJ 317, 322, Australia (murder due to provocation, Aboriginal People)

R. v. Noboi-Bosai [1971–1972], P. and N.G.L. R. 271, Papua New Guinea (necrophagia, Aboriginal People)

R. v. Rankin, [1966] QWN 16, Australia (murder due to provocation, Aboriginal People)

Ressler v. The Knesset [the Parliament], 21 February 2012, Israel (exemption from military service, ultra-Orthodox Jews)

State of Gujaratv.Mirzapur Moti Kureshi Kasab Jammat and others Appeals n. 4937–4940, 1998, Supreme Court of India, India (prohibition to kill cows during Bakrid Muslim celebration, Hinduism)

Supranational courts

Awas Tingi v. Nicaragua, 31 August 2001, Interamerican Court (man–land relationship, Indigenous People)

Chapman v. the United Kingdom, ECHR, 27238/95, 18 January 2001 (nomadism, Roma people)

G. and E. v. Norway, Appl. n. 9278/81 e 9415/81, decision 3 October 1983 (former European Commission for Human Rights) (territories, Sami Indigenous People)

Ivan Kitok v. Sweden, Communication No. 197/1985 UN Doc CCPR/C/33/D/197/1985, IHRL 2484 (UNHRC 1988), 27th July 1988, UN Human Rights Committee [UNHRC] (reindeer herding, Sami Indigenous People)

Lautsi v. Italy and others, ECHR, 30814/06, 22 March 2011 (crucifixes in schools, Italy)

Lovelace v. Canada, Communication No. R.6/24, U.N. Doc. Supp. No. 40 (A/36/40) at 166 (1981), UN Human rights Committee [UNHRC] (right to live in a Indian reservation, Indigenous People)

Lubicon Lake Band v. Canada, Communication No. 167/1984 (26 March 1990), U.N. Doc. Supp. No. 40 (A/45/40) at 1 (1990), UN Human rights Committee [UNHRC] (Industrial exploitation of ancestral territories, Indigenous People)

S.A.S. v. France, ECHR 695, 1° July 2014 (*burqa*, Islam)

Table of tests

Test used by judges

Religious test USA (Supreme Court, *Sherbert* 1963, codified in RFRA 1993–1997)

1 Defining the religious practice
2 Is the subject sincere?
3 Is there a substantial burden over a mandatory practice?
4 Is there a compelling state interest to limit the practice?

Cultural defense test USA (not official)

1 Defining the cultural practice
2 How would the reasonable Mexican, Chinese, Japanese etc. person have behaved in the same circumstances? (*reasonable cultural person test*)
3 How long has the person lived in the USA?

Cultural test Canada (Supreme Court, *Van Der Peet* 1996, applied only to indigenous)

1 Defining the cultural practice
2 Is the practice "essential and integral" to the cultural survival of the group?
3 Is the practice "distinctive" from other majority practices?
4 Did the practice exist prior to the contact with Europeans? (*pre-contact test*)
5 Were indigenous people consulted? (question inserted by *Haida* 2004)

Religious test Canada (Supreme Court, *Amselem* 2004)

1 Defining the religious practice
2 *Non-trivial burden* and possible alternative for the subject
3 Is the subject sincere?
4 Is the practice harmful?
5 Balancing with other rights
6 Is the limitation reasonable in a democratic society?

Reasonable accomodation Canada (since 1990)

1 Accomodation case by case
2 Double reasonableness: Is the practice reasonable? Is the limit to it reasonable?
3 Which effort did the employer or the public institution make to reach an accomodation?

4 Which burden or restriction would fall on the employee or public institution if he accomodates? (undue hardship or burden)
5 Balancing with other rights

Cultural test UN Human rights committee (from 1980)

1 Defining the religious practice
2 Is the practice "essential" to the cultural survival of the group?
3 Reasonableness of the limit imposed by the state
4 Has the minority been consulted?
5 Is the practice being destroyed or just altered?

Cultural test European Court of Human Rights (not official)

1 Is the practice essential and characterizing of that group?
2 Is the practice traditional?
3 Diversity needs protection as public good, value for the whole society
4 Is the practice being destroyed or just alterated?

Tests proposed in scholarship

Test proposed by Alison Dundes Renteln (*The Cultural Defense*, 2004)

1 Is the litigant a member of the ethnic group?
2 Does the group have such a tradition?
3 Was the litigant influenced by the tradition when he or she acted?
4 Does the practice cause an irreparable harm?

Test proposed by Avigail Eisenberg (*Reasons of Identity*, 2009)

1 *Jeopardy condition*: Will important and otherwise unrealizable dimensions of a group's or individual's identity be severely jeopardized in the absence of granting the claim?
2 *Validation condition*: Is the practice suitably validated through legitimate processes internal to the community and, where relevant, between communities?
3 *Safeguard condition*: Will the claim, if protected, place people at risk of serious harm?

Test proposed by Cristina De Maglie (*I reati culturalmente motivati – Culturally Motivated Crimes*, 2010)

1 *Cultural motivation*: Was the crime committed for a cultural reason?
2 *Coincidence of reaction*: Is there a "coincidence of reaction" with the average person of that group? (*reasonable person test*)

3 *Distinctiveness between cultures*: Is the cultural practice distinctive from others of the majority?

Test proposed by Fabio Basile (*I reati cd. 'culturalmente motivati' commessi dagli immigrati: (possibili) soluzioni giurisprudenziali – The So-called 'Culturally Motivated' Crimes Committed by Immigrants: (Possible) Solutions in Case-law*, 2017)

1 *Offensiveness of the conduct*: How does the right or interest compromised by the conduct rank within the relevant legal system?
2 *The features of the cultural norm*: Is the cultural norm also a religious norm? Is it legally recognized in the immigrant home country? Is it compulsory? Is it shared or contested within the group?
3 *Personal background of the offender*: Which is the level of integration of the person within the host country and his or her knowledge of the new legal system?

Test proposed by Isaak I. Dore (*Homo juridicus*, 2016)

1 Genuine membership in a native class
2 Motivation on the part of the defendant by a cultural belief system
3 Innocent nature of defendant's conduct
4 Uniform acceptance of such conduct by the native class of culture
5 The absence of victim harm
6 The lack of violence
7 The lack of intent
8 Absence of culpable mental state
9 Absence of extraneous proof of blameworthiness
10 Lack of moral turpitude
11 Legislative intent regarding unanticipated cases
12 In sexual cases, absence of sexual gratification

Test proposed by Ilenia Ruggiu (*Culture and the Judiciary: The Anthropologist Judge*, 2019)

1 Does the matter adjudicated fall within the *category of culture*?
2 *Describe* the cultural practice and the group
3 *Relate* and *link* the practice to the wider cultural *web of significances*
4 Is the practice *essential* (to the group's survival), *compulsory* or *optional*?
5 Is the practice *shared* or *contested* within the group?
6 Is the group *vulnerable* within a society? Is it discriminated against?
7 How would a *reasonable person in that group* behave in the same circumstances?
8 Is the subject *sincere*?
9 Is there a *cultural equivalent*, a similar or comparable practice, in the majority culture?

10 Is the practice *harmful*? Is the harm irreparable?
11 What is the impact of the practice on the culture, fundamental rights, and value system of the *majority*?
12 Does the practice perpetuate *patriarchy*?
13 What *value* does the minority ascribe to the practice at issue? Does this value reflect the choice of a *meaningful life*?

References

Abu-Laban J., C. Gabriel (2002) *Selling diversity. Immigration, multiculturalism, employment, equity and globalization*, Peterborough: Broadview;

Abu-Lughod L. (1991) "Writing against culture", in R.G. Fox (ed.), *Recapturing anthropology. Working in the present*, Santa Fe-New Mexico: School of American Research Press, 137 et seq.;

Ahmed A.S., C.N. Shore (eds.) (1995) *The future of anthropology: its relevance to the contemporary world*, London: Athlone;

Aime M. (2004) *Eccessi di culture*, Torino: Einaudi;

Al Hibri Azizah Y. (1999) "Is Western patriarchal feminism good for Third world/minority women?", in J. Cohen, M. Toward, M.C. Nussbaum (eds.), *Is multiculturalism bad for women? Susan Moller Okin with respondents*, Princeton: Princeton University Press, 256 et seq.;

Alfred T. (2005) *Wasáse: indigenous pathways of action and freedom*, Peterborough: Broadview Press;

Allievi S. (2010) "Multiculturalism in Italy: the missing model", in A. Silji (ed.), *European multi-culturalism rivisited*, London-New York: Zed Books, 145 et seq.;

American Anthropological Association (1947) "Statement on Human Rights", *American Anthropologist* Vol. 49, No. 4, 539 et seq.;

Anderson B. (1983) *Imagined communities. Reflections on the origins of nationalism*, London: Verso and New Left Books;

Appadurai A. (1988) *The social life of things: commodities in cultural perspective*, Cambridge: Cambridge University Press;

Appadurai A. (1991) "Global ethnoscapes. Notes and queries for a transnational anthropology", in R.G. Fox (ed.), *Recapturing Anthropology. Working in the present*, Santa Fe-New Mexico: School of American Research Press, 191 et seq.;

Appiah K.A. (2005) *The ethics of identity*, Princeton: Princeton University Press;

Appignanesi R., C. Garrat (2003) *Introducing postmodernism*, Malta: Gutemberg Press;

Arfini E.A.G. (2010), "Istruzioni per diventare disabile. Un'analisi narrativa del progetto sul corpo transabile", *Studi culturali*, No. 3, 343 et seq.;

Aritotle (2012) *The Organon: the works of Aristotle on Logic* (ed. R. Bishop Jones), Book 5 *Topics* (translated by W.A. Pickard-Cambridge), CreateSpace Independent Publishing Platform;

Asad T. (1973) *Anthropology and the colonial encounter*, London: Ithaca Press;

Asad T. (1986) "The concept of cultural translation in British social anthropology", in J. Clifford, G. Marcus (eds.), *Writing culture: the poetics and politics of ethnography*, Berkeley: University of California Press, 148 et seq.;

Asch M. (2000) "The judicial conceptualization of culture after Delgammukv and Van der Peet", *Review of Constitutional Studies* Vol. 2, 119 et seq.;
Azzariti G. (2012) *Diritto e conflitti*, Roma-Bari: Laterza;
Balibar E. (1991) "Is there a 'neo-racism'?", in E. Balibar, I.M. Wallerstein (eds.), *Race, nation, class, ambigous identities*, London: Verso, 17 et seq.;
Banting K., W. Kymlicka (eds.) (2006) *Multiculturalism and the welfare state. Recognition and redistribution in contemporary democracies*, Oxford: Oxford University Press;
Baraggia A. (2010) "Il referendum svizzero contro l'edificazione di minareti", *Quaderni costituzionali*, No. 1, 126 et seq.;
Barry B. (2001) *Culture and equality: an egalitarian critique of multiculturalism*, Cambridge: Harvard University Press;
Barry B. (2009) "The muddles of multiculturalism", *New Left Review*, No. 8 Mar/Apr., 49 et seq.;
Barsh R., J.Y. Henderson (1997) "The Supreme Court's Van der Peet trilogy: naïve imperialism and ropes of sand", *McGill Law Review* Vol. 42, No. 4, 993 et seq.;
Bascherini G. (2007) *Immigrazione e diritti fondamentali. L'esperienza italiana tra storia costituzionale e prospettive europee*, Napoli: Jovene;
Basile F. (2010) *Immigrazione e reati culturalmente motivati. Il diritto penale nelle società multiculturali*, Padova: Cedam;
Basile, F. (2017) "I reati cd. 'culturalmente motivati' commessi dagli immigrati: (possibili) soluzioni giurisprudenziali", *Questione giustizia* No. 1, 26 et seq.;
Baubock R. (2003) "Farewell to multiculturalism? Sharing values and identities in societies of immigration", *Journal of International Migration and Integration* No. 3, 1 et seq.;
Beaman L.G. (2008) "Defining religion: the promise and the peril of legal interpretation", in R. Moon (ed.), *Law and religious pluralism in Canada*, Toronto-Vancouver: UBC Press, 192 et seq.;
Beger R.R., J. Hein (2001) "Immigrants, culture, and American courts: a typology of legal strategies and issues in cases involving Vietnamese and Hmong litigants", *Criminal Justice Review* Vol. 26, No. 1, spring, 38 et seq.;
Benedetti G. (2010) "L'elogio dell'interpretazione traducente nell'orizzonte europeo", *Persona e Mercato* Vol. 1, 3 et seq.;
Benedict R. (1934) *Patterns of culture*, New York: Penguin Books;
Benhabib S. (2002) *The claims of culture*, Princeton: Princeton University Press;
Bernardi A. (2006) *Modelli penali e società multiculturali*, Torino: Giappichelli;
Bernardi A. (2007) "L'ondivaga rilevanza penale del 'fattore culturale'", *Politica del Diritto*, 3 et seq.;
Bernardi A. (2010) *Il "fattore culturale" nel sistema penale*, Torino: Giappichelli;
Bertossi C. (2010) "Conclusions. Mistaken models of integration? A critical perspective on the crisis of multiculturalism in Europe", in A. Silji (ed.), *European multiculturalism rivisited*, London-New York: Zed Books, 235 et seq.;
Bidney D. (1944) "The concept of culture and some cultural fallacies", *American Anthropologist* No. 46, 30 et seq.;
Bidney D. (1968) "Cultural relativism", in D. Sills (ed.), *International encyclopedia of the social science*, Vol. 3, New York: Free Press, 543 et seq.;
Bin R. (1992) *Diritti e argomenti. Il bilanciamento degli interessi nella giurisprudenza costituzionale*, Milano: Giuffrè;
Bin R., G. Brunelli, A. Pugiotto, P. Veronesi (eds.) (2004) *La laicità crocifissa? Il nodo costituzionale dei simboli religiosi nei luoghi pubblici*, Torino: Giappichelli;

Birket-Smith K. (1963) *Primitive man and his ways*, New York: Mentor Books;

Boas F. (1930) "Anthropology", *Encyclopedia of the social science*, Vol. 2, New York: Macmillan, 73 et seq.;

Boas F. (1938) *The mind of primitive man* (1st edition 1911), New York: The Macmillan Company;

Bognetti G. (2009) "L'oggetto e il metodo", in P. Carrozza, A. Di Giovine, G.F. Ferrari (eds.), *Diritto costituzionale comparato*, Roma-Bari: Laterza, 5 et seq.;

Bohannan P. (1973) "Rethinking culture: a project for current anthropologists", *Current Anthropologist*, No. 14, 357 et seq.;

Bork R.H. (2002) *Coercing virtue: the worldwide rule of judges*, Washington: AEI Press;

Borrows J. (1997–98) "Frozen rights in Canada: constitutional interpretation and the trickster", *American Indian Law Review* Vol. 22, 37 et seq.;

Borrows J. (2008) "Living law on a living earth: aboriginal religion, law, and the Constitution", in R. Moon (ed.), *Law and religious pluralism in Canada*, Toronto-Vancouver: UBC Press, 161 et seq.;

Bouchard G., C. Taylor (2008) "Building the future: a time of reconciliation. Report of the Commission de consultation sur les practiques d'accomodement reliées aux differences culturelles", Quebec: Gouvernment du Quebec, www.accomodements.qc.ca/documentation/rapports/raport-final-integral-en.pdf;

Bourdieu P. (1960) "Guerre et mutation sociale en Algèrie", *Etudes Meditèrranèenes* No. 7, 27 et seq.;

Bramadat P. (2005a) "Beyond Christian Canada: religion and ethnicity in a multicultural society", in P. Bramadat, D. Seljak (eds.), *Religion and ethnicity in Canada*, Toronto-Buffalo-London: University of Toronto Press, 1 et seq.;

Bramadat P. (2005b) "Toward a new politics of authenticity: ethno-cultural representation in theory and practice", *Canadian Ethnic Studies/Ètudes ethniques au Canada* Vol. XXXVII, No. 1, 1 et seq.;

Braunmühl, C. (2012) *Colonial discourse and gender in U.S. criminal courts: cultural defenses and prosecutions*, New York: Routledge;

Breidenbach J., I. Zukrigl (1998) *Tanz der Kulturen: Kulturelle Identität in einer globalisierten Welt*, München: Kunstmann;

Brettel C.B. (2006) "Introduction: global spaces/local places: transnationalism, diaspora and the meaning of home", *Identities* Vol. 13, No. 3, 327 et seq.;

Brown L.R., McGrath, P.L., Stokes, B. (1976) "Twenty-two dimensions of the population problem", in *Worldwatch paper* (USA), No. 5, Washington DC: Worldwatch Inst., 83 et seq.;

Brubaker R., F. Cooper (2000) "Beyond 'identity'", *Theory and Society* Vol. 29, No. 1. Feb., 1 et seq.;

Brumann C. (1999) "Writing for culture: why a successful concept should not be discarded", *Current Anthropology* Vol. 40, 1 et seq.;

Bryant T.L. (1990) "Oya-ko shinju: death at the center of the heart", *Pacific Basin Law Journal* UCLA, 8, 1 et seq.;

Burke S. (2016) "Doctors are applauding the end of a unique Tennessee law threatening addicted mothers with jail for assault if they gave birth to babies with drug dependence", *Associated Press*, April 1st.

Caggia F. (2010) "Le mutilazioni genitali femminili: uno spazio nel diritto dell'Unione europea?", *Quaderni costituzionali*, Vol. 1, 101 et seq.;

Camerlengo Q. (2007) *Contributo ad una teoria costituzionale del diritto cosmopolitico*, Milano: Giuffrè;

Caponio T. (2013) "Multiculturalism Italian style: soft or weak recognition?", in R. Taras (ed.), *Challenging multiculturalism: European models of diversity*, Edinburgh: Edinburgh University Press, 216 et seq.;

Caputi J., D.E.H. Russell Diana (1992) "Femicide: sexist terrorism against women", in J. Radford, D.E.H. Russell (eds.), *Femicide. The politics of woman killing*, New York: Twayne Publishers, 13 et seq.;

Cartabia M. (2009) "L'universalità dei diritti umani nell'età dei 'nuovi diritti'", *Quaderni costituzionali* No. 3, 537 et seq.;

Carter H. (2009) "Jedi religion founder accuses Tesco of discrimination over rules on hoods", *The Guardian*, 18 September;

Cassell E. (2009) "Anthropologists in the Canadian courts", in M. Freeman, D. Napier (eds.), *Law and anthropology*, Oxford: Oxford University Press, 187 et seq.;

Cavalla F. (1992) "Topica giuridica", *Enciclopedia del diritto*, Vol. XLIV, Milano: Giuffrè, 720 et seq.;

Cerrina Feroni G. (2008) "L'esperienza tedesca di multiculturalismo: società multietnica e aspirazioni di identità etnoculturale", http://archivio.rivistaaic.it;

Charlton G.C. (2007–2008) "Letting go of culture. A comment on R. v. Sappier; R. v. Gray", *Ottawa Law Review/Revue de droit d'Ottawa* Vol. 39, 317 et seq.;

Chase C. (2002) "'Cultural practice' or 'reconstructive surgery'? U.S. genital cutting, the intersex movement, and medical double standards", in S.M. James, C.C. Robertsone (eds.), *Genital cutting and transnational sisterhood. Disputing U.S. polemics*, Urbana and Chicago: University of Illinois Press, 126 et seq.;

Chienhan Cheng C. (1997) "Touring the museum: a comment on R. v. Van der Peet", *University of Toronto Faculty Law Review* No. 55, 419 et seq.;

Christensen, E. (2012) "Revisiting multiculturalism and its critics", *The Monist* Vol. 95, No. 1, January, 33 et seq.;

Clifford J. (1988) *The predicament of culture. Twentieth century ethnography, literature, and art*, Cambridge: Harvard University Press;

Clifford J., G. Marcus (eds.) (1986) *Writing culture: the poetics and politics of ethnography*, Berkeley: University of California Press;

Cohan J.A. (2010) "Honor killings and the cultural defense", *California Western International Law Journal* Vol. 40, No. 2, 177 et seq.;

Cohen A.P. (1996) "Personal nationalism: a Scottish view of some rites, rights, and wrongs", *American Ethnologist* Vol. 23, No. 4, 802 et seq.;

Cohen J., M. Toward, M. C. Nussbaum (eds.) (1999) *Is multiculturalism bad for women?/ Susan Moller Okin with respondents*, Princeton: Princeton University Press;

Comaroff J. (2010) "The end of anthropology. Again: on the future of an in/discipline", *American Anthropologist* Vol. 112, issue 4, 524 et seq.;

Connolly A.F. (1988) *Cultural difference on trial. The nature and limits of judicial understanding*, Burlington: Ashgate;

Coomaraswamy, R. (2005) "Violence against women and 'crimes of honour'", in Welchman L. and Hossain S. (eds.), *'Honour': Crimes, paradigms and violence against women*, London: Zed Books, xi et seq.;

Coombe R.J. (1995) "The properties of culture, and the politics of possessing identity. Native claims in the cultural appropriation controversy", in D. Danielsen, K. Engle (eds.), *After identity. A reader in law and culture*, New York and London: Routledge, 251 et seq.;

Courtois S. (2008) "A liberal defence of the intrinsic value of cultures", *Contemporary Political Theory* Vol. 7, 31 et seq.;

Crate S.A., M. Nuttall (2016) "Introduction", in S.A. Crate, M. Nuttall (eds.), *Anthropology and climate change from actions to transformations*, New York: Routledge, 9 et seq.;

Crenshaw K., N. Gotanda, G. Peller, K. Thomas (eds.) (1995) *Critical race theory. The key writings that formed the movement*, New York: New Press;

Croce M. (2009) "C'è un giudice a Valladolid: la rimozione del crocifisso dalle aule scolastiche in Spagna", *Quaderni costituzionali* Vol. 1, 108 et seq.;

Dalton C., Schneider E.M. (2001) *Battered women and the law*, New York: Foundation Press, Thomson West;

Damian M. (2008) "Fictions of intention in the cultural defence", *American Anthropologist* Vol. 110, No. 4, 432 et seq.;

Davis W. (2002) "Vanishing cultures", www.nationalgeographic.com, June 28;

De Maglie C. (2010) *I reati culturalmente motivati. Ideologie e modelli penali*, Pisa: Edizioni ETS;

De Martino E. (2004) *Sud e magia* (1st edition 1959), Milano: Feltrinelli;

De Roover J., S. Claerhout, S.N. Balagangadhara (2011) "Liberal political theory and the cultural migration of ideas: the case of secularism in India", *Political Theory* Vol. 39, No. 5, 571 et seq.;

Desi B. (2007) "Diversità culturale e principio di uguaglianza nel processo penale", lecture for the conference *Multiculturalismo e processo penale*, Bologna, April 13, www.giuristidemocratici.it;

Dillow G. (1985a) "When legal system and culture collide", *Los Angeles Herald*, February 18;

Dillow G. (1985b) "Community gathers to express concerns for Kimura", *The Rafu Shimp, Los Angeles Daily News*, April;

Dolan M. (1985) "Two cultures collide over act of despair; mother facing charges in ceremonial drowning", *Los Angeles Times*, February 24;

Dominijanni I. (2006) "Patriarcati trasversali", *Il Manifesto*, August 22;

Donovan J.M., H. Edwin Anderson III (2003) *Anthropology and law*, Oxford NY: Berghahn books;

Dore I.I. (2016) *Homo Juridicus. Culture as a normative order*, Durham: Carolina Academic Press;

Dundes Renteln A. (1988) "Relativism and the search of human rights", *American Anthropologist* Vol. 90, issue 1, 56 et seq.;

Dundes Renteln A. (1990) *International human rights. Universalism versus relativism*, Newbury Park: Sage Publications;

Dundes Renteln A. (2002) "In defense of culture in the Courtroom", in R.A. Shweder, M. Minow, H.R. Markus (eds.), *Engaging cultural differences. The multicultural challenge in liberal democracies*, New York: Russell Sage Foundation, 194 et seq.;

Dundes Renteln A. (2004) *The cultural defense*, Oxford: Oxford University Press;

Dundes Renteln A. (2009a) "Cross-cultural justice and the logic of reciprocity. When Westerners run afoul of the law in other countries", *Judicature* Vol. 92, No. 5, March-April, 238 et seq.;

Dundes Renteln A. (2009b) "The influence of culture on the determination of damages: how cultural relativism affects the analysis of trauma", in R. Grillo, R. Ballard, A. Ferrari, A.J. Hoekema, M. Maussen, P. Shah (eds.), *Legal practice and cultural diversity*, London: Routledge, 199 et seq.;

Dundes Renteln A. (2010a) "Corporal punishment and the cultural defense", *Law and Contemporary Problems* Vol. 73, 253 et seq.;

Dundes Renteln A. (2010b) "Making room for culture in the court", *The Judges' Journal* (monograph issue *Cultures in Court*) Vol. 49, No. 2, spring, 7 et seq.;

Dundes Renteln A. (2011) "Cultural defenses in international criminal tribunals: a preliminary consideration of the issues", *Southwestern Journal of International Law* Vol. XVIII, No. 1, 267 et seq.;

Dundes Renteln A., A. Dundes (eds.) (1994) *Folk law. Essays in the theory and practice of lex non scripta*, New York and London: Garland publishing Inc.;

Eco U. (1962) *Opera aperta*, Milano: Bompiani;

Eisenberg A. (1994) "The politics of individual and group difference in Canadian jurisprudence", *Canadian Journal of Political Science/Revue Canadienne de Science Politique* Vol. 27, No. 1, Mar., 3 et seq.;

Eisenberg A. (2007) "Identity, multiculturalism, and religious arbitration: the debate over Shari'a law in Canada", in B. Arneil, M. Deveaux, R. Dhamoon, A. Eisenberg (eds.), *Sexual justice/cultural justice*, London: Routledge, 211 et seq.;

Eisenberg A. (2009) *Reasons of identity. A normative guide to the political and legal assessment of identity claims*, Oxford: Oxford University Press;

Eisenberg A. (ed.) (2006) *Diversity and equality. The changing framework of freedom in Canada*, Toronto-Vancouver: UBC Press;

Eisenberg A., J. Spinner-Halev (eds.) (2005) *Minorities within minorities. Equality, rights and diversity*, Cambridge: Cambridge University Press;

Eisenberg A., W. Kymlicka, (eds.) (2011) *Identity politics in the public realm. Bringing institutions back in*, Toronto-Vancouver: UBC Press;

Ellington T. (2001) *The myth of the noble savage*, Berkeley and Los Angeles: University of California Press;

Engineer A.A. (2012) "Child marriage and Islam", www.dawn.com, August 3;

Engle K. (2001) "From skepticism to embrace: human rights and the American Anthropological Association from 1947–1999", *Human Rights Quarterly* Vol. 23, 536 et seq.;

Fabian J. (1983) *Time and the other. How Anthropology makes its object*, New York: Columbia University Press;

Fabian J. (2007) "On recognizing things. The 'ethnic artifact' and the 'ethnographic object'", in J. Fabian (ed.), *Memory against culture. Arguments and reminders*, Durham and London: Duke University Press, 52 et seq.;

Fabietti U. (1995) *L'identità etnica. Storia e critica di un concetto equivoco*, Roma: Nuova Italia Scientifica;

Fanon F. (1965) *A Dying colonialism*, New York: Monthly Review Press;

Federico V. (2010) "La Francia si interroga sulla poligamia", *Quaderni costituzionali* No. 2, 371 et seq.;

Ferlito S. (2005) *Le religioni, il giurista e l'antropologo*, Soveria Mannelli: Rubbettino;

Firth R. (2004) *We, the Tikopia: a sociological study of kinship in primitive Polynesia* (1st edition 1936), London-New York: Routledge;

Fisher J. (1992) "In search of the 'inauthentic': disturbing signs in contemporary Native American art", *Art Journal* Fall, 44 et seq.;

Foblets M.C. (2016) "The body as identity marker. Circumcision of boys caught between contrasting views on the best interest of the child", in M. Jänterä-Jareborg (ed.), *The child's interests in conflict. The intersections between society, family, faith and culture*, Cambridge-Antwerp-Portland: Intersentia, 126 et seq.;

Foblets M.C., A. Dundes Renteln (eds.) (2009) *Multicultural jurisprudence: comparative perspectives on the cultural defense*, Oxford: Hart Publishing;

Fornasari G. (2008) "Mutilazioni genitali femminili e multiculturalismo: premesse per un discorso giuspenalistico", in A. Bernardi, B. Pastore, A. Pugiotto (eds.), *Legalità penale e crisi del diritto, oggi. Un percorso interdisciplinare*, Milano: Giuffrè, 179 et seq.;

Foucault M. (2002) *The archaeology of knowledge*, London-New York: Routledge;
Fox-Genovese, E. (1982) "Placing women's history in history", *New Left Review* No. 133, May/June, 5 et seq.;
Fraser N., Honneth A. (2003) *Redistribution or recognition? A political-philosophical exchange*, London-New York: Verso;
Freeman M., Napier D. (eds.) (2009) *Law and anthropology*, Oxford: Oxford University Press;
French R.R. (2009) "Ethnography in ordinary case law", in Freeman M., Napier D. (eds.), *Law and anthropology*, Oxford: Oxford University Press, 126 et seq.;
Fromm E. (1956) *The art of loving*, New York: Harper & Row;
Gadamer H.G. (1960) *Wahrheit und Methode. Grundzüge der philosophischen Hermeneutik*, Tübingen: Mohr;
Galli C. (2006) *Multiculturalismo. Ideologie e sfide*, Bologna: il Mulino;
Gallie W.B. (1956) "Essentially contested concepts", *Proceedings of the Aristotelian Society*, Vol. 56, 167 et seq.;
Gallo F. (2005) *L'interpretazione del diritto è "affabulazione"?*, Milano: Edizioni universitarie di lettere, economia, diritto;
Gavison R. (2005) "Days of worship and days of rest", www.gavison.com/a2695-days-of-worship-and-days-of-rest;
Geertz C. (1973a) *The interpretation of cultures*, New York: Basic Books;
Geertz C. (1973b) *Thick description: toward interpretive theory of culture*, New York: Basic Books;
Geertz C. (1983) *Local knowledge. Further essays in interpretative anthropology*, New York: Basic Books;
Geller P.L., M.K. Stockett (2006) *Feminist anthropology: past, present and future*, Philadelphia: University of Pennsylvania Press;
Giddens A. (1991) *Modernity and self-identity. Self and society in the late modern age*, Stanford: Stanford University Press;
Giglioli P., P. Ravaioli (2004) "Bisogna davvero dimenticare il concetto di cultura? Replica ai colleghi antropologi", *Rassegna Italiana di Sociologia* Vol. 2, 267 et seq.;
Gilman L. (1999) "Barbaric rituals", in J. Cohen, M. Toward, M. C. Nussbaum (eds.), *Is multiculturalism bad for women? Susan Moller Okin with respondents*, Princeton: Princeton University Press, 57 et seq.;
Giuliani A. (1984) "Droit, mouvement et reminiscence", *Archives de Philosophie du Droit* Vol. 29, 101 et seq.;
Glendon M.A. (2006) *Traditions in turmoil: essays on law, culture and human rights*, Ann Arbor: Sapientia Press;
Goel R. (2004) "Can I call Kimura crazy? Ethical tensions in the cultural defense", *Seattle Journal for Social Justice* Fall/Winter No. 3, 443 et seq.;
Goldberg D.T., M. Musheno, L.C. Bower (eds.) (2001) *Between law and culture. Relocating legal studies*, Minneapolis-London: University of Minnesota Press;
Grandi C. (2009) "I reati culturalmente motivati nella giurisprudenza italiana: una categoria negletta?", in O. Giolo, M. Pifferi (eds.), *Diritto contro. Meccanismi giuridici di esclusione dello straniero*, Torino: Giappichelli, 179 et seq.;
Gruenbaum E. (2001) *The female circumcision controversy. An anthropological perspective*, Philadelphia: University of Pennsylvania Press;
Guazzarotti A. (2001) *Giudici e minoranze religiose*, Milano: Giuffrè;
Gupta A., J. Ferguson (1992) "Beyond 'culture'. Space, identity, and the politics of difference", *Cultural Anthropology* Vol. 7, No. 1, 6 et seq.;

Gustafsson A. (2011) "Kulturkrocken – Barnaga väcker debatt i Italien", *Svenska Dagbladet*, September 7 (Italian translation: "Scontro culturale. Picchiare i bambini desta un dibattito in Italia", www.italiadallestero.info, September 7);

Gutmann A. (2003) *Identity in democracy*, Princeton and Oxford: Princeton University Press;

Häberle P. (1999) "Per una dottrina della Costituzione europea", *Quaderni costituzionali* Vol. 1, 3 et seq.;

Habermas J. (1992) "Kampf um anerkennung im demokratischen rechtsstaat" in C. Taylor (ed.), *Multikulturalismus und die politik der anerkenmung*, Frankfurt am Main: Suhrkamp, 147 et seq.;

Haddock B., Sutch P. (eds.) (2003) *Multiculturalism, identity, and rights*, London-New York: Routledge;

Haldane D. (1989) "Culture clash or animal cruelty? Two Cambodian refugees face trial after killing dog for food", *Los Angeles Times*, March 13;

Hamilton G. (2001) "Montreal enclave. Hasidic residents fight 'turf war'", *National Post*, https://wwrn.org/articles/3854/, June 7;

Hannerz U. (1992) *Cultural complexity. Studies in the social organization of meaning*, New York: Columbia University Press;

Hannerz U. (1996) *Transnational connections. Culture, people, places*, London: Routledge;

Harris M. (1968) *The rise of anthropological theory: a history of theories of culture*, New York: Thomas Y. Crowell;

Harris M. (1979) *Cultural materialism: the struggle for a science of culture*, New York: Random House;

Harris P. (1997) *Black rage confronts the law*, New York-London: New York University Press;

Harrison L.E., Huntington S.P. (2000) *Culture matters: how values shape human progress*, New York: Basic Books;

Hatch E. (1983) *Culture and morality: the relativity of values in anthropology*, New York: Columbia University Press;

Herskovits M. (1950) *Man and his works: the science of cultural anthropology*, New York: Alfred A. Knopf;

Herzfeld M. (1987) *Anthropology trough the looking-glass: critical ethnography in the margins of Europe*, Cambridge: Cambridge University Press;

Hirschmann N. (1998) "Western feminism, eastern veiling and the question of free agency", *Constellations* No. 3, 5 et seq.;

Hobsbwam E.J., Ranger T. (1983) *The invention of tradition*, Cambridge: Cambridge University Press;

Hoffman J. (2009) "Feminism and difference", *Politics Review* Vol. 18, No. 4, April, 2 et seq.;

Holden L. (ed.) (2011) *Cultural expertise and litigation: patterns, conflicts, narratives*, New York-London: Routledge;

Honneth A. (1992) *Kampf um Anerkennung. Grammatik sozialer konflikte*, Frankfurt am Main: Suhrkamp;

Honneth A. (2005) *Verdinglichung: Eine anerkennungstheoretische studie*, Frankfurt am Main: Suhrkamp;

Huntington S.P. (1996) *The clash of civilizations and the remaking of world order*, New York: Simon&Schuster;

Hylland Eriksen T. (2004) *What is anthropology?*, London: Pluto Press;

Hymes D. (1974) *Reinventing anthropology*, New York: Vintage;

Jalki D., S. Pathan, and P. Shah (2017) *Western foundations of the caste system*, New York: Palgrave Macmillan;

Judicial Studies Board (1994) *Handbook on ethnic minority issues*, distributed by *Judicial Studies Board*, London: Judicial Studies Board, June;

Kandiyoti D. (1988) "Bargaining with Patriarchy", *Gender and Society* Vol. 2, No. 3, Sep., 274 et seq.;

Kawanishi Y. (1990) "Japanese mother-child suicide: the psychological and sociological implications of the Kimura case", *Pacific Basin Law Journal*, UCLA Vol. 8, No. 1, 32 et seq.;

Keane W. (2003) "Self-interpretation, agency, and the objects of anthropology: reflections on a genealogy", *Comparative Studies in Society and History* Vol. 45, No. 2, Apr., 222 et seq.;

Kelly P. (ed.) (2002) *Multiculturalism reconsidered. "Culture and equality" and its critics*, Cambridge: Polity Press;

Kluckhohn C. (1944) *Mirror for man*, New York-Toronto: McGraw-Hill;

Kompridis N. (2005) "Normativizing hybridity", *Political Theory* Vol. 33, No. 3, June;

Kotler N., P. Kotler, W. Kotler (2008) *Museum strategy and marketing. Designing missions, building audiences, generating revenue and resources* (2nd edition), San Francisco: Jossey-Bass;

Kroeber A.L. (1952) *The nature of culture*, Chicago: University of Chicago Press;

Kroeber A.L., C. Kluckhohn (1952) *Culture. A critical review of concepts and definitions*, New York: Vintage Books;

Kukathas C. (2001) "Is feminism bad for multiculturalism?", *Public Affairs Quarterly* Vol. 15, No. 2, 83 et seq.;

Kuper A. (1996) *Anthropology and anthropologists: the modern British school*, London: Routledge and Kegan Paul;

Kurt Barth W. (2008) *On cultural rights: the equality of nations and the minority legal traditions*, Leiden-Boston: Martinus Nijhoff publishers;

Kymlicka W. (1995) *Multicultural citizenship: a liberal theory of minority rights*, San Francisco: Jossey-Bass;

Kymlicka W. (2007) *Multicultural odysseys. Navigating the new international politics of diversity*, Oxford: Oxford University Press;

Kymlicka W., Baogang He (eds.) (2005) *Multiculturalism in Asia*, Oxford: Oxford University Press;

Kymlicka, W., C. Lernestedt, and M. Matravers (eds.) (2014) *Criminal law and cultural diversity*, Oxford Scholarship Online;

Laffaille F. (ed.) (2010) *Laïcité(s)*, Paris: Mare&Martin;

Leach E. (1954) *Political systems of highland Burma: a study of Kachin social structure*, Cambridge: Harvard University Press;

Lear J. (2006) *Radical hope. Ethics in the face of cultural devastation*, Cambridge: Harvard University Press;

LeBaron M. (2003) *Bridging cultural conflicts. A new approach for a changing world*, San Francisco: Jossey-Bass;

Lee C. (2003) *Murder and the reasonable man: passion and fear in the criminal courtroom*, New York: Critical America, New York University Hardcover;

Lee C. (2007) "Cultural convergence: interest convergence theory meets the cultural defense", *Arizona Law Review* Vol. 49, No. 4, Winter, 911 et seq.;

Legrand P. (1997) "The impossibility of legal transplants", *Maastricht Journal of European and Comparative Law* No. 4, 111 et seq.;

Lentin A., G. Titley (2011) *The crises of multiculturalism. Racism in a neoliberal age*, London-New York: Zed Books;

Lerner G. (1986) *The creation of patriarchy*, Oxford: Oxford University Press;

Levesque R.J.R. (2000) "Cultural evidence, child maltreatment, and the law", *Child Maltreatment* Vol. 5, No. 2, 146 et seq.;

Lévi-Strauss C. (1969) *The elementary structures of kinship* (*Les structures élémentaires de la parenté* (1949), London: Eyre and Spottiswoode;

Levy A. (2010) "Political correctness strikes back: Jedi believer wins apology after being kicked out of jobcentre for wearing a hood", *The Daily Mail*, March 17;

Lollini A. (2007) "La circolazione degli argomenti: metodo comparato e parametri interpretativi extra-sistemici nella giurisprudenza costituzionale sudafricana", *Diritto pubblico comparato ed europeo* Vol.1, 479 et seq.;

Lombroso C. (1876) *L'uomo delinquente*, Milano: Hoepli;

Luther E. (2010) "Whose "distinctive culture"? Aboriginal feminism and R. v. Van der Peet", *Indigenous Law Journal* Vol. 8, No. 1, 27 et seq.;

Luther J. (2006) "Il velo scoperto dalla legge: profili di giurisprudenza costituzionale comparata", in S. Ferrari (ed.), *Islam ed Europa*, Roma: Carocci, 78 et seq.;

Lyotard J.F. (1979) *La condition postmoderne*, Paris: Les Editions de Minuit;

MacIntosh C. (2009) "From judging culture to taxing 'Indians'. Tracing the legal discourse of the 'Indian mode of life'", *Osgoode Hall Law Journal/Revue juridique d'Osgoode Hall* No. 47, 399 et seq.;

Macklem P. (2001) *Indigenous difference and the Constitution of Canada*, Toronto-Buffalo-London: University of Toronto Press;

Mahamdallie H. (ed.) (2011) *Defending multiculturalism*, London: Bookmarks publications;

Maier S. (2009), "Honor killings and the cultural defense in Germany", in M.C. Foblets, A. Dundes Renteln (eds.), *Multicultural jurisprudence. Comparative perspectives on the cultural defense*, Oxford and Portland: Hart Publishing, 229 et seq.;

Malik, K. (2015) "The failure of multiculturalism: community versus society in Europe", *Foreign Affairs* Vol. 94, No. 2, March/April;

Malinowski B. (1922) *Argonauts of the Western Pacific. An account of native enterprise and adventure in the archipelagoes of Melanesian New Guinea*, London: Routledge and Kegan Paul;

Malinowski B. (1937) "Culture", *Encyclopedia of the social science*, E.R.A. Seligman ed., 621 et seq.;

Malinowski B. (1989) *A diary in the strict sense of the term* (1st edition 1967), Palo Alto, California: Stanford University Press;

Mancini S. (2012) "Patriarchy as the exclusive domain of the other: the veil controversy, false projection and cultural racism", *International Journal of Constitutional Law [ICON]* Vol. 10, No. 2, 411 et seq.;

Margalit A., M. Halbertal (2004) "Liberalism and the right to culture", *Social research* Vol 71, No. 3, 529 et seq.;

Marinopoulos S. (2008) *Dans l'intime de mères*, Paris: Fayard;

Markell P. (2003) *Bound by recognition*, Princeton: Princeton University Press;

Markesinis B., J. Fedtke (2006), *Judicial recourse to foreign law. A new source of inspiration?*, London-New York: Routledge;

Martìn Alcoff L. (2003) "Introduction. Identities: modern and postmodern", in L. Martìn Alcoff, E. Mendieto (eds.), *Identities. Race, class, gender and nationality*, Oxford: Blackwell, 1 et seq.;

Mauss M. (1990) *The gift: forms and functions of exchange in archaic societies*, (*Essai sur le Don: forme et raison de l'échange dans les sociétés archaïques*, 1950, trans. W.D. Halls), London-New York: Routledge;

McCaslin M. (1985a) "Immigrant's suicide attempt marks death of a dream, birth of a cause. Japanese American's trial widely followed in homeland", *The Washington Post*, September 5;
McCaslin M. (1985b) "When imported practice is criminal conduct", *San Jose Mercury News*, August 26;
McCrone D., A. Morris, R. Kiely (1995) *Scotland-the brand. The making of Scottish heritage*, Edinburgh: Edinburgh University Press;
Mead M. (1928) *Coming of age in Samoa: a psychological study of primitive youth for Western civilization*, New York: Morrow;
Mengoni L. (1996) *Ermeneutica e dogmatica giuridica*, Milano: Giuffrè;
Mengoni L., F. Modugno, F. Rimoli (2003) *Sistema e problema. Saggi di teoria dei sistemi giuridici*, Torino: Giappichelli;
Menski W.F. (2006) *Comparative law a global context: the legal systems of Asia and Africa* (2nd edition), Cambridge: Cambridge University Press;
Miller B.G. (1998) "Culture as cultural defense. An American Indian sacred site in court", *American Indian Quarterly* Vol. 22, No.1/2, 83 et seq.;
Milot M. (2009) "Modus co-vivendi: Religious diversity in Canada", in P. Bramadat, M. Koenig (eds.), *International migration and the governance of religious diversity*, Montreal-Kingston: McGill-Queen's University Press Metropolis, 105 et seq.;
Miner H. (1956) "Body rituals among the Nacirema", *American Anthropologist* Vol. 58, 503 et seq.;
Modood T. (1998) "Anti-essentialism, multiculturalism and the recognition of religious groups", *Journal of political philosophy* Vol. 6, No. 4, 378 et seq.;
Modood T. (2007) *Multiculturalism: a civic idea*, London: Blackwell Publishing Polity Press;
Modood T. (2011) "Multiculturalism and integration: struggling with confusion", in H. Mahamdallie (ed.), *Defending multiculturalism*, London: Bookmarks publications, 61 et seq.;
Monaghan J., P. Just (2000) *Social and cultural anthropology. A very short introduction*, Oxford: Oxford University Press;
Moore H.L., T. Sanders (eds.) (2006) *Anthropology in theory. Issues in epistemology*, Oxford: Blackwell;
Moore J.D. (2009) *Visions of culture. An introduction to anthropological theories and theorists* (3rd edition), Plymouth: Altamira Press;
Mootz F.J III, F. Cerrone, S. Niccolai, G. Repetto, G. Bascherini (2013) "Law and community: Alessandro Giuliani's Aristotelian Vision", www.federalismi.it, No. 16, 1 et seq.;
Mootz F.J. III (2010a) "In search of the reasonable woman: anti-discrimination rhetoric in the United States", in S. Niccolai (ed.), *Antidiscrimination discourse and practices*, Jean Monnet Symposium, http://papers.ssrn.com/sol3/papers.cfm?abstract_id=1697256;
Mootz F.J. III (2010b) *Law, hermeneutics and rhetoric*, Burlington: Ashgate;
Morris N., C. Howard (1964) *Studies in criminal law*, Oxford: Clarendon Press;
Morrissey J. (2009) *Environmental change and forced migration: a state of the art review*, Oxford: Refugee Studies Centre, University of Oxford;
Mulhern, F. (2009) "The idea of culture", *New Left Review* No. 55, Jan./Feb., 31 et seq.;
Murphy M. (2005) *Reconfiguring aboriginal state-relations*, Kingston: Institute of Intergovernmental relations, Queen's University;
Nader L. (1989) "Orientalism, occidentalism and the control of women", *Cultural Dynamics* Vol. 2, issue 3, 323 et seq.;
Nader L. (ed.) (2015) *What the rest think of the West. Since 600 AD*, Berkeley: University of California Press;

Nafziger J.A.R., R. Kirkwood Paterson, A. Dundes Renteln: (2010) *Cultural law. International, comparative, and indigenous*, Cambridge: Cambridge University Press;

Narayan U. (1998), "Essence of culture and a sense of history: a feminist critique of cultural essentialism", *Hypatia* Vol. 13, No. 2 (spring), 86 et seq.;

Newman D.G. (2007) "You still know nothin' 'bout me. Toward cross-cultural theorizing of aboriginal rights", *McGill Law Journal/Revue de Droit de McGill* No. 52, 725 et seq.;

Niccolai S. (2005) "Donne col viso coperto", in VV.AA., *Il rispetto delle regole. Scritti degli allievi per Alessandro Pizzorusso*, Torino: Giappichelli, 25 et seq.;

Niccolai S. (2007) "Differenze come cose e come valutazioni. La lezione interpretativa degli scritti di Sergio Panunzio sull'età e la capacità", in F. Cerrone, M. Volpi (eds.), *Sergio Panunzio. Profilo intellettuale di un giurista*, Napoli: Jovene, 475 et seq.;

Obiora L.A. (2000) "Bridges and barricades. Rethinking polemics and intransigence in the campaign against female circumcision", in A.K. Wing (ed.), *Global critical race feminism. An international reader*, New York-London: New York University Press, 260 et seq.;

Okin S. (1999) "Is multiculturalism bad for women?" in J. Cohen, M. Toward, M.C. Nussbaum (eds.), *Is multiculturalism bad for women? (with respondent)*, Princeton: Princeton University Press, 7 et seq.;

Orestano R. (1989) *Edificazione del giuridico*, Bologna: il Mulino;

Palermo F., G. Toggenburg (eds.) (2003) *European constitutional values and cultural diversity*, Quaderni No. 43, Bolzano: European Academy;

Palermo F., J. Woelk (2011) *Diritto costituzionale comparato dei gruppi e delle minoranze*, Padova: Cedam;

Pannia, P. (2016) "Quando la cultura entra nell'aula giudiziaria: uno studio sulle argomentazioni dei giudici italiani", *Sociologia del diritto* Vol. XLIII, No. 3, 133 et seq.;

Parekh, B. (2000) *Rethinking multiculturalism: cultural diversity and political theory*, Basingstoke: Macmillan;

Parolari P. (2014) "La violenza contro le donne come questione (trans)culturale. Osservazioni sulla Convenzione di Istanbul", *Diritto e questioni pubbliche* No. 14, 858 et seq.;

Parolari P. (2016) *Culture, diritto, diritti: diversità culturale e diritti fondamentali negli stati costituzionali di diritto*, Torino: Giappichelli;

Pateman C. (1988) *The sexual contract*, Cambridge: Polity;

Pedullà L. (2009) "Principi fondamentali e reati culturali: il criterio d'imparzialità versus le soggettive convinzioni religiose", www.forumcostituzionale.it;

Perelman C., L. Olbrechts-Tyteca (1969) *The new rhetoric: a treatise on argumentation (La Nouvelle Rhètorique; traitè de l'argumentation*, 1st edition 1958), Paris: University of Notre Dame Press;

Petrillo F. (2005) *La decisione giuridica. Politica, ermeneutica e giurisprudenza nella teoria del diritto di Emilio Betti*, Torino: Giappichelli;

Phillips A. (2003) "When culture means gender: issues of cultural defence in the English courts", *Modern Law Review* Vol. 66, No. 4, 510 et seq.;

Phillips A. (2005) "Dilemmas of gender and culture: the judge, the democrat and the political activist", in A. Eisenberg, J. Spinner-Halev (eds.), *Minorities within minorities. Equality, rights and diversity*, Cambridge: Cambridge University Press, 113 et seq.;

Phillips A. (2007) *Multiculturalism without culture*, Princeton: Princeton University Press;

Picardi N. (2005) "La funzione del giudice nell'interpretazione e nell'applicazione del diritto", in VV.AA., *Studi in onore di Gianni Ferrara*, Torino: Giappichelli, Vol. III, 115 et seq.;

Pigliaru A. (1959) *La vendetta barbaricina come ordinamento giuridico*, Milano: Giuffrè;

Piguet E., A. Pécoud, P. de Guchteneire (eds.) (2011) *Migration and climate change*, Cambridge: Cambridge University Press;

Pomorski S. (1997) "On multiculturalism, concepts of crime, and the 'de minimis' defense", *B.Y.U.L. Rev.* No. 51, 1 et seq.;

Porto B.L. (2005) "Annotation. Downward departure under United States sentencing guidelines based on 'cultural assimilation'", *American Law Reports ALR Federal 2d*, 6 A.L.R. FED. 2d, 317;

Pospisil L. (1967) "Legal levels and multiplicity of legal systems in human societies", *Journal of Conflict Resolution* Vol. 11, No. 1, 2 et seq.;

Pospisil L. (1971) *Anthropology of law: a comparative theory*, New York: Harper and Row;

Poulter S. (1986) *English law and ethnic minority customs*, London: Butterworth;

Poulter S. (1998) *Ethnicity, law, and human rights. The English experience*, Oxford: Clarendon press;

Prisco S. (2011) "Le radici religiose dei diritti umani e i problemi attuali", in VV.AA., *Studi in onore di Franco Modugno*, Napoli: ESI, Vol. III, 2683 et seq.;

Provera A. (2010) "Il 'giustificato motivo': la fede religiosa come limite intrinseco alla tipicità", *Rivista italiana di diritto processuale penale*, 964 et seq.;

Pusateri V. (2012) "Escluso il reato di esercizio abusivo della professione medica se la circoncisione maschile cd. rituale è stata eseguita per motivi culturali", *Diritto, immigrazione e cittadinanza* No. 1, 94 et seq.;

Rabinow P. (1986) "Representations are social facts: modernity and post-modernity in anthropology", in J. Clifford, G.E. Marcus (eds.), *Writing culture. The poetics and politics of ethnography*, Berkeley and Los Angeles: University of California Press, 234 et seq.;

Reddy R. (2008) "Gender, culture and the law: approaches to 'honour crimes' in the UK", *Feminist Legal Studies* No. 16, 305 et seq.;

Reddy S. (2002) "Temporarily insane: pathologising cultural difference in American criminal courts", *Sociology of Health and Illness* Vol. 24, No. 2, 667 et seq.;

Reese M. (1985a) "A tragedy in Santa Monica", *Newsweek*, May 6;

Reese M. (1985b) "She took her kids everywhere – even to die", *The Miami Herald*, June 7;

Remotti F. (1996) *Contro l'identità*, Roma-Bari: Laterza;

Ricca M. (2008) *Dike meticcia. Rotte di diritto interculturale*, Soveria Mannelli: Rubettino;

Roberts J.T., B.C. Parks (2009) "Ecologically unequal exchange, ecological debt, and climate justice: the history and implications of three related ideas for a new social movement", *International Journal of Comparative Sociology* Vol. 50, No. 3–4, 385 et seq.;

Robins K. (2006) *The challenge of transcultural diversities. Cultural policy, and cultural diversity*, Strasbourg: Council of Europe Publishing;

Robinson I. (2013) "Reflections on antisemitism in French Canada", *Canadian Jewish Studies* Vol. 21, 90 et seq.;

Rodrigañez C. (1995) *La represión del deseo materno y la génesis del estado de sumisión inconsciente*, Madrid: Madre Tierra;

Rombinson A.M. (2007) *Multiculturalism and the foundations of meaningful life. Reconciling autonomy, identity and community*, Toronto-Vancouver: UBC Press;

Rosen L. (1977) "The anthropologist as expert witness", *American Anthropologist* Vol. 79, Issue 3, 555 et seq.;

Rubin, G. (1975), 'The traffic in women: notes on the political economy of sex' in R. Reiter (ed.), *Toward an anthropology of women*, New York: Monthly Review Press, 157 et seq.;

Ruggiu I. (2013) "The crucifix and the margin of appreciation", in G. Repetto (ed.), *The constitutional relevance of the ECHR in domestic and European law*, Cambridge: Intersentia, 149 et seq.;

Ruggiu I. (2015) "From culture to patriarchy: recent changes in judicial reasoning and in normative classifications of multicultural conflicts", in E. Olivito (ed.), *Gender and Migration in Italy. A Multilayered Perspective*, London: Ashgate, 161 et seq.;

Ruggiu I. (2016) "Is begging a Roma cultural practice? Answers from the Italian law and anthropology", *Romanì Studies* Vol. 26, No. 1, 31 et seq.;

Sacco R. (2007) *Antropologia giuridica. Contributo ad una macrostoria del diritto*, Bologna: il Mulino;

Sagnotti S.C. (2005) *Forme e momenti del ragionare nel diritto*, Torino: Giappichelli;

Said E. (1989) "Representing the colonized: anthropology's interlocuters", *Critical Inquiry* No. 15, 205 et seq.;

Said E. (1993) *Culture and imperialism*, New York: Vintage Books;

Sapir E. (1968) "Culture, genuine and spurious", in D. Mandelbaum (ed.), *Selected writings of E. Sapir on language*, Berkeley: University of California Press, 308 et seq.;

Sarat A., J. Simon (2003) *Cultural analysis, cultural studies, and the law. Moving beyond legal realism*, Durham and London: Duke University Press;

Scaccia G. (2000) *Gli "strumenti" della ragionevolezza nel giudizio costituzionale*, Milano: Giuffrè;

Schauer F. (2003) *Profiles, probabilities, stereotypes*, Cambridge: Harvard University Press;

Schönwälder K. (2000) "Minority rights at home and abroad: the German debate", in R. Hudson, F. Rèno (eds.), *Politics of identity. Migrants and minorities in multicultural states*, New York: Palgrave, 115 et seq.;

Scudieri L. (2018) "Dalla cultural defense al 'test culturale': luci e (soprattutto) ombre del dibattito italiano", *Sociologia del diritto* Vol. 1, 125 et seq.;

Sellin T. (1938) *Culture and conflict in crime*, New York: Social Science Research Council;

Sen A. (2006) *Identity and violence. The illusion of destiny*, New York and London: W.W. Norton;

Sen A. (2009) *The idea of justice*, Cambridge: Belknap Press of Harvard University Press;

Sen, P. (2005) "'Crimes of honour': value and meaning", in L. Welchman and S. Hossain (eds.), '*Honour': crimes, paradigms and violence against women*, London: Zed Books, 42 et seq.;

Shachar A. (2001) *Multicultural jurisdictions. Cultural differences and women's rights*, Cambridge: Cambridge University Press;

Shah P. (2015a) "Legal responses to religious diversity (or to cultural diversity)?" in S. Ferrari (ed.), *Routledge handbook of law and religion*, London: Routledge, 119 et seq.;

Shah P. (2015b) "The difference that religion makes: transplanting legal ideas from the west to Japan and India", *Asian Journal of Comparative Law* Vol. 10, Issue 1, 81 et seq.;

Shweder R.A. (2001) "Culture: contemporary views", *International encyclopedia of the social and behavioral sciences* Vol. 5, 3151 et seq.;

Shweder R.A., M. Minow, H.R. Markus (eds.) (2002) *Engaging cultural differences. The multicultural challenge in liberal democracies*, New York: Russell Sage Foundation;

Sigler J.A. (1983) *Minority rights. A comparative analysis*, London: Greenwood Press;

Simoni A. (2009) "La qualificazione giuridica della mendicità dei minori rom tra diritto e politica", *Diritto, immigrazione e cittadinanza* No. 1, 99 et seq.;

Song S. (2005) "Majority norms, multiculturalism and gender equality", *American Political Science Review* Vol. 4, 99 et seq.;

Song S. (2007) *Justice, gender and the politics of multiculturalism*, Cambridge: Cambridge University Press;

Song S. (2009) "The subject of multiculturalism: culture, religion, language, ethnicity, nationality, and race?" in B. de Bruin, C.F. Zurn (eds.), *New waves in political philosophy*, New York: Palgrave MacMilliam, 177 et seq.;
Sorio C. (2008) "I reati culturalmente motivati: la cultural defense in alcune sentenze statunitensi", *Stato, Chiese e pluralismo confessionale*, www.statoechiese.it, November;
Spadaro A. (2008) *Libertà di coscienza e laicità nello stato costituzionale. Sulle "radici" religiose dello stato "laico"*, Torino: Giappichelli;
Spigno I. (2012) *Tra le tessere del mosaico culturale canadese non c'è la poligamia*, www.diritticomparati.it, January;
Spiro M.E. (1986) "Cultural relativism and the future of anthropology", *Cultural Anthropology* Vol. I, 259 et seq.;
Stocking G.W. Jr. (1968) *Race, culture, and evolution*, London: Collier-Macmillan;
Stocking G.W. Jr. (1985) *Objects and others. Essays on museums and material culture*, Madison: University of Wisconsin Press;
Stolzenberg N.M. (2002) "The return of the repressed: illiberal groups in a liberal state", *Journal of Contemporary Legal Issues* No. 12, 897 et seq.;
Stolzenberg N.M. (2010) "Board of education of kiryas Joel village school district v. Grumet. A religious group's quest for its own public school", in L.C. Griffin (ed.), *Law and religion: cases in context*, New York: Aspen Publishers, 203 et seq.;
Stolzenberg N.M., D.N. Myers (1992) "Community, constitution, and culture: the case of the Jeweish kehilah", *University of Michigan Journal of Law Reform* Vol. 25, No. 3, 633 et seq.;
Strathern, M. (1984) "Domesticity and the denigration of women, or nature and culture out of place", in D. O'Brien, T. Sharon (eds.), *Rethinking women's roles*, Berkeley: University of California Press, 13 et seq.;
Sultana Brelvi F. (1996–97) "'News of the weird'. Specious normativity and the problem of cultural defence", *Columbia Human Rights Law Review* Vol. 28, 657 et seq.;
Taras R. (ed.) (2013) *Challenging multiculturalism: European models of diversity*, Edinburgh: Edinburgh University Press;
Tavani C. (2012) *Collective rights and the cultural identity of the Roma*, The Netherlands: Martinus Nijhoff;
Taylor C. (1989) *Sources of the self. The making of modern identity*, Cambridge: Cambridge University Press;
Taylor C. (1992) *The politics of recognition: an essay*, Princeton: Princeton University Press;
Taylor C. (2007) *A secular age*, Cambridge: Harvard University Press;
Thornton R.J. (1988) "The rhetoric of ethnographic holism", *Cultural Anthropology* Vol. 3, 285 et seq.;
Tierney S. (ed.) (2007) *Multiculturalism and the Canadian constitution*, Toronto-Vancouver: UBC Press;
Trouillot M.R. (1991) "Anthropology and the savage slot: the poetics and politics of otherness", in R.G. Fox (ed.), *Recapturing anthropology. Working in the present*, Santa Fe-New Mexico: School of American Research Press, 17 et seq.;
Tucci A. (2004) "Ripensare l'identità all'epoca della globalizzazione. Il contributo delle discipline sociali e antropologiche", *Sociologia del diritto* Vol. 1, 108 et seq.;
Tully J. (1995) *Strange multiplicity. Constitutionalism in an age of diversity*, Cambridge: Cambridge University Press;
Tully J. (2007) "The practice of law-making and the problem of difference: an introduction to the field", in O.A. Payrow Shabani (ed.), *Multiculturalism and law. A critical debate*, Cardiff: University of Wales Press, 19 et seq.;

Tylor E.B. (1871) *Primitive culture: researches into the development of mythology*, Vol. II, London: Murray;

Ubertis G. (2011) "Multiculturalismo e processo penale", in P. Bonetti, A. Simoni, T. Vitale (eds.), *La condizione giuridica di Rom e Sinti in Italia*, Milano: Giuffrè, Vol. II, 1127 et seq.;

UNESCO (1968) "UNESCO statement on race and racial prejudice", *Current Anthropology* Vol. 9, No. 4, 270 et seq.;

Vallace N. (2011) "The misuse of 'culture' by the Canadian Supreme Court of Canada", in A. Eisenberg (ed.), *Diversity and equality. The changing framework of freedom in Canada*, Toronto-Vancouver: UBC Press, 97 et seq.;

Van Broeck J. (2001) "Cultural defence and culturally motivated crimes (cultural offences)", *European Journal of Crime, Criminal Law and Criminal Justice* Vol. 9, No. 1, 1 et seq.;

Van Praagh S. (2008) "View from the Succah: religion and neighbourly relations", in R. Moon (ed.), *Law and religious pluralism in Canada*, Toronto-Vancouver: UBC Press, 21 et seq.;

Veronesi P. (2012) "Diritti costituzionali e multiculturalismo", *Diritto e società* No. 1, 19 et seq.;

Vespaziani A. (2001) "Il bilanciamento dei diritti nella cultura giuridica statunitense", *Diritto pubblico* Vol. 3, 475 et seq.;

Vespaziani A. (2002) *Interpretazioni del bilanciamento dei diritti fondamentali*, Padova: Cedam;

Viehweg T. (1962) *Topica e giurisprudenza* (Italian translation ed. G. Crifò, *Topik und jurisprudenz*, Munich: Beck 1953), Milano: Giuffrè;

Viganò F. (2011) "La giurisprudenza sui reati commessi da Rom e Sinti", in P. Bonetti, A. Simoni, T. Vitale (eds.), *La condizione giuridica di Rom e Sinti in Italia*, Milano: Giuffrè, Vol. II, 1109 et seq.;

Volpe G. (2000) *Il costituzionalismo del Novecento*, Roma-Bari: Laterza;

Volpp L. (1994) "(Mis)identifying culture. Asian women and the 'cultural defense'", *Harvard Women Law Review* Vol. 17, 57 et seq.;

Volpp L. (1996) "'Talking culture'. Gender, race, nation and the politics of multiculturalism", *Columbia Law Review* Vol. 96, 1573 et seq.;

Volpp L. (2000) "Blaming culture for bad behaviour", *Yale Journal of Law & the Humanities* No. 12, 89 et seq.;

Volpp L. (2001) "Feminism versus multiculturalism", *Columbia Law Review* Vol. 101, 1181 et seq.;

Walby S. (1990) *Theorizing patriarchy*, Oxford: Basil Blackwell;

Walker L.E. (1979) *The battered woman syndrome*, New York: Harper and Row;

Watson A. (1993), *Legal transplants: an approach to comparative law* (2nd edition), Athens and London: The University of Georgia Press;

Watson G. (1991) "Rewriting culture", in R.G. Fox (ed.), *Recapturing anthropology. Working in the present*, Santa Fe-New Mexico: School of American research press, 73 et seq.;

Webber J. (2007) "A judicial ethic for a pluralistic age", in O.A. Payrow Shabani (ed.), *Multiculturalism and law. A critical debate*, Cardiff: University of Wales Press, 67 et seq.;

Welsh J.F. (2008) *After multiculturalism: the politics of race and the dialectics of liberty*, Lanham: Lexington Books;

Winant H. (2004) *New politics of race: globalism, difference, justice*, Minnesota: University of Minnesota press;

Wong C.M. (1999) "Good intentions, troublesome applications: the cultural defence and other uses of cultural evidence in Canada", *Criminal Law Quaterly* No. 42, 367 et seq.;

Woo D. (1989) "The People v. Fumiko Kimura: but which people?", *International Journal of the Sociology of Law* Vol. 17, 415 et seq.;

Woo D. (2004) "Cultural 'anomalies' and cultural defenses: towards an integrated theory of homicide and suicide", *International Journal of the Sociology of Law* Vol. 32, 279 et seq.;

Woodman G.R. (2009) "The cultural defence in English common law: the potential for development", in M.C. Foblets, A. Dundes Renteln (eds.), *Multicultural jurisprudence. Comparative perspectives on the cultural defense*, Oxford and Portland Oregon: Hart Publishing, 7 et seq.;

Yastrzhembskiy S. (2013) *Patriarchal Africa. The last sunrise. Photo-chronicle of the vanishing life* (two volumes), Milano: Skira;

Yldirim S. (2004) "Expanding secularism's scope: an Indian case study", *American Journal Comparative Law* No. 52, 901 et seq.;

Yoshitomo Takahashi M.D., M.D. Douglas Berger (1996) "Cultural dynamics and the unconscious in suicide in Japan", in A. Leenaars, D. Lester (eds.), *Suicide and the unconscious*, Northvale, NJ: Jason Aronson, 248 et seq., www.japanpsychiatrist.com/Abstracts/Shinju.html;

Young I.M. (1990) *Justice and the politics of difference*, Princeton: Princeton University Press;

Young I.M. (2000) *Inclusion and democracy*, Oxford: Oxford University Press;

Zanchetta P.L. (2007) "Fazzoletti, spugnette, accendini e minori stranieri", *Diritto, immigrazione e cittadinanza* No. 2, 105 et seq.

Index

Note: personal names used to identify litigants in referenced case law are displayed in *italics* to distinguish them from the names of authors quoted in the text.